Nelson's Annual Preacher's Sourcebook

2009 EDITION

ROBERT J. MORGAN AND
JOSHUA D. ROWE, EDITORS

THOMAS NELSON
Since 1798

NASHVILLE   DALLAS   MEXICO CITY   RIO DE JANEIRO   BEIJING

Published in Nashville, Tennessee, by Thomas Nelson. Thomas Nelson is a trademark of Thomas Nelson, Inc.

Thomas Nelson, Inc., titles may be purchased in bulk for educational, business, fund-raising, or sales promotional use. For information, please email SpecialMarkets@Thomas Nelson.com.

Typesetting by ProtoType Graphics, Mount Juliet, Tennessee.

Morgan, Robert J. (ed.)
   Nelson's annual preacher's sourcebook, 2009 edition.

ISBN 10: 1-4185-2536-7
ISBN 13: 978-1-4185-2536-1

Printed in the United States of America

1 2 3 4 5 6 7 8 — 12 11 10 09 08

Contents

SPECIAL FEATURES:

Introduction and Acknowledgments

Recently a pastor told me, "I am pastoring my church with all my energy, but I also work another fulltime job, and I just can't stay as fully prepared as I'd like. The *Preacher's Sourcebook* is a lifesaver."

That's the purpose of this eighth edition of *The Preacher's Sourcebook*.

Yes, we should all prepare our sermons "from scratch" each week; that's the ideal. But sometimes we need help—some ideas, some illustrations, a usable outline, a new wedding ceremony, or a bit of inspiration from a classic book or a Christian hero.

The *Sourcebook* is packed with hints, helps, and ideas for preaching and pastoring. If this volume is useful to you, I'd love to hear from you. You can reach me at www.robertjmorgan.com.

Michael Stephens, my Thomas Nelson editor and respected friend, is a great encouragement to me in putting together this resource, and I can't thank him enough. And hats off to Chris Ferebee of Yates & Yates, for his clear insight and hard work.

Corey Hawkins, my colleague at The Donelson Fellowship, who worked with me in compiling fifty-two weeks of suggested hymns and songs (actually he did the whole thing), is a great friend and gifted musician. This 2009 edition of the *Preacher's Sourcebook* is gratefully dedicated to him.

Daily Devotions

Not long before he passed away, Dr. Stephen Olford was speaking at Southern Seminary in Louisville, and I drove up from Nashville to see him. Years before when I'd been a college student in South Carolina, he had encouraged me to establish the practice of having a daily "Quiet Time." Now, many years later, the subject came up again.

He candidly told me that he had a friendly difference of opinion with his pastor, Dr. Adrian Rogers of Memphis. Dr. Olford was a staunch advocate of having a morning devotional period separate from his study and sermon preparation time. Dr. Rogers evidently considered his daily Bible study time as a two-in-one affair—a time both for feeding his soul and for preparing his sermons.

Both men are in heaven now, but I've thought of that conversation several times.

My own practice is to go to my desk after awakening in the morning, and, with a cup of hot coffee, to open my Bible to where I left off the day before. I might read a verse or a chapter or a book—whatever I feel like reading for that morning; but I look for a verse, a truth, a promise, a prayer, or a command to take with me into the day. I jot it in my journal, then turn to my prayer pages and spend the next few minutes in thanksgiving, confession, and intercession. I've also purchased a small kneeling bench, and I usually begin or end my prayer time on my knees, often with a hymn.

Then, my devotions finished, I turn to the news pages on the Internet and check the headlines of a half-dozen newspapers around the world, and I often read a few pages in some current book; and then I plunge into my Bible study, sermon preparation, and writing assignments.

Here's the way it works in my mind.

Suppose I were a student at a university or seminary, and there was one professor whom I admired above all others. His lectures were the highlight of my day, and I counted it a great honor to sit at his feet during three class sessions each week. But suppose that every morning before class I showed up early in the classroom with a thermos of coffee. Before the other students arrived, we sat down together—professor and pupil—informally chatting, fellowshiping, and developing a mutual friendship. It'd be a chance to ask questions I might not ask in class, and to gain some insights that were more personal and treasured than the ones in my professor's allocutions.

In my mind, that's the way I picture my Quiet Time. It's a personal time with the Teacher before the day's work really begins.

The Bible doesn't give us a specified regimen for every pastor to follow, of course; we all have different backgrounds, different perspectives, different needs, and different schedules. Many bi-vocational pastors have scarce time for prolonged study or advanced preparation. Some consider their "Quiet Time" as a day-long affair in which they pray without ceasing and practice the presence of God continually. Others prefer a quiet half-hour at bedtime. Some use their commuting time in the car or on the train for such purposes. But however it's done, we can't stand in the pulpit with power if we haven't first stood in the counsel of the Almighty.

There's a powerful verse about ministry tucked away in the middle of Jeremiah 23, where the Lord said: *If they had stood in My council, and had caused My people to hear My words, then they would have turned them from their evil way and from the evil of their doings* (Jer. 23:22).

This passage describes the careless shepherds of Jeremiah's day who didn't properly feed and tend to the flock. The Lord prescribed three corrective steps, all of which the shepherds had missed.

1. We stand in His counsel.
2. We cause the people to hear His words.
3. They turn from their evil ways and from the evil of their doings.

We're unlikely to have success with the third step if we neglect the first and the second steps.

Standing in God's counsel, of course, involves more than having a morning Quiet Time, as rich as that habit may be. It's a matter of abiding in Christ and letting His Word dwell richly in us (John 15:7; Col. 3:16); of hiding His Word in our hearts and meditating on it day and night (Ps. 119:11, 1:1–3); of rightly dividing the Scriptures and of using knowledge rightly (2 Tim. 2:15; Prov. 15:2). It's a matter of setting our hearts to study the Word of the Lord, to obey it, and to teach it in the power of the Holy Spirit (Ezra 7:10; 1 Cor. 2:4).

The French devotional writer François Fénelon (1651–1715) said, "There is no interpreter of the Divine Word like that of a holy heart;

or, what is the same thing, of the Holy Ghost dwelling in the heart. If we give ourselves wholly to God, the Comforter will take up His abode with us, and guide us into all that truth which will be necessary for us. Truly holy souls, therefore, continually looking to God for a proper understanding of His Word, may confidently trust that He will guide them aright."

Whether it's a half-hour in the morning, an open Bible on the car seat, a bedtime ritual of devotional practice, or a keen awareness of the Lord's presence during your study time, take time to be holy, speak oft with your Lord. Abide in Him always, and feed on His Word.

Create a Sermon Series!

If you would like to publicize and preach a series of messages, you can assemble your own by mixing and matching various sermons and sermon outlines in this *Sourcebook*. Here are some suggestions:

The Path of Wisdom
- The Path of Wisdom (January 18)
- Live Different: Wisdom (March 15)
- The Path of Wisdom: Our Relationship with God (May 31)
- Practical Proverbs (December 27)

Great Expectations: Living in Anticipation of Christ's Return
- A Threefold Duty (January 25)
- A Blessed Hope (February 8)
- A Bridesmaid's Rules (March 8)
- I'll Be Back (June 21)
- What Does the Future Really Hold? (November 22)

Church Matters
- Portrait of a New Testament Church (April 26)
- More Than Food (June 14)
- Life Together (September 13)
- The Body of Christ (September 13)
- Becoming an Excellent Church (September 20)
- The Communion of Saints (November 8)
- Do You Remember? (Communion Sermon)
- Saved from Wrath (Baptism Sermon)

Victory in Jesus: Conquering Life's Trials and Temptations
- Live Different: Patience (January 11)
- The Warrior Seed and the Way We Live (January 25)
- The Best Person on Earth (February 15)
- Hard Times (February 22)
- Temptation Planet (June 14)
- Fighting the Battle for Purity (July 26)
- The Battle Line Has Been Drawn (August 23)
- The Christian's Armor (September 20)
- Where Is God When All Hell Breaks Loose? (November 8)

Can You Hear Me Now? Lessons on Practical Praying

- The Prayer for Divine Plentitude (February 15)
- iPray: A Lesson in Prayer for the iPod Generation (May 24)
- How to Pray Jesus' Way (May 31)
- Prayer for Discerning Love (July 19)
- The Prayer for Enlightened Behavior (October 25)
- The Power in Persistence (November 29)
- You Just Call Out My Name (November 29)
- The Prayer for Spiritual Illumination (December 6)

God's Guys

- Noah and the Great Flood (August 2)
- Unexpected Heroism (September 27)
- The Influence and Integrity of Isaac (August 9)
- Meet Moses (May 31)
- Moses' Mandate and Mission (September 20)
- The Best Person on Earth (February 15)

Crucial Questions

- Understand? (July 26)
- Why Are You Afraid? (October 11)
- What Happens When a Christian Dies? (October 18)
- Where Is God When All Hell Breaks Loose? (November 8)
- What Does the Future Really Hold? (November 22)
- What's Wrong? (December 6)
- What If Jesus Had Never Been Born? (December 13)

Contributors

Dr. Timothy K. Beougher
Billy Graham Professor of Evangelism and Associate Dean of the Billy Graham School of Missions, Evangelism and Church Growth, The Southern Baptist Theological Seminary, Louisville, Kentucky

A Faith That Pleases (January 18)
Gradually (March 8)
Looking Within (March 29)
Portrait of a New Testament Church (April 26)
More than Food (June 14)
Do You Want to Be Free? (July 5)
Faith and Freedom (July 5)
The Cost of Discipleship (August 23)
Rest for the Weary (September 6)
Why Are You Afraid? (October 11)
Dying from the Inside Out (November 29)
Do You Remember? (Communion Sermon)

Pastor Al Detter
Senior Pastor, Grace Baptist Church, Erie, Pennsylvania

From Bondage to Freedom (January 4)
Getting Along with People (January 25)
Fighting the Battle of Anger (February 8)
Some Essentials for Living a Godly Life (April 19)
What a Woman Needs (May 10)
God Is Worth Knowing (May 17)
Hey, Mr. President (July 5)
Fighting the Battle for Purity (July 26)
Principles for Confronting Others About Sexual Sin (July 26)
Painless Giving (August 9)
Suffering: A Survival Guide (August 30)
Fighting the Battle of Unbelief (October 11)
Practicing a Converted Life (November 1)
Charge! (November 22)
Setting Things Straight (December 20)
Moving with God (Church Building/Relocation Sermon)
Tired of War (Patriotic Sermon)
Thankfulness Reexamined (Thanksgiving Sermon)

Dr. Ed Dobson
Pastor, Calvary Church in Grand Rapids, Michigan, and Moody Bible Institute's 1993 Pastor of the Year

The Romans Road Signs (February 15)
The Attitude of Christ (April 5)
Life Together (September 13)
Walk This Way (November 22)

Pastor Jonathan Falwell
Senior Pastor, Thomas Road Baptist Church, Lynchburg, Virginia. Executive Vice President of Spiritual Affairs at Liberty University, Lynchburg, Virginia

Live Different: Patience (January 11)
iServe: A Lesson in Service for the iPod Generation (February 8)
Live Different: Wisdom (March 15)
iWill: A Message About God's Will for an iPod Generation (April 5)
iForgive: A Lesson in Forgiveness for an iPod Generation (April 19)
iPray: A Lesson in Prayer for the iPod Generation (May 24)
The Battle Line Has Been Drawn (August 23)
iTell: A Lesson in Evangelism for the iPod Generation (September 6)
iKnow: A Lesson in Truth for the iPod Generation (October 4)
What If Jesus Had Never Been Born? (December 13)
Leaving a Legacy (December 27)

Rev. Billie Friel
Pastor, First Baptist Church, Mt. Juliet, Tennessee

Redundancy (February 22)
Worry (March 15)
How Is Your Faith? (May 10)
The Great Rule of Life (August 16)
Caleb: Model Senior Citizen (September 13)
Paul's Thorn in the Flesh (October 4)
Unity in the Church (November 15)

Rev. Peter Grainger
Pastor, Charlotte Baptist Chapel, Edinburgh, Scotland

Rights and Rewards (March 1)
Learning from the Past (June 7)

Rev. Larry Kirk
Christ Community Church, Daytona Beach, Florida

The Warrior Seed and the Way We Live (January 25)
It Is Good to Go Forward (March 22)
Choose Faith (April 5)
The Victory of Christ and the Kiss of Faith (May 3)
Temptation Planet (June 14)
Essential Encouragement (August 2)
What Does it Take to Get God's Blessing (September 27)
Revealed (November 1)
The Communion of Saints (November 8)
The Power in Persistence (November 29)
Christmas and the Cause of Hope (December 13)
A Light Has Dawned (December 13)
The Real Meaning of Christmas (December 20)

Dr. Woodrow Kroll
President and Senior Bible Teacher of Back to the Bible Broadcast

Noah and the Great Flood (August 2)

Dr. Robert M. Norris
Senior pastor of Fourth Presbyterian Church in the Washington suburb of Bethesda, Maryland

Horror and Hope (March 22)
The Refining Fire of God (June 14)
Ruler Over All (July 12)
Unexpected Heroism (September 27)
An Unexpected Inheritance (December 6)
Death Knell for Death (December 27)

Dr. Larry Osborne
Senior Pastor, North Coast Church, Vista, California

Blessed by God (January 11)
Losing My Religion (and Gaining God's) (February 1)
The Three Voices of God (February 22)
Sin in the Camp (March 8)
There's a Hole in Your Pocket (March 29)
Resurrection Responses (April 12)

Dr. Kevin Riggs
Former Pastor, Franklin Community Church, Franklin, Tennessee

Joshua D. Rowe
Assistant Editor to Robert J. Morgan, Summa Cum Laude Graduate of Columbia International University, Master of Divinity Student at The Southern Baptist Theological Seminary

William Graham Scroggie (1877–1959)
Scottish minister and writer

Rev. Melvin Tinker
Vicar of The Church of St. John Newland since 1994. Editor of "Restoring the Vision—Anglican Evangelists Speak Out," and "The Anglican Evangelical Crisis"

Hope and Holiness (January 4)
God Is at Work (January 11)
Robbing God (February 1)
Hard Times (February 22)
From Poverty to Praise (March 29)
A New Covenant (April 19)
Don't Forget (May 3)
It Was the Best of Times? (June 7)
The God Who Is (June 28)
Lord of All or Not at All (July 12)
A Redemption Story (August 2)
The God Who Tests (August 23)
Family Ties (September 27)
True Religion (October 18)
What Does the Future Really Hold? (November 22)
What's Wrong? (December 6)

Dr. Melvin Worthington
Executive Secretary, National Association of Free Will Baptists

The Tempestuous Tongue (March 1)
The Resurrection Record (April 12)
The Tamed Tongue (May 24)
Meet Moses (May 31)
Facts for the Family (June 21)
The Influence and Integrity of Isaac (August 9)
The Lord Lives (August 30)
Moses' Mandate and Mission (September 20)

(Note: Bold Print indicates main outlines)

All other outlines are from the pulpit ministry of the general editor, Rev. Robert J. Morgan, of The Donelson Fellowship in Nashville, Tennessee. Special appreciation goes to Brad R. Heyne—Cum Laude graduate of Columbia International University and student at the Southern Baptist Theological Seminary—for his invaluable assistance with this volume. Thanks also to Corey Hawkins, music minister of the Donelson Fellowship, for his hard work in compiling the suggested hymns for each weekly segment.

2009 Calendar

January 1	New Year's Day
January 4	
January 6	Epiphany
January 11	**The Feast of the Lord's Baptism**
January 18	**Sanctity of Human Life Sunday**
January 19	Martin Luther King, Jr., Day
January 25	
January 26	Australia Day
February 1–28	Black History Month
February 1	**National Freedom Day, Super Bowl Sunday**
February 2	Groundhog Day
February 8	**Boy Scout Day**
February 12	Lincoln's Birthday
February 14	Valentine's Day
February 15	
February 18	Presidents Day
February 22	**Washington's Birthday; Transfiguration Sunday**
February 25	Ash Wednesday
March 1	**First Sunday of Lent**
March 8	**Second Sunday of Lent, Daylight Savings Time**
March 15	**Third Sunday of Lent**
March 17	St. Patrick's Day

March 20	First Day of Spring
March 21	Purim
March 22	**Fourth Sunday of Lent**
March 29	**Fifth Sunday of Lent**
April 5	**Palm Sunday; Sixth Sunday of Lent**
April 8	Spy Wednesday
April 9	Maundy Thursday
April 10	Good Friday
April 11	Holy Saturday
April 12	**Easter**
April 19	**Passover**
April 22	Earth Day
April 25	National Arbor Day
April 26	
April 29	Administrative Professionals Day
May 3	
May 7	National Day of Prayer
May 10	**Mother's Day**
May 16	Armed Forces Day
May 17	
May 21	Ascension Day
May 24	
May 25	Memorial Day
May 31	**Pentecost**
June 7	**Trinity Sunday**

June 14	**Flag Day**
June 20	First Day of Summer
June 21	**Father's Day**
June 28	
July 4	Independence Day
July 5	
July 12	
July 19	
July 26	**Parent's Day**
August 2	**Friendship Day**
August 6	Transfiguration Day
August 9	
August 15	Assumption Day
August 16	
August 23	
August 30	
September 6	
September 7	Labor Day
September 11	Patriot Day
September 13	**Grandparents Day**
September 19	Rosh Hashanah
September 20	
September 22	First Day of Autumn
September 25	Native American Day
September 27	

September 28	Yom Kippur
October 1–31	Pastor Appreciation Month
October 4	
October 5	Child Health Day
October 11	**National Children's Day**
October 12	Columbus Day
October 16	Boss's Day
October 18	
October 24	United Nations Day
October 25	**Reformation Day**
October 27	
October 31	All Hallows Eve
November 1	**All Saints Day**
November 2	Daylight Saving Time Ends; All Souls Day
November 3	Election Day
November 8	**International Day of Prayer for the Persecuted Church**
November 11	Veterans Day
November 15	
November 22	
November 26	Thanksgiving Day
November 29	**First Sunday of Advent**
November 30	St. Andrews Day
December 1	AIDS Awareness Day
December 6	**Second Sunday of Advent**

December 7	National Pearl Harbor Remembrance Day
December 10	Human Rights Day
December 12	Hanukkah Begins
December 13	**Third Sunday of Advent**
December 19	Hanukkah Ends
December 20	**Fourth Sunday of Advent; First Day of Winter**
December 24	Christmas Eve
December 25	Christmas Day
December 26	Kwanzaa Begins
December 27	
December 31	New Year's Eve

Boldface dates are Sundays

SERMONS AND
WORSHIP SUGGESTIONS
FOR 52 WEEKS

JANUARY 4, 2009

Redeeming the Time

Date preached:

Scripture: Ephesians 5:15–16
See then that you walk circumspectly, not as fools but as wise, redeeming the time, because the days are evil.

Introduction: John Maxwell suggests that we make only a handful of important decisions during our lifetimes. The key to success is managing those decisions in our daily schedule. He wrote, "If we want to do something with our lives, then we must focus on today . . . . But how do you win today? How do you make today a great day instead of one that falls to pieces? Here's the missing piece: The secret of your success is determined by your daily agenda."[1] When we make Jesus our Lord and Master, He assigns our work; and success isn't found in results or achievements, but in simply doing what He appoints for us day by day. Psalm 139:16 says in the *Living Bible:* "You saw me before I was born and scheduled each day of my life before I began to breathe. Every day was recorded in Your Book!" As we enter a new year, let's look at how to live on God's schedule.

1. **Your Agenda Today, Lord.** Learn to say every morning: "Your agenda today, Lord." Offer your body as a living sacrifice, saying, "Lord, this is the day You have made. May Your will be done today in my life, as it is done in heaven."

2. **Plan Your Schedule Carefully**. When I was in college, I decided to make a weekly agenda; it was my first attempt at a self-imposed schedule in my life. I made seven vertical columns on a piece of paper, and drew horizontal lines to create the hours of the day. Then I shaded in my obligations and looked at what was left, asking myself how I needed to spend my remaining time. I shaded those in and began living by that calendar. It proved to be one of the best experiments I've ever conducted, and I'm still doing the same thing today. My system is a little more sophisticated now; but the basic

---

[1] John Maxwell, *Today Matters* (New York: Warner Faith, 2004), p. 14.

method remains the same. Psalm 90 tells us to number our days that we may present to the Lord a heart of wisdom.

3. **Accept Interruptions Wisely.** Having established disciplined schedules and minimized interruptions, when an interruption *does* occur, it frequently represents God's agenda for that day. Read through the Gospels and notice the ministry of Christ. How often interruptions became the ministry!

4. **Take Disappointments as Divine Appointments.** Sometimes a disappointment is God's way of showing us what He does *not* want us to do. It's His way of de-cluttering our schedule. Closed doors become His way of opening windows, and disappointments become His appointments for keeping us on His plan.

5. **Look for Open Doors.** We also need to train ourselves to look for open doors. Each day certain opportunities show up on either side of us. In Acts 17:17, Paul preached "in the marketplace daily with those who happened to be there."

6. **Perform Small Tasks Gladly.** The little things we do are bigger than the great things we do; and we must learn the importance of the "sacred ordinary." "Whatever you do, whether in word or deed, do it all in the name of the Lord Jesus, giving thanks to God the Father through him. . . . Whatever your hand finds to do, do it with all your might. . . . So whether you eat or drink or whatever you do, do it all for the glory of God" (Col. 3:17, Eccl. 9:10, 1 Cor. 10:31 NIV).

7. **Leave the Undone in God's Hands.** After we have done our best, we have to leave the undone in God's hands. Years ago I discovered that one of the hardest aspects of pastoring was the utter impossibility of doing everything needing to be done each day. Then I discovered a helpful verse—Acts 10:38: Jesus Christ went around doing good. What impressed me was that it said *good* and not *everything*. Not even Jesus, in His human person, could visit every village, touch every person, heal every sickness, or witness to every soul. He simply finished the work the Father had given Him to do, and left the undone in the Father's hands.

Conclusion: The years of our lives are threescore and ten, or if by reason of strength they be fourscore, yet they are soon cut off and we fly away. So teach us to number our days that we may present You a heart of wisdom, redeeming the time because the days are evil.

Father, lead me day by day,
Ever in Thine own sweet way;
Teach me to be pure and true;
Show me what I ought to do.
—JOHN HOPPS (1877)

STATS, STORIES, AND MORE

God portions out our work day-by-day, and He assigns our duties as He sees fit. We live our lives in day-by-day increments. The Lord could have designed the solar system and the size of our planet so as to make each day forty-eight hours—or forty-eight months for that matter. But in His wisdom He created each day as exactly 24 hours, no more, no less. We live in day-by-day increments. We can review the past and plan for the future—but we can only live our lives day-by-day.

François Fénelon wrote, "Cheered by the presence of God, I will do at each moment, without anxiety, according to the strength which He shall give me, the work that His Providence assigns me. I will leave the rest without concern; it is not my affair. I ought to consider the duty to which I am called each day, as the work that God has given me to do, and to apply myself to it in a manner worthy of His glory, that is to say, in exactness and peace."

Anna Waring put it this way:

I love to think that God appoints
My portion day by day;
Events of life are in His hand,
And I would only say,
Appoint them in Thine own good time,
And in Thine own best way.

PRAYER FOR THE PASTOR'S CLOSET

Lord, I do not know what I ought to ask of You. You only know what we need. You love me better than I know how to love myself. O Father, give to Your child that for which he himself does not know how to ask.
—FRANÇOIS FÉNELON

APPROPRIATE HYMNS AND SONGS

"Another Year Is Dawning," Frances R. Havergal, Public Domain.

"Fill Me Now," Michael Hansen & Christina Peppin, 2005 Mercy/Vineyard Publishing.

"Show Me Your Ways," Russell Fragar, 1995 Russell Fragar/Hillsongs Publishing (Admin. in U.S. and Canada by Integrity's Hosanna! Music).

"The Longer I Serve Him," William J. Gaither, 1965 Gaither Music Company.

"Day by Day," Carolina Sandell Berg & Oscar Ahnfelt, Public Domain.

FOR THE BULLETIN

On January 4, 1528, Holy Roman Emperor Charles V issued a decree to put the Anabaptists to death. This was the first secular mandate forbidding the Anabaptist movement. ● Hans Bret, a young believer in Holland was arrested and tortured for his faith. Early on Saturday, January 4, 1577, the executioner clamped an iron screw on his tongue, and seared the end of his tongue with a hot iron so he couldn't preach at his execution. He was burned alive. ● January 4, 1581, is the birthday of James Ussher, Archbishop of Armagh, Ireland. He is remembered for his calculations regarding the origin of earth, which he determined was created on November 23, 4004 B.C. ● On January 4, 1866, missionary James Chalmers sailed aboard the *John Williams* for a lifetime of successful service in the South Pacific. He was martyred on Easter, 1901, trying to reach a new island with the gospel. His head was cut off and his torso was cooked. News of the attack stunned the West, leading to a flood of new recruits for missions. ● Kaj Munk grew up in a pietistic setting and, in 1924, was ordained a priest in Denmark. He became an outspoken opponent of the Nazis, and on January 4, 1944, he was taken from his home by the Gestapo and shot. His Bible was found 20 meters from his body. He is considered Denmark's greatest modern martyr. ● On January 4, 1947, Peter Marshall was elected chaplain of the U.S. Senate.

WORSHIP HELPS

Call to Worship
Stand up and praise the Lord your God, who is from
everlasting to everlasting. Blessed be your glorious name, and
may it be exalted above all blessing and praise. You alone are
the Lord. You made the heavens, even the highest heavens, and
all their starry host, the earth and all that is on it, the seas and
all that is in them. You give life to everything, and the
multitudes of heaven worship you (Neh. 9:5b–6 NIV).

Welcome
Whether you're here today as a guest, a regular attendee, or a
member, you've come to the right place at the right time. As we
begin a new year, there is no more fitting place or situation
than where you find yourself this very moment. You've come to
a place of new beginnings and fresh starts. As we worship
together, fellowship with one another, and learn how to be
conformed to the image of Jesus Christ, I ask you to reflect on
what needs a fresh start in your life. Maybe you need to commit
yourself to this congregation as a member; perhaps there is sin
in your life that needs to be confessed and turned away from;
maybe you are hurting and need help to get through your
circumstances. Whatever your need may be, let today be a new
beginning as you commit yourself to the Lord Jesus and to His
church.

Benediction
Teach us to number our days, that we may gain a heart of
wisdom (Ps. 90:12).

Additional Sermons and Lesson Ideas

Hope and Holiness
By Rev. Melvin Tinker

Date preached:

SCRIPTURE: 1 Peter 1:13–2:3

INTRODUCTION: We are called to be holy as God is holy (v. 15). But what does it mean to be holy and how are we to be stirred so that we will desire holiness?

    1. A Glorious Hope (vv. 13–16).
    2. An Awesome Father (v. 17).
    3. A Precious Savior (vv. 18–21).
    4. A Powerful Word (vv. 1:22–2:3).

CONCLUSION: We are called to holiness and godliness. It is important to receive good biblical teaching so that we are growing in a healthy manner. God in His awesomeness sets before us our eternal hope, offers to us His Son as our Savior, and gives to us His Word to guide us in our new life. He gives us all that is needed for life and godliness (2 Pet. 1:3) and He says to us "Be holy because I am holy" (Lev. 11:44).

From Bondage to Freedom
By Pastor Al Detter

Date preached:

SCRIPTURE: Psalm 81:6a–10

INTRODUCTION: We can get ourselves trapped in situations that we are unable to get out of. Whether it is a financial situation, a tempting situation, or some other type of situation, we cannot save ourselves. This psalm offers direction from God as to how we can be freed from bondage by relying on Him.

    1. Admit That You Are in Bondage (v. 6).
    2. Get Some Help (v. 7).
    3. Follow God's Advice (v. 8).
    4. Remove Other Gods (v. 9).
    5. Trust God to Meet Your Needs (v. 10).

CONCLUSION: God's desire is for us to be free in Him so that we may be able to serve Him wholeheartedly. However, if we are in bondage, we will end up being subject to that and will be unable to allow God to use us in the ways He desires.

JANUARY 11, 2009

SUGGESTED SERMON

Live Different: Patience

Date preached:

By Pastor Jonathan Falwell

Scripture: James 1:1–12, especially verse 4
But let patience have its perfect work, that you may be perfect and complete, lacking nothing.

Introduction: Today, we're going to look at what James has to say about patience, about endurance. What to do in the midst of life's trials? What to do in the midst of life's pains? In the book of James, James likens "patience" to the idea of "being content as you endure" through what God wants us to go through in our lives. Sometimes in life, people become impatient and they miss out on the fullest blessing that God intended. In America especially, we have a consumer mindset: "I want it now! I want it fast! And if I don't get it from you, I will go to someone else who will serve me now and fast!" It's the fast food philosophy of life! Because this is the way we live now, we lack the ability (or desire) to "be content as you endure." But because God is all-wise, all-powerful, and never-changing, He knows what is best for us . . . and having everything NOW is not the best thing!

1. **Four Thoughts on the Trials of Life:**

   A. **Life's Not Easy (v. 2).** Notice that James says, "count it all joy when you fall into various trials" not "*if* you fall into various trials." Simply becoming a believer in Christ doesn't make life easier. If you recently accepted Jesus Christ as your Savior, please know that life will not get amazingly easier now. However, now you have both a God and godly friends to walk this path with you! If we patiently endure, we can have a powerful testimony of trust in God.

   B. **Our Trials Have a Purpose (v. 3).** The word "testing" in this verse is always used in the Bible to describe a challenge or situation that provides the opportunity for the recipient to prove himself. It's always spoken of as a positive thing to happen to us. This same word for testing was used to describe the refining process of metals like gold. They would melt the metal into liquid form so that impurities would rise to the top and be skimmed off. The precious metal was then much more valuable. That's the purpose of our testing too! God removes impurities from our lives as our faith is tested.

C. **You Don't Have to Worry (v. 2; John 16:33).** James tells us to count it all joy! Jesus taught this way too: "These things I have spoken to you, that in Me you may have peace. In the world you will have tribulation; but be of good cheer, I have overcome the world" (John 16:33).

D. **You Can Count on God (John 14:1).** We learn from James that God has a purpose and will bring us through the trials of life. Jesus reminded His disciples before His ascension of the same thing. He said, "Let not your heart be troubled; you believe in God, believe also in Me" (John 14:1). Jesus wants us to lean on Him to endure trials rather than worrying.

2. **Three Guarantees If We Endure Life's Trials:**

A. **Patience Perfects Us (James 1:4).** The word "perfect" in this verse should catch our attention. James is teaching us that patience is our tutor. If we stick with it we will enjoy all that God wants us to learn through patience.

B. **Patience Completes Us (vv. 4, 12).** The word "complete" in verse 4 means "whole, well, physical or spiritual well-being." This word is often used of people Jesus healed in the first century. James refers to the day in which our patience is complete and we will be rewarded: "God blesses those who patiently endure testing and temptation. Afterward they will receive the crown of life that God has promised to those who love him" (v. 12 NLT).

C. **Patience Prepares Us (v. 4; 5:10).** The phrase "lacking nothing" in verse 4 means "not deficient with regard to spiritual strength." With each trial endured, we're that much stronger to endure the next one. James mentions Job as an example of perseverance that was ultimately rewarded exceedingly above the trials Job endured (5:10).

Conclusion: What trials are you facing today? Whether you're having trouble with bills, your marriage, a coworker, friends at school, grades, or just finding your place in life, know today that what you're going through is not meaningless! Trust in Jesus and lean on Him. He promises to bless you in the end.

STATS, STORIES, AND MORE

James Then and Now

In the book of James, there are five chapters and 108 verses. Out of these 108 verses, this little book of the Bible contains fifty-four imperatives/commands/encouragements. This demonstrates how practical James is; it will help guide us in daily living.

The book of James was arguably the first New Testament Book written. They didn't have any other New Testament Books of the Bible available to them. They were living approximately fifteen years after the death/burial/resurrection of Jesus Christ. So, what people want to know is "how do the scriptures and the resurrected life of Jesus Christ relate practically to my life?"

Life was tough for the first-century readers of this little book because they were getting persecuted during this time. In fact, if you want to read about the various persecutions that were going on during this time, all you have to do is read Acts chapters 8–12. These people were literally running for their lives! Their anxieties were high. Fear was on high-alert. They were gripped with insecurity, gripped with fear, gripped with confusion on how to live! Sound familiar?
—*Pastor Jonathan Falwell*

Count It All Joy . . .

I have a friend who is a very successful businessman. We were talking about trials and how we handle going through these periods in our lives. He shared a very powerful truth with me. He said that his own prayer life has always been made up of about 98 percent praises. This is "count it all joy" in practice.
—*Pastor Jonathan Falwell*

APPROPRIATE HYMNS AND SONGS

"Rejoice, the Lord Is King," Charles Wesley & George Handell, Public Domain.

"'Tis So Sweet to Trust in Jesus," Louis M. R. Stead & William J. Kirkpatrick, Public Domain.

"Jesus, Lover of My Soul," Paul Oakley, 1995 Kingsway's ThankYou Music (Admin. in North America by EMI Christian Music Publishing).

"There Is Joy in the Lord," Cheri Keaggy, 1992 Sparrow Song (Admin. by EMI Christian Music Publishing)/BMI.

FOR THE BULLETIN

Muhammad arrived in Mecca on January 11, 630, with ten thousand troops. ● St. Paulinus of Aquileia, a favorite preacher of Charlemagne, died on this day in A.D. 804. He had been born into a family of Italian farmers, but his brilliant mind, godly heart, and gifted oratory propelled him into the ministry. During his lifetime, he fought heresy and promoted missions. ● It's well known that Dorothy Carey, the first wife of William Carey, suffered severe mental illness, aggravated by William's insistence on being a missionary in India. On this day in 1796, William's colleague, John Thomas, discussed the problem in a letter to supporting pastor Andrew Fuller: "Mrs. C has taken it into her head that C (William) is a great whoremonger; and her jealousy burns like fire unquenchable. . . . (She) declares in the most solemn manner that she has catched him with his servants, with his friends, with Mrs. Thomas, and that he is guilty every day and every night." ● January 11, 1782, marks the birth of Robert Morrison, first Protestant missionary to China. Arriving there, he lived in a cellar and was rarely seen until he mastered the language. The number of his converts during his twenty-seven years in China was no more than five, but he paved the way for future missions work in that country. ● On January 11, 1813, the first pineapples were planted in Hawaii. ● Today marks the death of Timothy Dwight, who passed away in 1817. As president of Yale University, Dwight led many students to faith in Christ. His chapel sermons are published under the title Theology Explained and Defended, and he is the author of the hymn, "I Love Thy Kingdom, Lord." ● Christian lawyer, statesman, and hymnist, Francis Scott Key, died on this day in 1843. ● The Church of God, headquartered in Cleveland, Tennessee, adopted its current name on this day in 1907, although its history goes back to the late 1800s.

Kid's Talk

Bring a one-pound weight and a five-pound weight with you and show them to the children. Ask for two volunteers (older children capable of responsibly handling the weights). Show them a simple exercise with the weights and ask each child to demonstrate the exercise. As they do, address the other children with a question: "If (the child with the one-pound weight) were to do this exercise for one day and (the other child with the heavier weight) were to do it for three weeks, who do you think would get stronger?" As they answer, explain that when we encounter difficulties, that often the harder they are and the longer they last, the stronger they make us. We might not enjoy hard times while they are happening, but God uses them to make us more patient and more capable to do His work.

WORSHIP HELPS

Call to Worship

Come, let us sing for joy to the LORD; let us shout aloud to the Rock of our salvation. Let us come before him with thanksgiving and extol him with music and song. Come, let us bow down in worship, let us kneel before the LORD our Maker; for he is our God and we are the people of his pasture, the flock under his care (Ps. 95:1–2, 6–7 NIV).

Suggested Scriptures

- Isaiah 40:30–31
- 1 Peter 1:3–9
- Matthew 10:22
- 1 Corinthians 1:8

Benediction

Therefore, my beloved brethren, be steadfast, immovable, always abounding in the work of the Lord, knowing that your labor is not in vain in the Lord (1 Cor. 15:58).

Additional Sermons and Lesson Ideas

Blessed by God

Date preached:

By Dr. Larry Osborne

SCRIPTURE: James 1:21–25

INTRODUCTION: God wants to bless us in everything we do. But He also desires for us to become more and more like Him.

1. Clean Out the Crud (v. 21a). We must be removing the moral filth from our lives.
2. Humbly Submit to the Bible (v. 21b). We must be submitting ourselves to God's saving Word.
3. Do What It Says (vv. 22–24). We must be obeying the Word we hear.
4. Now Take It to a Deeper Level (v. 25). We must be continuing to push ourselves to a fuller understanding of the Word.

CONCLUSION: God is looking for progress, not for perfection. As we grow in Christ, we will need to daily remove sin from our lives, humbly submit to the Word, obey the Word, and push ourselves deeper. As we grow in holiness, blessings will abound.

God Is at Work

Date preached:

By Rev. Melvin Tinker

SCRIPTURE: 1 Kings 19:1–18

INTRODUCTION: God leads Elijah to a place of restoration, reveals Himself to Elijah, and makes a promise regarding Israel.

1. Elijah and God's Provision (vv. 3–9a).
2. Elijah and God's Presence (vv. 9b–14).
3. Elijah and God's Promise (vv. 15–18).

CONCLUSION: The powers of this world will not prevail against God and His people. God sent Jesus that the world might be reconciled to Him and His Holy Spirit that we might be indwelt by Him. God has built His church and hell will not overcome it (Matt. 16:15–20).

Fénelon's Maxims of the Saints

Sometimes the best books are the ones that are at least 300 years old, not too long, and penned by writers who knew how to be still and pray and think.

François Fénelon (François de Salignac de la Mothe-Fénelon) was born into nobility on August 6, 1651, in the southwest of France in the town of Périgueux, not far from Bordeaux. He was educated in childhood by tutors, and early in life he decided on a career in the church. His first sermon was delivered when he was fifteen.

After studies at St. Sulpice Seminary in Paris, he thought of becoming a missionary to the American Indians or to the inhabitants of Greece, but his family and superiors thought otherwise, and Fénelon was ordained to the priesthood in 1675. He oversaw a girl's school in Paris, then wrote a book about it and went off to preach to French Protestants in a government-sponsored crusade to reconvert the Huguenots to Catholicism. He later became the personal tutor to the grandson and eventual heir of King Louis XIV.

In 1688, Fénelon met the famous French mystic, Madame Guyon, who was popular among the social circles of France but not so well received by the Pope, the Bishop of Chartres, and by church authorities. He found himself attracted to her teachings about prayer and quietism, and at the risk of his own prestige he defended and supported her. Even after he was appointed archbishop of Cambrai, he continued to defend her.

His *Explications des Maximes des Saints,* or *Maxims of the Saints,* was published in 1697 amid the Madame Guyon controversy. Today it's regarded as his masterpiece, but at the time it unleashed a tempest of political and spiritual criticism.

Fénelon's main point is that too much self-love hinders our love for the Master. When the soul is completely absorbed by the love of God, it becomes virtually indifferent to anything else. As with all the French mystics, we can certainly find fault with some of their views, but how beautiful and true are other of their sentences.

In November of 1714, Fénelon was returning from a trip into the country, and one of his horses was spooked by a windmill, upsetting the carriage. The accident seems to have shocked his nervous system, and he went into a decline. His attendants read the Bible to him continuously, and he passed away quietly shortly after five o'clock in the morning on January 7, 1715.

If you're interested in the French mystics, Madame Guyon and François Fénelon are a popular starting point, and their words are readily available in English.

Here are some brief excerpts from Fénelon's *Maxims:*

The motive of God's glory so expands itself and so fills the mind, that the other motive—that of our own happiness—becomes so small as to be practically annihilated. It is then that God becomes what He ever ought to be—the center of the soul, to which all its affections tend; the great moral sun of the soul, from which all its light and all its warmth proceed.

***

We know that it is impossible for God to forsake those who put their trust in Him. He can just as soon forsake His own word; and what is more, He can just as soon forsake His own nature. Holy souls, nevertheless, may sometimes, in a way and under circumstances that we may not fully understand, believe themselves to be forsaken, beyond all possibility of hope; and yet such is that faith in God and their love to Him, that the will of God, even under such circumstances, is dearer to them than anything and everything else.

***

It does not follow, because the love of ourselves is lost in the love of God, that we are to take no care and to exercise no watch over ourselves. No man will be so seriously and constantly watchful as he who loves himself IN and FOR God alone. Having the image of God in himself, he has a motive strong (we might perhaps say as that which controls the actions of angels) to guard and protect it. Continued on the next page

CLASSICS FOR THE PASTOR'S LIBRARY—*Continued*

***

Vocal prayer, when attended by right affections, ought to be both recognized and encouraged as being calculated to strengthen the thoughts and feelings it expresses, and to awaken new ones, and also for the reason that it was taught by the Son of God and His Apostles, and that it has been practiced by the whole Church in all ages . . . . Silent prayer, in its common form, is also profitable. Each has its peculiar advantages, as each has its place.

***

The principles of holy living extend to everything. For instance, in the matter of reading, he who has given himself wholly to God can read only what God permits him to read . . . In reading this may be a suitable direction, namely, to read but a little, and to interrupt the reading by intervals of religious recollection, in order that we may let the Holy Spirit more deeply imprint in us Christian truths.

***

Christ is the way, and the truth, and the life. The grace which sanctifies as well as that which justifies is by Him and through Him. He is the true and living way; and no man can gain the victory over sin and be brought into union with God without Christ.

***

One of the remarkable results in the soul of which faith is the sole governing principle is that it is entirely peaceful. Nothing disturbs it. And being thus peaceful, it reflects distinctly and clearly the image of Christ, like the placid lake.

***

Souls that have experienced the grace of sanctification in its higher degrees have not so much need of set times and places for worship as others. Such is the purity and the strength of their love that it is very easy for them to unite with God in acts of inward worship at all times and places. They have an interior closet. The soul is their temple, and God dwells in it. This, however, does not exempt them from those outward methods and observances which God has prescribed.

***

True holiness of heart is the object at which the Christian aims.

JANUARY 18, 2009

SUGGESTED SERMON

The Path of Wisdom

Date preached:

By Dr. David Jackman

Scripture: Proverbs 8:22–36, especially verses 34–35
Blessed is the man who listens to me, watching daily at my gates, waiting at the posts of my doors. For whoever finds me finds life, and obtains favor from the LORD.

Introduction: The beginning of Proverbs 8 is a sales pitch for wisdom. Wisdom is found in the marketplace carrying out a marketing campaign. You can't get away from the message as she raises her voice (v. 1). You can't help but see the billboards, as she is found at the heights, at the crossroads, and in the entrance to the town (v. 2). Wisdom is commending herself and the entire population is targeted (v. 4). The Bible is telling us wisdom is something we really need. In today's passage, we will see the bridge that this eighth chapter provides into the New Testament experience of wisdom and apply it to our lives.

I. **Creation Reveals the Wisdom of God (vv. 22–31).** In verse 12 we see that wisdom takes on a personality, a personification. Wisdom is referred to as "she" all the way through. Wisdom, in this passage, is commending herself which means that God is commending her to us. Verse 22 begins the section that really nails down why we should respond to the sales pitch. We're taken back to creation and given two reasons why we should love and seek God's wisdom:

A. **Wisdom's Pedigree (vv. 22–26).** The origin of the wisdom is God Himself. This wisdom isn't a human achievement but a divine attribute. The verbs "possessed" (v. 22) and "brought forth" (v. 24) can be literally translated "fathered." It comes to mean, in Hebrew, acquiring and possessing. God has wisdom— it existed before the rest of creation because it's an attribute of God Himself.

B. **Wisdom's Activity (vv. 27–31).** Not only did wisdom precede creation, but she was actively taking part in this creative work. The way God created was by wisdom. We see an entire list of creative acts of God in these verses, about which wisdom says,

"I was beside Him" (v. 30). Wisdom rejoices in humanity (v. 31) because humanity is the one creation in all of the cosmos that is able to relate to and appreciate wisdom.

2. **Redemption Requires the Wisdom of God (1 Cor. 1:30).** As Christian people we take seriously Jesus' teaching that He is the center of all the Scriptures and that the Bible finds its entire fulfillment in Him. He's the Supreme Prophet—the Word made flesh; He's the Supreme Priest—He presents His life as a sacrifice for us; He's the Supreme King—risen from the dead; He is the Shepherd Sovereign—the Leader who guides us into truth. But, He is also the Supreme Wise Man. He's the fulfillment of the picture of wisdom in the Old Testament (Luke 11:31). Paul teaches us: "But of Him you are in Christ Jesus, who became for us wisdom from God—and righteousness and sanctification and redemption" (1 Cor. 1:30). Just as we see the wisdom of God at work in creation, so we recognize wisdom even more clearly in the new creation: redemption.

3. **Those Who Are Wise Will Respond and Receive This Wisdom (vv. 32–36).** If Jesus has fulfilled all this wisdom and offers reconciliation with God, how can we grow in practical wisdom? Let's take a look at the verbs in these verses:

   A. **Listen and Obey (vv. 32–34).** Listening is the proper response to wisdom's teaching; it's not passive but an active receptivity that listens *and* says "yes." If you read through Proverbs, you'll find that the wise man is a portrait of Jesus; take heed and walk in His way!

   B. **Watch and Wait (v. 34).** These verbs are all about appetite. If you're watching at someone's gates, as this verse says, you're eager for them to come out. This is a picture of enthusiasm to find out how God wants us to live.

   C. **Find and Obtain (vv. 35–36).** God's grace and favor are offered to us; we would be very foolish to reject this offer throughout life. The wisdom is of this God who created this world, redeemed it all, and who can guide us through it perfectly.

Conclusion: The call of wisdom in Proverbs 8—with all the pedigree of the original power of wisdom in creation—now becomes the invitation of the crucified Jesus to enter into life through faith in Him. Won't you accept His invitation?

STATS, STORIES, AND MORE

Go to the Ant You Sluggard

My wife and I had some sabbatical leave one year between Christmas and Easter. We were privileged to spend six weeks of it in Singapore staying at a theological college there. Our flat was very accommodating and helpful, but one difficulty was a kitchen door that did not lie flat to the floor. Under this door there were all sorts of gaps through which various uninvited visitors came. On one occasion we were away for two or three nights and we made the mistake of leaving an open package of crackers on the counter. While we were gone, the ants seized their moment. Not hundreds of ants, but thousands of ants that came through the door and were processing across the floor, up the cupboard, onto the counter, taking crackers, and going back. They were extremely organized, surprisingly efficient, and very difficult to get rid of. Scripture tells us, "Go to the ant you sluggard! Consider her ways and be wise" (Prov. 6:6). If God can build into tiny ants the ability to seize the opportunity of a small pack of crackers, what kind of reflection of His character can He build into a human being who is in the market for wisdom? —*Dr. David Jackman*

Wisdom and Christology

In the second century of Christianity, the Christian apologist Justin Martyr noted that wisdom in Proverbs 8 was preexistent as the agent of creation. He linked this with verses such as Colossians 1:15–16: "He is the image of the invisible God, the firstborn over all creation. For by Him all things were created." Justin Martyr said that wisdom in Proverbs 8 must be Jesus. On this interpretation the Arian heresy, which was so devastating to the early church, grew up. It said that Jesus was, therefore, a created being—very highly exalted but not in very nature God. If you want the contemporary version of that heresy it's the Jehovah's Witnesses' distortion of Christianity. Still later in our day, Proverbs 8 is embraced by some feminist theologians who have seized the female personification of Christ, as they say, to argue that there's a mix of genders in the godhead. Thus God can be referred to as both father and mother, both he and she. A whole mother-god liturgy has grown up around this idea.

Wisdom in Proverbs 8 is *not* Jesus. Wisdom was created *by* God, but Christ is the eternal Son—not a created being, but in very nature, God. Wisdom in Proverbs 8 is at God's side, witnessing the creation, but Christ *is* the Creator. Wisdom is not the *agent* of creation, but the attribute of God manifested through the masterful design exhibited in His creation through His Son Jesus. —*Dr. David Jackman*

APPROPRIATE HYMNS AND SONGS

"Immortal, Invisible, God Only Wise," Walter Chalmers Smith, Public Domain.

"Be Thou My Vision," Irish Hymn c. 8th Century, Trans. by Mary E. Byrne, 1905; Versified by Eleanor Hall, 1912; Arr. by Donald Hustad, 1973, Public Domain.

"Above All," Lenny LeBlanc & Paul Baloche, 1999 Integrity's Hosanna! Music/ASCAP/Lensongs Publishing.

"Open the Eyes of My Heart," Paul Baloche, 1997 Integrity's Hosanna! Music.

"Abide with Me," Henry Francis Lyte & William Henry Monk, Public Domain.

FOR THE BULLETIN

After the outbreak of the Protestant Reformation in 1517, Roman Catholic officials convened the Council of Trent to articulate the principles of the Catholicism. The first meeting took place in 1545, and met periodically for years as decisions were made and published. The third era of these periodic sessions convened on this day in 1562, with all hope of reconciliation with the Protestants gone. ● On January 18, 1674, Scottish "Worthy" James Mitchell was executed after having been tortured for his faith. Being led to the Grassmarket in Edinburgh to be hanged, he was forbidden from preaching to the crowds, so he flung a manuscript of his message to the crowd. It said in part: "I am brought here that the work of God may be made manifest for the trail of faith, that I might be a witness for His despised truths and interests in this land, where I am called to seal the same with my blood. . . . Farewell to all earthly enjoyments; and welcome Father, Son, and Holy Ghost into whose hands I commit my spirit." ● Taylor University was established in Fort Wayne, Indiana, by Methodists on January 18, 1846. ● Today marks the birthday of John Stam (1907), who, along with his wife Betty, was murdered by the Communists in China in 1934. ● Andrew Murray, Dutch Reformed pastor in South Africa and famous devotional writer, died on this day in 1917. ● Missionary Amy Carmichael died on January 18, 1951.

Call to Worship

Brethren, we have met to worship and adore the Lord our
* God;*
Will you pray with all your power, while we try to preach the
* Word?*
All is vain unless the Spirit of the Holy One comes down;
Brethren, pray, and holy manna will be showered all around.
                                    —GEORGE ATKINS, 1819

Offertory Comments

How are you doing with your New Year's resolutions? It usually
doesn't take long for the hustle and bustle of life to overwhelm
our commitments. I wonder if you made financial commitments
this year to the Lord to give regularly and generously. Ecclesiastes
5:4–5 reminds us: "When you make a vow to God, do not delay
to pay it; for He has no pleasure in fools. Pay what you have
vowed—better not to vow than to vow and not pay." I want
to remind you today that the Lord expects us to fulfill our
commitments, and this church depends on your financial
support.

Pastoral Prayer

Heavenly Father, we praise You that what was mystery has now
been revealed, and what could not be known has now been
disclosed. We thank You that in Jesus we see the Wise Man and
we pray that we may be wise men and women as we hear His
teachings: listening, obeying, and making them the foundation
of our lives and so build on the Rock who is Christ. Thank You
that it is the cross that is the place where wisdom is fully and
finally revealed. We stand on the grounds of His work on the
cross and ask that in our lives, we may be more and more like
Jesus who is our wisdom. Hear our prayer for the honor and
glory of Your name, Amen.

Additional Sermons and Lesson Ideas

A Faith That Pleases God

Date preached:

By Dr. Timothy K. Beougher

SCRIPTURE: Mark 7:24–30

INTRODUCTION: God desires faith. He is not interested in how much money you make or how good you look. He wants you to trust in Him. Here we see a woman of low standing who in her persistence and faith delighted Jesus and stands as an example to us.

1. The Person of Faith (vv. 25–26a).
2. The Persistence of Faith (v. 26b).
3. The Test of Faith (v. 27).
4. The Response of Faith (v. 28).
5. The Result of Faith (vv. 29–30).

CONCLUSION: God often brings growth in our life through struggles; true growth in faith does not come easily. We must come to the Lord. We must approach Him humbly. We must display a persistent faith.

How to Defeat Desperation

Date preached:

By Dr. Michael A. Guido

SCRIPTURE: Psalm 42

INTRODUCTION: In our hour of desperation where can we turn? The psalmist speaks of needing God in order to survive. Throughout all of the tests and the troubles, God is there sustaining His people. He causes us to triumph because He is our strength and our life.

1. The Thirst (vv. 1–2).
2. The Tests (vv. 4–7).
3. The Taunts (vv. 3, 9–10).
4. The Triumph (vv. 8, 11).

CONCLUSION: God makes beautiful things out of broken things. He is not one to leave us in our pain. At times, He may send tests upon us so that He may show Himself trustworthy and turn us back to Him. He is Savior and God; is He yours?

JANUARY 25, 2009

SUGGESTED SERMON

The Warrior Seed and the Way We Live

By Rev. Larry Kirk

Date preached:

Scripture: Genesis 3:8–15, especially verse 15
I will cause hostility between you and the woman, and between your offspring and her offspring. He will strike your head, and you will strike his heel (NLT).

Introduction: Do you ever feel like life is a battlefield? Scripture tells us something about the inevitability of struggles in this present world and how to face them with strength and hope. It's Scripture that enables us understand what is going on in our world, what we need to do because of it, and where our true hope is found in the midst of it. Let's turn to Genesis 3 to learn how to face the battlefield of life:

1. **We Must Be Prepared to Face Life's Struggles (vv. 14–19).** Adam and Eve had turned away from God. They didn't trust His goodness or obey His commandment. They immediately experienced a spiritual death. When God came, He came with both grace and judgment.

   A. **The Judgment on the Serpent Is Both Symbolic and Real (v. 14).** When God cursed the serpent, He said it will eat dust. Satan was literally cursed as he appeared in the serpent form. At the same time, the snake is a symbol of the real Serpent's ultimate defeat. That's what it means to "eat dust" (cf. Ps. 72:9).

   B. **The Judgment on the Woman Affects Her Most Important Relationships (v. 16).** Even the greatest blessings will be accompanied by pain, and the most intimate relationship will be wounded by power struggles.

   C. **The Judgment on the Man Affects His Most Basic Responsibilities (vv. 17–19).** There was meaningful work to do before the Fall, but now there would be painful toil and a perennial battle with thorns and thistles until life is over.

2. **God Will Create a People to Stand with Him (v. 15).** Notice that God says to the serpent. "I will put enmity between you and the woman, and between your seed and her Seed." "Enmity" is opposition. God

is saying He is going create a people who will stand with Him against Satan. God was announcing that from this point on there would be two streams of humanity.

A. **The Offspring of Satan.** I know this may sound disturbing, and it should. Consider what Jesus teaches: "Why do you not understand My speech? Because you are not able to listen to My word. You are of your father the devil, and the desires of your father you want to do . . ." (John 8:43–44). Those who do not yield to the Word of Christ are ultimately the offspring of the evil one.

B. **The Offspring of God's Promise.** Colossians 1:13–14 puts it this way: "He has delivered us from the power of darkness and conveyed us into the kingdom of the Son of His love, in whom we have redemption through His blood, the forgiveness of sins." God will always have and sustain a people who will stand with Him. Are you one of those people?

3. **God Will Send a Savior to Crush the Serpent (v. 15).** "I will cause hostility between you and the woman, and between your offspring and her offspring. He will strike your head, and you will strike his heel" (NLT). Not only would there be enmity in a broad sense, but God speaks specifically about a single male individual: "He will strike your head, and you will strike his heel" (NLT).

4. **The One Who Crushes the Head of the Serpent Is Jesus Christ (1 John 3:8).** "The Son of God came to destroy the works of the devil" (NLT). The passage from Genesis also foreshadows that:

A. **In Crushing the Head of the Serpent, the Savior Will Be Wounded (Gen. 3:15).** "You will strike his heel" (NLT). Peter later explains that Jesus bore our sins in His body and that His wounds were for our healing (1 Pet. 2:24). In redeeming us, Jesus defeated Satan.

B. **Despite Being Wounded, the Savior Will Win the Battle (v. 15).** ". . . He will crush your head . . ." (NIV). The Bible tells us the decisive battle between God and Satan has already been won in the crucifixion and resurrection of Jesus Christ.

Conclusion: We stand at the other end of history from Adam and Eve. And yet, we still have a lot in common with them. The most important thing we have in common is this: the presence of sin has turned our world into a battlefield in which our only salvation is to receive God's grace and stand with Him.

STATS, STORIES, AND MORE

He Will Strike His Heel

In June of 1968, just after the Six Day War of 1967, Jewish authorities wanted to erect new homes in recently acquired property. It was just northeast of Jerusalem. But as the workers were excavating for the buildings, they unexpectedly broke through the rocky soil into several large caverns that turned out to be ancient burial chambers. It was a cemetery used by the Jews during the time of Jesus Christ. There were several skeletons, and one of them was a young man, somewhere in age between twenty-four and twenty-eight. He had been crucified by the Romans, just as Jesus was. Thousands of Jews were crucified by the Romans, but this skeleton was the first authenticated physical evidence of crucifixion in biblical times. We even know the young man's name. The inscription on the vault revealed it as "Yehohanan, the son of Hagakol." He was about five foot six, graceful in build and he had suffered no traumatic injury prior to his crucifixion. But his death had been excruciating. His arms had been tied to the crossbeam, and perhaps his wrists were nailed fast to it. The evidence for that is uncertain. His legs had been broken. But the interesting thing is this. For many centuries, Christian artists painted Jesus with his arms outstretched but with his feet crossing and a single large nail driven through his ankles. But Yehohanan's corpse told a different story and shows us just how the Romans executed their victims. The legs had been positioned so as to straddle the upright beam, and each foot was attached to the cross with a separate nail driven through the heel bone.

A thick iron nail is still embedded in the bone of the heel as it is displayed now in the Israel Museum in Jerusalem. He will crush your head, but you will strike his heel.

APPROPRIATE HYMNS AND SONGS

"A Mighty Fortress Is Our God," Martin Luther, Public Domain.

"Guide Me, O Thou Great Jehovah," John Hughes, Peter Williams, & William Williams, Public Domain.

"You Are My Strength," Reuben Morgan, 2007 Hillsong Publishing Company.

"Onward, Christian Soldiers," Sabine Baring-Gould & Arthur S. Sullivan, Public Domain.

FOR THE BULLETIN

In Christian tradition, this day commemorates the conversion of St. Paul to Christianity. ● The Roman Emperor, Nerva, dying suddenly on January 25, A.D. 98, was succeeded by his adopted son, Trajan, who proved a tireless and able administrator. It was Trajan who sent his advisor Pliny the Younger to Bithynia in 110, to check out disturbances relating to Christian activity. Pliny wrote back his famous letter, which is now our earliest extant Roman document regarding Christianity. It said, in part: On an appointed day, they meet before daybreak, recite a hymn antiphonally to Christ, as to a god, and bind themselves by an oath to abstain from theft, robbery, adultery and breach of faith. After the conclusion of this ceremony it was their custom to depart and meet again to take food. ● On January 25, 1527, Felix Manz, thirty, became the first Swiss Anabaptist to die for the faith. He was drowned by followers of Zwingli in the Limmat River in Zurich. ● Mendelssohn's "Wedding March" was presented for the first time on this day in 1858, as the daughter of Queen Victoria married the Crown Prince of Prussia. ● January 25, 1949, marks the death of Scottish-born Peter Marshall, chaplain to the United States Senate. ● On January 25, 1959, Pope John XXIII announced the Second Vatican Council to bring Roman Catholic worship and practice up to date. He attributed the idea of convening such an assembly to a sudden inspiration by the Holy Spirit. ● President John F. Kennedy was buried in Arlington National Cemetery on January 25, 1963.

WORSHIP HELPS

Call to Worship

We praise Thee, Lord, with earliest morning ray;
We praise Thee with the glowing light of day:
All things that live and move, by sea and land,
Forever ready at Thy service stand.

The nations all are singing night and day,
"Glory to Thee, the mighty God, for aye!
By Thee, through Thee, in Thee all beings are!"
The listening earth repeats the song afar.
　　　　　　　　　　　　—JOHANN FRANCK, 1869

Invitation

Have you given control of your life over to Jesus as Lord, trusting Him to save you from your sins as you turn from them? If you haven't, your life is at stake, and not just the years you have on earth. You were created for eternity and you know that, but you also sense that something is terribly wrong. You feel as if you have a mortal enemy and you feel guilty for wrongs you've done. Jesus came to destroy the works of the devil (1 John 3:8) and to free you from the punishment for your sins (Matt. 1:21). Today, the Lord wants you to join His side of the battle, the battle that He won on the cross. Give your life to Him today.

Benediction

May the LORD answer you in the day of trouble; may the name of the God of Jacob defend you . . . Save, LORD! May the King answer us when we call (Ps. 20:1, 9).

Additional Sermons and Lesson Ideas

A Threefold Duty

Date preached:

By William Graham Scroggie

SCRIPTURE: Mark 13:32–37

INTRODUCTION: The teaching of Jesus in regards to His Second Coming is always to promote conformity of life to revealed truth.

1. We Should Pray (v. 33). Pray at all times and be alert with perseverance (Eph. 6:18).
2. We Should Work (v. 34). Each of us has his own task to accomplish.
3. We Should Watch (vv. 33–37). We are told four times in this passage to be on the alert.

CONCLUSION: We are not to work just to fill up time. We have received a practical exhortation to work in and for God's kingdom. If we are to do our best work, we must recognize that to watch expectantly encourages readiness without laziness. Work without prayer is useless and vigilance without prayer is shortsighted weakness.

Getting Along with People

Date preached:

By Pastor Al Detter

SCRIPTURE: Romans 12:3–21

INTRODUCTION: The degree of our transformation is measured more by our difficult relationships than by our easy relationships. There are four behaviors that must be evident in our relation to others if we are in the process of being transformed (Rom. 12:1–2). All four of these behaviors must be evident in our lives for transformation to happen:

1. We Must Minimize the "I" Factor (Rom. 12:3).
2. We Must Serve the Church (Rom. 12:4–8).
3. We Must Concentrate on Treating People Well (Rom. 12:9–16).
4. We Must Forgive Those Who Mistreat Us (Rom. 12:17–21).

CONCLUSION: God's goal is to transform us. He gave us a new heart to make it possible and as we cooperate with Him, we'll see renewed minds, redirected bodies, and loving relationships in our lives. But, we must be willing to be transformed and we must be willing to live selfless lives.

FEBRUARY 1, 2009

SUGGESTED SERMON

The Cycle of Discipleship

Date pre(

By Dr. Kevin Riggs

Scripture: Mark 3:13–19; 6:7–13, especially 3:14
Then He appointed twelve, that they might be with Him and that He might send them out to preach.

Introduction: Life is a cycle. The planets travel around the sun; there are twenty-four hours in a day; seven days in a week; fifty-two weeks in a year. Our spiritual life is a cycle as well. Understanding this cycle will help you understand where you are and how God wants to use you. From the life and ministry of Jesus' disciples we uncover "the cycle of discipleship."

1. **Spending Time with Jesus (Mark 3:13–19).** The Bible says, "And He went up on the mountain and called to Him those He Himself wanted. And they came to Him. Then He appointed twelve, that they might be with Him and that He might send them out to preach" (Mark 3:14). The first thing Jesus wanted from His disciples was their time. The first thing Jesus wants from you when He calls you is your time. He is more concerned about your walk with Him than He is your work for Him. He would rather you *hang out with* Him than *burn out* doing ministry *for* Him. He is more interested in doing something great in you, than you doing something great for Him. Jesus wants your time, and no time spent with Jesus is wasted time. When was the last time you spent in the Scriptures, on your knees, or singing praises to Him in your car?

2. **Learning Through Experience (Mark 3–6).** Even though Jesus chose His apostles in chapter 3, He doesn't send them out until chapter 6. A lot happens between chapters 3 and 6 and the apostles are with Jesus every step of the way. In these three chapters, Jesus encounters Beelzebub, teaches in parables, calms the storm, heals a demon possessed man, raises a young girl from the dead, heals many sick people, and is rejected by His home town. These experiences were invaluable to the disciples when they were sent out by Jesus to do ministry on their own. Right now, wherever you are, whatever you

are doing, Jesus is teaching you something. Are you learning the lessons He is trying to teach you? The experience you are going through may be tough, but God will use it to teach you incredible truths.

3. **Doing Ministry for Jesus (Mark 6:8–11).** After sufficient time with Jesus had gone by, and after enough lessons had been learned through experience, Jesus sent His disciples out to put into practice what they had learned. He gave them authority to do everything He had been doing: "He commanded them to take nothing for the journey except a staff—no bag, no bread, no copper in their money belts—but to wear sandals, and not to put on two tunics. Also He said to them, "In whatever place you enter a house, stay there till you depart from that place. And whoever will not receive you nor hear you, when you depart from there, shake off the dust under your feet as a testimony against them" (vv. 8–11). What are you doing for Jesus? What does He want you to do? It is no accident that you are where you are, doing what you are doing, experiencing what you are experiencing. God wants you to use all of your experiences, and all of your gifts and talents to serve others, letting everyone know of His grace and mercy.

4. **Spending Time with Jesus (Mark 6:30).** The cycle starts all over again. "Then the apostles gathered to Jesus and told Him all things, both what they had done and what they had taught" (Mark 6:30). The importance of returning to this step cannot be overstated. You cannot continue ministering for Jesus if you do not take time out to spend with Jesus.

Conclusion: A disciple of Jesus will submit himself to this cycle, without skipping a step, or spending too much time at a step. The question for today is: Where are you in this cycle? Where do you need to be? If you don't know, the best place to start is by spending time with Jesus.

STATS, STORIES, AND MORE

A Quote from the Prince of Prayer Writers, E. M. Bounds (1835–1913)
"Today, there is no scarcity of preachers who deliver eloquent sermons on the need and nature of revival, who advance elaborate plans for the spread of the kingdom of God. But the praying preachers are rare. The greatest benefactor this age can have is a person who will bring the preachers, the church, and the people back to the practice of real praying. The reformer needed just now is the praying reformer. The leader Israel requires is one who, with clarion voice, will call the ministry back to their knees. There is considerable talk in the air about revival, however we need the vision to see that the revival we need, and the only one worth having, is the one that is born of the Holy Spirit. This kind of revival brings deep conviction for sin and regeneration of those who seek God's face. Such a revival comes at the end of a season of the Holy Spirit operating in His distinctive office, and this is conditioned on much earnest praying. Such a revival will begin in pulpit and pew alike; it will be promoted by both preacher and layman working in harmony with God."

A Quote from Vance Havner
Our Lord never put discipleship in fine print in the contract. He called on us to forsake all, take up our cross, deny self, love him more than anything else. We are not our own, we are bought with a price, the personal property of Jesus Christ with no right to anything. "Love so amazing, so divine, demands my soul, my life, my all." —*Vance Havner*[1]

APPROPRIATE HYMNS AND SONGS

"I Need Thee Every Hour," Annie S. Hawks & Robert Lowry, Public Domain.

"Still," Rebuen Morgan, 2002 Reuben Morgan/Hillsong Publishing (Admin. in U.S. by Integrity's Hosanna! Music).

"Sweeter," Israel Houghton, Meleasa Houghton & Cindy Cruse-Ratcliff, 2003 Integrity's Praise! Music, Lakewood Ministries Music & My Other Publishing Company.

"Take My Life and Let It Be," Frances R. Havergal & Henri A. Cesar Malan, Public Domain.

"I Will Serve Thee," Gloria Gaither & William Gaither, 1969 by William J. Gaither, Gaither Music Company.

[1] Vance Havner, *Playing Marbles with Diamonds* (Grand Rapids: Baker Book House, 1985), p. 18.

FOR THE BULLETIN

According to *Foxe's Book of Martyrs,* Trypho and Respicius, two eminent men, were seized as Christians and imprisoned at Nice. Their feet were pierced with nails; they were dragged through the streets, scourged, torn with iron hooks, scorched with lighted torches, and then beheaded, on February 1, A.D. 251. ● February 1, 435, is the traditional date and the Feast Day for Bridgit, famous Irish Christian and the founder of a monastery. ● On February 1, 1738, John Wesley arrived back in England following his unfruitful trip to America. Shortly thereafter at a Moravian meeting on Aldersgate Street, his heart was "strangely warmed." ● February 1, 1750, marks the marriage of John Newton and Mary Catlett. They lived together until her death forty years later, and their love story is one of the tenderest in Christian history. John Newton, a British pastor, was the author of "Amazing Grace." ● Today is the birthday of Thomas Campbell (1763), founder of the Disciples of Christ. ● Julia Ward Howe published her famous "Battle Hymn of the Republic" on February 1, 1862, in *The Atlantic Monthly.* ● American missionaries Charles and Lettie Cowman set sail for Japan, as missionaries on this day in 1901. During the course of their ministry, they founded the Oriental Missionary Society which supported mission works in Japan, Korea, Formosa, and China. Mrs. Cowman later became famous for her devotional book, Streams in the Desert. ● February 1, 1909, is the birthday of George Beverly Shea, America's beloved gospel singer.

Quote for the Pastor's Wall

Finish each day and be done with it. . . . You have done what you could; some blunders and absurdities no doubt crept in; forget them as soon as you can. Tomorrow is a new day; you shall begin it well and serenely.

—RALPH WALDO EMERSON

WORSHIP HELPS

Call to Worship

"My heart rejoices in the LORD; my horn is exalted in the LORD. I smile at my enemies, because I rejoice in Your salvation. No one is holy like the LORD, for there is none besides You, nor is there any rock like our God" (1 Sam. 2:1–2).

Reader's Theater

Reader 1:   His divine power has given to us all things that pertain to life and godliness, through the knowledge of Him who called us by glory and virtue (2 Pet. 1:3).

Reader 2:   And you, who once were alienated and enemies in your mind by wicked works, yet now He has reconciled in the body of His flesh through death, to present you holy, and blameless, and above reproach in His sight—if indeed you continue in the faith, grounded and steadfast, and are not moved away from the hope of the gospel which you heard (Col. 1:21–23).

Reader 1:   Now by this we know that we know Him, if we keep His commandments. He who says, "I know Him," and does not keep His commandments, is a liar, and the truth is not in him. But whoever keeps His word, truly the love of God is perfected in him. By this we know that we are in Him. He who says he abides in Him ought himself also to walk just as He walked (1 John 2:3–6).

Benediction

". . . let all Your enemies perish, O LORD! But let those who love Him be like the sun when it comes out in full strength" (Judg. 5:31).

Additional Sermons and Lesson Ideas

Losing My Religion (and Gaining God's)
By Dr. Larry Osborne

Date preached:

SCRIPTURE: James 1:26–27

INTRODUCTION: Our religion can often look nothing like that of God. Our religion ought to include three things.

1. Controlling My Tongue (v. 26). It's vital to keep a tight rein on this most dangerous of muscles.
2. Helping the Helpless (v. 27a). We are to be socially active in protecting those who have no protection.
3. Keeping High Standards (v. 27b). The world will be trying to pollute us and we must recognize and combat this attack.

CONCLUSION: Religion can often become a byword steeped more in tradition than in God's Word. But, God's desire is that we learn to bite our tongues, lend a helping hand to those in need, and keep ourselves pure and undefiled while remaining lights in this world.

Robbing God
By Rev. Melvin Tinker

Date preached:

SCRIPTURE: Malachi 3:6–12

INTRODUCTION: We are called to give sacrificially all we have to God. If we give up all that is ours, He promises to give us all that is His. However, we often clutch tightly the things that we deem ours and in so doing steal from God.

1. The Need for Radical Repentance (vv. 6–7). God explains that He has stayed the same and it is Israel that has strayed. He calls them to return to Him that He may return to them.
2. The Problem of Relentless Robbery (vv. 8–10a). Israel had been stealing from God by holding back their tithes and offerings. God told them to return to Him that which was rightfully His.
3. The Beauty of Real Renewal (vv. 10–12). God tells Israel to test Him and see that if they just give Him back what is His than He will bless them immeasurably and make them a blessing to all nations.

CONCLUSION: We have held back for too long. It is time to repent of our robbery and give to God what is His. Then, He can renew us as He desires and through us bless the nations in the name of Jesus Christ.

Thirty Years and Counting

This year, my wife Katrina and I celebrated our thirty-first wedding anniversary and our thirtieth anniversary pastoring. If it hadn't been for my friend, Bob Thomas, we'd be celebrating thirty-one years in both pursuits. When I finished my studies at Wheaton in 1976, I returned home and began looking for a job. I didn't expect a problem. There were many small churches throughout the mountains, and I thought I'd be settled into a pastorate in time for our wedding.

Nothing opened up. Katrina and I were married, and we visited a dozen churches needing a pastor. None of them called back. Finally, on our first wedding anniversary, August 28, 1977, we started our ministry at Harris Memorial Church in Greeneville, Tennessee. From there, we moved to Nashville to become part of The Donelson Fellowship on January 1, 1980.

Only later my friend Bob told me of his specific prayer when Katrina and I were married. In studying through Deuteronomy, Bob read this verse: *If a man has recently married, he must not be sent to war or have any other duty laid on him. For one year he is to be free to stay at home and bring happiness to the wife he has married.*

Bob prayed specifically that God would keep us out of pastoral work until our first wedding anniversary, and it happened just as he prayed. As a result, we have exactly one more year of marriage than of pastoring. This year as we celebrate our thirty-first wedding anniversary, we're also celebrating our thirtieth year in ministry.

I know less about pastoring than I knew then, but here are some lessons I've learned for what they're worth.

First, ministry is overflow. I used to claim immunity from burnout, but I realize that isn't completely true. We all have to guard against breakdowns. But emotional and spiritual exhaustion is rarer when we minister from the overflow. If I'm pouring myself into God's Word every day for my own nourishment, if I'm guarding my quiet time and replenishing my heart daily before the Throne, if I'm taking heed to myself and then to the

Continued on the next page

THOUGHTS FOR THE PASTOR'S SOUL—*Continued*

flock under my care as Paul instructed in Acts 20:20, and if I've learned to encourage myself in the Lord as David discovered in 1 Samuel 30:6—if I do those things, then I'm more resistant to what the old divines called *accidie*—a state of motivation-less fatigue.

At this point in life, I realize I need more breaks, more prayer, more rest, more study, and more faith than I've ever had before. In other words, it takes a little more effort to keep my bucket full and my energy replenished. But the old durable habits of prayer, Bible study, journaling, physical exercise, occasional getaways, and good nutrition are as workable now as ever, and praise God for that!

Second, success isn't correlated with size. While in college I attended a mega-church, and during graduate school I worked in crusades attended by mega-crowds. When I began pastoring The Donelson Fellowship, I thought we'd have one or two thousand in one or two years. When that didn't happen, I wondered what was wrong with me.

I came to realize that the Lord wants us to track numbers and value souls, but we can't use numbers as a basis for success or esteem. Nor can we get too discouraged when attendance is down. Jesus did His best work with one or two, or twelve; the multitudes proved fickle. He uses small churches in big ways, small works to achieve lasting results, and humble servants to plant acorns that become mighty forests.

Now, years later, we can look back with amazement at how God has used The Donelson Fellowship. Over time, we've ministered to thousands of people, many of whom I can't remember or indeed never met. Our missionaries are everywhere. Our pulpit ministry in printed form encircles the globe and literally reaches millions of people.

Yet the small things we do are usually larger than the big things we attempt, and success in God's eyes is faithfulness to His calling, whether large or small. That single awareness was a great help to me, and tremendously liberating. At the end of the day, the Lord isn't going to say, "Well done, thou good and *successful* servant . . . ," but hopefully we'll hear Him say, "Well done, thou good and *faithful* servant."

Third, methods change but the message remains the same. When I first started pastoring, I knew very well how to do it. Now, I hardly have a clue. As we grow older we increasingly realize how much we *don't* know. But church work has also become progressively more trendy, creative, innovative, difficult, technologically savvy, and consumer-driven. Reaching a new generation demands techniques the older generation didn't try, and some of them are good. It's just hard to keep up with it all.

Our confidence, however, comes from our unchanging message. I'm not a scholar, a theologian, or an intellectual. I wish I were. My area of concentration is the devotional exegesis and exposition of Scripture; and I'm more fascinated with God's Word than I've ever been. The more I study this Book, the more amazing it seems—its structure, its form, its beauty, its symmetry that runs full circle, its depth, its promises, its nature, its specific books, chapters, and verses.

I try to keep up with the new trends and techniques—our younger staff members help me stay current—but sometimes it all seems to go by me in a blur. It's the unchanging message of God's revealed Word that anchors my ministry and gives me the confidence to pastor a while more.

Fourth, fatigue is sometimes unavoidable but it's always an enemy. Some years ago, I spent a week in France. One afternoon I found a café, ordered a cup of coffee, and read from Henry David Thoreau's *Walden*.

It came in a flash that I was exhausted in body and spirit, and had been for a long time. On the spot I made a little list of corrective steps, things like a little extra sleep at night and a regular day off. Coming home, I implemented my list with checkered success.

Then our Building Program started just as other things were hitting me, and I became worn out again. One day I realized I was on the verge of becoming an IP—an Irritable Person (Pastor). Well, irritability in the pastorate is understandable but not helpful. So I've had to rededicate myself to my Paris list again, this time with slightly more success. *Continued on the next page*

All of which is to say, guard your energy and don't live in a state of chronic fatigue. It's not good for your family, your church, your job, or yourself. Jesus told the disciples to "come apart and rest" when they were tired, and to rest *in* Him when they were weary of heart. Even the rugged prophet Elijah needed his rest, the Israelites needed their Sabbaths, and Jesus needed a nap in the boat. Sometimes we do more by doing less.

Fifth, bitterness is a sure sign we're taking ourselves too seriously. Over the years a spot of criticism has sometimes drifted my way from one source or another, and sometimes I've bristled when it's entered my air space. But I've learned that our *righteous indignation* is usually *offended pride,* and we need to shake it off like dust from our clothes.

James wrote that our anger does not bring about the righteous life that God desires (James 1:20). If we can clear up a misunderstanding, we should reasonably try to do so; and then let it go. It's impossible to be effective when we're mad at other people, and that's why the apostle Paul said, "If it is possible, as far as it depends on you, live at peace with everyone" (Rom. 12:18 NIV).

If I've offended someone, I should apologize sincerely, then put it under the blood of Christ. If I've been slandered, I should tell the Lord about it and forget it. If others have sinned against me, I should forgive them and not let it eat at me week after week. If I've been criticized, I should consider whether the criticism is valid. If it is, I need to change; if it's not, I need to praise God and go on my way.

That's true in all areas. Take a marriage, for example. Katrina and I have learned that sulking, ranting, raving, scowling, glowering, pouting, shouting, silence, and touchiness are not good for our relationship. When we boil over, blow up, or boycott—those are the tools of the immature. Far better to lighten up, smile, roll with the punches, focus on the other person, and not take ourselves too seriously.

Much of the criticism I endured came earlier in my career when our denominational climate was more restrictive and suspicious. I have some interesting stories from those days and they make for good entertainment at staff retreats; but somehow the Lord gave me the ability to smile, overlook it, go my way, and not take any of it too seriously. I feel sorry for people who let a root of bitterness spring up within them; but the Holy Spirit is a good Gardener, and if we let Him He can uproot every bitter spirit and restore our good humor.

Sixth, there's no substitute for good leaders. My greatest blessing at The Donelson Fellowship—apart from souls saved—has been the caliber of leaders the Lord has given to us, especially among our staff, our great deacons, and our ministry committees. Decade after decade, we've had as solid and supportive a team as any church anywhere. Our musicians, our Global Outreach team, our Finance Committee, our children's and youth workers, our small group leaders, our paid and volunteer staff . . . , well, I could go on and on. God has given us great men and women with a passion for the kingdom and the ability to be team players. It's not my church or theirs—it's His, and we're all co-laborers and partners together in the work. But it sure helps to have a handful of great leaders in the pews.

PS from Katrina: Being the pastor's wife for thirty years (and in the same church for nearly twenty-eight of them) has certainly had its ups and downs. But it's been a good life. One Sunday some years ago, however, wanting out of the fishbowl, I went to a neighboring church to worship where no one knew me—but it was a disappointing experience and I never did it again. My own personal Bible study has been my anchor through the decades of mothering, homemaking, and "pastoring." When I've looked in the Bible for heroes, most women quietly went about faithfully doing their work and keeping low profiles. And I'm grateful for the many friends who have prayed regularly for Rob, the girls, and me over the years. "The fervent prayer of a righteous man/woman is the greatest force in the world" (James 5:16, my paraphrase).

FEBRUARY 8, 2009

SUGGESTED SERMON

Fighting the Battle of Anger

Date preached:

By Pastor Al Detter

Scripture: Numbers 20:2–13, especially verse 12
Then the LORD spoke to Moses and Aaron, "Because you did not believe Me, to hallow Me in the eyes of the children of Israel, therefore you shall not bring this assembly into the land which I have given them."

Introduction: Anger by itself is not a bad emotion. It's an emotional alarm system that says we're feeling hostility. But when anger takes control, people can do some pretty nasty and terrible things. Christians, like anyone else, can experience times when tempers flare. As we look at the story of Moses, I see four powerful lessons we must learn to help us control our anger.

Lessons:

1. **Restrain Yourself When Dealing with Angry People (vv. 2–5).** Angry people incite others. In verse 2, everyone in the congregation is reinforcing each other's frustration and anger; they decide to get together to let Moses and Aaron have it. They're in this big meeting pointing fingers at Moses. If you're an anger-prone person, being confronted like this is a perfect formula for a serious shouting match. When angry people come at you, things tend to escalate. We must restrain ourselves when angry people engage us. Or they'll drag us right into the fray. Moses did the perfect thing. He listened to them out and didn't retort. He didn't defend himself. He may have been churning inside, but he restrained himself.

2. **Get Before God About Upsetting Situations (vv. 6–8).** Verse 6 tells us that Moses and Aaron left the presence of the people and fell face down before the Lord at the doorway of the tabernacle. They both got pounded and they wanted to get next to God before they did a thing. That was a good move. When people are angry at us and criticize us, the sensible thing to do is to retreat before the Lord, to get away from the source of agitation and settle down. The tabernacle was where the Lord was present and where God would

speak with Moses. God told Moses exactly what to do: to gather up all the people and speak to the rock. Water would come out of the rock for everyone. These were simple instructions with miraculous results. When we retreat in our anger and bring it before the Lord, He will give us an answer through His Word.

3. **Obey God's Instructions Completely (vv. 9–11).** Up to this point, Moses was doing everything right. Now comes the part where he's supposed to do what God told him to do. Verse 9 says that Moses took the rod; that was good. Verse 10 says that Moses gathered the people before the rock; that too was good. But here's where things go south. God told Moses to speak to the rock. What did Moses do? He spoke to the people. Actually, he blasted them, "Hear now, you rebels! Must we bring water for you out of this rock?" (v. 10). He then raised his hand with Aaron's rod and struck the rock twice (v. 11). His anger had finally bubbled over. Moses obeyed God's instructions only so far and then did his own thing. Moses crossed a line. Partial obedience is sin and it's dangerous.

4. **Realize That Unrighteous Angry Behavior Is Always Harmful (vv. 12–13).** Sometimes we think angry behavior is no big deal. God thinks otherwise. God told Moses and Aaron in verse 12 that their angry behavior would prevent them from leading Israel into the Promised Land. Verse 12 reveals that Moses *didn't believe God.* Verse 24 says Moses *rebelled against God.* Moses also *compromised the holiness of God.* In 1 Corinthians 10:4, the rock is identified as Christ; Moses struck this symbol in anger not treating it as holy (Deut. 32:49–52). As Christians, how we handle our anger reflects upon God. People will form opinions about God based on how we behave when we are angry. How are you representing Him when you're angry?

Conclusion: Perhaps some of you are fighting a battle with anger. Or maybe people are angry with you and you're at a crossroads. Do what Moses and Aaron did before they sinned. Get on your face before the Lord. Let His glory surround you. And expect to hear a word from Him. Manage your anger in the power of the Lord and blessing rather than loss will be yours!

STATS, STORIES, AND MORE

More from Pastor Al Detter: Safety in Obedience

I'll never forget an afternoon I took my son, Jason, hunting. He was about fourteen at the time. We saw absolutely nothing, so I told him to stay exactly where he was—by this big tree—and not to move for *any* reason. I would make a big circle and try to drive a deer his way. We were in huge woods with deep ravines. I started to circle but I couldn't find my way back to him. A bad storm blew in and I got lost. I found my way to a blacktop road over a mile away. In less than two hours, it would be dark. I was beginning to panic.

I ran to the nearest house. The man got on the phone and within 10 minutes, we had a search party. We entered the woods where we had begun the day. I was certain he would have left the tree to find his way out. About half an hour later, I could hear shouts, "We found Jason!"

The relief I felt was so overwhelming that I cried for joy. I ran over to Jason and there he was, standing right by the tree. He never moved. I told him I was afraid that with my long time away and with the storm, he would try to get out of the woods. He said, "Dad, you told me to stay by that tree and not to move for any reason. That's what I did." The story ended well because Jason completely obeyed his dad.

A Close Call

I remember the day I sat in a worship service a few years ago. Something went on in the service that made me very angry. It had happened a number of times before, but this time, I had had it. In a few minutes, I was to preach and I was madder than a hornet.

As the music played during the offering, I had this *daydream.* I saw myself getting up in front of the church and venting my frustration. I saw myself bawling some people out and saying some pretty nasty things. I was right at the edge.

I stood up and mounted the platform. I had no idea what was going to come out of my mouth. But this little voice inside of me said, "If you do what you just did in your mind, you will not treat Me as holy in the sight of the people." I thought about Moses and his fall. In an instant of time, I started the sermon as usual. Had I done what I wanted to do, it would have been very embarrassing and I would have disrespected the Lord. One little footnote. I spoke rather directly to a few people after the service.

APPROPRIATE HYMNS AND SONGS

"Again and Again," Robert Sterling & Claire Cloninger, 2004 Juniper Landing Music/Two Fine Boys Music/Word Music, LLC.

"Lifesong," Mark Hall, 2005 Club Zoo Music/SWECS Music.

"Joyful, Joyful, We Adore Thee," Henry Van Dyke & Ludwig van Beethoven, Public Domain.

"Spirit of the Living God," Daniel Iverson, Public Domain.

FOR THE BULLETIN

On February 8, 1587, Mary Queen of Scots (Mary Stuart), age forty-four, was beheaded. An ardent Roman Catholic, she was viewed as a threat by England's Queen Elizabeth I. The Roman Catholics of England considered Mary the rightful queen and formed many conspiracies to place her on the throne. For alleged complicity in one of these she was executed. Her son later became James I of England, for whom the King James Version of the Bible is named. ● On February 8, 1693, the College of William and Mary was chartered in Williamsburg, Virginia, for the purpose of training young men for the Anglican ministry. ● Evangelist George Whitefield returned home on this day in 1744 after a preaching trip, eager to be reunited with his wife, Elizabeth, and four-month-old son, John. George was met at the door by tearful family members who told him little John had just died of a stroke or seizure. The heartbroken evangelist gathered his family for prayer. He felt he should fulfill a preaching obligation on the day of the child's burial, and he chose for his text Romans 8:28, almost breaking down as he said, "All things work together for good. . . ." ● February 8, 1865, marks the birth of Louis E. Jones, author of the gospel song, "There Is Power in the Blood." ● The Boy Scouts of America was chartered and incorporated on February 8, 1910.

WORSHIP HELPS

Call to Worship

Let us then with gladsome mind
Praise the Lord for He is kind:
For His mercy shall endure,
Ever faithful, ever sure.
                    —JOHN MILTON

Scripture Reading Medley

Mockers stir up a city, but wise men turn away anger. A fool gives full vent to his anger, but a wise man keeps himself under control. Do not be quickly provoked in your spirit, for anger resides in the lap of fools. Get rid of all bitterness, rage and anger, brawling and slander, along with every form of malice. Be kind and compassionate to one another, forgiving each other, just as in Christ God forgave you. My dear brothers, take note of this: Everyone should be quick to listen, slow to speak and slow to become angry, for man's anger does not bring about the righteous life that God desires (Prov. 19:8, 11; Eccl. 7:9; Eph. 4:31–32; James 1:19–20 NIV).

Kid's Talk

Read Proverbs 15:1: "A soft answer turns away wrath, but a harsh word stirs up anger." Explain that we are often prone to speak rudely to our siblings or friends when we get upset at each other. But the Bible says to do the opposite. Tell the children to think of something nice they can say to their brother, sister, friend, or parent next time they get upset. Ask for a few volunteers to give their answers—their kind words prepared for someone—as examples.

Additional Sermons and Lesson Ideas

A Blessed Hope
Date preached:
By Dr. Michael A. Guido

SCRIPTURE: Various

INTRODUCTION: As believers we have a hope; a blessed hope in the glorious appearing our God and Savior Jesus Christ (Titus 2:13).

1. It Is a Certain Hope (John 14:3; Acts 1:11; Rev. 22:7, 12).
2. It Is a Comforting Hope (1 Thess. 4:16–18).
3. It Is a Cleansing Hope (1 John 3:2–3; John 1:12).
4. It Is a Constraining Hope (1 Thess. 1:9–10).

CONCLUSION: We as children of God have a great and blessed hope in the return of our Savior Jesus Christ. But, there are many who will find their destruction in that day. Christ is coming soon and we must be willing to lead them to new life in Jesus Christ. In this way, they will also be partakers of the blessed hope of Christ's coming.

iServe: A Lesson in Service for the iPod Generation
Date preached:
By Pastor Jonathan Falwell

SCRIPTURE: Various

INTRODUCTION: Jesus came to serve and set an example for us as His followers. Here are four principles of a servant's lifestyle:

1. Serve Intentionally (Matt. 20:26–28).
2. Serve Continually (John 13:12–17).
3. Serve Thankfully (Col. 3:15–23).
4. Serve Compassionately (Gal. 5:13; 6:2).

CONCLUSION: The best way to serve people is not just to give them what they need physically but to provide for what they need spiritually! Charitable deeds and actions do indeed reflect the love of Christ but you need to explain to them why you are so passionate about serving them. Your life has been touched and changed by a Holy God who has given you an eternal hope and joy—a God who came and humbled Himself as a servant in the person of Jesus Christ. We also ought to humble ourselves and serve others.

FEBRUARY 15, 2009

SUGGESTED SERMON

The Best Person on Earth

Date preached:

Scripture: Job 1:1–8, especially verse 8
Have you considered My servant Job . . . ?

Introduction: "Have you considered My servant Job?" That's the question the Lord asked the devil in the book of Job, chapter 1; and that's the question I'd like to ask you today. Have you given consideration to the biblical character of Job and what he can teach us? There's one thing to notice right off the bat—Job was a man of incredible moral character, and there aren't many people like that around today. We're prone to think of Job in terms of suffering and anguish, but there are two sides to the story of Job. That's what I'd like to show you today.

1. **Integrity Comes When We Exercise Our Faith in Times of Prosperity (Job 1:1–8, 29, 31).** If we can remain true to God when things are going well, then we have integrity. The love of money is the root of all kinds of evil; but Job, a wealthy man, practiced a deep faith in God and maintained a sterling character. The book of Job begins with a summary statement about this. Job was a blameless, upright, God-fearing, evil-shunning man (v. 1), the greatest man in the east (v. 3) and the best man on earth (v. 8). He was a man commended by God and whose righteousness frustrated Satan (vv. 8–9). That's a digest of his life, but if we really become acquainted with Job, we need to turn over to chapters 29 and 31, where Job opened his heart and assessed his own life as honestly as he could, telling his friends, in essence: "I don't know why these things have happened to me, because I've tried my best to be a man of character and integrity. Let me tell you how I have lived . . . ." Notice these aspects to his life:

   A. **His Spiritual Life Is Described in Job 29:3–6.** God watched over him, and with God's light he walked through darkness, enjoying the friendly counsel of the Lord.

   B. **His Public Life Is Described in Job 29:7–11,** where he was respected by young and old as a city leader.

C. **His Generosity Is Described in Job 29:11–17,** where he cared for the poor, the fatherless, the widow, the blind, the lame, and the innocent.

D. **His Ministry Is Described in Job 29:18–25,** where he gave wise counsel and a warm countenance to those needing his encouragement.

E. **His Moral Life Is Described in Job 31,** where he made a covenant with his eyes to keep himself sexually pure (v. 1), keeping his marriage vows with diligence (v. 9). He was as honest as the day was long (vv. 5–8). The rest of chapter 31 lists additional ways in which Job had lived a life of relentless integrity. This is the way we see Job before his troubles. He was true to God amid an affluent, powerful, popular, successful life. Yet, though he was the best man on earth, by the end of the book he was an even better man—deeper, wiser, and more effective. To his integrity God added new levels of maturity.

2. **Maturity Comes When We Exercise Our Faith in Times of Adversity (whole book of Job).** The story of the book of Job has to do with suffering. Why did God allow it? One of the reasons is to take Job from good to great, to take him further into maturity, insight, understanding, and blessing than he'd ever known before (see Rom. 5:1–5 and James 1:2–8). By the end of the book, Job has a depth of character, wisdom, and influence that put him at the very heart of the Bible, in the center of the human story, and at the forefront of encouragement for millions of people over thousands of years. Trouble is never wasted in the lives of God's children. God wants us to be righteous amid affluence and faithful amid suffering.

Conclusion: If you are enjoying the blessings of God now, it's because He wants to teach you integrity. If you're going through hardship, He wants to teach you maturity. Integrity comes by trusting God in prosperity, and maturity comes by trusting Him in adversity, like the old song that says:

> When peace, like a river, attendeth my way,
> When sorrows like sea billows roll;
> Whatever my lot, Thou has taught me to say,
> It is well, it is well, with my soul.

Though Satan should buffet, though trials should come,
Let this blest assurance control,
That Christ has regarded my helpless estate,
And hath shed His own blood for my soul.

STATS, STORIES, AND MORE

Integrity
Several years ago, there was a financial journalist named B. C. Forbes who started a magazine, which today is one of the premier publications in the world of finance—*Forbes Magazine.* One day Mr. Forbes interviewed multimillionaire John D. Rockefeller, asking him for his ideas and advice. Rockefeller said, "The most important thing for a young man starting life to do is to establish a credit, a reputation, character. He must inspire the complete confidence of others."[1]

At roughly the same time B. C. Forbes was eliciting this advice from John D. Rockefeller, another journalist named Douglas Freeman, who was a journalist and historian, was writing a book about George Washington. Freeman was one of the proponents of the theory that history is largely biographical—it's not so much the story of great events, but of great men and women who inspired and caused the events. Of Washington, he wrote, "The great big thing stamped across that man is character." And by character he meant integrity, self-discipline, dependability, honesty, and resolve.[2]

Queen of the Dark Chamber
The Chinese Christian Christiana Tsai suffered from a debilitating disease much of her life. In her book, *Queen of the Dark Chamber,* we find these words: "Once a great scholar in China said, 'A sage seeks opportunities in difficulties, and a fool finds difficulties in opportunities.' We are born to overcome difficulties through the power of the Holy Spirit."[3]

[1]Charles E. Watson, *What Smart People Do When Dumb Things Happen at Work* (New York: Barnes & Noble Books, 1999), p. 69.

[2]David Hackett Fischer, *Washington's Crossing* (New York: Oxford University Press, 2004), p. 446.

[3]Christiana Tsai, *Queen of the Dark Chamber* (Chicago: Moody Press, 1953), p. 12.

APPROPRIATE HYMNS AND SONGS

"Holy Is the Lord," Chris Tomlin & Louie Giglio, 2003 Worshiptogether.com Songs/sixsteps Music.

"Ancient Words," Lynn Deshazo, 2001 Integrity's Hosanna! Music.

"When I Can Read My Title Clear," Isaac Watts, Public Domain.

"Shout to the North," Martin Smith, 1995 Curious? Music (Admin. in North America by EMI Christian Music Publishing).

FOR THE BULLETIN

February 15, A.D. 37, marks the birthday of Nero (Claudius Drusus Germanicus Caesar Nero), the Roman emperor who condemned Peter, Paul, and a multitude of Christians to death for their faith. ● February 15, 1497, is the birthday of Philipp Melanchthon, German reformer and Martin Luther's closest associate. ● On February 15, 1386, King Jagiello of Lithuania was baptized, making Lithuania the last European people to leave organized Paganism. ● The Italian scientist, Galileo, was born on this day in 1562. ● The eloquent British preacher, John Donne, preached his last sermon on this day in 1631. It was entitled, "Death's Duel." Five weeks later he passed away. He is chiefly remembered as the dean of St. Paul's Cathedral in London where he often preached before King Charles I. ● America's first foreign missionary, Adoniram Judson, found himself imprisoned in Burma, accused of spying. He was placed in a dark cell filled with vermin. Every evening he was hanged upside down with only his head and shoulders resting on the ground. His wife, Ann, was pregnant. On February 15, 1825, eight months after his arrest, she showed up at his prison carrying a small bundle, their newborn daughter Maria. Unfortunately, both Ann and Maria were later to die of fever. ● On February 15, 1860, Wheaton College is chartered in Wheaton, Illinois, "for Christ and His Kingdom." ● Lew Wallace died on this day in 1905 at age seventy-seven. He was a military leader, a lawyer, and a novelist who wrote *Ben Hur: A Tale of Christ.*

WORSHIP HELPS

Call to Worship

God is faithful, by whom you were called into the fellowship of His Son, Jesus Christ our Lord (1 Cor. 1:9).

Stewardship Emphasis

The word "stewardship" is showing up in the headlines, especially in articles about global warming, environmental care, and natural conservations. We're reading about environmental stewardship, land stewardship, and the stewardship of our natural resources. Our culture is becoming aware that we don't "own" the earth; we're borrowing it and are responsible for its keeping and care. The concept of stewardship says, in essence, that we are responsible for what belongs to another. When we talk about Christian financial stewardship, we're saying that God owns all we are and all we have. As Job 1:21 says, "Naked I came from my mother's womb, and naked shall I return there." Or as Paul put it in 1 Timothy 6:7, "We brought nothing into this world, and it is certain we can carry nothing out." The Lord holds the deed to it all, but He has entrusted its management to us. Giving a portion of it back to Him for the special work of His church and for the advancement of the gospel is a part of that stewardship trust. So let us give as we have purposed in our hearts, not grudgingly or of necessity; for God loves a cheerful giver (2 Cor. 9:7).

Benediction

Now dismiss us with Your peace, Your grace, Your guidance, Your blessing, and with Your Spirit. Work in us what is pleasing to You. And may we go forth into the battle, into service, into another week of progress and praise for the sake of Jesus Christ our Lord. Amen.

Additional Sermons and Lesson Ideas

The Prayer for Divine Plentitude
Date preached:
By William Graham Scroggie

SCRIPTURE: Ephesians 3:14–21

INTRODUCTION: The fullness of God is just God Himself as revealed in Christ and ministered by the Spirit.

    1. The Approach to Prayer (vv. 14–15).
        A. Bowed Knees (v. 14).
        B. Before the Father (v. 14).
        C. The Great Creator (v. 15).
    2. The Appeal for Plenitude (vv. 16–19).
        A. The Necessary Preparation for the Divine Fullness (vv. 16–17).
        B. The Growing Illumination in the Divine Fullness (vv. 18–19a).
        C. The Final Realization of the Divine Fullness (v. 19b).
    3. The Ascription of Praise (vv. 20–21).
        A. He Who Is Able (v. 20a).
        B. He Who Has Power (v. 20b).
        C. He Who Receives Glory (v. 21).

CONCLUSION: May we know the unfathomable and inconceivable blessing of being "filled with all the fullness of God" (v. 19).

The Romans Road Signs
Date preached:
By Dr. Ed Dobson

SCRIPTURE: Various Romans Passages

INTRODUCTION: In Romans, we see many signs that help us on the road of the Christian life.

    1. There Is a STOP Sign (Rom. 1:20; 3:22–23). God has revealed Himself to everyone.
    2. There Is a ONE WAY Sign (Rom. 5:1). Justification comes only through faith in Jesus.
    3. There Is a YIELD Sign (Rom. 6:11–14). Yield to God.
    4. There Is a RIGHT TURN ONLY Sign (Rom. 8:28). Everything is worked for good.
    5. There Is a MEN AT WORK Sign (Rom. 12:6). Exercise your God-given gifts.
    6. There Is a PASS WITH CARE Sign (Rom. 14:1; 15:1). Take care of the weak.

CONCLUSION: If we follow these signs we will be on the road to a greater understanding of Christ, our relationship to Him, other believers, the world, and how we can live our faith.

FEBRUARY 22, 2009

SUGGESTED SERMON

The Three Voices of God

Date preached:

By Dr. Larry Osborne

Scripture: Various, especially 2 Timothy 3:16
All Scripture is God-breathed and is useful for teaching, rebuking, correcting and training in righteousness (NIV).

Introduction: How many of you love cell phones? How many of you hate them at the same time? Nothing is more frustrating than a dropped call—you keep talking and have no idea that someone else is no longer on the line. Some of us feel that way in our walk with God. We have no idea whether He is "on the line" or how to tell whether He's communicating with us. Today we'll take a look at the three ways in which God speaks to us.

I. **The Bible.** Scripture is the most powerful and direct communication we have from God.

   A. **It Provides God's Point of View (2 Tim. 3:16; 2 Pet. 1:20–21).** If you want to know what God thinks about something, go to the Bible! In His point of view we get His commands, His promises, and His principles. Though it's different in each book depending on the author and the circumstance, it's exactly what God intends to communicate to us.

   B. **It Contains Real Letters to Real People.** Many people treat the Bible as a very different book, which is right in the sense that it contains the Word of God. But, they also get confused because ultimately the Bible is a compilation of literature throughout thousands of years: history, narrative stories, poetry, letters, etc.— all these are somewhat mutually exclusive, but together form the whole counsel of God's Word. We're always *reading over the shoulder* of the writers. The Bible was written *for* us but not *to* us, so that we need to understand the context of the Word.

   C. **Worry About Clear Stuff Not Obscure Stuff (2 Pet. 3:15–16).** Peter, an apostle, in these verses refers to Paul's letters as hard to understand. He also says that ignorant people distort these things. This should come to us as somewhat of a warning: it's easy to get caught up in the obscure or difficult portions of Scripture, to fight over those things to the detriment of the rest of the Bible, most of which is crystal clear. The purpose of the Bible is not to make us theologically smart, but for correction and instruction in righteousness—to change how we live (Titus 3:8–9).

2. **The Holy Spirit.**

   A. **He Provides Spiritual Insight and Understanding (Eph. 1:17; 1 Cor. 2:13).** The Bible tells me what's right and wrong, who God is, who Jesus is, how I'm supposed to live; the Holy Spirit guides me through living out this knowledge with spiritual insights and understanding.

   B. **He Changes Us from the Inside Out (John 16:6–13).** When you step over the line and give Jesus the steering wheel of your life, He forgives your sins, He adopts you into His family, and He comes and literally invades your life (Phil. 2:13).

   C. **He Primarily Guides Us Through Our Thought Processes (1 Cor. 2:10–16; Rom. 8:6–9).** Paul consistently taught that the Holy Spirit gives us the mind of Christ. It's not natural for us to see God in everything; on the contrary we tend to look at everything from our own perspective. But as we grow in Christ, our minds are informed by Scripture and guided by the Spirit to have God's perspective.

3. **Wise Counsel.**

   A. **Together We Can Decipher Things We'd Otherwise Miss (Eph. 4:11–15).** Because of our maturity level or sin in our lives, we often misinterpret Scripture or miss relevant passages completely. The body of Christ works in unison, supporting the other members. You may be in a Bible study and someone gives you a verse or an insight you hadn't considered. This is exactly how the body is intended to operate—not in isolation but in unison.

   B. **Isolation Is a Sign of Spiritual Arrogance (Prov. 13:10; Heb. 10:24–25).** If we go through life with the attitude of "all I need is my Bible and the Spirit" it may sound spiritual, but it's arrogant.

Anyone unwilling to turn to wise counsel is someone who will, sooner or later, make a fatal decision.

Conclusion: If you ever find that the voices conflict, understand that the Bible is the most clear and should be the ruling factor in any discrepancy (Acts 17:11; 2 Tim. 3:15–16; 1 Kin. 13). God has been gracious enough to give us His Word, to give us His Spirit, and to give us each other to speak to us. Are you listening?

STATS, STORIES, AND MORE

Wise Counsel

When Lou Gehrig was starting his baseball career, he went into a slump and grew so discouraged he was thinking of quitting. After several bad games, he doubted his talent and ability, and his spirits collapsed. A friend named Paul Krichell heard that Lou was slumping, and he took a train to Hartford, Connecticut, and invited Lou to join him for a steak dinner at the Bond Hotel. Lou poured out his frustrations, and Paul could see that the player's confidence was shot. Paul spent the evening telling Lou that all hitters go through slumps, that the best ones—even Ty Cobb—fail to get hits six or seven out of every ten tries. But eventually good hitters start hitting again, and, said Paul, you're a good hitter. After dinner, Gehrig walked with Paul to the train station and thanked him for coming. The next day, Lou started blasting the ball again, and over the next eleven games he came through with twenty-two hits, including six home runs—and his career took off. "I decided not to quit after all," he said.

Sometimes we need to take a train, track someone down, buy them a steak, and encourage them. We do it in many ways. Our children need encouragement. Their self-image is going to be based, in large measure, by their perceptions of what we think of them. We need to find ways to affirm their strengths and express our love and admiration for them. Our husbands and wives need encouragement more than they need harping criticism. Our coworkers and leaders and friends and neighbors need to be built up.

Blessed is the person who knows how to give and receive wise counsel.

APPROPRIATE HYMNS AND SONGS

"Be Still and Know," Traditional, Public Domain.

"Draw Me Nearer," Fanny Crosby & Diane Sheets, 2004 Word Music.

"Untitled Hymn (Come to Jesus)," Chris Rice, 2003 Clumsy Fly Music.

"I Give You My Heart," Reuben Morgan, 1995 Reuben Morgan/Hillsongs Publishing.

"Sweet Hour of Prayer," William W. Walford, Public Domain.

FOR THE BULLETIN

On February 22, 1661, Scottish Covenanter James Guthrie was placed on trial for his faith in Christ. In his defense, he said: "I beseech you to ponder well what profit there is in my blood . . . My blood, bondage, or banishment will contribute more for the propagation of these things than my life in liberty would do, though I should live many years." He was hanged in Edinburgh on June 1, 1661. ● February 22, 1680, marks the death of famed English Nonconformist preacher, Thomas Goodwin, seventy-nine. His last words were: "Ah, is this dying? How I have dreaded as an enemy this smiling friend." ● George Washington was born on this day in 1732. ● February 22, 1805 is also the birthday of hymnist Sarah F. Adams, born in Harlow, Essex, England. Sarah was a noted London actress, but when her career was disrupted by poor health she began writing poetry and hymns, her best known being "Nearer, My God, to Thee." ● On February 22, 1807, as William Wilberforce watched, the second reading of his bill to ban slavery in the British Empire was read in Parliament. He had written in his diary that morning, "God can turn the hearts of men," but prospects for victory were uncertain. To his amazement, the entire House rose, cheering and applauding his lifelong efforts. The motion carried 283 to 16. ● On February 22, 1906, the African-American evangelist, William J. Seymour, arrived in Los Angeles. He began holding revival meetings there, and the famous "Azusa Street Revival" broke out under his leadership, launching the Pentecostal movement in America.

WORSHIP HELPS

Call to Worship

"You are worthy, O Lord, to receive glory and honor and power; for You created all things, and by Your will they exist and were created" (Rev. 4:11).

Responsive Reading

Worship Leader: Man shall not live by bread alone, but by every word that proceeds from the mouth of God (Matt. 4:4).

Congregation: The word of God is living and powerful, and sharper than any two-edged sword, piercing even to the division of soul and spirit, and of joints and marrow, and is a discerner of the thoughts and intents of the heart (Heb. 4:12).

Worship Leader: Now therefore, listen to me, my children; Pay attention to the words of my mouth; Listen carefully to Me, and eat what is good, And let your soul delight itself in abundance (Prov. 7:24; Is. 55:2).

Congregation: I will hear what God the LORD will speak, for He will speak peace to His people and to His saints; but let them not turn back to folly . . . We speak the wisdom of God . . . the hidden wisdom which God ordained before the ages . . . But God has revealed them to us through His Spirit. We have received . . . the Spirit who is from God, that we might know the things that have been freely given to us by God (Ps. 85:8; 1 Cor. 2:7, 10, 12).

Benediction

Grow in the grace and knowledge of our Lord and Savior Jesus Christ. To Him be the glory both now and forever. Amen (2 Pet. 3:18).

Additional Sermons and Lesson Ideas

Redundancy
Date preached:

By Rev. Billie Friel

SCRIPTURE: Judges 3:5–11

INTRODUCTION: The predictability of humanity can be seen vividly in the book of Judges.

1. Rebellion (v. 7). The people of God began serving other Gods while dwelling among the other nations (vv. 5–6).
2. Retribution (v. 8). God is not mocked: rebellion leads to retribution. God must be the only One we serve.
3. Repentance (v. 9). God is rich in mercy and awaits our humility and our cry for help.
4. Rescue (vv. 9–10). God delivered His people through Othniel and delivers us through Christ (Luke 4:18).
5. Rest (v. 11). Peace with God brings the peace of God.

CONCLUSION: All of humanity can be found at some stage of this cycle. Run from temptation, cry out to God for help if in bondage, and be thankful and watchful if at rest. Where are you in this cycle?

Hard Times
Date preached:

By Rev. Melvin Tinker

SCRIPTURE: Ruth 1:1–22

INTRODUCTION: Sometimes God must deal with us harshly to bring about beautiful change.

1. Elimilech—A Man in Crisis (vv. 1–5). He leads his family away from God, God's land, and God's judgment to find salvation from their troubles.
2. Naomi—A Woman in Mourning (vv. 6–13). She is bitter about her misfortune but realizes that only the Lord can save her from her troubles.
3. Ruth—A Woman in Love (vv. 14–22). She turns to God recognizing that He is the only way of salvation.

CONCLUSION: God uses difficult times to shape us. At times, we run from His judgment seeking refuge in other things. Yet, His provision and mercy may drive us back into His arms. And, difficult times can often bring people who do not know Christ into a saving knowledge of Him.

COMMUNION SERMON

Do You Remember?

Date preached:

By Dr. Timothy K. Beougher

Scripture: Revelation 1:4–6, especially verses 5–6
. . . To Him who loved us and washed us from our sins in His own blood, and has made us kings and priests to His God and Father, to Him be glory and dominion forever and ever. Amen.

Introduction: You may have heard the story of the man who went to the doctor because he was struggling with his memory. He told the doctor, "Doc, I can't seem to remember anything from one minute to the next." The doctor asked him, "How long has this been going on?" The man replied, "How long has what been going on?" We may feel like that at times; we realize that we are very good "forgetters." Jesus knew all too well our tendency to forget, and one of the reasons He instituted the Lord's Supper was so that we would not forget His sacrifice for us. I would like for us to reflect on five important truths found in Revelation 1:4–6 that we should remember as we prepare to take the Lord's Supper together:

1. **God Is in Control (vv. 4–5).** Verse 4 refers to Jesus' throne in heaven; verse 5 says Jesus is "the ruler over the kings of the earth." We live in a day of great uncertainty. Many of us wake up in the morning and turn on the television or radio to see what has happened around the world overnight. There is great uncertainty in the world, but there is perfect calm in heaven. There is fear in the world, but there is perfect peace in heaven. Why? Because all the angels in heaven, all the redeemed in heaven, know full well that God is in control. From heaven's perspective it is easy to see that truth, but it is hard for us to see it sometimes.

2. **God Loves Us (v. 5b).** John refers to Jesus as "Him who loved us . . ." in verse 5. How much does God love us?

   > "God demonstrates His own love toward us, in that while we were still sinners, Christ died for us" (Rom. 5:8).

   > "Behold what manner of love the Father has bestowed on us, that we should be called children of God!" (1 John 3:1).

"In this the love of God was manifested toward us, that God has sent His only begotten Son into the world, that we might live through Him. In this is love, not that we loved God, but that He loved us and sent His Son to be the propitiation for our sins" (1 John 4:9–10).

God shows His love by meeting our greatest need: our need for forgiveness. If we want proof of God's love for us, we only need to look at the cross. Calvary is the absolute, irrefutable proof of God's love for us. We need to remember His great love for us and celebrate that love as we prepare our hearts to partake of the Lord's Supper.

3. **Our Sins Have Been Forgiven (v. 5b).** John refers to Jesus again as Him who "washed us from our sins in His own blood." Hebrews 9:22 tells us "without the shedding of blood there is no forgiveness" (NIV). Under the old covenant, that blood was of an innocent bull, goat, or lamb. When that animal was sacrificed in the temple, the blood conveyed reconciliation with God. As we reflect on the new covenant, brought by Jesus Christ, the apostle Peter reminds us in 1 Peter 1:18–19: "knowing that you were not redeemed with corruptible things, like silver or gold, from your aimless conduct received by tradition from your fathers, but with the precious blood of Christ, as of a lamb without blemish and without spot." It is only through Christ that we can be delivered from judgment, and experience forgiveness of sins and eternal life in heaven with God. As we celebrate the Lord's Supper, we need to remember our sins have been forgiven.

4. **We Are Called to Serve Him (v. 6a).** John continues to explain that Jesus "has made us kings and priests to His God and Father." It has been said that believers "Gather to worship, then depart to serve." That is never truer than when we celebrate the Lord's Supper.

"How much more, then, will the blood of Christ, who through the eternal Spirit offered himself unblemished to God, cleanse our consciences from acts that lead to death, so that we may serve the living God!" (Heb. 9:14 NIV).

"For we are God's workmanship, created in Christ Jesus to do good works, which God prepared in advance for us to do" (Eph. 2:10 NIV).

We need to be reminded that His sacrifice was not just so that we might be forgiven, but also so that we can serve Him.

5. **We Must Live for His Glory (v. 6b).** John concludes this paragraph: "to Him be glory and dominion forever and ever. Amen." We are to live for His glory. One of the truths that celebrating the Lord's Supper reminds us of is that *it is SO not about us!* It's all about Him and His glory. As Paul reminds us in 1 Corinthians 10:31: "So whether you eat or drink or whatever you do, do it all for the glory of God" (NIV). He also reminds us that recognizing God's grace destroys our pride: "For it is by grace you have been saved through faith—and this not from yourselves, it is the gift of God—not by works, so that no one can boast" (Eph. 2:8–9 NIV). We are to live for His glory.

Conclusion: In a few moments we are going to celebrate the Lord's Supper together, but first let's have a time of quiet meditation. May God's Word penetrate our hearts with these five important truths: God is in control; God loves us; our sins have been forgiven; we are called to serve Him; and we must live for His glory. Let's reflect on these truths as we prepare our hearts, confessing any known sin to the Lord.

When Your Denomination Changes

Rev. Melvin Tinker

Vicar of the Church of St. John Newland, Hull, England;
Editor of "Restoring the Vision—Anglican Evangelists
Speak Out," and the Anglican Evangelical Crisis

What can you tell us about events in the last few years that have brought major challenges to the Anglican Church?

In England, the attendance at Anglican Churches has shown an overall decline during the last decade or so—8 percent in the 1980's and 17 percent in the 1990's (more than a million people from 1989–99). The liberal churches have especially declined. The only area in which growth was seen was amongst those who would designate themselves evangelical. There has been increasingly centralization, with more power being taken away from the local church and an overall downsizing. Many Dioceses are in financial difficulty, but there is a reluctance to see this as a symptom of a deeper spiritual malaise. Along with the increasing feminization of the denomination and the ordaining of more women, there is also increased pressure to legitimize the ordination of practicing homosexuals. This liberal trend is a feature of the West in general. However, the largest numbers of Anglicans are in Africa. Here the gospel is thriving and orthodoxy is championed. There could well be a significant shift in the Anglican world away from Canterbury and the West and to Africa and the Southeast Asian countries.

How have you responded to these challenges?

The primary problem is a spiritual one. We aren't battling with flesh and blood, but principalities and powers, and so we respond accordingly. We pray, we proclaim, we evangelize, teach God's Word, care for God's people, and contend for the faith. We put the gospel first and work with like-minded evangelical believers within and outside the denomination. We also work politically with fellow evangelicals through networks such as REFORM and

Continued on the next page

CONVERSATIONS IN THE PASTOR'S STUDY—*Continued*

Anglican Mainstream. We seek to train up gospel workers and deploy them with or without the help of the denomination. Historically this has been the genius of British evangelicalism as we see with the likes of George Whitefield, the Wesley Brothers, William Wilberforce, Charles Simeon and others—getting on with the task whatever the opposition.

What advice can you give pastors who may see similar challenges brewing in their own denominations?

First, realize that God does not change nor does the gospel. We have been here before, and God has often shown mercy and worked despite the denomination. This is an "Ephesus" situation, so what Paul said to Timothy about the church of Ephesus in 2 Timothy 2:14–4:7 really applies directly to us. We are to keep on preaching the Word in season and out of season.

Second, we need to have a proper biblical view of the church. Thankfully, the denomination is **not** a church (though we call it that)—it is a para-church body. The church is always a congregation, either the local gathering of believers or the heavenly gathering of the universal/heavenly/catholic church; and it is this which is central to God's purposes in the world, which Christ is building and against which the gates of Hades will not prevail. These are the sheep we're to protect from the wolves and feed with God's Word. We are to keep them uppermost in our hearts. With Timothy we are not to 'lose our head' but do what is right and leave the consequences to God. It is not easy (especially if we want to be liked), but it is what God expects of us. After all, the Great Shepherd died for His sheep; often we simply have to suffer abuse for them by the powers that be.

MARCH 1, 2009

Rights and Rewards

Date preached:

By Rev. Peter Grainger

Scripture: 1 Corinthians 9:1–18, especially verse 18
What is my reward then? That when I preach the gospel, I may present the gospel of
Christ without charge, that I may not abuse my authority in the gospel.

Introduction: Living in a free country has engrained in us the idea of
"inalienable rights." But would you be willing to lay down these rights
if it meant the spread of the gospel? Paul is an excellent example of
one who was willing and who did just this. As an apostle, he deserved
certain things, but laid them down for the sake of Christ.

1. **Rights (vv. 1–14).** Before dealing with the rights of an apostle, Paul
   began (in vv. 1–2) by defending his credentials, arguing that he was
   a genuine apostle who qualified for these rights. The *experience of Paul*
   (Acts 9:1–6) and the *existence of the Corinthian church* prove genuine
   apostleship. Paul then moved to establish rights which every apostle
   should expect:

   A. **The Right to Food and Drink (v. 4).** An apostle should receive
   the basic necessities of hospitality and care.

   B. **The Right to Take a Wife on His Travels (v. 5).** The issue here is
   not whether an apostle should be married or not, but that he should
   be allowed to take his wife on his travels and she should receive
   the same hospitality as her husband.

   C. **The Right to Pay (v. 6).** Should Paul and Barnabas be the only
   ones who must work for a living? The answer is clearly "No."
   Every apostle should have the right to be supported. And to back
   this up, he gave supporting evidence from four sources:

   1) **Common Practice (v. 7).** The soldier is paid a salary for his
   services, the viniculturist can eat some of the grapes from the
   vines he tends, and the shepherd can drink milk from the flock
   he looks after.

   2) **Scriptural Precedent (vv. 8–12; Deut. 25:4).** The law of Moses, given by God, said that an ox which was treading out the grain in preparation for winnowing should not be muzzled but allowed to eat some of the grain (Deut. 25:4). In the same way, those who work in God's service should benefit from their work.

   3) **Temple Practice (v. 13; Lev. 7).** In every temple in the ancient world, the priests who served and offered sacrifices on behalf of the worshiper were given some of the offerings for their own use, not least in the Jewish temple (Lev. 7).

   4) **Christ's Command (v. 14; Matt. 10:8–10; Luke 10:4–7).** Paul refers to Christ's teaching; the right to pay is legitimate. What is surprising is that, having taken so much time to defend these rights, he chooses not to use them.

2. **Reward (vv. 15–18).** Paul wasn't writing about forfeiting his right to pay in the hope that the Corinthians would take the hint and pay him (v. 15). It's the privilege of preaching the gospel, the good news about Jesus, that takes precedent over everything else.

   A. **Not a Choice but a Calling (v. 16).** Paul was under a divine compulsion, called by God to preach the gospel of Jesus. His calling was so strong that, if he were to abandon it, he would be under divine judgement.

   B. **Not a Salary but a Reward (vv. 17–18).** If preaching the gospel were simply a matter of a career choice, then Paul should expect some reward, some pay for the job; but that is not the case for Paul. His reward is to preach the gospel without pay!

3. **Reasons.** Why did Paul abandon his right for pay in this particular situation in Corinth? For at least two reasons:

   A. **To Avoid Compromising the Messenger (v. 19).** Paul knew that the Corinthians, influenced by their own cultural practices and predisposition, would want some return for their money if he allowed them to pay his salary.

   B. **To Avoid Confusing the Message (v. 12).** In Corinth, the value of a message was evaluated by how much the preacher charged to pass it on. But the gospel of Jesus Christ was a message about

God's grace, His free gift of forgiveness and new life which could not be bought or earned.

Conclusion: We must seek out any hindrances to the gospel being preached in and through our lives. We should freely and joyfully lay down our own rights that the gospel may be advanced.

STATS, STORIES, AND MORE

More from Rev. Peter Grainger

First Corinthians 9 may seem very strange to us: not just that Paul refused a salary but also that the church members were upset about it. Surely, it would be every church's dream to get the services of a pastor like Paul free of charge! So, the first thing we need to do is to understand the background to the situation in Corinth, which is very different from ours. In the Greek and Roman world of the first century, itinerant philosophers and religious teachers could support themselves in one of four ways: charging fees for their services, staying in well-to-do households supported by a patron, begging, or working for a living. Working for a living was the least popular and least esteemed. People reasoned that anything worthwhile was worth paying for, and so the more important the message and the more important the messenger the more the pay.

The followers of Jesus claimed that their message was the most important message the world had ever received: a final and definitive message from God concerning His Son, Jesus. And the most important custodians of this message were the apostles, those especially commissioned by Jesus to preserve and promulgate His teaching. The Christians in Corinth knew about these apostles of Jesus and some had even visited their city and accepted pay and perks for their services. But Paul hadn't and didn't. So, if Paul didn't charge for his services, it threw into doubt whether he was the genuine article. And, if he wasn't a proper apostle, then he had no real authority over them. Thus they didn't need to pay any attention to what he wrote in his letters to them, let alone follow his example on issues such as eating meat which had been offered to idols.

APPROPRIATE HYMNS AND SONGS

"Take My Life," Scott Underwood, 1994 Mercy/Vineyard Publishing.

"Rock of Ages," Rita Baloche, 1997 Maranatha Praise, Inc.

"Joy Unspeakable," Barney E. Warren, Public Domain.

"Doxology," Thomas Ken (tune of OLD HUNDRETH), Public Domain.

FOR THE BULLETIN

George Wishart, an early Scottish Reformer, began preaching in Dundee from the book of Romans. Throngs attended his sermons, among them a young man named John Knox, who began serving as Wishart's bodyguard. Archbishop David Beaton sought to repress Protestants; and as Wishart's arrest grew more certain, Knox asked to remain at his side. "No," said Wishart, "one is sufficient for a sacrifice at this time." On the morning of March 1, 1546, Wishart was led to the stake where he told the crowds, "I exhort you, love the Word of God and suffer patiently. I know surely that my soul shall sup with my Saviour this night." He was then strangled and his body burned to ashes. ● On March 1, 1562, a group of French Protestants (Huguenots), meeting in a barn at Vassy for religious exercises, was attacked, and many of them were massacred by the followers of the Duke of Guise. ● Today marks the death, in 1625, of Pastor James Robinson of Pilgrim Fathers fame. ● John Berridge, an unusual and effective evangelical revivalist and hymnist, was born on this day in 1716 in Kingston, Nottinghamshire, England. ● Hudson Taylor arrived in China on this day in 1854. ● March 1, 1861 is the birthday of Carrie E. Rounsefell, a New Hampshire native best remembered for her hymn, "I'll Go Where You Want Me to Go, Dear Lord."

PRAYER FOR THE PASTOR'S CLOSET

I myself need Thy support, comfort, strength, holiness,
that I might be a pure channel of Thy grace,
and be able to do something for Thee;
Give me then refreshment among Thy people,
and help me not to treat excellent matter in a defective way,
or bear a broken testimony to so worthy a redeemer,
or be harsh in treating of Christ's death, its design and end,
from lack of warmth and fervency.
And keep me in tune with Thee as I do this work.
                    —AN OLD PURITAN PRAYER, taken from
                    The Valley of Vision

WORSHIP HELPS

Call to Worship

And now my head shall be lifted up above my enemies all around me; therefore I will offer sacrifices of joy in His tabernacle; I will sing, yes, I will sing praises to the LORD (Ps. 27:6).

Suggested Scriptures

- Genesis 14:22–23
- Leviticus 2:1–3; 27:30–32
- Deuteronomy 14:23–25
- Malachi 3:10
- Mark 12:33

Offertory Comments

As we focus today on 1 Corinthians 9, it's easy to get confused about tithes and offerings. Paul seems to reject the Corinthians' desire to give him money for his ministry. However, many times throughout the Scriptures Paul and others in ministry do take, distribute, and even live off of what is given to the Lord. The key is that when we tithe, we're not giving money to a building, to a preacher, or to a youth pastor, but to the Lord. The Lord will do His work with or without our offerings, but what a privilege to be a part of it and what a blessing for our staff and me to give our lives more freely to ministry as our financial burdens are shared with this body.

Quote for the Pastor's Wall

Efficiency is doing things right; effectiveness is doing the right things.

—PETER DRUCKER

Additional Sermons and Lesson Ideas

Sowing
By Dr. Michael A. Guido

Date preached:

SCRIPTURE: Psalm 126:5–6

INTRODUCTION: Lives are changed when God's Word is preached.

1. Mark the Task (v. 6). We are to go and preach (Mark 16:15).
2. Mark the Tears (vv. 5–6). Our sowing should be marked with tears for the sins of others.
3. Mark the Treasure (v. 6). The seed we have is the precious life-giving gospel of Christ.
4. Mark the Triumph (vv. 5–6). When we sow, God will reap.

CONCLUSION: When you stick to sowing the seed, you can depend upon this—your labor isn't in vain. We must be willing to sacrifice our lives and our tears for the good of the gospel and the hope of the world.

The Tempestuous Tongue
By Dr. Melvin Worthington

Date preached:

SCRIPTURE: Various Passages from James

INTRODUCTION: What would you say if someone asked you the percentage of your speech that is glorifying to God in comparison to that which is not? If we think about this for a moment, we realize the intensity of our struggle with godly speech. Perhaps no New Testament writer illustrates this more extensively than James. He describes many ways in which we misuse our mouths:

1. The Hasty Tongue (1:19).
2. The Hypocritical Tongue (1:26).
3. The Heartless Tongue (2:15–16).
4. The Hellish Tongue (3:6).
5. The Heathen Tongue (5:12).

CONCLUSION: No man can tame the tongue (3:8); we must rely upon the Holy Spirit to sanctify our speech (Rom. 12:1–2).

TECHNIQUES FOR THE PASTOR'S DELIVERY

Charles Spurgeon's Advice on the Voice
Condensed from His Lectures to His Students

One of the surest ways to kill yourself is to speak from the throat instead of the mouth. Open your mouths when you speak, for much of inarticulate mumbling is the result of keeping the mouth half closed. It is not in vain that the evangelists have written of our Lord, "He *opened His mouth* and taught them."

Moreover, brethren, avoid the use of the nose as an organ of speech, for the best authorities are agreed that it is intended to smell with. Time was, when the nasal twang was the correct thing, but in this degenerate age you had better obey the evident suggestion of nature and let the mouth keep to its work without the interference of the olfactory instrument.

Demosthenes took, as you know, unbounded pains with his voice, and Cicero, who was naturally weak, made a long journey into Greece to correct his manner of speaking. With far nobler themes, let us not be less ambitious to excel.

Always speak so as to be heard. I know a man who weighs sixteen stone, and ought to be able to be heard half-a-mile, who is so gracelessly indolent, that in his small place of Worship you can scarcely hear him in the front of the gallery. What is the use of a preacher whom men cannot hear? It is hateful to hear a big fellow mutter and whisper when his lungs are quite strong enough for the loudest speech; but at the same time, let a man shout ever so lustily, he will not be well heard unless he learns to push his words forward with due space between.

Do not as a rule exert your voice to the utmost in ordinary preaching. Two or three earnest men, now present, are tearing themselves to pieces by needless bawling; their poor lungs are irritated, and their larynx inflamed by boisterous shouting, from which they seem unable to refrain.

Now it is all very well to "Cry aloud and spare not," but "Do thyself no harm" is apostolical advice. When persons can hear you

Continued on the next page

TECHNIQUES FOR THE PASTOR'S DELIVERY—*Continued*

with half the amount of voice, it is as well to save the superfluous force for times when it may be wanted.

"Waste not, want not" may apply here as well as elsewhere. Be a little economical with that enormous volume of sound. Do not give your hearers headaches when you mean to give them heartaches: you aim to keep them from sleeping in their pews, but remember that it is not needful to burst the drums of their ears. The Lord is not in the wind. Thunder is not lightning. Men do not hear in proportion to the noise created; in fact, too much noise stuns the ear, creates reverberations and echoes, and effectually injures the power of your sermons.

Adapt your voice to your audience; when twenty thousand are before you, draw out the stops and give the full peal, but not in a room which will only hold a score or two.

Whenever I enter a place to preach, I unconsciously calculate how much sound is needed to fill it, and after a few sentences my key is pitched. If you can make the man at the end of the chapel hear, if you can see that he is catching your thought, you may be sure that those nearer can hear you, and no more force is needed, perhaps a little less will do—watch and see.

Observe carefully the rule to *vary the force of your voice*. The old rule was to begin very softly, gradually rise higher, and bring out your loudest notes at the end. Let all such regulations be blown to pieces at the cannon's mouth; they are impertinent and misleading. Speak softly or loudly, as the emotion of the moment may suggest, and observe no artificial and fanciful rules.

Do not start at the highest pitch as a rule, for then you will not be able to rise when you warm with the work; but still be outspoken from the first. Lower the voice when suitable even to a whisper; for soft, deliberate, solemn utterances are not only a relief to the ear, but have a great aptitude to reach the heart.

Do not be afraid of the low keys, for if you throw force into them they are as well heard as the shouts. You need not speak in a loud voice in order to be heard well. Macaulay says of William Pitt, "His voice, even when it sank to a whisper, was heard to the remotest benches of the House of Commons."

It is not the loudness of your voice; it is the force which you put into it that is effective. I am certain that I could whisper so as to be heard throughout every corner of our great Tabernacle, and I am equally certain that I could holler and shout so that nobody could understand me.

A bell will be heard much further off than a drum; and very singularly, the more musical a sound is the farther it travels. It is not the thumping of the piano which is needed, but the judicious sounding of the best keys. You will therefore feel at liberty to ease the strain very frequently in the direction of loudness, and you will be greatly relieving both the ears of the audience and your own lungs.

Try all methods, from the sledgehammer to the puffball. Be as gentle as a zephyr and as furious as a tornado. Be, indeed, just what every common-sense person is in his speech when he talks naturally, pleads vehemently, whispers confidentially, appeals plaintively, or publishes distinctly.

We are bound to add—*endeavor to educate your voice.* Grudge no pains or labor in achieving this, for as it has been well observed, "However prodigious may be the gifts of nature to her elect, they can only be developed and brought to their extreme perfection by labor and study."

We are bound to use every possible means to perfect the voice by which we are to tell forth the glorious gospel of the blessed God. Take great care of the consonants, enunciate every one of them clearly; they are the features and expression of the words. Practice indefatigably till you give every one of the consonants its due; the vowels have a voice of their own, and therefore they can speak for themselves.

Observe the statues of the Roman or Greek orators, look at Raphael's picture of Paul, and, without affectation, fall naturally into the graceful and appropriate attitudes there depicted, for these are best for the voice. Get a friend to tell you your faults. What a blessing an irritating critic will be to a wise man!

MARCH 8, 2009

A Bridesmaid's Rules

Date preached:

By Rev. Todd M. Kinde

Scripture: Matthew 25:1–13, especially verses 10 and 13
". . . the bridegroom came, and those who were ready went in with him to the wedding; and the door was shut . . . Watch therefore, for you know neither the day nor the hour in which the Son of Man is coming."

Introduction: One festive custom that is part of the wedding day is showering the married couple with rice, bird seed, or bubbles as they proceed to the car after the ceremony. Similarly, weddings in the ancient days were family celebrations. The feast itself could last up to a week. In preparing for the actual ceremony, a processional would move from the bride's house escorting her to the bridegroom's house where the ceremony and feast would occur (cf. Ps. 45). Torches lit the way in the darkness so the bridesmaids would have to have enough oil to keep the torches lit for the full length of the processional.

Rules:
1. **You Can Sleep—God May Delay His Coming Longer than We Expect (vv. 1–5).** Jesus tells this parable as an illustration of the kingdom of heaven. The Groom of this parable is the ultimate Groom, the King Himself on His wedding day. The parable likens us to the bridesmaids. These are all active participants in the procession but five are foolish and five are wise. There is, however, a delay in the arrival of the bridegroom. The delay is so long that all ten bridesmaids fall asleep. There is nothing wrong with sleep. The wise can sleep with a clear conscience for they are prepared—all the provisions have been made (Ps. 4:8; 127:1–2). The foolish sleep, but perhaps with a guilty conscience, filled with anxieties about their needs, or completely ignorant of their true situation and need (Prov. 6:6–11; 10:5; 26:14). The coming of Christ is delayed. We do not know the hour of His coming so we must be prepared. We must be ready and waiting.

2. **But You Can't Borrow—Discipleship May Be More Difficult than We Thought (vv. 6–9).** Discipleship may be more difficult than we

first anticipated (Luke 14:26–33). To be a follower of Christ is not merely praying some prayer once and then letting your light go out (Matt. 5:14, 16). When the King does return for His bride, the foolish maidens are found lacking oil for their lamps. They ask if they can borrow from the others and the answer is, "No." If the wise maidens who had brought a supply of oil had shared, then they all would run out and the Groom would arrive with no one to receive Him. The lesson is this, in the life of faith you cannot borrow from others (Ezek. 14:12–20). You cannot assume that church attendance or a life of good deeds necessarily indicates salvation. Where there is no submission to the rule and reign of King Jesus in the life, there is no membership in the kingdom of heaven. Many can be deceived into thinking that they are saved when they really are not and never have been. They have no oil and no light.

3. **Don't Be Late—When the End Comes It May Be Too Late to Prepare (vv. 10–13).** To confirm this thought look at verses 10a–13. The foolish bridesmaids did go to the shops and find some oil, but in their absence the Groom arrived. When they did return from their errand they met a closed door. They pleaded for the door to be opened but it was too late to join the party. The Groom says, "I do not know you." Now you may knock and the door will be opened and the Lord will eat with you (Rev. 3:20) but wait too long and the door will be shut not to be opened again. For this we might consider the flood of Noah's day. Eight went into the ark and were saved. Multitudes remained outside but "the LORD shut him in" (Gen. 7:16).

Conclusion: The time of repentance is now. You need wisdom from God to live in His kingdom under His rule. The wisdom of God is found in Christ (1 Cor. 1:24). Count the personal cost of following Jesus and yield to His reign and rule over you now. You cannot borrow from anyone else but Christ. Don't be too late to get the wisdom of Christ!

STATS, STORIES, AND MORE

Waiting Too Long

In the autobiography of Peter Cartwright, the Methodist frontier evangelist told of preaching in a particular city where he met a young man from one of the Eastern states. This fellow was well-educated and well-mannered. He was staying in the same hotel as Cartwright, and the two men struck up a friendship. Cartwright shared the gospel, but the man said (in paraphrase), "I know I need to get myself right with God. I certainly intend to do it. I'm not quite ready right now." Nothing Cartwright could do or say would change the young man's mind. Shortly afterward, Cartwright was given a message. The young man had fallen ill and was suffering a dangerously high fever. His body began shutting down, and the doctors fell back in helpless horror as some kind of disease took over his body. Cartwright rushed to the young man's bedside, and this is what the dying man said: "Oh, if only I had taken your advice a few days ago . . . I would now be ready to die. But I was stubborn and resisted it. If I had yielded then, I believe God would have saved me from my sins, but now, racked with pain almost insupportable and scorched with burning fevers, and on the very verge of an eternal world, I have no hope in the future; all is dark, dark and gloomy. . . . And I must now make my bed in hell, and bid an eternal farewell to all the means of grace, and all hope of heaven. Lost! Lost. Forever lost!" And with those words he died. He had waited too long. We may not have very much time left, and the Bible says, "Today is the day of salvation."

APPROPRIATE HYMNS AND SONGS

"When the Night Is Falling," Dennis Jernigan, 1991 Shepherd's Heart Music.

"Better Is One Day," Matt Redman, 1995 Kingsways ThankYou Music.

"Rejoice, the Lord Is King," Charles Wesley, Pubic Domain.

"When He Shall Come," Almeda J. Pearce, Copyright 1934 by Almeda J. Pearce.

"Jesus Is Coming Again," John W. Peterson, 1987 by John W. Peterson Music Company.

FOR THE BULLETIN

March 8, 1607, is the birthday of Johann Rist, German clergyman and hymnist, best known for the Lutheran hymn, "Break Forth, O Beauteous Heavenly Light." ● A dramatic earthquake occurred this day in 1750 in London (the last earthquake to have an epicentre in London). One of the most unusual hymnbooks ever published came out of this event—Charles Wesley's *Hymns Occasioned by the Earthquake, March 8, 1750.* Included is the hymn "Woe to the Men on Earth Who Dwell." One stanza says, "Lo! From their seats the mountains leap, the mountains are not found; / transported far into the deep, and in the ocean drowned. / Who then shall live, and face the throne, / and face the Judge severe? / When heaven and earth are fled and gone, / O where shall I appear?" ● On March 8, 1839, Phoebe Palmer Knapp was born in New York City, the daughter of evangelists Walter and Phoebe Palmer. Phoebe grew up to become a wealthy socialite in New York, but she always maintained her Christian zeal. One of her closest friends was hymnist Fanny Crosby. It was Phoebe Palmer who wrote a delightful tune and played it for the blind hymnist who immediately clapped her hands and exclaimed, "That says 'Blessed Assurance!'" Thus was born one of history's favorite gospel songs. ● March 8, 1857 is the birthday of William Young Fullerton, who came to Christ under the preaching of Charles Spurgeon. He later became a powerful Baptist preacher in England and the President of the Baptist Union. He was also a hymnist and the author of "I Cannot Tell." ● American pastor Henry Ward Beecher died on this day in 1887. His last words were, "Going out into life, that is dying." ● On March 8, 1948, the United States Supreme Court ruled that religious instruction in public schools was unconstitutional.

Quote for the Pastor's Wall

If I should write of the heavy burden of a godly preacher, which he must carry and endure, as I know by my own experience, I should scare every man from the office of preaching.

—MARTIN LUTHER

WORSHIP HELPS

Call to Worship
I will declare Your name to My brethren; in the midst of the assembly I will praise You. You who fear the LORD, praise Him! My praise shall be of You in the great assembly; I will pay My vows before those who fear Him. All the ends of the world shall remember and turn to the LORD, and all the families of the nations shall worship before You (Ps. 22:22, 23a, 25, 27).

Invitation to Recommitment
I'd like to take a moment to ask if anyone here has been trying to borrow oil from another's lamp. Have you been coming to church, but without engaging or getting involved, just to get your spiritual "fix" for the week? Do you ask for prayer but never pray for others? Are you prepared for the return of Christ? I ask today that you confess your sin before the Father and turn away from a lifestyle of attempting to live off others' faith without living out your own with them. Hear the words of Jesus from the book of Revelation—a book about being prepared for His return—as he calls the church of Laodicea to this kind of repentance: "Those whom I love I rebuke and discipline. So be earnest, and repent. Here I am! I stand at the door and knock. If anyone hears my voice and opens the door, I will come in and eat with him, and he with me" (Rev. 3:19–20 NIV).

Benediction
Seek the LORD and His strength; seek His face evermore! Remember His marvelous works which He has done, His wonders, and the judgments of His mouth (1 Chr. 16:11–12).

Additional Sermons and Lesson Ideas

Gradually
By Dr. Timothy K. Beougher

Date preached:

SCRIPTURE: Mark 8:22–26

INTRODUCTION: God often works in ways that don't make sense to us. He doesn't follow a standard method when He works. However, He is sovereign and knows what is best for us. It's not our duty to question His methods. Instead we should trust Him and seek to obey and follow His leadings so that we may be changed and glory brought to His name.

1. God Can Work However He Wants—He Is Sovereign (vv. 22–23).
2. We Must Respond Obediently to God's Promptings (vv. 22–23).
3. Faith Sometimes Comes Gradually (vv. 24–25).
4. God Opens Blind Eyes (v. 25).

CONCLUSION: We shouldn't expect God to work according to our time schedule or according to the ways we think best. We should instead allow Him to lead and trust that His ways are good. God will heal our spiritual blindness if we will simply and obediently look to Him.

Sin in the Camp
By Dr. Larry Osborne

Date preached:

SCRIPTURE: 1 Corinthians 5:1–13

INTRODUCTION: How should the church respond to sin within the church?

1. The Situation (v. 1). Sexual immorality of a horrible kind pervaded the Corinthian church. Paul wasn't about to turn a blind eye or join in the church's acceptance of this behavior.
2. The Church's Strange Response (v. 2). The church actually affirmed rather than rejected this immorality.
3. How to Respond to Sin in the Camp (vv. 3–5). With Scripture as our authority, believers are called to remove sin from their midst; if someone is blatantly sinning and will not repent they are to be removed.
4. Why the Big Deal? Sin Is Contagious (vv. 6–8). The body of Christ is to remain pure since He is pure. Paul explains that allowing immorality is a recipe for disaster!
5. Clearing Up Some Major Confusion (vv. 9–13). Paul explained that believers are certainly to associate with those who are immoral and sinful outside the church to win them to Christ, but that we are to remove those who call themselves believers and yet indulge in this behaviour.

CONCLUSION: We must expose sin to the Light and exercise church discipline. This is God's way to keep the church pure and to incite the sinning brother or sister toward restoration.

MARCH 15, 2009

SUGGESTED SERMON

Live Different: Wisdom

Date preached:

By Pastor Jonathan Falwell

Scripture: James 1:4–5; 3:13–18, especially 1:5
If any of you lacks wisdom, let him ask of God, who gives to all liberally and without reproach, and it will be given to him.

Introduction: Today, we talk about Wisdom. In order to *live different,* one of the major goals of our lives must be the seeking of wisdom. Proverbs is full of verses calling us to the pursuit of wisdom. It is an essential ingredient to the successful Christian life.

1. **The Invitation (1:5a).** James starts, "If any of you . . ." in verse 5. God's wisdom is available to his children, but they must sense the need, ask, and receive it. Wisdom, like patience, is not automatically applied. Not just the rich, not just the poor, not just the ones who serve God, not just the babes in Christ. It says, "if **any** of you"! Right off the bat, this message is applicable to everyone: fathers, mothers, children, grandmothers, grandfathers—anyone.

2. **The Application (1:5a).** James continues, "If any of you lacks wisdom . . ." James is about to tell us what to do if we find ourselves lacking wisdom. We are going to have to do something. We will need to take some steps to find what it is that God wants us to do in seeking wisdom. We need to realize that while God is the Source of our strength, the Source of our power, we don't automatically have everything we need in ourselves to face life. We must tap into that power, tap into that strength. God provides the power, but you must tap into that power! You must seek it with all of your heart.

3. **The Request (1:5b).** If we lack wisdom, James explains, we should "ask of God" (1:5b). This could be translated that we should *continually* be asking God: "God, what do I do? God where do I go? God, what do You want me to do? God, show me the right thing in this situation." Asking God for wisdom is a never-ending prayer request! Seeking God's face will bring us to the point of absolute dependence on Him, which is exactly where our weakness is made strong.

4. **The Promise (1:5c).** Wisdom is available to all who desire it. And if you are willing to daily, continually ask for it, He will give it to you! God "gives to all liberally and without reproach" and when we ask God for wisdom, "it will be given" (1:5c).

   A. **He Will Give Liberally: "God Who Gives . . . Liberally."** This word is used in 2 Corinthians 8 to describe how the Macedonian churches gave "generously" or "liberally" to help others in need and in 2 Corinthians 9 to describe how the Church of Corinth should sow "generously" so they will reap "generously." This word means that God will give "liberally . . . out of an abundance of His riches!"

   B. **He Will Give Graciously: "Without Finding Fault" (NIV).** God gives to us regardless of our condition, regardless of our status, regardless of our actions. He finds no fault in us when we come to Him, laying down our lives before Him. Remember, when we pray God is our Father, "Abba," Dad! Any true loving Father who sincerely wants the best for his children would be very proud that we are coming to him for counsel and guidance on how to live our lives!

5. **The Evidence (3:13–18).** James illustrates what wisdom looks like practically in 3:13–18. There is no place for envy or strife with true wisdom. Wisdom yields recognizable fruit of righteousness. If we go through life with God's wisdom, we will have a power source that will deliver us during the trials, will guide us in the victories, and will help us to help others in their lives as well.

Conclusion: The heart of revival, the heart of a wise Christian, always results from the power of the Holy Spirit in that heart. I can stand up here all day and tell you what you need to know about salvation, about living a Godly life, about living a victorious life, about how to live different. But my friend, unless you take a step of faith and tap into the power of Christ, the power of the Holy Spirit, my words will be wasted and so will the power that is there for the asking. Seek Him today!

STATS, STORIES, AND MORE

Wisdom from Above

In his book *Your Inner You,* pastor Leslie Flynn tells of his conversion to Christ during an evangelistic campaign led by Dr. Oscar Lowry, author of the book *Scripture Memorizing for Successful Soul-Winning.* Lowry admits that he entered Christian service as a young man with an undisciplined mind. Thinking he could not memorize Scripture, he filled the flyleaf of his Bible with references useful for counselling and evangelism, but it proved awkward to stop his conversations long enough to track down the right verse. Finally he determined to succeed at Scripture memory.

"If I can memorize one verse, I can memorize one more," he said, "and ten more, and even one hundred." He rose early the next morning and chose what seemed to him a difficult passage, Romans 10:9–10. He paced the room, saying to himself, "I will do this thing." He struggled with this passage for half an hour, but finally succeeded in memorizing it completely. The next morning, he reviewed and reinforced those verses in his memory, then added a new one. He keep reviewing his chosen passages and adding new ones until it dawned on him one day that he could repeat one hundred verses without looking in his Bible.

By the end of his life, he had learned over 20,000 verses, and he could locate each by chapter and verse without his Bible. No wonder his Christian life was full of joy, his mind full of wisdom, and his evangelistic efforts full of success.[1]

APPROPRIATE HYMNS AND SONGS

"Be Thou My Vision," Irish Hymn, c. 8th Century, Trans. by Mary E. Byrne, 1905; Versified by Eleanor H. Hall, 1912; Arr. by Donald Hustad, 1973, Public Domain.

"Where He Leads Me," E. W. Blandy, Public Domain.

"All I Once Held Dear (Knowing You)," Graham Kendrick, 1994 Make Way Music.

"Come, Now Is the Time to Worship," Brian Doerksen, 1998 Mercy/ Vineyard Publishing.

---

[1]Adapted from Leslie B. Flynn, *Your Inner You* (Wheaton, IL: Victor Books, 1984), p. 60, and taken from the author's book *From This Verse* (Nashville: Thomas Nelson, 1998), installment for October 14th.

FOR THE BULLETIN

Julius Caesar was assassinated on this day, the Ides of March, in 44 B.C., ambushed by his friend Brutus and a group of coconspirators. ● On March 15, 1493, Christopher Columbus returned to Spain from America. ● On March 15, 1517, Pope Leo X announced a special sale of indulgences to raise funds to rebuild St. Peter's basilica. Johann Tetzel became the chief agent of the sale in Germany, angering Martin Luther and sparking the Protestant Reformation. ● On March 15, 1540, Francis Xavier, under orders from Loyola, slipped out of Rome to report to King John III of Portugal, who longed to have Catholic missionaries evangelize far-flung Portuguese colonies, starting Xavier's dramatic history as the first Jesuit missionary. ● British evangelist George Whitefield arrives in London on Sunday morning, March 15, 1740, with an increasing worry that John Wesley was teaching error. Had Wesley been in London that day, the breach between the two men might have been avoided; but Wesley was in Bristol. George later wrote, "Ten thousand times would I rather have died than part with my old friends." ● March 15, 1859 is the birthday of Henry Jeffreys Zelley in Mount Holly, New Jersey, who wrote the gospel songs, "Heavenly Sunlight" and "He Brought Me Out." ● Archbishop John McCloskey became the first American to be named a cardinal of the Roman Catholic Church of St. Patrick's Cathedral in New York City on March 15, 1875. ● Two great inventions were born on this day in 1892. The first escalator was patented by Jesse Reno in New York on March 15, 1892, and on the very same day New York unveiled the first voting machines.

Kid's Talk

Bring a piece of candy or a small toy. While the children watch, have a tall member of your congregation place the item somewhere too high for the children to reach. Ask them what they think the best way to get it would be. They will likely answer to use a ladder or a stool. Answer that there is no ladder or stool around. Tell them that you have an idea. Ask the same person who put the item out of reach to get it down for you. Explain that the Bible also teaches us how to reach wisdom. We might have lots of ideas to become wise, but the best way is to ask God who is the Author of wisdom and the One who can place it within our reach.

WORSHIP HELPS

Call to Worship

Awake, my glory! Awake, lute and harp! I will awaken the dawn. I will praise You, O Lord, among the peoples; I will sing to You among the nations (Ps. 57:8–9).

Reader's Theater

Reader 1:   Happy is the man who finds wisdom, and the man who gains understanding; for her proceeds are better than the profits of silver, and her gain than fine gold.

Reader 2:   Receive my instruction, and not silver, and knowledge rather than choice gold; for wisdom is better than rubies, and all the things one may desire cannot be compared with her.

Reader 3:   Riches and honor are with me, enduring riches and righteousness. My fruit is better than gold, yes, than fine gold, and my revenue than choice silver.

Reader 1:   Poverty and shame will come to him who disdains correction, but he who regards a rebuke will be honored (Prov. 3:13–14; 8:10–11, 18–19; 13:18).

Additional Sermons and Lesson Ideas

The Lord Watches Over You

Date preached:

SCRIPTURE: Psalm 1:6a (NIV)

INTRODUCTION: The Lord watches over the way of the righteous. We are righteous if we have the righteousness of Christ imputed to us through the process of justification. It's also important to practice practical daily righteousness in our personal conduct. The righteous have the great assurance that God Himself is watching over us. He is watching over our:

1. Footsteps—Guiding Us Day by Day.
2. Families—Keeping an Eye on Each Member.
3. Feelings—Concerned About Our Worries, Attitudes, and Emotional Needs.
4. Finances—Meeting Each and Every Need.
5. Friendships—Giving Us Needed, Healthy Relationships with Others.
6. Failures—Turning Them and Using Them for Good.
7. Futures—Promising a City in Heaven.

CONCLUSION: This one phrase in the Old Testament, borne in mind and claimed by faith, can banish a multitude of anxieties and reassure us through day and night.

Worry

Date preached:

By Rev. Billie Friel

SCRIPTURE: Matthew 6:25–34

INTRODUCTION: Why does Jesus tell us not to worry?

1. Worry Is a Detriment to One's Health (v. 25). The body is worth more than clothes.
2. Worry is Distrust in God's Ability and Care (vv. 26–31). Trust God to work out the details of life.
3. Worry Is a Distortion of Reality (v. 27). Worries distort the image of the problem.
4. Worry Is a Detraction of Our Testimony (v. 32). Worry makes us no different from unbelievers.
5. Worry Is a Distraction from Our Main Purpose in Life (v. 33). If we seek God first, He will provide for our needs.
6. Worry Is a Dissipation of Today's Strength (v. 34). Today has enough troubles of its own.

CONCLUSION: Nothing can be changed by our worrying. Instead, we ought to trust our Father who is good and provides for us.

When You're Worried About a PK

It's not easy being a preacher's kid, but it's even harder being the preacher who has the PK. I know what it's like to stand up to preach on parenting (or on any other subject) when you don't know where your own kid is, or what he's doing, or what kind of trouble he's in. Only another pastor can realize how much it hurts when the parsonage kids go astray.

One night when our child was prodigalizing, I woke up feeling helpless—helpless to help my child or his friends. Then it dawned on me that I had three indomitable weapons, code-named PTL, in my fight with Satan for the souls of my children.

The "P" stands, of course, for *prayer*, which is "an offering up of our desires unto God for things agreeable to His will, in the name of Christ, with confession of our sins and thankful acknowledgement of His mercies (Westminster Shorter Confession). Prayer is drawing near to God, into His very presence, coming to His footstool, and pleading with Him for that which He alone can do—until He does it. It isn't that we're trying to persuade Him to do what He doesn't choose to do. As Archbishop Trench put it, "We must not conceive of prayer as overcoming God's reluctance, but as laying hold of His highest willingness."

The Kneeling Christian says that there are two aspects to prayer, and only two: Seeking God's glory and obtaining God's grace. Coming into His presence without sensing His glory is a waste of both God's time and ours. Prayer is, at its essence, a coming into His glorious court. The greatest purpose of prayer is recognizing the presence of our heavenly Father. As we do so, we recognize that His throne is a throne of Grace where we may obtain mercy and find grace to help in this time of need (Heb. 4:16).

The "T" stands for *time*. It took a while for the young prodigal in Luke 15 to come to his senses. Maturity, recovery, and rehabilitation are *processes*, and time is on our side, for our times are in the hands of Jehovah-M'Kaddesh, the God who Sanctifies (Lev. 20:8). Think of how long it has taken the Lord to work on you and me. "Please be patient," a friend once said, "God isn't finished with me yet."

For my child, I'm claiming the promise of Philippians 1:6: ". . . being confident of this very thing, that He who has begun a good work in you will complete it until the day of Jesus Christ."

Wisdom and maturity are found in learning to tell time on God's clock, in developing a sense of His timing, in knowing when to work and when to wait, when to move and when to tarry. We don't mind the working and moving, but we chafe at the waiting and tarrying, but that's an element of faith that God values very highly.

God has built into our children a process of maturation that they cannot escape. Sooner or later, they'll mature—whether they want to or not. Time is on our side; and while waiting is hard, the process goes forward under the watchful eye of the Lord Himself.

The "L" is *love*. We may not think of love as a weapon, but it sends a radioactive blanket over its target for which there is no known antidote. Paul said, "Love never fails" (1 Cor. 13:8), and I've claimed that promise for my child. Love simply means that I'm going to do what's best for my child regardless of whether or not it seems best for me. It is putting the needs of my child ahead of my own desires. Sometimes that means exercising "tough love," perhaps even telling my child he can't continue to live in our house if he's going to persist in a lifestyle that consistently disrupts our home. That's exceedingly painful for a parent, yet it might be the wisest and most helpful words we ever speak to our child.

Angry words, however, and demeaning comments or name-calling must stop—at least on our part. Remember that love is kind and does not behave rudely; it always seeks the best for the other person. It can be firm and forthright, but it never tears down those to whom it's directed.

And according to 1 Corinthians 13:7, "Love never gives up, never loses faith, is always hopeful, and endures through every circumstance" (NLT). *Continued on the next page*

So if you wake up in the middle of the night feeling helpless, just remind yourself that you have an arsenal of weapons—prayer, time, and love. Those weapons have broken down many a strong-hold and reclaimed many a life. Those are God's weapons that He has put at your disposal. You're not powerless after all.

PTL—Praise The Lord![2]

***

I used to love the nights, dear Lord,
The fading of the evening lights,
The quiet routine;
The bedtime prayers;
A tale or two; then nodding heads,
three weary kids in cozy beds;
The silent hours of healing rest.
I loved the evenings best.

I hate the evenings now, dear Lord.
A speeding car out in the night,
Dives and dens and worthless ends,
Flashing lights, unworthy friends,
An empty heart, a search for love,
When all he needs is found above.

I'm going to trust You through this night,
I'm going to walk by faith, not sight.
You slumber not, nor do you sleep,
Your wakeful eye can always keep,
My children in your care.
To Him who tucks me into bed:
Please station angels around his head,
And guard my child where're he be,
And bring him back, dear Lord, to Thee.

—ROB MORGAN

---

[2]Adapted from the editor's book, *Moments for Families with Prodigals,* published by NavPress in 2003.

MARCH 22, 2009

SUGGESTED SERMON

Horror and Hope

Date preached:

By Dr. Robert M. Norris

Scripture: Malachi 3:1–6, especially verse 2b
For He is like a refiner's fire and like launderers' soap.

Introduction: Are you facing difficulty? Could it be that the Lord is using your situation to purge sin from your life? Throughout Scripture, God purges sin from the lives of His people through adversity. This was the case for Israel as revealed through Malachi. The people were questioning God and whining because He had not met their expectations. Through the mouth of His prophet Malachi the Lord therefore warns His people that He will come with refining fire!

1. **God Will Come as a Refiner (vv. 1–6).** The picture of the ancient refiner of silver is used by the prophet to describe the actions of God in the life of His people: "For He is like a refiner's fire and like launderers' soap" (3:2). The description is both vivid and deliberate. A refiner's fire melts down a bar of silver or gold, separates out the impurities that ruin its value, burns them up, and leaves the silver and gold intact. Yet the Lord does come with fire, and that is both fearful and painful. Christianity is never a play thing because the God with whom we have to deal is like fire, and fire is serious. But at the same time, the furnace of affliction in the experience of the family of God is always for refinement, not for destruction (v. 3, 6). In addition, God the Father is promising to send one who is "the Messenger of the covenant" (v. 1) who will come as the refiner and whose coming will be prepared for by a prophet (4:5). What Malachi is predicting is nothing less than the coming of Jesus the Christ whose way is prepared by John the Baptist.

2. **God Will Come to Refine His People (vv. 3–6).** We were created in the image of God with the potential and the obligation to reverence God, to trust, obey, and glorify Him. However, the Scriptures make clear that we are all guilty of sin. We are shot through with the impurity of rebellion and unbelief, and we fall short of God's glory

again and again (Rom. 3:23). If He were not a refiner's fire, heaven would be empty, for we would be left in our sins unable to stand in His presence. God did not want to leave us in a sinful state and covenanted to preserve His people (v. 6). This never changes—the free and sovereign choice of God to save sinners: "For I am the LORD, I do not change; therefore you are not consumed . . ." (v. 6). Therefore, Jesus comes as a refiner of His people and not their destroyer!

3. **God Seeks and Provides an Acceptable Sacrifice (vv. 3–4).** "He will purify the sons of Levi, and purge them as gold and silver, that they may offer to the LORD an offering in righteousness. Then the offering of Judah and Jerusalem will be pleasant to the LORD, as in the days of old, as in former years." Malachi spends a great deal of his book on the issue of proper sacrifice, because worship is a basic indicator of overall faithfulness to the covenant. On that day, "the sacrifices" will delight God. God has provided in His Christ the right and only acceptable offering. This is the great truth of the grace of God: that what He demands from sinners He Himself provides! God does not want a restoration of Israel's worship and sacrificial system because the ability to delight God cannot be attributed to ability of those skilled in offering. All the Old Testament sacrifices were emblems pointing to the one great sacrifice of Christ on Calvary. Our worship to delight God must glory in His grace in Christ and trust in His gospel, which is our salvation and the provision of His perfect sacrifice.

Conclusion: All men and women experience the fires of life in different forms. We must repent and get rid of our own sin, for then we would need no refining! We cannot refine ourselves; instead we must trust in the purifying mercy of God. Don't doubt His expertise as a Refiner. The way to experience the fire of Christ as refining and not consuming is to trust His promise to bring us through the fire to endless joy. Salvation is by grace through faith in the purifying mercy of God.

STATS, STORIES, AND MORE

Missionary Amy Carmichael worked with children in India, and one day she took them on a field trip to see a goldsmith refine his gold after the ancient manner of the East. He was sitting beside a little charcoal fire, and in the fire was a little curved roofing tile. Another tile covered it as a lid. This was the crucible.

The goldsmith had concocted a solution, put it in the tile crucible, placed the lump of gold in the solution, and put the whole thing in the fire. As the fire did its work, the impurities in the gold began to leak into the solution and the gold become more pure. The goldsmith would occasionally take the gold out of the crucible with a pair of tongs, let it cool, and rub it between his fingers. Then he put it back into fresh solution in the tile and heated it up again.

Every time this happened, the goldsmith blew the fire hotter than before. Looking up at the children, the goldsmith said, "The gold could not bear the fire this hot to begin with; it would have destroyed it. But now it helps it."

One of the children asked, "How do you know when the gold is purified?" Here was the man's answer: "When I can see my face in it (the liquid gold in the crucible) then it is pure."

Of course, Amy Carmichael couldn't miss the lesson for her own life. When our Great Refiner sees in us His own image, He has brought us to maturity and wholeness. He uses truth to cultivate wisdom; trials to cultivate faith; tasks to cultivate faithfulness, and temptation to cultivate obedience until He can see His face in us and we have grown into the image of Christ. Is that process happening in your life?

APPROPRIATE HYMNS AND SONGS

"Trust and Obey," James H. Sammis, Public Domain.

"Purify My Heart," Jeff Nelson, 1993 HeartService Music.

"Made Me Glad," Miriam Webster, 2001 Miriam Webster/Hillsong Publishing.

"The Potter's Hand," Darlene Zschech, 1997 Darlene Zschech/Hillsong Publishing.

"Spirit of the Living God," Daniel Iverson, Public Domain.

FOR THE BULLETIN

March 22 was an important day in the world of fourth-century Christianity. At the Counsel of Nicea, summoned by Emperor Constantine to resolve disputes within the Christian world, it was determined that Easter would always be celebrated on the Sunday after the first full moon following the Spring equinox. That means that March 22nd is the earliest possible date in any given year when Easter can be celebrated. Then, on March 22, 337, Constantine died at age forty-seven. ● While it can't be proved, many authorities and almanacs say that the famous Gutenberg Bible, the first book ever printed, was first published on March 22, of 1457. ● On March 22, 1630, the Massachusetts Bay colonists sailed for America led by Puritan John Winthrop. But on March 22, 1638, religious dissident Anne Hutchinson was expelled from Massachusetts Bay Colony for insisting she had received divine revelations. ● Today is the feast day of England's Nicholas Owen. Roman Catholics were persecuted in England during the days of Queen Elizabeth I, and Owen, probably a builder by trade, designed countless hiding places for them. He hid them in secret rooms and between the walls and under the floors. He designed nooks and crannies that looked like anything but hiding places. He also proved a master at devising getaways, and he invented brilliant schemes for helping Catholics escape prison. He was an escapist himself, having several aliases and disguises. Perhaps no one saved the lives of more Catholics in England during these days than Nicholas Owen. But Nicholas was at last betrayed. Taken to the Tower of London, his arms were fixed to iron rings and he was hung for hours, his body dangling. He was canonized and is honored each year on March 22.

Quote for the Pastor's Wall

The Christian's life should put his minister's sermon in print.

—William Gurnall (1618–1679)

WORSHIP HELPS

Call to Worship

Rejoice, rejoice, believer,
And let thy joy and glory ever be
In Him, the great Deliverer,
Who gave Himself a sacrifice for thee.
—FANNY CROSBY in *Rejoice,*
Rejoice, Believer

Scripture Reading Medley

O LORD, do not be far from Me; O My strength, hasten to help Me! Do not forsake me, O LORD; O my God, be not far from me! Make haste to help me, O Lord, my salvation! Help me, O LORD my God! Oh, save me according to Your mercy, that they may know that this is Your hand—that You, LORD, have done it! Hear my prayer, O LORD, give ear to my supplications! In Your faithfulness answer me, and in Your righteousness. Answer me speedily, O LORD; my spirit fails! Revive me, O LORD for Your name's sake! For Your righteousness' sake bring my soul out of trouble. I am poor and needy; yet the LORD thinks upon me. You are my help and my deliverer; do not delay, O my God. Hear, O LORD, and have mercy on me; LORD, be my helper! My soul follows close behind You. In the multitude of my anxieties within me, Your comforts delight my soul (Ps. 22:19; 38:21–22; 109:26–27; 143:1, 7a, 11; 40:17; 30:10; 63:8; 94:19).

Benediction

"For I am the LORD, I do not change; therefore you are not consumed, O sons of Jacob. Yet from the days of your fathers you have gone away from My ordinances and have not kept them. Return to Me, and I will return to you," says the LORD of hosts . . . (Mal. 3:6–7).

Additional Sermons and Lesson Ideas

The Christian
By Dr. Michael A. Guido

Date preached:

SCRIPTURE: Various

INTRODUCTION: There is a great deal of confusion about the title "Christian." What is a Christian? How do you become a Christian? How should a Christian act? What does a Christian do?

1. The Birth (John 1:12–13).
2. The Behavior (Phil. 1:27).
3. The Business (John 17:18; Luke 19:10; Matt. 4:19).

CONCLUSION: The Bible tells us that it is by grace through faith in Jesus Christ that one becomes a Christian (Eph. 2:8–9). We are to be emulating Christ. We need to love each other, love the world, and love God. We need to conduct ourselves in a manner worthy of the life we have been called to (Phil. 1:27). Lastly, we need to be about the business of the Father. We are to be telling about Jesus, baptizing people, and making disciples in the faith (Matt. 28:19–20).

It Is Good to Go Forward
By Rev. Larry Kirk

Date preached:

SCRIPTURE: Luke 9:23–35

INTRODUCTION: Jesus pointed His disciples to the glory of His kingdom, and how that ought to affect the way they lived their lives.

1. The Promise of the Kingdom of Christ Provides the Perspective for Today's Struggle (vv. 23–27).
2. Christ Gives Us, in This Life, a Powerful Promise of His Coming Kingdom (vv. 28–32).
3. Those Who Have Received the Promise of the Kingdom Must Learn to Live Life from That Perspective (vv. 32–35).

CONCLUSION: Listen to Jesus when He says; Glory is coming, the kingdom of God will come, but now is the time for taking up your cross daily, denying yourself and following Me.

MARCH 29, 2009

SUGGESTED SERMON

From Poverty to Praise

Date preached:

By Rev. Melvin Tinker

Scripture: Matthew 15:29–39, especially verse 31
So the multitude marveled when they saw the mute speaking, the maimed made whole, the lame walking, and the blind seeing; and they glorified the God of Israel.

Introduction: Today it's widely believed that since we live in a world that has come from nowhere and is going nowhere, our sense of well being is only to be found through what we wear, what we eat, what we drink, and where we live. The Western world is actually lapsing into a form of paganism. It's the self-help spirituality through the possession of things. But while it may superficially provide some short term gain, it can never satisfy the deep aching inside. Like all idols it leaves us short changed. But what happens when the true God steps into our situation? When our felt needs are seen for what they are: symptoms of a deeper need? Well, to find out the answer, turn with me to that fascinating account we have of an episode in the life of Jesus as recorded for us in Matthew 15.

1. **Universal Need (vv. 29–31).** Just like all fallen people in this world, Jesus' audience was spiritually impoverished. They needed:

   A. **The Teaching of Jesus (v. 29).** Jesus first goes to the mountain and sits down. The mountain would have provided a natural amphitheatre to carry His voice. In that day, the sitting position was the posture of an authoritative teacher. These crowds are not made up of Jews, the chosen people, but of mostly Gentiles— those who have no relationship with the one true God. Obviously God wants them to; that is why Jesus is here, teaching them as He taught others, bringing God's Word to their needy situation.

   B. **The Healing of Jesus (vv. 30–31).** Matthew could have given us more of a description of what went on, but all he says is "He healed them." While Matthew may not have given us much by way of description of the healings themselves, he does tell us the reaction of the people to the effects of the healings: "So the multitude marveled when they saw the mute speaking, the maimed made whole, the lame walking, and the blind seeing; and they glorified the God of Israel" (v. 31). Here is a visible, tangible demonstration of the nature of the one true God in Jesus Christ.

2. **A Universal Concern (vv. 32–34).** The real God is not stuck up on Mount Olympus out of reach and out of sight in perfect seclusion from the plight of His subjects, as many of these Gentiles would have believed before they encountered Jesus. No, He is there on that mount. His brow is getting hot, His hands are getting sweaty, His body is getting tired as hour after hour and day after day He heals and teaches, and still the people keep coming, thousands of them. What moved Jesus to such lengths? The key word is *compassion* (v. 32). Here the word means much more than pity; it refers to an emotion which moves a person to the very depths of his being.

3. **Universal Provision (vv. 35–37).** The number "7" is the figure of wholeness, the number of completion. Seven baskets were left over after all the people were fed. In other words, Jesus' power and supply is sufficient for the *whole* world not just the whole of Israel. What's more, a different word is used here to describe the baskets from that used in chapter 14. There it was *kophinos*—a small Jewish container. Here it is *spuridas*—a container Gentiles used, so large it could contain a man. Between ten and twenty thousand people are fed to bursting point and still there is plenty to spare. And you wonder whether Jesus is sufficient to meet your needs?

Conclusion: There is one Person we can turn to who fills it perfectly: Jesus. No one who ever came to Him on His terms ever felt short changed. Sure, He never promises a life of health and wealth, for the world remains broken until His return. But to be rightly related *now* to the One who made you and who loves you and cares for you is surely what life is all about. So whether you are a Bantu living in Africa or a docker living in Grimsby—your deepest needs remain the same: life with God and Jesus is the one who meets it.

STATS, STORIES, AND MORE

Jack Welch, former Chief Executive Officer to General Electric in the United States. When he retired, the company continued to provide him with a luxury apartment in central park, free travel on company jets, together with flowers, furniture, opera tickets and even stamps. And when he had a close brush with death a few years ago requiring heart surgery, do you know what conclusion he came to about life? He said, "I learned I didn't spend enough money." As a result he vowed he would never again drink wine that cost less than $100 a bottle. But, if this life is *all* there is, then why not?

More from Rev. Melvin Tinker
In A.D. 250, a measles epidemic swept through the Roman Empire with devastating effect. Here is a description from the time of what the non-Christians did: "At the first onset of the disease, they pushed the sufferers away and fled from their dearest, throwing them into the roads before they were dead and treating unburied corpses as dirt, hoping thereby to avert the spread and contagion of the fatal disease." And the Christians? "Heedless of the danger; they took charge of the sick, attending every need and ministering to them in Christ, and with them departed this life serenely happy; for they were infected by others with the disease, drawing on themselves the sickness of their neighbors and cheerfully accepting their pains." And do you know that resulted in tremendous numbers of people being converted to Christianity. Not surprising really because they *saw* the difference, as did these people. And that always remains the challenge for God's people—to have the compassion of Christ and to show it.

APPROPRIATE HYMNS AND SONGS

"That's Why We Praise Him," Tommy Walker, 1999 We Mobile Music and Duolos Publishing.

"Praise Ye the Lord, the Almighty," Joachim Neander, Public Domain.

"Praise Him! Praise Him!," Fanny Crosby, Public Domain.

"Let Everything That Has Breath," Matt Redman, 1999 Kingsway ThankYou Music.

"I Will Sing Praise," Michael Popham, 2002 Tayken Music/BMI/Experience Worship Music Publishing.

FOR THE BULLETIN

John Lightfoot, English scholar and rabbinical scholar, was born on this day in 1602. ● In January of 1788, Methodist leader and hymnist Charles Wesley was too weak to go out, and in February he was confined to his bed. He had neither illness nor pain, but weariness and weakness. Late in March he became too feeble to use a pen or write any more of his famous hymns. His final hymn was dictated to his wife: "In age and feebleness extreme, / Who shall a sinful worm redeem? / Jesus, my only hope Thou art, / Strength of my failing flesh and heart; / Oh, could I catch a smile from Thee, / and drop into eternity." Shortly afterward, Charles slipped into a state of unconsciousness and passed away peacefully on March 29, 1788. During his lifetime he wrote over 7,000 hymns. ● Another famous hymnist died on this day in 1887—Ray Palmer, author of "My Faith Looks Up to Thee." But today is the birthday of Winfield Scott Weeden, born in 1847. He's the author of "I Surrender All." ● On March 29, 1848, Niagara Falls stopped flowing for thirty hours due to an ice jam.

PRAYER FOR THE PASTOR'S CLOSET

Most merciful Father, we beseech Thee to send down upon this Thy servant Thy heavenly blessings; and so endue him with Thy Holy Spirit, that he, preaching Thy Word, may not only be earnest to reprove, beseech, and rebuke with all patience and doctrine; but also may be to such as believe a wholesome example, in word, in conversation, in love, in faith, in chastity, and in purity; that, faithfully fulfilling his course, at the latter day he may receive the crown of righteousness laid up by the Lord the righteous Judge, who liveth and reigneth one God with the Father and the Holy Ghost, world without end. Amen.

—From the BOOK OF COMMON PRAYER (the Church of England)

WORSHIP HELPS

Call to Worship
I will give You thanks in the great assembly; I will praise You among many people (Ps. 35:18).

Offertory Comments
I'd like us to take just a moment to think about our own personal finances. First, think of the last purchase you made that was probably unnecessary or exorbitant. Now, think of the last time you gave an offering over and above your regular tithes. Think of the last time you went out to eat. Then think of the last time you donated to missions to help feed those who hunger both spiritually and physically. No one here wants to guilt you into tithing, but it's my responsibility as your pastor to help you evaluate your heart. As Scripture teaches: "Where your treasure is, there your heart will be also" (Matt. 6:21).

Scripture Reading Medley
Heal me, O LORD, and I shall be healed; Save me, and I shall be saved. O LORD my God, I cried out to You, and You healed me. By [His] stripes you were healed. For you were like sheep going astray, but have now returned to the Shepherd and Overseer of your souls. He will feed His flock like a shepherd; He will gather the lambs with His arm. So they all ate and were filled (Jer. 17:14; Ps. 30:2; 1 Pet. 2:24a, 25; Is. 40:11a; Matt. 15:37a).

Benediction
May He grant you according to your heart's desire, and fulfill all your purpose. We will rejoice in your salvation, and in the name of our God we will set up our banners! May the LORD fulfill all your petitions (Ps. 20:4–5).

Additional Sermons and Lesson Ideas

There's a Hole in Your Pocket

Date preached:

By Dr. Larry Osborne

SCRIPTURE: Haggai 1:1–2:9

INTRODUCTION: The people of Israel ignored God's house and instead refurbished their own houses. They claimed that they didn't have enough money to give to God. God was angry and gave them a message through His prophet Haggai.

1. Why There Is Never Enough (1:1–11). God rebuked Israel for freely spending money on themselves but withholding offerings to Him. So, God held back His blessings from them just as they had held back their offerings.
2. Quick Obedience (1:12). When the people heard this, they obeyed God because they believed His warning and feared Him.
3. God's Immediate Response (1:13–2:9). God reassured Israel with the promise of His presence and a reminder of His covenant. He promised to renew them and give them peace.

CONCLUSION: We often live the same way. We fall back on that old excuse of "enough." What is enough? God may hold back because we are being stingy in order that we might return to Him and honor Him.

Looking Within

Date preached:

By Dr. Timothy K. Beougher

SCRIPTURE: Mark 7:14–23

INTRODUCTION: We are a culture obsessed with the external. However, the real problem of sin is not external but internal. In the same way, the solution to our sin is not something that changes the outside but Someone who changes the inside.

1. Preoccupation with the External (vv. 14–16).
2. Prominence of the Internal (vv. 17–23).
3. Power of the Eternal (2 Cor. 3:18).

CONCLUSION: The Bible makes it clear that the solution to sin is not a ceremony but a Savior. Jesus Christ died so that our sin might be forgiven. The things we do will not make us clean or good. We must rely on Christ for our righteousness.

APRIL 5, 2009

The Attitude of Christ

Date preached:

By Dr. Ed Dobson

Scripture: Philippians 2:5–11, especially verse 8
And being found in appearance as a man, He humbled Himself and became obedient
to the point of death, even the death of the cross.

Introduction: What does it mean to be Christlike? To think like Christ,
to act like Christ, to respond like Christ, to walk like Christ, to talk like
Christ. That ought to be one of the ultimate consuming desires of our
life, that whatever we do and whatever we say, we reflect Christ. In our
passage today, Paul illustrates how we can be like Jesus by giving us
an overview of Christ's life.

1. **The Nature of Christ's Obedience (vv. 5–7).** The nature of Christ's
   obedience was *voluntary*. One of the themes of this passage is that
   He humbled Himself. In other words, the obedience of Christ going
   to the cross was not an enforced obedience. Yes, it's true that that's
   what was necessary to redeem fallen mankind, but Jesus *willingly*
   laid down His life. In fact, He Himself said, "No one takes it from
   Me, but I lay it down of Myself. I have power to lay it down, and I
   have power to take it again" (John 10:18).

2. **The Extent of Christ's Obedience (v. 8a).** The extent of Christ's
   obedience ultimately led Him to death. Jesus did not come primarily
   to teach the way of salvation, although He taught that. He did teach
   the way of salvation, but that was not His ultimate mission. Jesus
   did not come to demonstrate a godly life, although in every way,
   shape and form and in every circumstance He demonstrated a godly
   life. But that's not *primarily* why He came. Jesus came for this
   purpose: to be obedient to the point of death, even death on a cross.

3. **The Sacrifice of Christ's Obedience (v. 8b).** ". . . even the death of
   the cross." We should understand a few things about death on a cross:

   A. **Jesus Died an Accursed Death.** Death on the cross was considered the ultimate and final disgrace: "If a man has committed a
   sin deserving of death, and he is put to death, and you hang him

on a tree, his body shall not remain overnight on the tree, but you shall surely bury him that day . . . for he who is hanged is accursed of God" (Deut. 21:22–23). A person hanged from a tree is under God's judgment. We stand condemned by God under the curse of the law, but Jesus died an accursed death to pay the price we owe.

B. **Jesus Died a Shameful Death.** To a Roman mind, the concept of the death of Christ on the cross was an affront (1 Cor. 1:23). How could anyone, including the Son of God, be put to such open shame by death on the cross? What we preach to the world is total foolishness (1 Cor. 1:18). When you preach Christ, crucified and raised to an unbelieving world it is often received as foolishness. To those who have experienced in a personal way, the foolishness of the preaching of the gospel of Jesus Christ— Christ crucified—Jesus is for us the power of God unto salvation (Rom. 1:16).

C. **Jesus Died a Painful Death.** The obedience which Christ demonstrated on the cross was an obedience that cost Him something: the agony and the pain of crucifixion. We need only to read the gospel accounts to understand the pain and agony of Jesus' death: being whipped, scourged, nailed by His hands and feet to a cross with thorns piercing His brow, hanging for hours left to die in humiliation.

D. **Jesus Died a Vicarious Death.** When Jesus died He took my sins and your sins and He endured the curse of God, the condemnation and judgment of God for my sin, for my benefit (Rom. 5:6–11). That's what the word "vicarious" means. When Jesus died, He died so that I might know and experience the power of God unto salvation—so that I could know the righteousness of God, the justification of God, the redemption of God, the forgiveness of God, and the indwelling of the Holy Spirit.

Conclusion: If Jesus, the supreme Son of God who deserves all glory and honor, went to die an accursed, shameful, painful death for us, how much more should we sinners saved through Him humble ourselves! Let's submit ourselves to His will and ask Him to give us the same attitude of humility.

STATS, STORIES, AND MORE

More from Dr. Ed Dobson
I remember when I was on the faculty of Liberty University and the president would announce a required faculty meeting. My natural response was "You won't see me there!" Now if he had said, "We'd like you to come." I probably would have gone. But once he said, "It is required" I said in my mind, "Over my dead body!" We are all like that; we have stubborn hearts that resist authority. The barrier that stands in our way to obedience is inside of us.

The Power of the Cross
In his book, *The Power of the Cross,* Tim LaHaye says that in writing the book he decided to conduct an experiment. Whenever he saw someone wearing a cross as a piece of jewelry, he would ask about it. He explained that he was writing a book on the subject, and that he was taking a survey of just two questions: Why do you wear that cross, and what does it mean to you? No one took offense, said LaHaye, but he got some very interesting replies. Born-again Christians were quick to identify themselves as followers of Christ, but other people had other reasons. One woman said, "I saw it in the display case of a shop and thought it was attractive. Because it was on sale for 50 percent off, I bought it." Another woman said, "I have never gone to church much, except on Easter and Christmas, but I consider myself a Christian. I wear it to identify myself—besides, I think it is a beautiful piece of jewelry. A young clerk with a beautiful gold cross on a chain around her neck said, "My boyfriend gave it to me for Christmas, and I love him very much. I wear it because it reminds me of him." And a receptionist at a computer shop said, "I wouldn't be without this cross; it goes with me everywhere I go. It brings me good luck."[1]

APPROPRIATE HYMNS AND SONGS

"All Glory, Laud, and Honor," Theodulph of Orleans, c. 800, Public Domain.

"Hosanna, Loud Hosanna," Jennette Threlfall, Public Domain.

"Above All," Lenny LeBlanc and Paul Baloche, 1999 Integrity's Hosanna! Music.

"Hosanna We Sing," Claire Cloninger & Robert Sterling, 2005 Word Music, LLC.

"Trust and Obey," James Sammis & Daniel Towner, Public Domain.

[1]Tim LaHaye, *The Power of the Cross* (Sisters, OR: Multnomah Books, 1998), 29–30.

FOR THE BULLETIN

On April 5, 1524, Swiss reformer Ulrich Zwingli married Anna Reinhart, breaking the ban (as Luther also did) on celibacy among members of the priesthood or clergy. ● Hans Nielsen Hague, twenty-five, had grown up in rural Norway and was a skilled cabinetmaker, blacksmith, and beekeeper. On April 5, 1796, as he worked outdoors singing hymns, he was caught in a dramatic experience. He felt the Holy Spirit flowing through him like a warm river. Running home, he shared the experience with his family, and then he set out to tell others about Christ. He traveled for eight years and 10,000 miles throughout Norway on foot, ski, and horse. Today he is known as the "Father of Scandinavian Pietism." ● Today marks the death in 1811 of Robert Raikes, English philanthropist and founder of Sunday school movement. ● Dietrich Bonhoeffer, born in 1906 to a distinguished neurologist, studied theology and taught in Berlin as a young man and quickly became one of Germany's most respected Lutheran clergymen. As the Nazis gained power, Bonhoeffer criticized the abuses of the Hitler regime, insisting that the church may criticize any unjust action of the state and assist victims of the injustice. After working in America and Britain, Bonhoeffer was called back to Germany in 1935 to direct a preacher's seminary in the remote village of Finkenwalde, and after it was closed by the police he continued his work underground. In April 1943, the Gestapo took Bonhoeffer into custody, and on April 5, 1945, Hitler ordered his execution. Four days later, Bonhoeffer, 39, went to the gallows—April 9, 1945. He left behind several powerful books including *The Cost of Discipleship,* published in 1937.

WORSHIP HELPS

Call to Worship
I will praise You forever, because You have done it; and in the presence of Your saints I will wait on Your name, for it is good. Come and hear, all you who fear God, and I will declare what He has done for my soul (Ps. 52:9; 66:16).

Exhortation
Eric Johnson was an esteemed man in Hollywood, the president of the Motion Picture Association of America. He had originally wanted to devote his career to the Marines, and he fought with valor in World War I. But during the conflict, he sustained a career-ending injury, so he retuned home to civilian life and

took up a job selling vacuum cleaners in Spokane, Washington. For many hours every day, he lugged his sample vacuum cleaner on his back, going up one street and down another, giving demonstrations and trying make a sale; but after three weeks he had not had a single success. He imagined his friends saying, "Too bad about Eric, isn't it? He's just not cut out to be a salesman." And Eric himself was beginning to agree with them. But somehow he just couldn't believe that there wasn't some family in Spokane that needed a vacuum cleaner, so he kept at it. Then one day it happened. He sold a vacuum cleaner. He went home jubilant, and, going home, he reviewed in his own mind what had happened during the interview that was different from the others. He became more confident of his selling abilities, and during the next several days he sold seven more vacuum cleaners. He later wrote out the lesson that he learned: "No is not an answer. It is merely a ringing challenge." I tell you this story to encourage you to invite people to our upcoming Easter services. Invite one person after another. Ask God to place some people on your heart, and keep asking them. Review your techniques and keep trying to be more and more effective in the way you witness and in the way you invite to church. Keep a little list, and let's see if we can't have more people here for Easter than we've had for a long, long time. If we invite enough people some will come; and if enough come, some will be saved.

Additional Sermons and Lesson Ideas

iWill: A Message About God's Will
for an iPod Generation
Date preached:
By Pastor Jonathan Falwell

SCRIPTURE: Various

INTRODUCTION: With God's power we can do what He has called us to do (Zech. 4:6b; Gal. 2:20). Here are four encouragements for you as you obey:

1. Let God's Word Do the Talking (1 Cor. 2:1–5).
2. Let God Guide Your Steps (Ex. 4:10–12).
3. Let God's Hand Ease the Stress (Jer. 1:17–19).
4. Let God Use You to Change Others (Is. 6:8; Rom. 10:14).

CONCLUSION: As believers, God gives us His power and backs us with His authority. He has given us all we need to live and to obey Him (2 Pet. 1:3–4). The question is will you? Will you listen, will you give, will you love, will you serve, and will you go? You can leave the results to Him for He will draw all men to Himself. You just have to be found faithful!

Choose Faith
Date preached:
By Rev. Larry Kirk

SCRIPTURE: Habakkuk 3:16–19

INTRODUCTION: God wants us to learn that because He is our Savior and our strength we can choose to have faith in Him every circumstance.

1. Through Faith in God We Can Have Courage When We Are Afraid (v. 16).
2. Through Faith in God We Can Have Patience When We Have to Wait (v. 16).
3. Through Faith in God We Can Have Joy When Times Are Tough (vv. 17–18).
4. Through Faith in God We Can Have Strength When We Are Weak (v. 19).

CONCLUSION: Trust in God gives us courage, patience, joy, and strength, not because trust itself is so powerful but because trust taps into the truth about God and His relationship to us. Trust Him. Choose faith.

When You Feel Underappreciated

I had a small handful of men who had grown disgruntled and embittered, and it made the job of pastoring well nigh impossible to do with a good attitude. So I took a page in my prayer journal, listed their names, and told the Lord about it. One by one the Lord dealt with each person, and they either changed their attitude or changed their church—all except one, about whom I'm still praying.

Let me tell you about a conversation I had with one of these men. I called and asked to see him, and for three hours we talked about the things that had displeased him. I was physically sick at the end of our session, but one snippet of the conversation was very telling. He said, "Pastor, you say that you love my family, but I don't think you really care for us. You haven't visited us, we don't talk much, you haven't asked about my work or my schooling, you haven't reached out to us. I don't think you care."

"Well, I should do better," I said, "But, Reggie, my job isn't to *do* those things, it to see that those things *are being done*. When our church had a hundred people, I could tend to every member like that. Now that we're larger, it's impossible for me. I can't personally provide constant pastoral care for each person, but I can see to it that our church is providing an environment in which everyone receives pastoral care."

Then I said, "But think about this. I have a large number of people to look after, I preach or teach several times a week, I put in sixty to seventy hours or more, I start at seven in the morning and finish at nine or ten at night, I never take time to watch a television show unless it's at bedtime with my wife, I'm married to a disabled person, I have to care for her and sometimes literally carry her from one place to another, I do the cooking and the shopping and the dry cleaning, and I've just been through a bruising stewardship campaign and building program. And I have writing deadlines. Not one time in the last three years have you come to me and asked how I was doing and inquired as to my wife or my family or showed any concern for us whatsoever."

Continued on the next page

"Yes," he replied, "but I'm not the pastor. You are. You're supposed to be the one doing those things."

I didn't have a good response to that, so we went on to the next topic, but I've been mulling over that exchange ever since. I suspect a lot of people share that attitude. They think that it's our job to take care of them, but not their job to care for us. We're in a consumer culture, and everyone is concerned about being ministered to, or catered to, or cared for. Sometimes the pastor's family feels underappreciated, and often they *are* underappreciated.

I'm happy to report that my conversation with Reggie wasn't wasted. A few weeks later, he called, we had coffee, and it was like a new friendship. Since then, we've become closer, happier, and I'm very grateful for him and for his loving, prayerful support. I understand him better, and I suspect the reverse is true too.

If you have a church that cares for you, thank God for it. It's an increasingly rare phenomenon.

If you don't, then remember the words of our Lord Jesus: "The Son of Man did not come to be served, but to serve, and to give His life a ransom for many" (Matt. 20:28).

Don't fall into self-pity or internal anguish. Don't let yourself acquire a flagging spirit, a weary heart, or a timid soul. We are servants, nothing more; and after we have done our best, we have only done our duty. Our Lord Jesus was underappreciated in His day, as were all the prophets and apostles. We shouldn't develop a martyr's complex unless, of course, we really are martyred. Even then a complex is more trouble than it's worth.

Take care of yourself, appreciate your supporters, leave your enemies in God's hands, don't let the conflicts eat at you for long, take a break, memorize a verse, play a round of golf, and work through the situations in your life.

Find someone to talk to. Get counseling from a trusted advisor. Or get away if you can. A little distance often diminishes the distress. An overnight stay at a state park gives us separation, rest, and needed time to process our emotions and regain our equilibrium. If possible and as a rule, we should make things better and not worse. If possible, as far as it lies with us, we should live at peace with everyone.

And remember . . .
. . . it's far better to be underappreciated than overvalued.

Go, labor on; spend, and be spent,
Thy joy to do the Father's will;
It is the way the Master went;
Should not the servant tread it still?
—HORATIUS BONAR, 1843

PRAYER FOR THE PASTOR'S CLOSET

Rest him, O Father! Thou didst send him forth
With great and gracious messages of love;
But Thy ambassador is weary now,
Worn with the weight of his high embassy.
Now care for him as thou hast cared for us
In sending him; and cause him to lie down
In Thy fresh pastures, by Thy streams of peace.
Let Thy left hand be now beneath his head,
And Thine upholding right encircle him,
And, underneath, the Everlasting arms
Be felt in full support. So let him rest,
Hushed like a little child, without one care;
And so give Thy beloved sleep tonight.
—From FRANCES RIDLEY HAVERGAL's
poem, "Sunday Night," a prayer
for her pastor

APRIL 12, 2009

Date preached:

I Know That My Redeemer Lives

Scripture: Job 1, 2, 13, 19, and 23, especially 19:25–26
I know that my Redeemer lives and He shall stand at last on the earth; and after my
skin is destroyed, this I know, that in my flesh I shall see God.

Introduction: You may never have heard of Robert King Merton, the
Columbia University sociologist who died in 2003, but I'll bet you've
heard some of the phrases he coined, like *self-fulfilling prophecy* and
unintended consequences. It was Merton who invented *focus groups* and
who popularized *serendipity*. And it was Merton who coined the phrase
role model to describe someone who provides an example of positive
behavior. The term may be new, but the concept is as old as the Bible;
and if you want a role model of someone transformed by the message
of Easter, you can find it in the book of Job. According to James 5:10–
11, Job is a role model for all of us. Despite intense tribulation and
unanswered questions, he verbally affirmed his commitment to the
Lord five times. Five great statements of faith are planted like signposts
in the book of Job.

1. **Blessed Be the Name of the Lord! (Job 1:20–22).** In Job 1, the devil
   stirred up trouble for Job. In responding, Job fell to the ground, not
   in despair, but in worship (v. 20), saying: "Naked I came from my
   mother's womb, and naked shall I return there. The LORD gave and
   the LORD has taken away; Blessed be the name of the LORD" (cf.
   1 Tim. 6:7).

2. **Shall We Accept Good and Not Bad? (Job 2:9–10).** The devil unleashed another attack, this time on Job's health. His wife said,
   "Are you still trusting God after all this?" Job rebuked her and said,
   "Shall we indeed accept good from God, and shall we not accept
   adversity?" In all this, Job did not sin with his lips. There are several
   insights woven into this verse, one of which is the importance of
   sanctified acceptance. See that word "accept" in the verse? Sometimes we have to accept things, even if we would wish them otherwise. Remember the old "Serenity Prayer" that begins: "God grant
   me the serenity to accept the things I cannot change. . . ." Some-

times we just have to accept things, trust God with them, and say, "Well, praise the Lord anyway."

3. **Though He Slay Me Yet Will I Trust Him! (Job 13:15).** Job 4–36 is an account of discussions between Job and his friends who suggested that his problems occurred because of unnamed and unconfessed sins. Job resisted that argument and reaffirmed his faith in God, though he could not explain his suffering. In one of the greatest statements of faith in the Bible, he said, "Though He slay me, yet will I trust Him." I've come to appreciate that attitude. It conveys a sense of utter trust that God will never do anything to us that will in any real or ultimate sense harm us. He only aims for our good, however it may look at the time.

4. **I Know That My Redeemer Lives! (Job 19:23–27).** And now we come to the Old Testament's great Easter text, Job's fourth declaration of faith. Notice the personal pronouns. Job isn't just making a theological statement; he's expressing his own feelings: *I know that **my** Redeemer lives. . . . And after **my** skin has been destroyed, yet in **my** flesh I will see God; I **myself** will see him with **my own** eyes—I, and not another* (NIV). Jesus rose from the dead, and one day the bodies of His children will be resurrected. This passage contains the truths of the redemption of the soul, the person of the Redeemer, the resurrection of the body, the Second Coming of Christ, the end of the world, and the promise of everlasting life.

5. **He Knows the Way I Take! (Job 23:10).** The final great declaration of faith in Job is in Job 23:8–12. Job asserts, in effect, "My troubles won't last forever, and they're not without purpose. He knows the way I take, and when it's over I will come forth as gold" (paraphrased).

Conclusion: Are you facing trials and troubles right now? The hope of the resurrection undergirded the heroes of the Old Testament, the saints in the New Testament, the champions of Christian history, and you and me and all of us today, and we can sing: "I know that my Redeemer liveth, / And on the earth again shall stand; / I know eternal life He giveth, / That grace and power are in His hand" (Jessie B. Pounds, 1893).

STATS, STORIES, AND MORE

One day while we were having lunch, I asked my wife a strange question. It was sort of out of the blue, and she didn't know what to make of it. I asked her, "What would you think of a good friend who would come up to you and slice you open with a knife?"

"Well," she said, shocked, "that would be terrible."

"Yes," I said, "but what if he were a surgeon and he was performing an operation that would save your life?"

Well, that's different, isn't it? We still wouldn't like it at the time, but we'd be grateful that we had a friend with enough skill to help us at a critical moment. When Job said, "Though He slay me, yet will I trust Him," he was saying, "I know that God loves me, that He is a Great Physician, and that He will never harm me but will always work all things for good. And even if it appears for a moment that He is harming me, I know it's in appearance only and that in reality it is for my benefit. So I'm going to trust Him completely. Though He slay me, yet will I trust Him."

I know that my Redeemer lives, and ever prays for me;
A token of His love He gives, a pledge of liberty.
—CHARLES WESLEY

APPROPRIATE HYMNS AND SONGS

"Worthy Is the Lamb," Darlene Zschech, 2000 Hillsong Publishing.

"Because He Lives," Gloria and William Gaither, 1971 by William J. Gaither; Gaither Music Company.

"In Christ Alone," Stuart Townend & Keith Getty, 2002 ThankYou Music.

"The Power of the Cross," Stuart Townend & Keith Getty, 2005 ThankYou Music.

"Christ the Lord Is Risen Today," Charles Wesley, Public Domain.

FOR THE BULLETIN

Today is the birthday of two great hymn composers. Felice de Giardini was born in 1716. He was an Italian composer and chorister, violinist, music instructor, conductor, and opera singer. He wrote the music for the great hymn "Come, Thou Almighty King." Arthur H. Messiter, a prominent New York City organist, was born on this day in 1834. He composed the stirring tune to "Rejoice, Ye Pure in Heart." ● On April 12, 1799, the Church Missionary was organized in London. ● Today marks the anniversary of William Wilberforce's last speech, in 1833. Wilberforce was an outspoken Christian and British statesman. In his last speech he spoke with difficulty at Maidstone and called for the freeing of all slaves, predicting that the struggle to abolish slavery was nearing its goal. ● America's first missionary, Adoniram Judson, died on this day in 1850 and was buried at sea. Two other notable Christian leaders passed away on this day in history. The American Presbyterian clergyman, T. DeWitt Talmage, died in 1902. He was one of America's most powerful preachers, and his sermons were published in over 3,500 newspapers around the world. ● The founder of the American Red Cross, Clara Barton, also died on this day in 1912. ● On April 12, 1861, Fort Sumter in South Carolina was shelled, starting the American Civil War. ● Today is the birthday, in 1867, of Samuel Marinus Zwemer, best remembered for his work with the Student Volunteer Movement. ● On April 12, 1914, a convention of Christians began in Hot Springs, Arkansas, which led to the founding of the Assemblies of God.

Quote for the Pastor's Wall

I told God that I had done all that I could and that now the result was in His hands; that if this country was to be saved, it was because He so willed it! The burden rolled off my shoulders. My intense anxiety was relieved and in its place came a great trustfulness!

—ABRAHAM LINCOLN

WORSHIP HELPS

Call to Worship

Praise be to the God and Father of our Lord Jesus Christ! In his great mercy he has given us new birth into a living hope through the resurrection of Jesus Christ from the dead, and into an inheritance that can never perish, spoil or fade—kept in heaven for you, who through faith are shielded by God's power until the coming of the salvation that is ready to be revealed in the last time. In this you greatly rejoice . . . (1 Pet. 1:3–6a NIV).

Hymn/Poem for the Day

> *I know that my Redeemer lives;*
> *What comfort this sweet sentence gives!*
> *He lives, He lives, who once was dead;*
> *He lives, my ever living Head.*
>
> *He lives to bless me with His love,*
> *He lives to plead for me above.*
> *He lives my hungry soul to feed,*
> *He lives to help in time of need.*
>
> *He lives triumphant from the grave,*
> *He lives eternally to save,*
> *He lives all glorious in the sky,*
> *He lives exalted there on high.*
>
> *He lives to grant me rich supply,*
> *He lives to guide me with His eye,*
> *He lives to comfort me when faint,*
> *He lives to hear my soul's complaint.*
>
> *He lives to silence all my fears,*
> *He lives to wipe away my tears*
> *He lives to calm my troubled heart,*
> *He lives all blessings to impart.*
>
> *He lives, my kind, wise, heavenly Friend,*
> *He lives and loves me to the end;*
> *He lives, and while He lives, I'll sing;*
> *He lives, my Prophet, Priest, and King.*
>   —SAMUEL MEDLEY, 1775

Additional Sermons and Lesson Ideas

The Resurrection Record
Date preached:

By Dr. Melvin Worthington

SCRIPTURE: Luke 24

INTRODUCTION: The truth of the bodily resurrection of the Lord Jesus Christ was the theme of the preaching of the early church.

1. The Distinct Reality (vv. 5–6). The fact of Christ's resurrection recorded.
2. The Direct Reminder (vv. 6–7). The truth of the resurrection had been predicted.
3. The Disciple's Recall (v. 8). Jesus' implication and instruction remembered.
4. The Dramatic Response (vv. 9–10). They told the apostles.
5. The Disbelief Revealed (vv. 11–12). The initial response was unbelief.
6. The Divine Revelation (vv. 13–49). The appearance of the risen Savior.
7. The Departure Recorded (vv. 50–51). Jesus *led* and then *left* them.
8. The Daily Rejoicing (vv. 52–53). The disciples worshiped God continually.

CONCLUSION: The foundational truth of Christianity is the bodily resurrection of the Lord Jesus Christ. Without it our faith would be in vain.

Resurrection Responses
Date preached:

By Dr. Larry Osbourne

SCRIPTURE: Matthew 28:1–20

INTRODUCTION: The resurrection is the ultimate life-changing truth. The way we respond to life-changing truth impacts the way God works in our life.

1. The Women's Delight (vv. 1–10).
2. The Soldiers' Denial (vv. 11–15).
3. The Disciples' Doubt (vv. 16–20).

CONCLUSION: We all must respond to the resurrection of Jesus Christ. We can deny it and shut it out, doubt it but leave room for investigation, or accept it in childlike faith. God desires to work in and through our lives, but we must believe that He is who He says He is (Heb. 11:6). Respond to Jesus today and let God's truth work in your life.

Protecting the Speaking Voice

Former President Bill Clinton's voice is judged by some experts to be growing more raspy and hoarse the longer he remains in public life. What was once a pleasing and easy-to-hear voice is becoming an often-mocked rough and husky voice, due, it seems, to poor public speaking techniques. Ronald Reagan's voice, on the other hand, never lost its velvet quality. He was a trained actor who knew how to use and protect his voice.

But even actors can mess up. Perhaps you remember the sad story of Julie Andrews, the movie star and vocalist, who, having damaged her voice through overuse, sought help at New York's Mt. Sinai Hospital. Surgeons were to remove a small, noncancerous polyp from her vocal cords, but the operation went badly. Miss Andrews later filed a medical malpractice lawsuit against the hospital and two doctors for ruining her vocal cords and her ability to sing.

Like a vocalist, pastors and preachers must guard their voices as cherished gifts. If your voice feels strained after a sermon, it's likely that your breathing and speaking techniques are flawed. In time, your voice could commit "voice suicide," as one expert put it. A clear, ringing voice can become a hoarse, raspy one over the years, losing much of its power and appeal.

How can we protect the speaking voice? Here are some tips from a handful of experts.

- Drink more water than caffeine. Ideally, as far as the voice is concerned, we should avoid caffeine all together, for it's a diuretic that can dehydrate the voice and dry out the vocal cords. But if total abstinence isn't possible or practical, make it a point to drink more water.

- Switch to "half-caff" coffee in the mornings, which contains only one-half the caffeine.

- Order water at restaurants.

- Drink a full glass of water after every teeth brushing.

- Don't clear your throat. If you have phlegm, swallow or try gently dislodging it. Clearing the throat is very harsh on the vocal cords.

- Avoid yelling or screaming at home, at ball games, or elsewhere. Avoid prolonged conversations in noisy environments.

- Rest your voice when it feels tired. Don't preach when your voice is hoarse. When the vocal cords are swollen, they're particularly susceptible to injury, including permanent damage. Whispering does not help. It's vital to rest the voice. Continuing to use a hoarse voice is like running with a sprained ankle.

- Hot showers and facial steamers are good for the voice, for they hydrate the vocal cords.

- Consciously relax your hands when you preach. This will relax your voice muscles, allowing them to do their work with less strain.

- Use a public address system whenever possible, even for smaller gatherings. Tell your audio technicians that you need a stage monitor as much as the musicians, for when you can hear your own voice, you know you're being heard by the audience without undue volume.

- Visit a speech therapist to learn proper warm-up exercises and abdominal breathing techniques, especially in the delivery of a speech or sermon.

- Don't smoke.

If hoarseness or voice problems persist for more than a few days, see an ear, nose, and throat specialist. Don't take any chances with your voice. It's your God-given tool for reaching those who need to hear what you have to say.

APRIL 19, 2009

SUGGESTED SERMON

iForgive: A Lesson in Forgiveness
for an iPod Generation   *Date preached:*

By Pastor Jonathan Falwell

Scripture: Various, especially 1 John 1:9
If we confess our sins, He is faithful and just to forgive us our sins and to cleanse us
from all unrighteousness.

Introduction: If anyone is to thrive spiritually and keep from drying
up inside spiritually, they need to first experience God's forgiveness;
then they need to be a forgiving person. We need to cultivate a forgiving
heart. The Lord agreed that this was indeed necessary as well. In fact,
He, too, promised that He would provide forgiveness for all who ask
Him (1 John 1:9). Let's look at four facts about forgiveness to learn
what Scripture expects of us:

Facts:

1. **Forgiveness Brings Peace.** The Bible sometimes uses the word "forgiveness," but often times, when speaking about how God forgives
   us of our sins and saves us, it uses the word "reconcile" or "reconciliation." The word "reconcile" means "to make peace." Therefore,
   when God forgives us, He makes a way to where we can have peace
   with God. The Bible also uses the imagery of being *afar off, far away,
   separated, or excluded* from God, but God brings us near through
   Jesus (Col. 1:20–22). Getting saved is like God tearing down any
   barrier that has kept you from having peace and intimacy with Him.
   Now you can approach God's throne because you are His child
   (Heb. 4:16). You see, prior to accepting Christ as our Savior, we
   were not "at peace" with Him. But upon requesting forgiveness
   from God, we become not recipients of His wrath, but recipients of
   His grace, peace, and mercy!

2. **Forgiveness Requires Work on Our Part.** On the cross, in order for
   the Lord to provide forgiveness for our sins, He had to bear the
   weight of sin upon His shoulders. He did not retaliate or react. He
   worked hard to bear the pain for you and me. God absorbed the

debt of sin on our behalf so that we could be forgiven (Rom. 6:23; 2 Cor. 5:21). You see, He had every right to retaliate (and the power to do it), but He said He would fulfill God's will. For us, this does not come naturally; it takes work. For example, when the Roman guards came to the Garden of Gethsemane to take Jesus away, Peter retaliated by cutting off a soldier's ear. Jesus responded, telling Peter to put away his weapon. God's way is to forgive and not retaliate in kind, but to trust God that He will do His part while you do your part (cf. Rom. 12:17–19).

3. **Forgiveness Is a Choice We Make.** Paul makes this evident in 1 Corinthians 2:7–8: "But we speak the wisdom of God in a mystery, the hidden wisdom which God ordained before the ages for our glory, which none of the rulers of this age knew; for had they known, they would not have crucified the Lord of glory." If forgiveness is any less than a choice, then it is based on emotions that fluctuate and change at a moment's notice. Choosing to forgive faces the sin and deals with it rather than avoiding it. God's forgiveness is much greater and deeper than forgiving and forgetting. If you try to forgive and forget, you may just run into the temptation, when you "remember" sinful acts again, to beat the other person up because of the way these memories made you feel. But remember this, my friend, forgiveness is a choice. You choose to say, "No matter how many times I remember the pain you caused me, the emotions I felt surrounding that situation in the past, I have accepted your confession and I have promised that I will never hold that sin to your account again!"

4. **Forgiveness Is a Gift—Salvation.** God is willing to forgive you for every wrong you've ever done if you will confess them and turn from them (1 John 1:9). Psalm 86:5 says: "You, Lord, are good, and ready to forgive, and abundant in mercy to all those who call upon You." Before you can become a *forgiving* person, you need to be a *forgiven* person.

Conclusion: As the body of Christ, it's not an option or a peripheral concern to become people who forgive one another (Col. 3:13). It's also our responsibility to tell others of God's forgiveness made possible through the cross of Christ (1 Cor. 5:18–20).

STATS, STORIES, AND MORE

The Problem with Forgiveness
An article on July 3, 2006, in the *London Telegraph* bore the headline:
"Vicar Who Can't Forgive Steps Down from Pulpit." The story was about a
British minister whose daughter was killed in the London bombings. Rev.
Julie Nicholson of Bristol was unable to return to the pulpit after the July
7th terror attack that left fifty people dead, including Nicholson's
24-year-old daughter, Jenny, who was a gifted musician. She said that she
repeats the name of her daughter's killer, Mohammed Sidique Khan,
bitterly every day. "I rage that a human being could choose to take another
human's life. I rage that someone should do this in the name of God. I find
that utterly offensive . . . Can I forgive what they did? No, I cannot. And I
don't wish to. . . . I believe that there are some things in life which are
unforgivable by the human spirit. . . . I will leave potential forgiveness for
whatever is after this life. I will leave that in God's hands. . . . Forgiving
another human being for violating your child is almost beyond human
capabilities. It is very difficult for me to stand behind an altar and celebrate
the Eucharist and lead people in words of peace and reconciliation and
forgiveness when I feel very far from that myself."[1]

And This Quote
Everyone says forgiveness is a lovely idea, until they have something to
forgive.   —*C. S. Lewis*[2]

APPROPRIATE HYMNS AND SONGS

"Free," Kirk Franklin, 2000 Kerrion Publishing/Lilly Mack (BMI).

"The Lord's Prayer," Matthew 6:9–13; Albert Hay Malotte, 1976 by
      G. Schirmer, Inc.

"Sing to the King," Billy James Foote & Charles Silvester Horne, 2003
      Worshiptogether.com Songs/sixsteps Music.

"Give Us Clean Hands," Charlie Hall, 2000 sixsteps Music/
      Worshiptogether.com Songs.

---

[1]"Vicar Who Can't Forgive Steps Down from Pulpit," by Richard Savill in the London
 Telegraph, July 3, 2006.
[2]C. S. Lewis, *Mere Christianity* (New York: The Macmillan Company, 1958), p. 89.

FOR THE BULLETIN

On this day in 1529, followers of the Reformation became known as "Protestants." It happened at the Diet of Speyer, in Germany, which was a congress convened by Emperor Charles V who was threatening to wipe out the Lutheran movement. Five reformation-minded political leaders and fourteen cities issued a written protest, saying, "In matters concerning God's honor and the salvation of souls, each one must for himself stand before God and give account." This protest gave birth to the term "Protestants." ● Today marks the death in 1560 of Philipp Melanchthon, Luther's coworker and one of the original leaders of the Reformation. ● Today also marks the death in 1813 of the Methodist pastor, John H. Stockton, who passed away in New Hope, Pennsylvania. He was a musician who wrote the tunes to "Come Every Soul by Sin Oppressed," "Down at the Cross," and "The Great Physician Now Is Near." ● Hymnist Anna L. Waring was born on this day in 1823. Her best known hymn is "In Heavenly Love Abiding," but all her hymns are rich. She was also a tireless worker in prison ministry. ● Presbyterian Missionary Henry Jessup was born on April 19, 1832, and the prominent Boston pastor, Dr. A. J. Gordon, was born on April 19, 1836. ● Charles Haddon Spurgeon, nineteen, was called to London on April 19, 1854, to become the pastor of the New Park Chapel. ● William Henry Havergal, hymnist, died in Leamington, on April 19, 1870. He was an Anglican clergyman who worked tirelessly to develop higher and improved musical standards for Christian worship, but he is best known as the father of the great hymnist and devotional writer, Frances Ridley Havergal.

Quote for the Pastor's Wall

My voice fails me again, and my thoughts too. I was weary this morning, when I came into this pulpit, and I am weary now. Sometimes I am joyous and glad, and feel in the pulpit as if I could preach forever; at other times I feel glad to close. . . .

—CHARLES SPURGEON during his sermon on Jonah

WORSHIP HELPS

Call to Worship
The LORD your God in your midst, the Mighty One, will save; He will rejoice over you with gladness, He will quiet *you* with His love, He will rejoice over you with singing (Zeph. 3:17).

Invitation
If you're listening today and you have never asked for the Lord's forgiveness, take a moment to open your heart and mind to God. Do you feel guilty? Do you know that you were meant to live for eternity and yet you know that something is terribly wrong? Have you rebelled against authority or the notion of a God who is in control of your life? Jesus offers you freedom and forgiveness. God sent His Son who was worthy of worship and praise to pay the price of our rebellion through His death. Yet, Jesus conquered death and sin—everything that is wrong with the world—that we might have the opportunity to be reconciled to God. I invite you and beg you to be reconciled to God through Jesus' blood and to live a new life without guilt in the power of His risen Spirit.

Suggested Scriptures
- Matthew 6:9–15
- Matthew 18:21–35
- Luke 6:37
- Luke 17:3–4
- Colossians 3:13
- 1 John 1:9

Benediction
Thus says the LORD of hosts: "Execute true justice, show mercy and compassion everyone to his brother" (Zech. 7:9).

Additional Sermons and Lesson Ideas

Some Essentials for Living a Godly Life
By Pastor Al Detter

Date preached:

SCRIPTURE: 1 Peter 2:1–12

INTRODUCTION: Putting these things into practice will help you grow to be more like God.

1. Nourish Yourself in the Word of God (vv. 1–3).
2. Practice Your Priestly Duties as Your Primary Spiritual Ministry (vv. 4–10).
3. Behave Like the People of God (vv. 11–12).

CONCLUSION: We see that godliness happens by a constant feeding on the Word of God, by offering up spiritual sacrifices to God as your number one ministry, and by behaving like a Christian in an unfriendly world. As a priest of God, apply what you've learned and grow to be more like Jesus Christ.

A New Covenant
By Rev. Melvin Tinker

Date preached:

SCRIPTURE: Jeremiah 31:29–36

INTRODUCTION: God's gift to His church is not a new law written on tablets of stone, but the Spirit who writes His truth in hearts of flesh. Through Jesus, God offers a new covenant which consists of:

1. An Individual Relationship Rather Than Corporate Affinity (vv. 29–32).
2. An Internal Transformation Rather Than External Conformity (v. 33).
3. Personal Knowledge Rather Than Second-Hand Acquaintance (v. 34).

CONCLUSION: Jesus came that we might be reconciled through this new covenant to God our Father. The Good News is that sin has been dealt with fully and finally in Jesus, as God exhausted His holy wrath on our sin in Him, bearing it away so that our relationship with Him can never be threatened again. God stamps His seal upon His promises in verses 35 and 36 swearing by His character and His name that what He says will come to pass.

APRIL 26, 2009

The High Price of an Untamed Ego

By Dr. Larry Osborne   *Date preached:*

Scripture: Daniel 4, especially verse 17
This decision is by the decree of the watchers, and the sentence by the word of the holy ones, in order that the living may know that the Most High rules in the kingdom of men, gives it to whomever He will, and sets over it the lowest of men.

Introduction: Today we're going to learn a lesson from Nebuchadnezzar. Daniel 4 was penned by Nebuchadnezzar himself.

1. **The Danger Zone (v. 4).** "I, Nebuchadnezzar, was at home in my palace, contented and prosperous" (NIV). When it comes to an untamed ego, there's no more dangerous situation than a place where you're content and prosperous, where everything in your life seems to be going right and you begin to think that maybe it's because you're so great.

2. **The Dream (vv. 5–17).** Nebuchadnezzar had a strange dream that terrified him. He brought in all the wise men, the magicians, the astrologers, and soothsayers to interpret but none could. Finally Daniel was brought before Nebuchadnezzar to interpret it.

3. **The Interpretation (vv. 18–27).** Daniel was troubled that he had to give the king such an interpretation, but proceeded to explain the dream. The tree in the dream symbolized Nebuchadnezzar, his expansive power and reign. But Nebuchadnezzar would be humbled, driven out of his kingdom, forced to live among cattle and even eat grass as they do until "you know that the Most High rules in the kingdom of men, and gives it to whomever He chooses" (v. 25). The stump that is left indicates that when he is humbled, Nebuchadnezzar will again be restored to the kingdom.

4. **The Fulfillment (vv. 28ff).** Later, as the king walked on his roof, he said one of the stupidest things ever to be uttered: "Is not this great Babylon, that I have built for a royal dwelling by my mighty power and for the honor of my majesty?" (v. 30). While he was still speaking, judgment came audibly from heaven (v. 31) and then physically to

fulfill what was foretold in the dream interpreted by Daniel (v. 33). Nebuchadnezzar lost his kingdom and was humbled to the point of living as cattle until he acknowledged God's sovereignty. He was only restored to his kingdom when he recognized God's ultimate authority.

Application: None of us are in a place of world dominion like Nebuchadnezzar, but we certainly are susceptible to an untamed ego whether it shows up in a marriage, a work environment, a school, or any other situation.

1. **Develop Healthy Pride and Rid Yourself of Arrogance.** Let's look at the differences between healthy pride and arrogance:

   A. **Healthy Pride.** There's nothing wrong with healthy pride that is confident in one's own abilities. God doesn't want you to go through life thinking you're bad at something you're good at. He doesn't want you to have a *lower* view of yourself, but an *accurate* view of yourself (Rom. 12:3). We are also supposed to find joy and satisfaction in our own success (2 Cor. 8:24). It's also acceptable to tell others about our successes in a way that glorifies God (Gal. 6:4). For example, we could all agree that Daniel was a great man and Daniel is the same person who wrote Daniel—a book filled with great things God did through him.

   B. **Arrogance.** It's absolutely wrong to have arrogance that looks down on others (Luke 18:9–14). It's okay to recognize things we're better at than others, but it's sinful to think we're simply better than others. A second way arrogance shows up is when we think rules that apply to others don't apply to us (Dan. 4:29–30). Another way this is displayed is in taking advantage of the weak (Dan. 4:26–27; Prov. 29:7). Finally, arrogance is blowing God off (Dan. 4:30). Blowing God off is *calculating without God in my equation.* We so easily forget that God has put us where we are and begin to think we don't need God. Arrogance is something that God *hates* and *attacks* (Prov. 8:13; 15:25)—a much bigger deal than we make of it.

2. **How to Keep Your Ego Well-Tamed.** These principles are in effect the antithesis of Nebuchadnezzar's statement in verse 30:

A. Share the Credit (James 1:16–17).

B. Remember the Helping Hand (Ps. 127:1; Eph. 4:11–14).

C. Ask "What's in It for God?" (1 Cor. 10:31; Prov. 16:2–3).

Conclusion: Whenever you see a tortoise on a post, you know he didn't get there alone. As you go, share the credit, remember the helping hands, and use it all for God's glory.

STATS, STORIES, AND MORE

Better than Average
A study done in Australia on 150,000 students asked the question "How good are you at getting along with others?" All of them said they were "better than average."

Raymond Who?
Raymond Lewis was the greatest high school basketball player to ever come out of California. Many people would call him the greatest high school basketball player in the country. He was the type of guy with hundreds of scholarships offered. Jerry Tarkanian, a famous coach of that era, said that without question, Raymond Lewis was the best basketball player he ever saw—not the best high school player, but the best basketball player, period. He was so incredible and left such a mark on anyone who saw him play that they didn't forget him. He came onto my radar screen because our team played his, and I had the chance to guard him (my coach didn't actually call it *guarding* but it was the best I could do). Ten years after he graduated from high school, I was leafing through a *Sports Illustrated* and saw a ten-page article entitled simply *Raymond, Where Are You?* When he died about thirty years after getting out of high school due to some complications after a surgery, the *Los Angeles Times* for two days ran major articles on Raymond Lewis. Yet when I ask almost any crowd "Remember Raymond Lewis?" Hardly anyone does.

Lewis is known as the greatest player *never* to play in the NBA. He was an early hardship case. He was drafted by the Philadelphia 76ers. Another young man was drafted that year named Doug Collins. Doug Collins was the first pick and Lewis was picked next. It's said that in one scrimmage, at half-time Lewis had scored fifty points guarded by Collins. The guy was unbelievable, but never played in the NBA. Why?

As he was running all over Doug Collins day after day, Lewis realized his own contract wasn't nearly as good. He and his buddies decided this wasn't good, and he decided to sit on the bench until he got what he wanted. The 76ers said, "Fine, we'll see you next year." The next year he tried to come back, but he was involved in legal battles because he played for another (smaller) league. Due to the legal battles, he sat out another year. This type of problem continued and Lewis never played in the NBA. Raymond Lewis's problem wasn't drugs, it wasn't women, it wasn't money; it was an untamed ego.

APPROPRIATE HYMNS AND SONGS

"Cry of My Heart," Terry Butler, 1991 Mercy/Vineyard Publishing.

"Shine on Us," Michael W. Smith & Deborah D. Smith, 1996 Milene Music, Inc. and Deer Valley Music.

"Holy, Holy, Holy," Reginald Heber, Public Domain.

"I Would Be Like Jesus," James Rowe, 1912 Hope Publishing Company; 1949 Rodeheaver Company.

FOR THE BULLETIN

In the 1400s, the family of Pope Sixtus IV (builder of the Sistine Chapel) clashed with the Medici family of Florence. The rivalry became so tense that in 1748, with the pope's knowledge, his nephews and bankers hatched a plan to murder Lorenzo and Julian Medici. On Sunday, April 26, 1478, the two Medici brothers entered the cathedral in Florence for Easter Mass. In the middle of the service, the brothers were attacked with knives. Julian was killed, but Lorenzo survived to track down the murderers and exact revenge. ● On April 26, 1772, Philip Gatch attended a Methodist prayer meeting at the home of a neighbor. He came under deep conviction of sin, but felt he was too evil to be saved. He left, but as he stood outside the building, a friend came out and entreated him to return. Upon reentering the house, he was saved and later became one of the first American-born Methodist preachers and circuit-riders. ● Today is the birthday, in 1806, of the Scottish missionary Alexander Duff. ● One of the saddest trials in church history began on April 26, 1832. Edward Irving was a brilliant and kindhearted Scottish pastor who served as assistant to the great Thomas Chalmers in Glasgow. In 1822, Irving moved to London where he accepted the pastorate of a dying church. Within a few months it grew from fifty people to over a thousand, and a new building was built at Regent Squire. Irving grew arrogant and his popularity with the people declined. At the same time, he was accused of heresy because he declared that Christ, though sinless, had a sinful nature. His views on other subjects grew more bizarre, and on April 26, 1832, a hearing was convened which led to his being expelled from the church he had built. ● Horatio Richmond Palmer, American Congregational clergyman, was born on April 26, 1834, in Little Compton, Rhode Island. He is best known for his hymn "Yield Not to Temptation," and "My Faith Looks Up to Thee," but he also wrote a lesser-known hymn entitled "Angry Words" that says, "Angry words! O let them never, / From the tongue unbridled slip. / May the heart's best impulse ever, / Check them ere they soil the lip." ● This is the anniversary of the Columbine massacre in Littleton, Colorado.

WORSHIP HELPS

Responsive Reading

Worship Leader: But you, do not be called "Rabbi"; for One is your Teacher, the Christ, and you are all brethren. Do not call anyone on earth your father; for One is your Father, He who is in heaven. And do not be called teachers; for One is your Teacher, the Christ. But he who is greatest among you shall be your servant (Matt. 23:8–11).

Congregation: And whoever exalts himself will be humbled, and he who humbles himself will be exalted (Matt. 23:12).

Worship Leader: When you are invited by anyone to a wedding feast, do not sit down in the best place, lest one more honorable than you be invited by him; and he who invited you and him come and say to you, "Give place to this man," and then you begin with shame to take the lowest place. But when you are invited, go and sit down in the lowest place, so that when he who invited you comes he may say to you, "Friend, go up higher." Then you will have glory in the presence of those who sit at the table with you (Luke 14:8–10).

Congregation: For whoever exalts himself will be humbled, and he who humbles himself will be exalted" (Luke 14:11).

Worship Leader: Two men went up to the temple to pray, one a Pharisee and the other a tax collector. The Pharisee stood and prayed thus with himself, "God, I thank You that I am not like other men—extortioners, unjust, adulterers, or even as this tax collector. I fast twice a week; I give tithes of all that I possess." And the tax collector, standing afar off, would not so much as raise his eyes to heaven, but beat his breast, saying, "God, be merciful to me a sinner!" I tell you, this man went down to his house justified rather than the other . . . (Luke 18:10–14a).

Congregation: For everyone who exalts himself will be humbled, and he who humbles himself will be exalted (Luke 18:14b).

Prayer

Father, teach us in the deepest part of our hearts how to enjoy every good and perfect gift You have given without confusing the root and the starting place of it all, Amen.

Additional Sermons and Lesson Ideas

How to Get Rid of Guilt
Date preached:
By Dr. Michael A. Guido

SCRIPTURE: Various Scriptures

INTRODUCTION: How do we find forgiveness and freedom?

1. Mark the Guilt.
    A. Guilt from the Savior (Rom. 3:10–18). We are guilty because of what we are.
    B. Guilt from Satan (Rev. 12:10–11). We are reminded of the past.
    C. Guilt from Self (Ps. 32:1–5). When guilt comes we should search our souls.
2. Mark the Grief.
    A. Physical Suffering (Ps. 32:3). Disobedience hurts the health.
    B. Emotional Suffering (Ps. 32:4). Disobedience manifests misery.
    C. Spiritual Suffering (Ps. 32:4). Disobedience delivers a drought.
3. Mark the Grace (1 John 1:9).
    A. Confession. Sin must be confessed to Jesus Christ.
    B. Compensation. Sin must be forgiven by Jesus Christ.
    C. Cleansing. Sin must be cleansed through Jesus Christ.

CONCLUSION: Our guilt and our grief can only be taken away through the grace of God.

Portrait of a New Testament Church
Date preached:
By Dr. Timothy K. Beougher

SCRIPTURE: 1 Corinthians 1:1–3

INTRODUCTION: 1 Corinthians gives us an actual portrait of a New Testament church. In these verses we are introduced to this church and what it is all about.

1. The Planter of the Church (v. 1). God uses real people to build up His body through evangelism and discipleship in the context of meeting together in congregations.
2. The Proprietor of the Church (v. 2a). The church doesn't belong to people but to God.
3. The People of the Church (v. 2b). True members of God's church are believers in Christ who are growing and being sanctified by Him.
4. The Pronouncement to the Church (v. 3). God, through Christ, has given us grace and peace.

CONCLUSION: We are called to take part in God's plan, but it's still God's plan. The church is not our church, it is God's church. We are not our own, we are the people of God. And, God desires to give us grace and peace through Jesus Christ.

MAY 3, 2009

SUGGESTED SERMON

The Life God Blesses

Date preached:

By Dr. David Jeremiah

Scripture: Acts 9:31–43, especially verse 36
At Joppa, there was a certain disciple named Tabitha, which is translated Dorcas. This
woman was full of good works and charitable deeds which she did.

Introduction: The violinist Paganini stood before a packed house and
played a number of difficult pieces, but one of the strings on his violin
broke. He improvised on three strings, but a second string broke. Near
the end of the concerto, a third snapped! Amazingly, he finished the
piece on one string. The audience stood and applauded till all hands
were numb. In the same way, think of what God can do with one man
or one woman whom He blesses and uses.

1. **A Life Marked by Ministry (Acts 9:32–33).** God uses a life marked
   by ministry. Peter was a go-getter, going everywhere with the gospel.
   God seems to use busy people. It seems like every biography I read
   tells the story of someone who's on the move, doing the work God
   has assigned. We find God's will by being about the will He's
   already revealed to us.

2. **A Life Marked by Humility (Acts 9:34–35).** As Peter itinerated, he
   came to Lydda where he found a certain man named Aeneas who
   had been bedridden for years. Peter told him, "Jesus the Christ
   heals you. Arise and make your bed." Peter approached Aeneas,
   not to seek glory for himself, but for the Lord. God will not use
   those who are not humble in His sight. If you want to be impressed
   with yourself, God won't bless you; but if you'll allow God to work
   in your life and if you'll give Him the glory, He will honor you.
   Peter wasn't the healer, just the instrument. This was a one-person
   miracle, but its impact affected the entire city and area. Peter dealt
   with one man, but many turned to the Lord. Was Peter a God-
   blessed minister? I guess he was!

3. **A Life Marked by Availability (Acts 9:36–39).** From the restoration
   of Aeneas, Peter moved to the resurrection of Dorcas. The second

miracle was a result of being available for the first one. If Peter hadn't been in Lydda, they wouldn't have come to get him. Walking with the Lord is an adventure. We start one place, and one opportunity leads to another. And Peter was willing to go. He didn't have any roots that would keep him from being where God wanted him to be. This woman (Tabitha is her Aramaic name, and Dorcas is her Greek name; both words mean *gazelle*) was apparently a very graceful woman. The Bible calls her a "certain disciple." She was full of good works and charitable deeds. Verse 39 says she sewed tunics and garments for those around her. She was a model of the verse saying we are His workmanship, created in Christ Jesus for good works" (Eph. 2:10). When Dorcas died, her friends washed her body, laid her in an upper room, and went for Peter.

4. **A Life Marked by Dependency (Acts 9:40–41).** Peter needed something in that hour he couldn't provide, so he knelt and prayed. We need a spirit of dependency: "Lord, if You don't do something here, nothing's going to happen." When Peter finished praying, he turned to Dorcas, and said, "Arise." She opened her eyes and sat up. Imagine the joy in the church that day.

5. **A Life Marked by Productivity (Acts 9:42).** The life God blesses is marked by productivity because everyone in Joppa heard of this, and as news spread more progress was recorded for the kingdom.

6. **A Life Marked by Flexibility (Acts 9:43).** This verse is about Peter's remaining among the Gentiles. Peter has yet to deal with the idea that Gentiles are included in the church. He'd grown up with traditional Jewish prejudices, so when he dwelt with Simon the tanner—oh my goodness, tanners dealt with dead bodies. To a Jew, a tanner was an outcast from synagogue and society. Now everyday Peter woke up to see stinking animal skins hanging through the house. God was teaching Peter that the legalistic life was over, and now in Christ, there is neither Jew nor Gentile.

Conclusion: God blesses a life that's marked by ministry. What are you doing to serve God? A life marked by humility. Do you give the glory to Christ for what He's doing in your life? A life marked by availability. Are you willing to go to Joppa? A life marked by dependency. When you do something for God, do you kneel and pray? A life marked by productivity. When you serve the Lord, something's going to happen. And a life marked by flexibility. Are you willing to serve God no matter the circumstances?

STATS, STORIES, AND MORE

More from Dr. David Jeremiah
A few weeks ago, I was asked to speak at the FCA meeting in Tampa. About 700 people came to this event, and I preached a message that I have preached on passion. It was kind of what was in my heart that day, and I thought this would be great for a bunch of athletes because they are passionate. I had no idea who was going to be there, but I preached, and we had a great time. I got home the next day, and I had a phone call from the head of the FCA down there, and he said, "You aren't going to believe what happened here. One of the guys on our staff had invited the number one high school football coach to come to that event. He's been coaching here for twenty years and has won more games than any other coach in the history of Tampa high school football. He heard you preach on passion, and when it was all over, he turned to the guy who brought him and said, "I don't have anything like that in my life. I don't have any passion like that in my life. Can I meet with you for lunch tomorrow?" The next morning he got up and he went to lunch with this coach, and over lunch he led him to Christ. He was the last person in the world you'd ever believe to be saved, and the word spread through the whole city. You never know what's going to happen when someone comes to Christ.

APPROPRIATE HYMNS AND SONGS

"Victory in Jesus," Eugene M. Bartlett, 1967 by Mrs. E. M. Bartlett.

"We Declare Your Majesty," Malcom Du Plessis, 1985 Maranatha Praise, Inc.

"We Want to See Jesus Lifted High," Doug Horley, 1993 Kingsways ThankYou Music.

"For Who You Are," Marty Sampson, 2006 Hillsong Publishing.

"Offering," Paul Baloche, 2003, 2004 Integrity's Hosanna! Music.

FOR THE BULLETIN

On May 3, 1675, a state law was enacted in Massachusetts requiring that church doors be closed and locked during worship services to prevent attendees from getting up and leaving church before the lengthy sermons were complete. ● On this day in 1721, missionary Hans Egede, the "Apostle of Greenland," sailed from Denmark with 46 people. He became an effective worker to the Eskimos of Greenland, and his work was continued by his son, Paul. ● On May 3, 1738, evangelist George Whitefield arrived in America for the first of his seven evangelistic tours. ● Charles Spurgeon was baptized on his mother's birthday, May 3, 1850. He later wrote, "I can never forget the 3rd of May, 1850; it was my mother's birthday, and I myself was within a few weeks of being sixteen years of age. I was up early, to have a couple of hours for quiet prayer and dedication to God. Then I had some eight miles to walk to reach the spot where I was to be immersed into the Triune name. . . . What a walk it was! What thoughts and prayers thronged my soul during that morning's journey!" ● William Whiting died on May 3, 1878. He was master of Winchester College Choristers' School for more than twenty years and is best known for writing the words of "Eternal Father, Strong to Save." This is frequently called the Navy Hymn, and it was played in 1963 as President John Kennedy's body was carried up the steps of the U.S. Capitol to lie in state. It was also the favorite hymn of President Franklin Roosevelt. ● The musician who wrote the score to "O Holy Night," Adolphe Charles Adam, died on this day in 1856 in Paris and was buried in the Cimetiere de Montmartre.

PRAYER FOR THE PASTOR'S CLOSET

Lord, I don't like some of the people to whom I preach,
Yet may I love them by Your grace!
I don't understand some of the passages from which I preach,
Yet make me effective by Your power.
I don't have the strength or skill to soar with pulpit oratory,
Yet may souls be saved by Your Spirit.
Lord, I don't want to work from inferior motives,
Yet my heart is deceitful and desperately wicked.
Make me content to be Your humble, cheerful servant,
and use me for heaven's sake.
Amen.

WORSHIP HELPS

Call to Worship
Blessed are the people who know the joyful sound! They walk, O LORD, in the light of Your countenance. In Your name they rejoice all day long (Ps. 89:15–16).

Pastoral Prayer Idea
Our churches are to be houses of prayer for all nations, and we're specifically commanded to pray for leaders and for those in authority. Spend some time this week checking out the international news, reports from the persecuted church, and letters from missionaries supported by your church. In your pastoral prayer, cover the globe. Pray for nations in conflict, for troops in harm's way, for famine relief efforts, and for gospel advances among unreached people. Pray for your national, state, and local leaders. And pray for a revival to sweep across our land and call us back to the Lord.

Offertory Comments
Colonel Sanders of fried chicken fame once said, "There's no good reason to be the richest man in the cemetery." The Bible teaches that Christians aren't on earth for very long, and we're to be laying up wealth in heaven through the good works that we do and by the ministries that are supported by our funds. May the Lord give us generous hearts and may He use what we're setting aside for His kingdom today.

Benediction
Lord, we want to be usable, useful, and used for You. Take our attitudes this week and brighten others. Take our deeds and glorify Yourself. Take our words, and may we be Your witnesses to the ends of the earth. In Jesus' name, Amen.

Additional Sermons and Lesson Ideas

The Victory of Christ and the Kiss of Faith
By Rev. Larry Kirk

Date preached:

SCRIPTURE: Psalm 2

INTRODUCTION: Psalm 2 tells us that Jesus Christ will ultimately be victorious on earth, and that's why we should serve Him with joyful submission.

1. The Ultimate Victory of Christ Will Come in Spite of the Rebellion of Mankind (vv. 1–3).
2. The Ultimate Victory of Christ Will Come Because of the Irresistible Power of God (vv. 4–6).
3. The Ultimate Victory of Christ Will Result in His Lordship Over All the Earth (vv. 7–9).
4. The Ultimate Victory of Christ Requires a Response of Faith and Submission (vv. 10–12).

CONCLUSION: Christ died as a willing sacrifice to pay for our sins, and He rose again as our King. Trust in Him; that's how you take refuge in Him and receive His blessing (v. 12).

Don't Forget
By Rev. Melvin Tinker

Date preached:

SCRIPTURE: Deuteronomy 8:1–19

INTRODUCTION: We are to remember what God has done and be thankful for those things.

1. Recall God's Word and Provision (vv. 1–6). God led and protected His people through the wilderness.
2. The Problem of Plenty and Pride (vv. 7–17). God warned the people lest they gain wealth and credit themselves rather than remembering God.
3. Remember and Praise with Gratitude (vv. 2, 10–11, 18). The people were incited to remember that the Lord was provider and they were to be grateful.

CONCLUSION: God provides so much for us, but like the Israelites our memories are short. Verse 19 holds a warning for us: ungratefulness, pride, and disobedience lead to destruction. Remember what the Lord has done in the past and trust Him for the future.

Duncan Campbell

Duncan Campbell grew up harnessed to a set of bagpipes, and he eventually became a sought-after entertainer in his Scottish village. But one night during a concert, he suddenly asked himself, "Is this all life offers a young man like me?" Excusing himself, he hurried home where his mother led him to Christ. He served the Lord in churches in his native highlands until age fifty when he left as a missionary to the Outer Hebrides Islands.

A mission church had already been established on Lewis Island, and several of its members had been pleading for revival. One night in a prayer meeting, a young man rose and read Psalm 24: "Who may ascend into the hill of the Lord? Or who may stand in His holy place? He who has clean hands and a pure heart. . . ."

"Brethren," the man said, "it seems just so much humbug to be waiting and praying as we are, if we ourselves are not rightly related to God." Instantly the Christians began confessing their sins to God and to one another.

When Duncan Campbell arrived soon afterward, he went straight to the church and preached, then dismissed the service. The crowd filed from the building; but instead of going home, they stood under the stars, weeping, praying and confessing their sins. The number soon swelled to 600, and all night the Holy Spirit moved through the village. Hundreds trusted Christ as Savior.

The revival spread to nearby villages, and Duncan traveled for three years, strengthening the converts. Night after night, churches were filled with worshipers, often until five o'clock the following morning. Duncan later said that during those days he could stop any passerby on the island and find him thinking about his soul.

Duncan Campbell lived until 1971, and he preached until the last week of his life. But the Lewis Revival proved the most fruitful period of his ministry.[1]

---

[1]From the editor's book, *From This Verse,* published by Thomas Nelson Publishers in 1998, entry for March 1.

MAY 10, 2009

MOTHER'S DAY SUGGESTED SERMON

What a Woman Needs

Date preached:

By Pastor Al Detter

Scripture: Selected texts in Proverbs, especially 31:10
Who can find a virtuous wife? For her worth is far above rubies.

Introduction: Proverbs sets a high goal for women. That goal is that she be a woman of moral excellence. By that, I don't just mean that she is pure. Moral excellence speaks of knowing the difference between right and wrong and conforming to a standard of right behavior. Proverbs talks about some of these traits. I want to highlight five of them.

I. **Five Characteristics of the Happy Woman.**

   A. **Grace (Prov. 11:16).** The word used here relates the idea of a kind, generous, hospitable, gentle woman. She's not hard and gruff. This verse says she will be honored.

   B. **Discretion (Prov. 11:22).** Discretion means that a woman has moral discernment. She sees moral and spiritual right and wrong and she chooses and advises the right thing. This verse says that a beautiful woman without discretion is like putting a ring of gold in a pig's nose. Doing that would be highly inappropriate. In just the same way, when you see a beautiful woman who compromises spiritual virtues, the disparity is obvious.

   C. **Virtue (Prov. 12:4).** A virtuous woman is a woman of moral character. She is sexually pure and she does the ethically right thing. She has godly character. She is a great asset to her husband. He doesn't have to be concerned about her lifestyle and what she does in secret. The second part of the verse says that if a man is married to a woman who lacks virtue, she will slowly but inevitably destroy him.

   D. **Wisdom (Prov. 14:1).** This quality is about possessing the knowledge of how to create a harmonious and orderly home resulting in happiness and fulfillment. She knows how to firmly connect the members of the household together. When a woman does not exercise care about how her family is doing, the family will begin to disintegrate and she will bear a large part of the blame. The wise woman realizes the strategic role she plays in the home.

E. **Prudence (Prov. 19:14).** Prudence basically means common sense. It's the ability to be shrewd in managing practical matters.

2. **The Unhappy Woman.**

A. **Her Description: Contentious.** The unhappy woman has one major characteristic—contention. The contentious woman is referred to five times in Proverbs, second only to the adulterous woman. The word for contentious can be translated in a number of ways—the angry woman, the nagging woman, the quarrelsome woman—and it comes from a word that means "discord" in Hebrew. She is upset, ill of mood, and mad about something and it has become her disposition. It's the contentious disposition; that's the problem. What Proverbs says about the contentious woman is almost humorous unless you happen to be married to one. But these are God's words: "Better to dwell in a corner of a housetop, than in a house shared with a contentious woman" (Prov. 21:9). In those days in Israel, houses had flat roofs. This verse basically says that living in a corner of a roof with its challenges is better than the challenge of sharing a very large house with an angry woman. Several other Scriptures support this idea (Prov. 21:19; 19:13; 27:15).

B. **Her Problem: Feeling Unloved.** I believe Proverbs 30:23 puts its finger on the root of the problem. It says following the set-up statement in verse 21, "Under three things the earth trembles, and under four it cannot bear up . . . an unloved woman who is married" (NIV). Let me paraphrase it according to my understanding: "Look out for the woman who feels unloved!" I think that's what Proverbs is trying to tell us. A woman who feels unloved sends strong signals! She does that by becoming contentious.

C. **Her Husband.** If a major problem with the contentious woman is feeling unloved, then husbands you have a responsibility to counteract this! Your role as a leader and as the love of her life is one of self-sacrifice (Eph. 5). Be willing to go as far as you need to in making her feel loved.

Conclusion: If we're married, didn't we marry to be friends? What use is it for men to ignore their wives' needs and for women to be contentious and quarrelsome? Life is too short to live that way. I know there will be problems in every marriage. But the deadly combination is an insensitive husband and a contentious wife. That's what I believe Proverbs is trying to stress and solve.

STATS, STORIES, AND MORE

More from Pastor Al Detter
I want to suggest a twenty-four-hour experiment. You can do it as a couple or as an individual. I'd like you to take an egg this week and for twenty-four hours, you will take it wherever you go. It can't be hard-boiled. It's never to leave your side. You will take it in the shower. You will take it to meals. You will take it in the car. It will be wherever you go at work. It will be by your side when you watch TV and when you answer the phone. You will find a way to sleep with it. You're mission is to watch and protect it so that nothing happens to it. Do that for twenty-four hours this week. And while you're doing that, tell yourself that if you can treat an egg that well, you can do that kind of thing with your spouse.

Presidential Moms
Her children rise up and call her blessed (Prov. 31:28).

🔖 "My mother was the most beautiful woman I ever saw. All I am I owe to my mother. I attribute all my success in life to the moral, intellectual, and physical education I received from her."
—*George Washington*

🔖 "There never was a woman like her. She was gentle as a dove and brave as a lioness. The memory of my mother and her teachings were, after all, the only capital I had to start life with, and on that capital I have made my way." —*Andrew Jackson*

🔖 "I remember my mother's prayers and they have always followed me. They have clung to me all my life."
—*Abraham Lincoln*

🔖 "She was one of the most remarkable persons I have ever known. . . . I seem to feel still the touch of her hand, and the sweet steadying influence of her wonderful character. I thank God to have had such a mother." —*Woodrow Wilson*

APPROPRIATE HYMNS AND SONGS

"Faith of Our Mothers," Henri F. Hemy, Public Domain.

"Before the Throne of God Above," Charitie Lees Bancroft and Vikki Cook, 1997 PDI Worship.

"Hungry," Kathryn Scott, 1999 Vineyard Songs.

"Because We Believe," Jamie Harvill & Nancy Gordon, 1996 Mother's Heart Music.

FOR THE BULLETIN

On May 10, 1310, fifty-four Knights Templar were burned alive in Paris on order of King Phillip I, and the rest of the Templars fled into hiding, eventually splitting into secret societies. ● Today is the birthday, in 1812, of Frances Elizabeth Cox, author of the English rendition of Johann Schutz's German hymn, "Sing Praise to God Who Reigns Above." The Anglican evangelical leader, John Charles Ryle, was also born on this day in 1816; and the Swiss theologian Karl Barth was born on this day in 1886. ● Thomas "Stonewall" Jackson, a brilliant general and staunch Presbyterian, credited his calmness in battle to his faith. "My religious belief teaches me to feel as safe in battle as in bed," he once said. "God has fixed the time for my death. I do not concern myself about that, but to always be ready, no matter when it may overtake me." It overtook him at the Battle of Chancellorsville, when Jackson was hit by friendly fire. His arm was amputated, but his condition worsened. His last words were, "Let us cross the river, and rest under the shade of trees." He died on May 10, 1863. ● On this day in 1908, the observance of Mother's Day began when Ana Jarvis arranged for her church in Philadelphia to honor the memory of her own mother and those of others. Afterward Ana waged a crusade to launch Mother's Day as a national day of celebration, and on May 9, 1914, President Wilson issued such a proclamation. ● Methodist preacher John Bunnell Sumner died on this day in 1918. He was a "Singing Methodist Preacher" who is best known for having written the music to "I'm a Child of the King."

WORSHIP HELPS

Call to Worship
Because Your lovingkindness is better than life, my lips shall praise You. Thus I will bless You while I live; I will lift up my hands in Your name. My soul shall be satisfied as with marrow and fatness, and my mouth shall praise You with joyful lips (Ps. 63:3–5).

Invitation to Prayer
This message was not meant to make people feel bad but to get husbands and wives out of sinful and harmful patterns. Perhaps the Spirit of God is telling you to make a mid-course correction. If you're a contentious woman, pray the following prayer in your heart and mean it. If you're a husband who is not sensitive to your wife's needs, pray it as well: "Lord Jesus, I realize that I'm a contentious woman or I admit that I don't love my wife as I should. Help me to see how I've failed and break me. Forgive me for the ways I have wounded my spouse. Make me to be a godly person regardless of how I may be treated. I realize this will not be automatic or easy, but I am expecting a new day. Help me, Lord! In the powerful name of Jesus, Amen."

Kid's Talk

If possible, have your church purchase carnations to give to all the mothers in your congregation. Bring the children to the front and show them the flowers. Ask them why they think their mothers deserve a flower? After accepting a few answers, have the mothers in your congregation stand and have the children deliver flowers to their own mothers and ask for a few volunteers whose children are not there to pass out the remaining flowers. Be sure to include mothers-to-be and mothers of all ages.

Additional Sermons and Lesson Ideas

Daughters of Sarah
By Rev. Todd M. Kinde

Date preached:

SCRIPTURE: 1 Peter 3:1–6

INTRODUCTION: Using Abraham's wife Sarah as a role model for every woman who is a part of the body of Christ, Peter tells us the characteristics of a godly woman:

1. A Godly Woman Is Reverent (v. 2).
2. A Godly Woman Is Pure (v. 2).
3. A Godly Woman Is Gentle (v. 4).
4. A Godly Woman Is Quiet in Spirit (v. 4).
5. A Godly Woman Is Hopeful (v. 5).
6. A Godly Woman Is Obedient (v. 6).
7. A Godly Woman Is Courageous (v. 6).

CONCLUSION: Women, does this describe you? Young men, is this the type woman you are looking for in a mate? It should be. Husbands, how can you encourage and strengthen your wives to build them up in these areas? Parents, are you instilling these values in your daughters?

How Is Your Faith?
By Rev. Billie Friel

Date preached:

SCRIPTURE: 1 Thessalonians 3:1–10

INTRODUCTION: Paul sent Timothy back to Thessalonica to check on the spiritual quality of the new church's faith (vv. 1–2).

1. Trouble Is Coming (vv. 3–4). The inevitability of trouble was affirmed by Jesus and Job. With trouble, it is not a matter of "if" but "when."
2. Troubles Will Test Our Faith (v. 5). When troubles come, they reveal the reality of our faith. A faith that has not been tested is not trustworthy.
3. Our Faith Encourages Others (vv. 6–10). The faith of the Thessalonian church brought comfort and joy to Paul. We are a blessing to others by our faithful stand in the faith.

CONCLUSION: Troubles will certainly come to us in this life. These troubles will test our faith. The way we respond to these tests will influence others. How is your faith?

MAY 17, 2009

SUGGESTED SERMON

Stranglers or Wranglers?

Date preached:

Scripture: 2 Corinthians 7:5–7, especially verse 5
Outside were conflicts, inside were fears.

Introduction: Everyone is a combination of strengths and weaknesses, good points and bad points. There's a sense in which we're all walking contradictions, because we often believe one thing and do another. In my case, I'm a preacher who believes what the Bible says about the peace of God that passes understanding. Yet I sometimes struggle with anxiety. Here in 2 Corinthians, Paul admits the same was true for him. The man who wrote Philippians 4 about the peace of God also wrote 2 Corinthians 7 about his own fears and phobias, saying, "When we came into Macedonia, this body of ours had no rest, but we were harassed at every turn—conflicts on the outside, fears within" (NIV).

1. **Encouragement Is One of Our Greatest Needs (v. 5).** In chapter 2, Paul wrote: Now when I went to Troas to preach the gospel of Christ and found that the Lord had opened a door for me, I still had no peace of mind, because I did not find my brother Titus there. So I said good-by to them and went on to Macedonia (v. 12 NIV). Corinth was Paul's premier church in Europe, but there were divisions and conflicts there, and false teachers and heretical doctrines. Titus had gone to manage the situation; but Paul was so worried he couldn't even preach in Troas when a door opened. The Greek says, "My spirit had no relaxing." Winston Churchill defined worry as an emotional spasm that occurs when the mind "catches hold of something and will not let it go." Not even Paul was immune from this; and here in Troas, he grew so upset and worried he couldn't even preach, so he went to Macedonia. Our text today picks up the story: When we came into Macedonia, this body of ours had no rest. He uses the same Greek word: (relaxing). In chapter 2, his mind could not relax; and in chapter 7, his body could not relax. He continued, we were harassed at every turn . . . conflicts on the outside, fears within. Paul needed encouragement just like we do. We live in a world in which encouragement is one of our greatest needs.

2. **Encouragement Is One of God's Greatest Provisions (v. 6).** The passage, however, doesn't stop with 7:5. Verse 6 opens with the words: *Nevertheless God.* What a memorable phrase! *Nevertheless God,* who comforts the downcast. If you are downcast today, congratulations. You qualify! But now, here's the question. How does God encourage and comfort us? I could say, "God comforts us with certain promises in His Word that meet our particular need. He comforts us through the act of worship. He comforts us through answered prayer and by the workings of His personal providence." But in this passage, God encouraged Paul through a fellow believer, through the arrival of Titus. God imparted comfort through another human who showed up with good news. Think of yourself as a fully commissioned dispenser of encouragement to others. It's fantastic to think that we are providers of God's own encouragement to another person.

3. **Encouragement Has a Never-Ending Pass-Along Quality (v. 7).** Furthermore, encouragement is the gift that keeps on giving. In this passage, the Corinthians, despite their problems, had somehow managed to encourage Titus, who had encouraged Paul, who wrote this book for us, and today we've been greatly encouraged by it. There's a ripple effect to our simple acts of encouragement that continues until Christ returns. In *The Fine Art of Friendship,* Ted Engstrom tells of a literary group that formed years ago at the University of Wisconsin, made up of gifted young men wanting to be writers. They met together to read and critique each other's work. They called themselves the Stranglers, and they tended to be hard on each other. They dissected the minutest literary expressions, and their sessions became critical as they surveyed each other's work. A group of women at the same university, not to be outdone, formed a group called the Wranglers. They, too, read their works to one another, but there was a difference. Their criticism was softer, more positive, more encouraging, and sometimes there was no criticism at all. Twenty years passed, and someone did an exhaustive study of the two groups. For all their determined potential, not one of the Stranglers had made a significant literary accomplishment of any kind. But from the Wranglers had come six or more successful authors, including Marjorie Kinnan Rawlings who wrote *The Yearling.*[1]

---

[1] Ted W. Engstrom, *The Fine Art of Friendship* (Nashville: Thomas Nelson, 1985), pp. 131–132.

Conclusion: Are you a Strangler or a Wrangler? We all need encouragement, and God is the God of all comfort. He uses us to encourage one another, and those simple acts and words of encouragement have a ripple effect that outlive us all.

STATS, STORIES, AND MORE

As a boy, Vincent van Gogh wrote: "I feel instinctively that I am good for something, that there is some point to my existence. . . . What could I be? What service could I perform?" Growing up, he searched for purpose in life. As a young man, he moved to Paris and became friends with a young Englishman with whom he studied the Bible. He began working in a little church and occasionally taught the Bible and gave the sermons. He wrote in one letter: "Woe is me if I do not preach the Gospel; if I do not aim at that and possess faith and hope in Christ, it would be bad for me indeed. . . . It is a delightful thought that in the future, wherever I go, I shall preach the Gospel." Vincent, however, failed to get into theological school. In 1879, he was assigned to preaching the Gospel among poverty-stricken miners in Belgium. He had no one to encourage him. The church authorities issued a report saying that while he aided the sick and wounded, his ability to preach was lacking. As a result he was dismissed. Vincent packed his things and plodded down the road in bare feet, head bent, carrying his few possessions on his shoulders. The children shouted after him, "He's mad! He's mad!" Vincent gave up on the ministry, turned away from the Lord, and decided to become an artist. Even there, he had no one to encourage him except his brother. During his entire lifetime, he sold only one painting. He became increasingly unstable and unhappy. During the final seventy days of his life he painted seventy paintings. He was in frenzy, losing touch with reality, until he finally borrowed a pistol and went out into a field and shot himself. I can't help wondering what would have happened in those early days of his ministry if he had just been given some encouragement.

APPROPRIATE HYMNS AND SONGS

"Blessed Be Your Name," Beth Redman & Matt Redman, 2002 ThankYou Music.

"Come Thou Fount," John Wyeth & Robert Robinson, Public Domain.

"Comfort, Comfort Now My People," Catherine Winkworth, Johannes Olearius, Louis Bourgeious, Public Domain.

"Straight to the Heart," Michael W. Smith & Brent Bourgeois, 1995 Sony/ATV Milene Music; ADC Music; W.B.M. Music; Deer Valley Music.

"A Shelter in the Time of Storm," Ira D. Sankey & Vernon J. Charlesworth, Public Domain.

FOR THE BULLETIN

Scottish philosopher and clergyman John Duns Scotus was ordained on May 17, 1291, at the age of twenty-five. ● On this day in 1527, Michael Sattler, an early Anabaptist leader, was placed on trial in Rotenberg for his faith. He refused legal counsel, saying the issues against him were spiritual and religious, not secular and legal. He was convicted and sentenced to be led to a place of execution where his tongue would be cut out, his body tortured with hot tongs, and his life taken by fire. On May 20th, he was executed at the stake, and shortly afterward his wife was martyred by drowning. ● On this day in 1776, Rev. John Witherspoon of Princeton preached a sermon that had a catalytic effect of the founding of the United States of America. Until then, Witherspoon had opposed the "rebellion," but his message that day centered on the biblical doctrine of divine providence, and he argued that even things that seem harmful and destructive can become instruments of God's will. He said that liberty was God's gift to all of creation. Witherspoon later became a signer of the Declaration of Independence and a member of the Continental Congress. ● On May 17, 1792, the New York Stock Exchange was founded by twenty-four merchants at 70 Wall Street. ● Today is the birthday of the Conservative Baptist Association of America, formed on May 17, 1947, in Atlantic City, New Jersey.

WORSHIP HELPS

Welcome
If you have come today with a heavy heart, this is a place to be encouraged. You will see that there are people here who genuinely care about you and will lift you up. You will also find power outside of yourself when you turn to the Lord. Meeting with us is meant to be an encouragement as the Scripture says: "Let us not give up meeting together, as some are in the habit of doing, but let us encourage one another—and all the more as you see the Day approaching" (Heb. 10:25 NIV).

Scripture Reading Medley
May our Lord Jesus Christ himself and God our Father, who loved us and by his grace gave us eternal encouragement and good hope, encourage your hearts and strengthen you in every good deed and word. For everything that was written in the past was written to teach us, so that through endurance and the encouragement of the Scriptures we might have hope. See to it, brothers, that none of you has a sinful, unbelieving heart that turns away from the living God. But encourage one another daily, as long as it is called Today, so that none of you may be hardened by sin's deceitfulness. Therefore encourage one another and build each other up, just as in fact you are doing (2 Thess. 2:16–17; Rom. 15:4; Heb. 3:12–13; 1 Thess. 5:11 NIV).

Benediction
May the God who gives endurance and encouragement give you a spirit of unity among yourselves as you follow Christ Jesus, so that with one heart and mouth you may glorify the God and Father of our Lord Jesus Christ (Rom. 15:5–6 NIV).

Additional Sermons and Lesson Ideas

God Is Worth Knowing
By Pastor Al Detter

Date preached:

SCRIPTURE: 1 Kings 8:22–61

INTRODUCTION: Solomon's dedication of the temple focuses on the glory of God and the beauty of a relationship with Him.

1. God Is Worth Knowing in a Personal Way Because He Is Incomparable in Greatness (vv. 23–29).
2. God Is Worth Knowing in a Personal Way Because He's So Incredibly Forgiving (vv. 30–53).
3. God Is Worth Knowing in a Personal Way Because He Wants to Bless Those Who Know Him (vv. 54–61).

CONCLUSION: God sent Jesus Christ so that a way would be made for us to join the family of God. Having a relationship with God allows us to see Him for who He is and permits us to experience His forgiveness and blessings. We are not to contain His name in a building but proclaim Him that the world may also know Him.

Staying Power
By Dr. Larry Osborne

Date preached:

SCRIPTURE: James 1:1–8

INTRODUCTION: Writing to a scattered congregation, James pleads for God's people to persevere and in so doing prove their faith genuine.

1. Rejoice Instead of Complain (vv. 2–3). We must have a different attitude when things are rough.
2. Stay Instead of Run (v. 4). We must give a different response when resistance arises.
3. Pray for Wisdom Instead of Deliverance (vv. 5–7). We must make a different request when we are challenged.

CONCLUSION: We are called to perseverance. Difficult times will come but we must trust that Jesus is who He says He is. Our race will be marked with trials, resistance, and challenges, but we serve a God who provides joy, strength, and wisdom.

The Active Silence of God
By Pastor Al Detter

If you read and obey the Bible, you'll be blessed in every area of your life as a pastor and you'll never have to experience a breaking.

That's what I thought for twenty years in the ministry as life sailed by so smoothly. Then came one heartbreak after another. My father was killed in a car accident. Two hundred people left my church. I entered a firestorm with my staff and elders that required a mediator. Our youngest son and his friends set fire to a wing of our church. Our unmarried teenage daughter became pregnant. Slowly I went from thriving to surviving.

But the most encompassing heartbreak of all was the tragic car accident of our oldest son, Jason, then nineteen. He was T-boned by a semi-truck. The first responders radioed a probable DOA to the emergency room. Two policemen woke us from sleep early in the morning to identify our son in the ER.

But he lived! He sustained a traumatic brain injury. Nineteen days in a coma. Five months in a rehab hospital. Once again a baby in every sense, he had to relearn how to walk, speak, and reason.

Fast-forward to more recent years. Adopted at birth and in his mid-twenties, Jason was still living at home due to his injuries. A letter arrives addressed to him. "Dear Jason, I'm not exactly sure how to begin this. I'm your paternal grandmother."

Jason's heart skipped with astonishment and excitement.

She continued, "Last October, your father died of cancer. He was forty-five. I wanted you to know something about your biological family's medical history, so I hired an investigator to find you. Your dad never married. You were his one and only son."

The letter invited Jason to call his grandmother. A two-hour conversation ensued after twenty-seven years of absolutely no contact.

"There's another reason I wanted to find you," she said on the phone. "Your father restored a car but he never got to drive it. His dying wish was for me to find you. Your father wants you to have his '69 Camaro."

In the letter was another piece of information—the name and number of his biological mother. She was willing for Jason to contact her if he wanted to. That very afternoon, Jason called her. He began, "Hi. This is your son, Jason. I've been waiting for this moment for as long as I can remember." She responded with a sigh followed by the tearful silence of a meaningful connection. Then she told Jason something about herself, "When my life got turned around, I married a pastor. And Jason, you have eight half-brothers and sisters."

Suddenly life had taken another incredible turn!

I've had some time to reflect on all of this and two lessons keep coming hard at me. I want to share them with you because you might find yourself in a sea of adversity doing all you can to survive in the ministry.

Lesson #1—Be Persistent in Your Prayers. Life over the years has forced me to my knees. I've hit a lot of whitewater and my only hope for survival was to reach out to God. Jason's accident became a clinic in prayer. We couldn't have survived without the divine connection. Today there's not much theology on waiting and praying through. But prayer is often more a time exposure than a snapshot. We have to pray patiently and look for God's hand across time to see how He's orchestrating the answers.

Philippians 4:6–7 became my rock for prayer. I discovered that the major answer to prayer is *peace* that guards our minds and hearts no matter what the circumstances. But there are times we can't get that peace. I believe that's a signal to keep on praying until either we get peace or we get the answers we're praying for.

Jason's recovery reached a plateau and it looked like he was going nowhere. Years began to tick by. I'd given God the right to bruise my son, but I couldn't get peace. So I began to pray four very specific prayers:

- Lord, would you give Jason his legs? He wants to walk so he can get around and drive a car.
- Lord, would you give him someone to love? The girls pass him by. He's so lonely. *Continued on the next page*

- Lord, would you give him a job? Those with brain injuries have a hard time finding and holding a job.

- Lord, would you bless him in other good ways to make up for his losses? He's such a great kid. Would you restore to him what the locusts have eaten?

For six long years I prayed the same four prayers, often sobbing with agonizing pain of spirit. No answers. No peace. I kept pleading sometimes hardly believing.

Without warning, it was like popcorn in a microwave oven. You hear the sound of the oven for several minutes but no popping. Then suddenly, profuse popping. Answers to prayer began to pop. Some procedures helped Jason's walking and he passed his driver's test—prayer #1. He met a Christian girl at a Bible study which led to marriage—prayer #2. He got a part-time job—prayer #3. And then this letter arrives about his biological family that could enrich his years ahead—prayer #4.

Many of you are in places of waiting and difficulty. Maybe not like mine. But you're crying out to God. You're not seeing immediate answers to prayer. Don't stop praying. Be persistent. God *is* at work.

Lesson #2—God's Writing a Bigger Story Than We Realize.
What particularly gets our attention is the hard stuff of life. When we go through those times, we wonder where God is and what He's up to. How could God allow such turmoil and intense difficulties? Why isn't He doing something about it?

There's no grander illustration of this than the story of Joseph in Genesis. We all know the obvious story. Then twice we're told about the bigger story (Gen. 45:5, 7; 50:19–20). God was behind the scenes working out the events so Joseph could save his family and keep the developing grand story of Israel alive. But Joseph didn't know or understand while it was happening.

We often find ourselves in that place. Difficult things are happening. God seems so inactive. Well, that's the active silence of God! He's faithfully at work. You've got to believe that with God, when nothing seems to be happening, something *is* happening!

We don't have the ability to see the big picture in the short run. We have a hard time seeing a good outcome in times of pain. But eventually, we begin to see the hand of God. He's been refining us into His image. And He's preparing us to be a force in the lives of other people in ways we could never have fathomed.

If you're in a place of bitter struggle and doubt, affirm in your heart once again—through it all, He's been faithful! And keep praying until you see the bigger story!

By the way, I'm still the senior pastor of the same growing church after twenty-nine years.

PRAYER FOR THE PASTOR'S CLOSET

Lord,
Help me to live this day
Quietly, easily.
Help me to lean upon Thy
Great strength
Trustfully, restfully,
To wait for the unfolding
Of Thy will
Patiently, serenely
To meet others
Peacefully, joyously,
To face tomorrow
Confidently, courageously.
Amen.
—St. Francis of Assisi

MAY 24, 2009

SUGGESTED SERMON

The Tamed Tongue

Date preached:

By Dr. Melvin Worthington

Scripture: James 3:1–12, especially verses 8–10

No man can tame the tongue. It is an unruly evil, full of deadly poison. With it we bless our God and Father, and with it we curse men, who have been made in the similitude of God. Out of the same mouth proceed blessing and cursing. My brethren, these things ought not to be so.

Introduction: The Bible says a great deal about the tongue. David prayed for the Lord to set a watch and keep the door of his lips. The writer of Proverbs declared that the hypocrite with his mouth destroyed his neighbor. Jesus warned about judgment regarding use of the tongue (Matt. 12:36–37). James said it takes a perfect person to not offend by words (James 3:3). The way we talk reveals what we think, for out of the abundance of his heart a man speaks. The use of the tongue either crowns or curses the Christian community. The index to our spiritual health is how we talk. Our speech reveals what kind of person we are.

1. **The Tongue's Power to Direct (James 3:3–5).** James 3:3–5 illustrates the great potential of the tongue in how it directs: like the bit to control a horse and the helm to control a ship. The power of the tongue is effective to direct the lives of others into right or wrong paths. We must ever be aware of the idle word, the questionable story, the deliberate lie, or a half-truth, which is in reality a whole lie. If the tongue is properly regulated, the whole man—as a horse is managed by the bit and a ship is steered by the helm—is brought under control. The problem with the tongue, however, is that it has the power to direct in the wrong way as well.

2. **The Tongue's Power to Destroy (James 3:6).** James gives us the tongue's description, comparing it to a fire, a world of iniquity (3:6). He further states that it defiles the whole body, sets on fire the course of nature and is itself set on fire of hell. What a powerful indictment! The tongue defiles, destroys and damns men by suggesting sin, committing sin, condoning sin, excusing sin, and defending sin.

Throughout his epistle, James describes the tongue's devastation: the hasty tongue (1:19), the hellish tongue (3:6), the heathen tongue (5:12), the hypocritical tongue (1:26), and the heartless tongue (2:15–16) are all described in this book.

3. **The Tongue's Power to Delight (James 3:9–17).**

   A. **The Illustrations (v. 11).** James uses a fountain and fruit trees to set forth this truth (3:9–17). He argues, "Does a spring send forth fresh water and bitter from the same opening? Can a fig tree, my brethren, bear olives, or a grapevine bear figs? Thus no spring yields both salt water and fresh."

   B. **The Impossibility (v. 10b).** James declares that it is impossible for a fountain to give both fresh and salt water at the same time. Likewise it is impossible for the tongue to speak blessings and cursing at the same time; in the end your blessings are contradicted and mean nothing.

   C. **The Imperative (vv. 8–10).** These verses make it obvious that the Christian must discipline his tongue. The holy tongue, happy tongue, honest tongue, and humble tongue characterize the Christian. He uses his tongue to pray for wisdom, help the afflicted, for healing, and for backsliders to be restored. He uses his tongue to praise his heavenly Father for His glory, goodness and greatness. He uses his tongue to proclaim the gospel.

   D. **The Inference (v. 8a).** The tongue can only be tamed by the Holy Spirit. James declares, "But no man can tame the tongue." If we cannot tame the tongue, we must rely on the Holy Spirit to do so in our lives. We are exhorted to yield our members (Rom. 6:13) to the Lord. That includes the tongue.

Conclusion: Perhaps it's time we all gave our tongues to the Lord and prayed, "Let the words of my mouth and the meditation of my heart be acceptable in Your sight, O LORD, my strength and my Redeemer" (Ps. 19:14).

STATS, STORIES, AND MORE

Horatio Richmond Palmer, a New Yorker born in 1834, began singing in the church choir (his father was the director) at age seven. He later became an accomplished musician and choir director himself. He wrote the music to several of our hymns, and the words to the gospel song, "Yield Not to Temptation." One of Palmer's lesser-known songs (he wrote both the words and music) is one of the very few hymns on the subject of the misuse of the tongue. Its title is "Angry Words," published in 1867, shortly after the end of the Civil War.

Angry words! O let them never,
From the tongue unbridled slip,
May the heart's best impulse ever,
Check them ere they soil the lip.

Love is much too pure and holy,
Friendship is too sacred far,
For a moment's reckless folly,
Thus to desolate and mar.

Angry words are lightly spoken,
Bitterest thoughts are rashly stirred,
Brightest links of life are broken,
By a single angry word.

Chorus:
Love one another thus saith the Savior,
Children obey the Father's blest command,
Love each other, love each other,
'Tis the Father's blest command.

APPROPRIATE HYMNS AND SONGS

"Every Move I Make," David Ruis, 1996 Mercy/Vineyard Publishing.

"O For a Thousand Tongues to Sing," Charles Wesley, Public Domain.

"Be the Centre," Michael Frye, 1999 Vineyard Songs.

"Lord, You Have My Heart," Martin Smith, 1992 ThankYou Music.

FOR THE BULLETIN

John Wesley's missionary labors in Georgia failed, and he returned to England saying, "I went to America to convert the Indians, but, oh, who shall convert me?" Back in London, Wesley attended a Moravian meeting in Aldersgate Street on May 24, 1738, and listened to someone reading from Luther's preface to Romans. He later said, "I felt my heart strangely warmed. I felt I did trust in Christ, Christ alone for salvation; and an assurance was given to me that he had taken away my sins, even mine." ● As a young man, Joseph Hart was a passionate opponent of Christianity, and he once wrote a pamphlet entitled "The Unreasonableness of Religion," which attacked one of Wesley's sermons. But after coming to Christ, Hart became a powerful preacher and hymnwriter, the author of "Come, Ye Sinners, Poor and Needy." He passed away on this day in 1768, and was buried in Bunhill Fields in London. ● This day marks the birth in 1824 of John G. Paton, Presbyterian missionary to the New Hebrides in the southwest Pacific. His exploits there are legendary, and his autobiography is a best-seller in Christian history. ● Inventor Samuel Morse, the son of a minister, planned a dramatic demonstration on this day in 1844. Before assembled dignitaries, he sent a message via telegraph wire from the U.S. Capitol to a railroad depot in Baltimore. The first words to ever be electronically transmitted were from Numbers 23:23: "What Hath God Wrought." He later explained, "It is all of God. He used me as His hand in all this. I am not indifferent to the rewards of earth and the praise of my fellow men, but I am more pleased with the fact that my Father in heaven has allowed me to do something for Him and for His word. Not unto us, but unto God be all the glory. Not what hath man, but what hath God wrought!"

Quote for the Pastor's Wall

*Work as though you would live forever, and
live as though you would die today.*

—OG MANDINO

WORSHIP HELPS

Call to Worship
O Lord, open my lips, and my mouth shall show forth Your praise (Ps. 51:15).

Scripture Reading
I will extol the LORD at all times; his praise will always be on my lips. My soul will boast in the LORD; let the afflicted hear and rejoice. Glorify the LORD with me; let us exalt his name together. Whoever of you loves life and desires to see many good days, keep your tongue from evil and your lips from speaking lies. The eyes of the LORD are on the righteous and his ears are attentive to their cry; The righteous cry out, and the LORD hears them; he delivers them from all their troubles (Ps. 34:1–3, 12–13, 15, 17 NIV).

Offertory Scripture
"No servant can serve two masters; for either he will hate the one and love the other, or else he will be loyal to the one and despise the other. You cannot serve God and mammon." Now the Pharisees, who were lovers of money, also heard all these things, and they derided Him. And He said to them, "You are those who justify yourselves before men, but God knows your hearts. For what is highly esteemed among men is an abomination in the sight of God" (Luke 16:13–15).

Additional Sermons and Lesson Ideas

Living by Faith
Date preached:

SCRIPTURE: Habakkuk 2:4

INTRODUCTION: The Bible says on four occasions that the just shall live by faith. Faith is so essential because it:

1. Saves Our Lives from Destruction (Rom. 3:23).
2. Supports Our Hearts in Difficulty (1 Pet. 1:3–7).
3. Shields Us from the Devil's Attacks (Eph. 6:16).
4. Sustains our Morale in Labor (1 Thess. 1:3).
5. Strengthens Our Days with God's Blessings (Rom. 1:17).
6. Sweetens Our Attitudes in Daily Life (1 Tim. 1:5).
7. Sends Our Souls to Heaven (2 Cor. 5:6–8).
8. Satisfies the Heart of God (Heb. 11:6).

CONCLUSION: A great example of this is Abraham, whom we can emulate. According to Romans 4:21 (NIV), faith, as Abraham practiced it, is being fully persuaded that God has the power to do what he had promised.

iPray: A Lesson in Prayer for the iPod Generation
Date preached:
By Pastor Jonathan Falwell

SCRIPTURE: Various Scriptures on Prayer

INTRODUCTION: Today, I want to share five principles with you that will help you understand what prayer is, why it is important, what it can do for us, and how God deeply desires that conversation with us on a regular basis. God desires to commune with us in a very real way. A way that can change our lives!

i —Individual (Luke 11:2).
P—Personal (Ps. 4:1).
R—Relational (Rom. 10:9; Luke 11:2b).
A—Assurance (Luke 11:9; 1 Pet. 1:3–4).
Y—Yield (Luke 11:2b; 1 Thess. 5:17–18).

CONCLUSION: Today, we've taken the letters of "iPray" and made an acronym. You could also summarize today's sermon this way: Pray to Have Peace with God; Pray to Have the Peace of God; Pray to Obey the Will of God!

MAY 31, 2009

The Path of Wisdom: Our Relationship with God

Date preached:

By Dr. David Jackman

Scripture: Proverbs 15:30–16:30, especially 15:31, 32b
The ear that hears the rebukes of life will abide among the wise . . . he who heeds rebuke gets understanding.

Introduction: From chapters 1–15, Proverbs focuses much attention on the contrast between the righteous and the wicked. Starting at chapter 16 the focus shifts to highlight the contrast between human righteousness and divine righteousness and also to give evidences of how the Lord intervenes in our daily lives, in our everyday thoughts and actions, in our plans and their outcomes. So here we're brought face-to-face with the God who stands behind this wise instruction and who is working out His providential will in our circumstances.

I. **Mind the Gaps (15:30–33).** These verses stand about halfway through the book as a reminder about what proverbs is all about, and how to use it. Verse 30 states "The light of the eyes rejoices the heart, and a good report makes the bones healthy." That reminds us why we study this great book: it's designed to bring rejoicing and refreshment. Just as the sun after a gloomy spell or just as a good report encourages us, that's exactly what wisdom is intended to do. The next three verses tell us how, specifically teaching us that there is no divide between what is secular and what is spiritual. We should mind these gaps; we should pay attention to where we mistakenly divide daily life from God's wisdom.

A. **Reproof (15:31, 32b).** "The ear that hears the rebukes of life will abide among the wise . . . he who heeds rebuke gets understanding." The promise in this verse is that we can gain wisdom and understanding if we subject ourselves to correction.

B. **Instruction (15:32a, 33a).** "He who disdains instruction despises his own soul . . . The fear of the LORD is the instruction of wisdom." To reject God's input on our lives is to despise ourselves, for what greater counselor to guide us through life than the One who created it?

C. Humility (15:33b). "And before honor is humility." It's not natural for us to subject ourselves to reproof and instruction, but humility is a prerequisite to gaining wisdom.

2. **Mark the Grace (16:1–30).** As we look at God's proactive involvement with us in the life of wisdom, we can see this clearly from the verses that contain the phrase: "but the LORD." Here we have God breaking in to our lives and wisdom enables us to see it, to understand it, and to cooperate with it. How does He do this?

A. Wise Speech (16:1). "The preparations of the heart belong to man, but the answer of the tongue is from the LORD." The contrast in this verse is not between our plans and God's answers as though it was wrong to plan. The contrast is what belongs to man and what belongs to God. As Christians, we should seek to make decisions prayerfully and wisely, but as the second half of this verse points out, sometimes it simply doesn't turn out the way we expect. However well we plan, God will overrule to advance His purposes. What an incentive to active trust in God!

B. Discerning Motives (16:2). "All the ways of a man are pure in his own eyes, but the LORD weighs the spirits." The first half of this verse is, perhaps, an attack on our complacency. We all tend to think we're right and can persuade ourselves quite readily about the appropriateness of our motives. But, as the second half of this verse points out, we can never understand those motives fully. God knows the heart and understands exactly why we do everything we do. Not only does God know, but He assesses it and goes on revealing it to us, motivating us to change.

C. Divine Direction (16:9). "A man's heart plans his way, but the LORD directs his steps." The steps are the stages of progression along the way. They stay firm because they are watched over and protected by the Lord of wisdom. We cannot achieve the ends we desire; only God can. Again, we must humble ourselves and rely upon divine grace.

D. Revealing Providence (16:33). "The lot is cast into the lap, but its every decision is from the LORD." Casting lots was an Old

Testament method of making decisions; doing so was still trusting that God would determine the outcome. God's providence is such that it overcomes the human circumstance to accomplish His will.

Conclusion: Nothing can thwart the plans of the Lord. Wisdom is depending upon Him completely in all the details of our lives: walking with God, talking to God, about every decision every day—this is the Christian life!

STATS, STORIES, AND MORE

More from Dr. David Jackman
The last use of casting lots in the Bible was the choosing of Matthias in Acts 1. This was the last time lots were used because it was before Pentecost. The gift of the Holy Spirit to the church in New Testament to every believer is the fulfillment of God's promise to guide us with His eye upon us, so the Spirit is the means by which we understand His providence today. It's the Holy Spirit who prompts us and teaches us from Scripture, and who controls our thought processes as we pray and lay out our lives before God.

Providence and Provision
Years ago when I felt called to go to theological college, my wife Heather and I did not have the means. I had been working for a Christian organization for six years, unable to save money and my church had no provisions for training either. It was an incredible adventure of faith. One day we were in considerable financial need and a sizeable check came through the post from a totally unexpected source. I would never have thought this particular person would have sent us money to support our ministry. What happened, though, was that at a previous Christian job I had been working with foreign students and a Swiss medical student was converted. He had now gotten back to Switzerland years later, was still a single man now working a good job with a good salary. Someone from the team visited him in Switzerland and he asked about me. They told him I was in theological college. He replied, "I suppose he could use some money. Most theological students can." So he sent a check. I wouldn't have thought of him if I had written a letter to every trust that I could imagine. But it's just a little example—and we see it all the time in our lives—that God is overruling in these ways; He is in charge; He does provide! —*Dr. David Jackman*

APPROPRIATE HYMNS AND SONGS

"Immortal Invisible," Walter Chalmers Smith, Public Domain.

"Be Thou My Vision," Irish Hymn, c. 8th Century; Trans. by Mary E. Byrne & Versified by Eleanor Hall, Public Domain.

"Friend of God," Michael Gungor & Israel Houghton, 2003 Vertical Worship Songs and Integrity's Praise! Music.

"Open the Eyes of My Heart," Paul Baloche, 1997 Integrity's Hosanna! Music.

"Open My Eyes That I May See," Clara H. Scott, Public Domain.

FOR THE BULLETIN

On May 31, 1578, the Christian catacombs in Rome were discovered by Italian archaeologist Antonio Bosio. ● On this day in 1660, in Boston, Mary Dyer was sentenced to death for defying a law banning Quakers from the colony. She was hanged the next day. Today a bronze statue of her stands in front of the Massachusetts State Capitol Building. ● Alexander Cruden was born in Scotland on May 31, 1699. His father, a strict Puritan, forbade games on the Lord's Day, and Alexander entertained himself by tracing words through the Bible. He enrolled in college at thirteen and graduated at nineteen. He eventually moved to London and began working on his *Concordance.* It was published in 1737 and became an immediate success. Cruden himself, however, suffered from repeated trips to the asylum. He spent his final days giving out tracts and studying the Bible. One morning in 1770, a servant found him on his knees, his head on the open Bible, dead. ● May 31, 1792, is the date of the famous missionary sermon preached by a cobbler named William Carey in which he famously said, "Expect great things from God; attempt great things for God." Carey preached at ten in the morning to his fellow Baptist preachers in Nottingham. His text was Isaiah 54:1–2. He was determined that his denomination do something for missions. At first, the response to the sermon seemed to go nowhere, but the next day, the gathering voted to take the first steps in establishing what came to be known as the Baptist Missionary Society, and William Carey became its first missionary and the "Father of Modern Missions."

WORSHIP HELPS

Call to Worship
Oh, bless our God, you peoples! And make the voice of His praise to be heard (Ps. 66:8).

Scripture Reading Medley
Only may the LORD give you wisdom and understanding, and give you charge concerning Israel, that you may keep the law of the LORD your God. But where can wisdom be found? And where is the place of understanding? Man does not know its value. Wisdom calls aloud outside; She raises her voice in the open squares. She cries out. . . The LORD gives wisdom . . . He stores up sound wisdom for the upright. If any of you lacks wisdom, let him ask of God, who gives to all liberally and without reproach, and it will be given to him. And in the hidden part You will make me to know wisdom. My mouth shall speak wisdom, and the meditation of my heart shall give understanding. I thank You and praise You, O God of my fathers; You have given me wisdom and might (1 Chr. 22:12; Job 28:12–13a; Prov. 1:20–21a; 2:6a, 7a; James 1:5; Ps. 51:6b; Ps. 49:3; Dan. 2:23a).

Pastoral Prayer
Lord, we do love You and worship You. Some of us can look back on years and years where You have proven Yourself again and again; You've never failed us. Every promise of the Lord has been fulfilled. We pray, therefore, that You would encourage us in this faith, that You would grant us the humility that trusts where we cannot see You, that You would grant us the faith that takes our hands off when we can't control things, and that acknowledges that there could not be wiser, safer, more loving hands than those that were nailed to the cross for our sins. Please help us to hear the Word, to trust You, and to follow the path of wisdom for Your name's sake, Amen.

Additional Sermons and Lesson Ideas

Meet Moses
By Dr. Melvin Worthington

Date preached:

SCRIPTURE: Exodus 1–2

INTRODUCTION: The Bible describes Moses as a mighty, meek, and ministering man. His life and ministry spans Exodus to Deuteronomy. Let's meet him.

1. His Background (Ex. 1).
   A. The Period (vv. 1–7).
   B. The Problem (vv. 8–14).
   C. God's Provision (vv. 15–22).
2. His Birth (Ex. 2:1–10).
   A. The Parents of Moses (vv. 1–3).
   B. Preservation of Moses (vv. 4–10).
3. His Boldness (Ex. 2:11–20).
   A. The Fear of Moses (vv. 11–14).
   B. The Fleeing of Moses (vv. 15–20).
4. His Bride (Ex. 2:21–22).
   A. His Contentment (v. 21).
   B. His Companion (v. 22).
5. His Boy (v. 22).
6. His Brethren (vv. 23–25).
   A. He Recorded Persecution (v. 23).
   B. He Remembered Promise (v. 24).
   C. He Respected People (v. 25).

CONCLUSION: God did not forget the Children of Israel. God remembered them and used Moses to deliver them from bondage. Great is His faithfulness!

How to Pray Jesus' Way
By Dr. Larry Osborne

Date preached:

SCRIPTURE: Matthew 6:9–13

INTRODUCTION: Jesus models for us five things our prayers should be concerned with.

1. The Enhancement of God's Reputation (v. 9).
2. The Advancement of God's Agenda (v. 10).
3. Our Material Needs (v. 11).
4. Forgiveness (v. 12).
5. Spiritual Protection (v. 13).

CONCLUSION: We must remember that prayer is based on our relationship with God and is a privilege we have received through Christ.

YOUTH SERMON

Abstinence Is in the Bible

Date preached:

By Dr. David Jeremiah

Scripture: 1 Thessalonians 4:1–8, especially verse 3
This is the will of God, your sanctification: that you should abstain from sexual immorality.

Introduction: Basketball pro A. C. Green once spoke at Los Angeles Lynwood High School about abstinence, saying: "I remember my first trip with the Lakers. Everyone was saying, 'A.C., you're not going to believe how wonderful the girls look who hang out after the game. You won't be talking about saving yourself for marriage after you've seen these girls. We give you six weeks before you give in, man.'" As he told the story to the students, Green laughed. "Well, nine years later they gave up on me. In the end, I respect myself more than I want to be a part of the crowd."[1] Today we're going to talk about abstinence as delicately as we can; but we have a lot of young people in this church, and this is a biblical subject. The city of Thessalonica was an immoral place. In fact, sexual immorality was part of their worship. The new Christians in this pagan environment were struggling with purity in the midst of perversion, just as we are today. In this passage Paul gave four reasons for abstinence.

1. **Abstinence Until Marriage Is God's Perfect Plan.** When you see the phrase, "This is the will of God . . . ," it's because God wants to be absolutely clear about something. His will for us is abstinence before marriage. Occasionally people living together outside of marriage tell me they've prayed about it and God has given them peace in their hearts. Well, I don't know who they're praying to, but it isn't the God who wrote this passage. He said, "You don't have to pray about this. I've already told you what to do." Sex is God's idea. He created it. Hebrews 13:4 says that marriage is honorable and the bed undefiled; but fornicators and adulterers God will judge. Sexual involvement within marriage is exciting. But if you're living together, you're out of God's will. I'm not making that up. It comes right out of this Book we believe.

---

[1] Tom McNichol, "Sex Can Wait," *The USA Weekend: The Tennessean,* March 25–27, 1994, 4–6.

2. **Abstinence Until Marriage Is God's Perfect Prevention Plan for Your Life.** This passage says that each of us should possess his own vessel (our bodies) in sanctification and honor (see 1 Cor. 6:18). When you engage in sexual activity outside covenantal marriage, you're sinning against your own body. On television people climb in and out of bed like so many sexual robots. Only nerds are shown to be chaste. The young actors in those steamy dramas never face consequences for their indulgences. But in real life, there are consequences. God is good to us! Not only has He provided a means for pleasure through sex, but He has given us boundaries in which to enjoy His gift. He has told us to wait until marriage because He wants us to have an abundant life.

3. **Abstinence Until Marriage Is a Powerful Testimony to a Watching World.** Verse 5 says we should not live in the passion of lust, like the Gentiles who do not know God. We should be different. Many teenagers engage in promiscuity because of peer pressure. But everybody is *not* doing it. One girl was badgered by her friends because she was supposedly the only one in their group still a virgin. One day she just said: "Anytime I want I can be like you are. But you can never again be like I am."

4. **Abstinence Until Marriage Is Your Best Possibility for a Good Marriage in the Future.** Verse 6 says we should live a chaste life because we don't want to defraud another person. In the context of sexual purity, you shouldn't cheat another person. We can cheat others by the way we practice our lives sexually. You cheat the person who sleeps with you. You cheat your future husband or wife. You even cheat yourself. The best way to have a wonderful family is to save yourself until marriage.

Conclusion: The world says you've got to shack up with someone to see if it's going to work, like testing out a new car. Well, we're not cars. We're made in the image of God. If you practice abstinence until marriage, you'll not be afraid of STDs. You'll not fear getting pregnant. You'll never go through the trauma of abortion. You'll not have to get married before you're ready. You'll never have to give your baby up for adoption. You won't get AIDS. You won't be overwhelmed by guilt. You'll protect the specialness of a relationship that belongs to marriage. And you will know in your heart that you are in the will of God!

JUNE 7, 2009

Learning from the Past

Date preached:

By Rev. Peter Grainger

Scripture: 1 Corinthians 10:1–13, especially verse 6
Now these things became our examples, to the intent that we should not lust after evil things as they also lusted.

Introduction: It has been well said, that "those who fail to learn from the mistakes of history live to repeat them." Although it wasn't Paul who said this (and the source is ultimately unknown), he would have certainly agreed with the sentiment. Looking back on Israel's experience in the desert, Paul gives us three warnings from the wilderness:

1. **A Warning Against Complacency (vv. 1–5).** Paul describes the wonderful privileges which the people of Israel enjoyed on their journey through the wilderness after leaving Egypt and heading for the Promised Land. He then describes their fall into sin despite the blessings of:

   A. **God's Salvation (vv. 1–2).** Paul recounts the famous story of how God made a miraculous path through the sea to safety for the Israelites when they were being pursued by Pharaoh and his army. Paul speaks of this as a "baptism" into Moses. This means they were fully identified with Moses as leader just as we are with Christ in our baptism.

   B. **God's Provision (vv. 3–4).** This is called "spiritual food" and "spiritual drink." The word "spiritual" doesn't mean that it wasn't real food and drink but rather that it was supernaturally provided by God—manna from heaven and water from a rock which Moses struck. Again Paul refers to this manna in Christian terms as spiritual food and drink. This may point to the Lord's Supper and the presence of Christ.

   C. **The Peoples' Reaction (v. 5).** "But with most of them God was not well pleased, for their bodies were scattered in the wilderness." No matter what our experiences of Christ in the past, they do not provide any immunity against displeasing God and suffering His judgment. This is a clear warning against complacency.

2. **A Warning Against Idolatry (vv. 6–12).** Look closely at what the Israelites did: "Now these things occurred as examples to keep us from setting our hearts on evil things as they did" (v. 6 NIV). The literal meaning of "setting on our hearts on evil" is "lusting or craving after evil." Paul describes four incidents from the wilderness wanderings of the people of Israel to illustrate this:

A. **Pagan Worship (v. 7; Ex. 32).** Verse 7 refers to the incident of the Golden Calf which was made and worshiped while Moses was on Mount Sinai receiving the Ten Commandments from the Lord. The result was God's judgment fell upon the people in the form of a plague.

B. **Sexual Immorality (v. 8; Num. 25).** This was when the prophet Balaam, unable to curse God's people, seduced them by means of Moabite women who come into the Israelite camp. Again, God's judgment by plague struck down thousands of them.

C. **Testing the Lord (v. 9; Num. 21:4–9).** The people of Israel complained against Moses and the Lord. To "test" someone means to see how far one can go before you provoke a reaction. The Israelites discovered that God's patience was not limitless when the snakes were sent as his judgment.

D. **Grumbling (v. 10; Num. 16).** This specifically refers to the rebellion of a man named Korah and his associates who challenged Moses' leadership. God's response was to open up the ground to consume the conspirators, followed by fire that incinerated their supporters.

3. **A Warning Against Despondency (v. 13).** Paul has stressed the certainty of God's judgment, whether on the people of Israel in the wilderness or the Christians in Corinth: anyone can fall. This could cause us to feel despondent—hopeless against temptations too strong for us. Paul responds by saying two things:

A. **No Temptation Is Unique.** Temptations or tests we face are not unique to us, but the same kind that all human beings face. That should be an encouragement to all of us, especially those who wrestle with secret sins that we are convinced are unique to us.

B. **God Is Faithful.** The word "way out" is used in the context of an individual or band of men that are encircled by a large force, so that it looks as though they will be overwhelmed. But then they spot a way out, a narrow mountain defile through which they can make an escape.

Conclusion: Jesus offers us escape from the snares of sin. Maybe you need forgiveness, maybe refreshing, maybe a fresh start. As you come to the Lord's Table today, come to the Lord of the Table.

STATS, STORIES, AND MORE

The Power of 1 Corinthians 10:13

In his autobiography, *Rebel with a Cause,* Franklin Graham wrote that after he committed himself to Christ, he was surprised to find his taste for cigarettes was strong as ever. He determined to quit smoking, but three days later, he awoke with *an absolutely overwhelming—almost terrifying—desire for a cigarette. I wanted to smoke so bad that I couldn't think of anything else. It intensified with each passing minute. Throughout the day, the yearning for a cigarette grabbed me like the jaws of a junkyard dog.*

He finally shared his struggle with his friend Roy Gustafson. "Roy, I quit smoking, but I don't think I can hold out. I just don't think I have the power to say no any longer."

"Oh, you don't, huh?" replied Roy, looking up from a hamburger. "Why don't you just get down on your knees and tell God He's a liar?"

"What? I can't do that!"

Roy quoted 1 Corinthians 10:13 to him, then said, "You need to tell God He's a liar. You claimed that verse and it didn't work."

"I'm not going to call God a liar," said Franklin. "Besides, I haven't claimed that verse yet!"

"You haven't?" said Roy, sounding shocked. "Why don't you, then?"

Franklin did claim that verse. And it did work.

Trying Not To!

"What are you doing, son?" the shopkeeper asked a little boy whose eyes were on a large basket of apples outside the storefront. "Trying to steal one of those apples?"

"No sir," replied the boy. "I'm trying not to."

APPROPRIATE HYMNS AND SONGS

"Salvation Is Here," Joel Houston, 2004 Hillsong Publishing.

"Hands and Feet," Bob Herdman, Charlie Peacock, Mark Stuart, Tyler Burkum & Will McGiniss, 1999 Up in the Mix Music.

"Refresh My Heart," Geoff Bullock, 1992 Word Music, Inc. & Maranatha Music.

"Wonderful, Merciful Savior," Dawn Rogers & Eric Wyse, 1989 Word Music, LLC; Dayspring Music, LLC.

"Great Is Thy Faithfulness," Thomas O. Chisholm, Public Domain.

FOR THE BULLETIN

The birth of Sir James Young Simpson was on June 7, 1811. He was a dedicated Christian and Scottish medical doctor who discovered how to use chloroform to put patients to sleep during surgery. When some in the clergy grew critical of anesthesia, Simpson pointed to Genesis 2, when God put Adam to sleep before removing one of his ribs. ● Following their wedding, missionaries Samuel and Marie Gobat left Beuggen, Germany, for Ethiopia and the Middle East on June 7, 1834. Their story is one of extreme suffering, but they eventually founded thirty-seven schools in Palestine, twelve churches, and several hospitals. ● Franz Xavier Gruber, Austrian church organist, died on this day in 1863. He is best known for having composed the music for the Christmas carol, "Silent Night." Another famous hymnist died on this day in 1878. Knowles Shaw, a singing evangelist in the west and the author of "Bringing in the Sheaves," was killed in a train wreck just outside of Dallas, Texas. ● And today marks the anniversary of Charles Spurgeon's last sermon at the Metropolitan Tabernacle in London. He was exhausted in ministry, burdened by denominational conflict, and physically heavy and weak. He ended his sermon without knowing these would be his last words in the pulpit: *These forty years and more have I served him, blessed be his name! And I have had nothing but love from him. I would be glad to continue yet another forty years in the same dear service here below if so it pleased him.* That afternoon he fell ill, and shortly afterward left for the south of France hoping for recovery. He passed away at the Hotel Beau Rivage in Menton, France. ● "The Old Rugged Cross" was sung for the first time on June 7, 1913, as its author, evangelist George Bennard, held meetings in Pokagon, Michigan.

WORSHIP HELPS

Call to Worship

> *The praises of Thy wonders, Lord,*
> *The heavens shall express;*
> *And in the congregation*
> *Of saints Thy faithfulness*
> —From the SCOTTISH BOOK
> OF PSALMS, 1886

Reader's Theater

Reader 1: Now these things became our examples, to the intent that we should not lust after evil things as they also lusted (1 Cor. 10:6).

Reader 2: Now when the people saw that Moses delayed coming down from the mountain, the people gathered together to Aaron, and said to him, "Come, make us gods that shall go before us . . . And the LORD said to Moses, "Go, get down! For your people whom you brought out of the land of Egypt have corrupted themselves . . . " (Ex. 32:1, 7–8).

Reader 3: Now . . . the people began to commit harlotry . . . They invited the people to the sacrifices of their gods, and the people ate and bowed down to their gods. So Israel was joined to Baal . . . , and the anger of the LORD was aroused against Israel. Then the LORD said to Moses, "Take all the leaders of the people and hang the offenders . . . that the fierce anger of the LORD may turn away from Israel." So the plague was stopped among the children of Israel. And those who died in the plague were twenty-four thousand (Num. 25:1–4, 8b–9).

Reader 4: And the people spoke against God and against Moses: "Why have you brought us up out of Egypt to die in the wilderness? For there is no food and no water, and our soul loathes this worthless bread." So the LORD sent fiery serpents among the people, and they bit the people; and many of the people of Israel died (Num. 21:5–6).

Reader 1: Now all these things happened to them as examples, and they were written for our admonition, upon whom the ends of the ages have come. Therefore let him who thinks he stands take heed lest he fall (1 Cor. 10:11–12).

" Quote for the Pastor's Wall

Before you enter on the study of a sermon, humbly pray to God for the gracious aid of the Holy Spirit. Our Heavenly Father, who knoweth all things, is the Fountain of Wisdom; and if any man lack wisdom, let him ask of God, that giveth to all men liberally, and unbraideth not; and it shall be given him. Before you proceed one step in your preparation for the pulpit, kneel down before Him, and pray for direction in the choice of a subject; pray for that light which will unfold the meaning of the passage which you may select; and pray for assistance in the selection of suitable matter to fill up your discourse. By earnest prayer and supplication the mind is well prepared for this important study; and when the Holy Spirit directs our thoughts, our compositions are pure and spiritual.

—Rev. J. Edmondson, in the 1884 manual, *Precepts for Preachers in the Pulpit and Out of It* "

Additional Sermons and Lesson Ideas

It Was the Best of Times?

Date preached:

By Rev. Melvin Tinker

SCRIPTURE: 1 Kings 17:1–16

INTRODUCTION: Elijah is sent by God to lead the people to repentance.

1. The Lord's Strange Provision (vv. 1–6). God provides for Elijah by sending ravens to feed him and a brook to give him water during the drought.
2. The Lord's Surprising Place (vv. 7–12). God sends Elijah to a poor widow in Jezebel's hometown. He is in a pagan country around people who do not believe in the Lord.
3. The Lord's Sure Promise (vv. 13–16). God provides mercifully for the pagan widow and her son.

CONCLUSION: God is to be taken at His word. He faithfully provides for those who obey and trust Him. His mercies extend to the entire world and if we would just have faith in Him, He is willing to provide life to us.

Harness Your Hearts

Date preached:

By Dr. Larry Osborne

SCRIPTURE: James 3:1–12

INTRODUCTION: All of us are put in a position to instruct at one time or another. We must be careful that our tongues do not get the best of us.

1. Watch Your Words Because You Will Be Judged by Them (v. 1).
2. Be Slow to Criticize Because We All Mess Up Big Time (v. 2).
3. Never Forget That Even Little Things Have Big Consequences (vv. 3–6).
4. Do Not Even Try to Tame Your Tongue; It Cannot Be Done (vv. 7–8).
5. Our Only Hope Is to Tame It Upstream in the Heart (vv. 9–12).

CONCLUSION: The human tongue is restless and impossible to control. It is the instrument through which God has ordained the teaching of His Word and yet it can also be used for the most disdainful evils. We must harness our hearts and in so doing, tame our tongues.

JUNE 14, 2009

SUGGESTED SERMON

The Refining Fire of God

Date preached:

By Dr. Robert M. Norris

Scripture: Malachi 4:1–3, especially verse 2

But to you who fear My name The Sun of Righteousness shall arise with healing in His wings; and you shall go out and grow fat like stall-fed calves.

Introduction: Have you ever heard of a "promise box"? They were once very popular among Christian people. They were little boxes containing rolled up verses of Scripture, and each verse contained a promise of God which you could select and think about during the day. The promise box has gone the way of much Christian trivia but the promises remain! These old promise boxes only contained positive promises of blessing. In these verses, Malachi records for us promises from God, but they are much more honest and realistic. They are promises made from God to His people.

1. **The Promise to All of Us (v. 1a).** Verse 1 gives the promise to everyone: "For behold, the day is coming . . ." Malachi speaks of "the day of the Lord" as a day that God has promised to come in judgment. The biblical view of history is not cyclical; it's linear. It has a definite beginning with God's creation of the universe, and is building to a final climax in which the present world is brought to its end. In this first verse of chapter 4, Malachi asserts the certainty that the Day of Judgment will come. The New Testament understands that will be the day of the return of Jesus Christ. Indeed, all our human history, mocked as it has been by war, pestilence, and famine have been pointers set in our history as a foreshadowing the great and dreadful day of the Lord (1 Thess. 5:1–3). Malachi sees the future after "the day of the Lord" when God's people will be pure, cleansed from all iniquity.

2. **The Promise That Makes Unbelievers Tremble (v. 1b).** The Lord has promised that He will come to His people: "'And all the proud, yes, all who do wickedly will be stubble. And the day which is coming shall burn them up,' says the LORD of hosts, 'That will leave them neither root nor branch'" (v. 1). Malachi warned that those

who proudly resist God will be consumed with fire on the coming Day of Judgment. The image employed by Malachi is the consuming heat of the sun which will burn like a furnace. There is no root left to start afresh. There is no branch or shoot that can be grafted from anywhere else to make a new beginning. The nature of the judgment is that it is final and irreversible.

3. **The Promise That Makes the Believer Rejoice (vv. 2–3).** God has a different word to say to those who fear the Lord. For them the future holds something vastly more wonderful. Here is a prophet writing 450 years before Jesus but full of expectation that the Messiah is coming: "But to you who fear My name the Sun of Righteousness shall arise with healing in His wings" (v. 2). The Sun of Righteousness was rising, and He has been rising all over this world since Jesus' First Coming (cf. Luke 1:78). One day His rise will reach its noonday brightness, and He will appear in glory. Clearly Jesus is in the mind of God as He speaks through the prophet Malachi, and Jesus is portrayed as a rising sun. The image is designed to convey to us:

A. **Light.** Malachi uses the imagery of the sun to indicate that Jesus would expose areas of darkness (1 Cor. 4:5). Jesus is the light of the world (John 8:12). He brings sense and meaning out of absurdity.

B. **Righteousness.** The sun is a sun with beams of righteousness. This means that Jesus makes things right. He makes man right with God through reconciliation (2 Cor. 5:18).

C. **Healing.** This Sun of Righteousness rises with healing in its wings. Jesus was a great healer. Although Jesus does not heal every disease in this life, He will heal every disease in the resurrection (Rev. 7:16–17).

D. **Liberty.** One effect of all this for those who fear the Lord will be a going forth from the stall: "And you shall go out and grow fat like stall-fed calves" (v. 2). The coming of Jesus means freedom, not bondage, and Jesus promises to give it (John 8:36).

Conclusion: Each of these great promises of God is designed for us to take heart. We can look forward with joy to the coming of Christ and live in that hope.

STATS, STORIES, AND MORE

Just as Sudden
One night, Earl Kelly, a pastor in Mississippi, was preaching about the Second Coming. He had just quoted Matthew 24:27, "For as the lightning comes from the east and flashes to the west, so also will the coming of the Son of Man be." Suddenly a large light bulb dropped from its socket in the ceiling and burst on the floor in front of the pulpit, startling the worshipers. Without missing a beat, Kelly said, "His coming will be just as sudden, and unexpected, and devastating to the dreams that are not Christ-centered."[1]

Any Day
Denis Lyle, a Baptist pastor in Belfast, Northern Ireland, tells of a tourist who visited a beautiful mansion on a lovely lakeshore in Switzerland. The house was surrounded by well-kept gardens connected by tidy pathways. Not a weed anywhere.

"How long have you been caretaker here?" the tourist asked the gardener.

"I've been here twenty years."

"And during that time how often has the owner of the property been in residence?"

The gardener smiled and said, "He has been here only four times."

"And to think," exclaimed the visitor, "all these years you've kept this house and garden in such superb condition. You tend them as if you expected him to come tomorrow."

"Oh no," replied the gardener, "I look after them as if I expected him to come today."[2]

APPROPRIATE HYMNS AND SONGS

"Refiner's Fire," Brian Doerksen, 1990 Mercy/Vineyard Publishing.

"Purify My Heart," Jeff Nelson, 1993 HeartService Music/Maranatha Praise, Inc.

"Purified," Michael W. Smith & Deborah D. Smith, 2001 Word Music, Inc./ Smittyfly Music.

"The Potter's Hand," Darlene Zschech, 1997 Darlene Zschech/Hillsong Publishing.

"Set My Soul Afire," Eugene M. Bartlett, 1965 by Albert E. Brumley & Sons.

---

[1]Paul Lee Tan, *Encyclopedia of 7700 Illustrations* (Rockville, Maryland: Assurance Publishers, 1979), pp. 1239–1240.
[2]Denis Lyle, *Countdown to Apocalypse* (Belfast: Ambassador Books, 1999), p. 21.

June 14, 1811 is the birthday of Harriet Beecher Stowe, author of *Uncle Tom's Cabin,* and of the hymn, "Still, Still with Thee." ● Catherine Munford Booth, the "Mother of the Salvation Army," was converted on this day in 1846. ● Today marks the death of Presbyterian missionary Eliza Agnes, in 1833, and of English author and journalist G. K. Chesterton in 1936. ● The first "Superman" comic book was issued by Action Comics on this day in 1938. ● On June 14, 1956, President Dwight Eisenhower signed a congregational resolution adding the words "under God" to the Pledge of Allegiance. ● On June 13 and 14, 1972, authorities in Mozambique rounded up several hundred people, including the leaders of the Presbyterian Church in that country. No official cause was given, and prisoners were snatched from their homes so quickly they were unable to take warm clothing or necessities. They were taken to an infamous prison for political prisoners. Among them were two elderly church leaders, who died in the prison under mysterious circumstances. Authorities later said they had committed suicide, but few believed the report.

PRAYER FOR THE PASTOR'S CLOSET

Lord, we want to live while we live. We do pray that we may not merely groan out an existence here below, nor live as earthworms crawling back in our holes and dragging now and then a withered leaf with us; but Oh! give us to live as we ought to live, with a new life that You have put in us, with the divine quickening which has lifted us as much above common men as men are lifted above the beasts that perish. —CHARLES HADDON SPURGEON

WORSHIP HELPS

Call to Worship

Save us, O God of our salvation; Gather us together, and deliver us . . . to give thanks to Your holy name, to triumph in Your praise. Blessed be the LORD God of Israel from everlasting to everlasting (1 Chr. 16:35–36)!

Responsive Reading

Leader: "Therefore, I urge you brothers, in view of God's mercy, offer your bodies as living sacrifices, holy and pleasing to God—this is your spiritual act of worship" (Rom. 12:1 NIV).

Congregation: ". . . present yourselves to God as being alive from the dead, and your members as instruments of righteousness to God" (Rom. 6:13).

Leader: ". . . let us continually offer the sacrifice of praise to God, that is, the fruit of our lips, giving thanks to his name" (Heb. 13:15).

Congregation: "I will freely sacrifice to You; I will praise Your name, O LORD, for it is good" (Ps. 54:6).

Leader: "I will sing to the LORD as long as I live; I will sing praise to my God while I have my being. May my meditation be sweet to Him; I will be glad in the LORD" (Ps. 104:33–34).

Congregation: "Accept, I pray, the freewill offerings of my mouth, O LORD" (Ps. 119:108a).

Benediction

Take all the failures, each mistake
Of our poor human ways,
Then, Savior, for Thine own dear sake,
Make them show forth Thy praise.
—MRS. F. G. BURROUGHS,
1920, from "Transformed"

Additional Sermons and Lesson Ideas

Temptation Planet
By Rev. Larry Kirk

Date preached:

SCRIPTURE: James 1:12–18

INTRODUCTION: None of us ever achieves immunity from temptation or total victory over sin in this life. God gives us four truths to help us face temptation.

1. Temptation Is an Inevitable Test of Life—Stand Up to It (vv. 12–13).
2. Temptation Is Your Responsibility—Own Up to It (vv. 13–14).
3. Temptation Is Predictable and Terrible—Understand It (vv. 14–15).
4. Temptation Is Conquered Through God's Goodness—Choose It (vv. 16–18).

CONCLUSION: Every temptation you face is an opportunity to glorify Him by choosing to believe in His goodness by the strength that Christ provides. Turn from temptation and do not try to back out slowly. If you do not deal with it swiftly it will destroy you. Turn away from temptation no matter what form it takes and choose to trust in the goodness of God.

More Than Food
By Dr. Timothy K. Beougher

Date preached:

SCRIPTURE: Romans 12:3–16

INTRODUCTION: Fellowship is often misunderstood. It's more than food and fun. Paul tells us we should do the following to achieve true fellowship:

1. Value One Another (vv. 3–8).
2. Love One Another (vv. 9–10).
3. Exercise Spiritual Fervor with One Another (vv. 11–12).
4. Share with One Another (v. 13).
5. Forgive One Another (v. 14).
6. Empathize with One Another (v. 15).
7. Practice Humility Toward One Another (v. 16).

CONCLUSION: Fellowship is not just getting together and eating food. It's a beautiful picture of our new life in Christ.

Three Friends

They were best friends, the three. Alanson Work was sandy-haired, married, father of four. George Thompson was young and single, with thick black hair and a five-feet frame. The third man, James Burr, was six-feet-four. But they were united by a common devotion to Christ and a joint hatred of slavery.

In 1841, arrested for trying to smuggle slaves from Missouri, they were chained to each other and held without bail. Outside, a mob chanted for their deaths, while inside the three knelt in prayer. Thompson later wrote: *Our singing and happy contentment in our prisonhouse much annoyed the consciences of the [town's] inhabitants.* They preached to the crowds before and during their trial, then were sentenced to twelve years hard labor at the state penitentiary.

Arriving in prison, the men's heads were shaved, they were garbed in prison rags, and were repeatedly threatened with forty lashes. Their food consisted of hard cornbread, rotting bacon, cold potatoes, and "various animal intestines." During the cold winters, they nearly froze until they were allowed to sleep together. *We could take turns getting into the middle. If an outside one was becoming frostbitten, he only had to request the middle one to exchange places awhile.*

Night after night, the men read to one another from the Bible and joined together in singing and praying. Soon they were evangelizing and teaching the other prisoners. On Sunday, May 14, 1843, George Thompson's sermon from Luke 9:23 sparked a prison revival.

The most glorious day I have seen! The power of God wonderfully displayed. In prayer meeting, four new cases of conversion; cell crowded to overflowing; converts mounting higher and growing stronger; while the long-harded tremble like Belshazzar. Preached to 12 converts, in my cell, from Luke 9:23. In the afternoon, a powerful sermon—six

Continued on the next page

HEROES FOR THE PASTOR'S HEART—*Continued*

new ones came forward. I talked and prayed with them, no man forbidding. Glory to God.

Work was finally released in 1845. Burr and Thompson were pardoned the next year, the latter becoming a missionary to Africa.[3]

Quote for the Pastor's Wall

Optimism and pessimism are infectious and they spread more rapidly from the head downward than in any other direction. Optimism has a most extraordinary effect upon all with whom the commander comes in contact. With this clear realization, I firmly determined that my mannerisms and speech in public would always reflect the cheerful certainty of victory—that any pessimism and discouragement I might ever feel would be reserved for my pillow.

—DWIGHT D. EISENHOWER, referring to the Allied Invasion of North Africa, November, 1942[4]

---

[3]From the editor's book, *From This Verse*, published by Thomas Nelson Publishers in 1998, entry for August 8.
[4]Quoted in *To America* by Stephen E. Ambrose (New York: Simon & Schuster Paperbacks, 2002), p. 97.

JUNE 21, 2009

FATHER'S DAY SUGGESTED SERMON

Facts for the Family

Date preached:

By Dr. Melvin Worthington

Scripture: Various, especially Ephesians 5:22, 25; 6:1
Wives, submit to your own husbands . . . Husbands love your wives . . . Children obey your parents . . .

Introduction: The first institution ordained by God was the family. Its well-being is essential if the country, community, and church are to be healthy. According to some sociologists the death of the family is at hand. Scripturally, fathers are to be the leader of the household; it's ultimately their responsibility to ensure the family functions in a proper manner. The Bible gives clear and concise instructions regarding the family. I'd like all of us here, but especially the fathers to consider the following facts regarding the family.

1. **The Providential Establishment of the Family (Gen. 1–2).** God *prescribed the family* when He perceived Adam's loneliness (Gen. 2:20). God *planned the family* to meet the social, spiritual, psychological, emotional needs of men, women and children. God *provided the family* as a teaching, training and tending agency. God *preserved the family*. The family unit will not disappear, for it is prescribed, provided, planned, and preserved by the Sovereign God. All the needs for human beings are met in the family. The family serves as an illustration of God's relationship to His children as well.

2. **The Practical Essentials for the Family.** For a family to be what God intended both the husband and wife must be Christians. When children come into the home, everything within parents' power should be done to both live and teach the Christian faith to their children. Being Christians does not mean there will be no problems, but gives the proper basis to resolve every potential problem. In the family, Scripture tells us, there should be:

   A. **Clear Oneness (Gen. 2:24a).** There must be an obvious unity between the husband and wife. This oneness is developed over a process of time. Mates become one in soul, spirit, and outlook. Children must see this oneness evidence in their parents.

B. **Coming Away (Gen. 2:24b).** Spouses must come away from their mother and father and cleave to one another.

C. **Communication (Eph. 5–6).** Happy families communicate with each other: husband with wife, parents with children, and children with children.

D. **Commitment (1 Pet. 3).** We must be committed to live out our proper role within the family structure that God has ordained. The husband is the leader of the family. Each must be content in his place or there will be household war. When the husband, help, and heritage accept their respective roles in the family unit, peace and harmony result.

3. **The Potential Enemies of the Family (Gen. 1–2; Eph. 5–6; Col. 3; 1 Pet. 3).**

A. **Immorality (Col. 3:5).** A loose and licentious lifestyle before marriage is an enemy in marriage. Reading the wrong books and magazines, watching profane TV programs, plays or movies contribute to destroying the family unit.

B. **Ignorance (Eph. 5–6; 1 Pet. 3).** Ignoring the pattern for marriage set forth in the Scriptures contributes to many broken and unhappy homes. All may not like the scriptural pattern for the family, but when followed it results in happiness which cannot be explained and when ignored there is chaos and confusion.

C. **Infidelity (Mal. 2:15–16).** Marriage is a solemn, sacred, and special covenant between a man and a woman. To break one's solemn vows is inexcusable and unjustified. Unfaithfulness on the part of married persons to their partners undermines a happy family. It devastates the companion and disillusions the children.

D. **Impatience (1 Pet. 3:1–7; Eph. 6:4).** Peter gives wonderful guidance to the wife who has been converted after marriage, but her husband has not. She should be patient and live out the role God has for her, allowing God to work in her husband's life (1 Pet. 3:1–6). He continues to tell believing husbands to bear with their wives (v. 7). Paul tells parents not to exasperate their children (Eph. 6:4); we must discipline children out of love and not impatience.

E. **Interference (Gen. 2:24).** Interference by in-laws almost guarantees an unhappy life. When a young couple marries and establishes their own family unit, Mom and Dad need to respect that new family unit. Many insignificant problems have been blown out of proportion by parental interference. Though there may be exceptions, a good rule to follow is to not interfere or to advise unless asked.

Conclusion: Marriages are not made for or in heaven. Marriage is designed to function on earth. Family life is designed for human beings, not angels. Fathers, I encourage you to step up to the challenge today and submit yourself to your heavenly Father. Ask Him to enable you to lead your family in His ways.

STATS, STORIES, AND MORE

Parenting Advice
Harry Ironsides warned, "Parents need to remember it is not enough to tell their little ones of Jesus and His rejection, or to warn them of the ways of the world, but they must see to it that in their own lives they exemplify their instructions. This will count above all else in the training of the young."

Honest Dads
Children learn to fear God and shun evil, they learn the power of biblical convictions, they learn to love the Lord from the example of those whom they most love and respect. It might be a friend or neighbor or teacher, but very often it's their dad and their mom. Devotional writer Henry G. Bosch once wrote in *Our Daily Bread* that when he was a boy he would often work with his father during the summer months. Leaving home each morning, they would stop at a particular store for a newspaper, which they read at coffee break. One day, arriving at work, Henry's dad discovered that he had taken two papers by mistake because they were so thin. After a moment's thought, he decided to return to the store immediately to pay for the extra paper. "I don't want the owner, who isn't a Christian, to think I'm dishonest," said Mr. Bosch.

About a week later, some expensive items were shoplifted from the same store. The police calculated that at the time of the robbery only two men had been shopping in the store—Mr. Bosch and another man. "I know John is honest," said the storekeeper. "Just last week he came all the way back here to return a newspaper he'd taken by mistake." The police questioned the other man instead and, in so doing, apprehended the culprit who made a full confession.

"Father's honesty and Christian character . . . not only made a deep impression on the storekeeper," Henry later wrote, "but his actions also left an indelible mark upon my young and pliable mind."

APPROPRIATE HYMNS AND SONGS

"Faith of Our Fathers," Frederick W. Faber & Henri F. Henry, Public Domain.

"Rise Up O Men of God," William P. Merrill, Public Domain.

"O Perfect Love," Dorothy Gurney, Public Domain.

"Come, Now Is the Time to Worship," Brian Doerksen, 1998 Vineyard Songs.

"Sing for Joy," Lamont Hiebert, 1996 Integrity's Hosanna! Music.

FOR THE BULLETIN

The first Anglican parish in America was established at Jamestown, Virginia, on June 21, 1607. ● John Livingstone was a popular and powerful preacher in Scotland in the early 1600s. His greatest sermon was preached on June 21, 1630, after a night of prayer, when he preached from Ezekiel 36:26–27, and 500 people were saved. ● Today is the birthday, in 1639, of the colonial pastor, Increase Mather, who preached in Boston and served as President of Harvard College from 1684 to 1701. ● In 1641, Georg Neumark, twenty, left home in the Thuringian forests to enroll at the University of Königsberg. Passing through Magdeburg, he was robbed on the Gardelegan Heath. Georg lost everything except his prayer book and a few hidden coins. His university hopes dashed, the young man was destitute; but suddenly an unexpected position opened—a tutoring job. On that very day he composed the great hymn, "If Thou But Suffer God to Guide Thee." *While tutoring, Georg saved his money, and the next year he proceeded to* Königsberg and enrolled in the university on June 21, 1643. ● On June 21, 1675, the foundation stone was laid for St. Paul's Cathedral in London. ● Today is the birthday, in 1892, of American theologian, Reinhold Niebuhr; and today marks the death, two years later, of Clara Scott, who wrote the hymn, "Open My Eyes, That I May See." She died when she was thrown from a runaway buggy.

WORSHIP HELPS

Call to Worship
Stand up and bless the LORD your God forever and ever! Blessed be Your glorious name, which is exalted above all blessing and praise (Neh. 9:5)!

Offertory Scripture Reading
Both riches and honor come from You, and You reign over all. In Your hand is power and might; in Your hand it is to make great and to give strength to all (1 Chr. 29:12).

Suggested Scriptures

- Ephesians 5
- Colossians 3:18–21
- Hebrews 12:9–11
- 1 Peter 3:1–7

Kid's Talk

Have some volunteers from your congregation ready to help you hand out materials for this Kid's Talk. Create a one-page document with an acrostic:

F — Funny	Forgiving	Fun
A — Amazing	Awesome	Artistic
T — Terrific	Talented	Talkative
H — Heroic	Huggable	Handsome
E — Energetic	Endearing	Extroverted
R — Respectable	Righteous	Reliable

Have volunteers pass out the sheets and pencils for the children. Tell the children to circle the adjective from each line/letter that most accurately describes their dad (or grandfather or other father figure). You might go through some of the adjectives to define them. Lead them in a prayer thanking God for their fathers and have them give these sheets to their dads.

Additional Sermons and Lesson Ideas

The Great Refusal
By Dr. Michael A. Guido

Date preached:

SCRIPTURE: Mark 10:17–22

INTRODUCTION: A wealthy young man came to Jesus to find out how to get eternal life. But, He didn't like the answer and walked away from Jesus.

1. Mark His Request (v. 17). He wanted to know how to have eternal life.
2. Mark the Response (vv. 18–21). Jesus told him to give up everything.
3. Mark His Refusal (v. 22). He walked away because his wealth was great.

CONCLUSION: The man "went away sad" because he couldn't give up his stuff. To follow Jesus, we have to let go of everything we own and allow Him to give us riches beyond measure. Give up everything for the Savior; He gave up everything for you and He wants to give you everything anew.

I'll Be Back
Based on a Sermon by William Graham Scroggie

Date preached:

SCRIPTURE: Various Scriptures

INTRODUCTION: Belief that the Lord will come again should produce:

1. Purity of Character (2 Cor. 7:1).
2. Steadfastness of Faith (Phil. 3:20–4:1).
3. Holiness of Walk (Rom. 13:11–14).
4. Compassion for Souls (1 Thess. 2:19–20).
5. Watchfulness of Disposition (1 Thess. 1:9–10).

CONCLUSION: If we really believe in and hope for the return of Jesus Christ, then our lives must reflect that. We ought to be vigilant, holy, steadfast, and pure, and we must be in service to others by carrying the glorious message of Christ's death and resurrection. Are you ready for His return? Are you acting like it?

JUNE 28, 2009

SUGGESTED SERMON

Christ the Source

Date preached:

By Rev. Todd M. Kinde

Scripture: 2 Peter 1:1–2
Simon Peter, a bondservant and apostle of Jesus Christ, to those who have obtained like precious faith with us by the righteousness of our God and Savior Jesus Christ: Grace and peace be multiplied to you in the knowledge of God and of Jesus our Lord.

Introduction: It is apparent in reading this letter that Peter knows his time of death is near (see 1:14). We discern that the plan of God in redemptive history is entering a new dimension with the removal of the apostles from this earth. The church is yet present but now progressively dependent upon the written word rather than the audible voices of the apostles. It is with this in mind that Peter exhorts the church not to forget the promises of God as they have been passed on by the prophets and apostles. It's in these promises that we fellowship with God and overcome the corruption of the world.

1. **We are Slaves in the Service of Jesus the Christ (v. 1a).** Peter comes with original and genuine apostolic authority delegated to him by our Lord. As such, he writes to us a message from God which we are to heed carefully. Peter comes also as a servant or bond servant of Jesus Christ. The term denotes one who is born into slavery and so serves another to the disregard of his own interests. Peter has been born anew by the Spirit of God to faith in Christ and so serves Christ to the disregard of his own self interests. Here we remember Jesus' call to Peter as they stand on the seashore looking at the fish he had caught—this was his career and his passion. Jesus asks Peter, "Do you love Me more than these?" (John 21:15). Peter responds, "Yes, Lord; You know that I love You." We, too, who are born anew by the Spirit unto faith in Christ are born into slavery to Christ which abandons any thoughts about self-interests.

2. **We Receive Faith by the Righteousness of Jesus Our Savior (v. 1b).** The righteousness of Christ is the basis for our faith. We actually receive faith as a gift by the righteousness of Jesus Christ our Savior. This faith is consistent and of absolute equality because it comes

from our Savior Himself (v. 1a). Faith is itself accomplished by Christ for us. The life Christ lived on earth as a man He lived by faith. He believed the promises of God. He believed the Father would fulfill the promises made to the Son who "for the joy that was set before Him endured the cross, despising the shame" (Heb. 12:2). The night before His crucifixion, Jesus cried out "not My will, but Yours, be done" (Luke 22:42). These are expressions of faith— "the substance of things hoped for, the evidence of things not seen" (Heb. 11:1). Faith is accounted to us by the righteousness of Jesus Christ. It's His faith accomplished in His perfect life of obedience and in His perfect sacrifice on the cross. It is this faith alone that saves us from sin and secures for us the blessings of God's intimate presence.

3. **We Receive Grace and Peace by the Knowledge of Jesus Our Lord (v. 2).** Peter gives us a blessing. His blessing is that grace and peace be multiplied. Grace and peace are to be understood in relation to God. May we continue to experience God's favor and have peace with God. Interestingly, grace and peace are abundantly ours through the knowledge of God and of Jesus our Lord. This knowledge is not a mere intellectual knowledge but is an intimate fellowship, an experience of what and who God is which comes from personal interaction with Christ Jesus. While the blessing here is typical of most letters of the day, the Old Testament background is for us the most important. In Numbers 6 we have read the Aaronic blessing given to the people of God after service in the tabernacle (Num. 6:24–27). In this blessing we find grace and peace bestowed by the experience of knowing God—seeing the light of His face and receiving His name.

Conclusion: Have you given your heart and life to the Lordship of Jesus Christ, who has lived a perfect life of faith? Cling to Jesus today, for He is our only hope of reconciliation with God.

STATS, STORIES, AND MORE

In his book, *My All in All,* Rob Morgan writes, "When I was a youngster, my parents built a home at the foot of Roan Mountain on the Tennessee and North Carolina border. My dad, who had grown up there, took countless hikes up the hillside looking for marshy ground indicating the presence of a spring. Using dynamite and a shovel, he dug back to the heads of springs, installed reservoirs, and piped the water down to the house. Many times I went with him to clean out the springs, and we were amazed at how these small creeks and brooks could perpetually run underground, never drying up, never exhausted, and always fresh and cool.

"Psalm 87 was a psalm of rejoicing for those living in Jerusalem, the Mountain of God. This city wasn't built on a river or lake; it depended on the Gihon Spring for its water supply. But when the psalmist said, "All my springs are in you," he meant that all his innermost resources were found in his ever-flowing and overflowing Lord—all his courage, all his joy, all his resilience, all his optimism, all his hope, all his love, all his wisdom, all his patience.

"The Lord Jesus is the Source of that which refreshes our personalities and of all that makes our personalities refreshing. As Matthew Henry put it, 'There is in Him an all-sufficiency of grace and strength; all our springs are in Him, and all our streams are from Him.'"

APPROPRIATE HYMNS AND SONGS

"Grace Flows Down," Louie Giglio, David Bell, & Rod Padgett, 2000 Worshiptogether.com Songs/sixsteps Music.

"Famous One," Chris Tomlin, 2002 Worshiptogether.com Songs/sixsteps Music.

"You Are Worthy of My Praise," David Ruis, 1999 Shade Tree Publishing.

"Mighty to Save," Reuben Morgan & Dean Fielding, 2006 Hillsong Publishing.

FOR THE BULLETIN

Today is the birthday of John Wesley, who was born in tiny Epworth, England, to Rev. Samuel Wesley and his wife Susanna, in 1703. At age five, he was rescued from the upper window of a burning building, "a brand plucked from the burning." He went on to establish the movement that came to be known as the Methodist denomination. ● June 28, 1796 is the birthday of John Williams, missionary to the South Seas. ● The English theologian and hymnist, Frederick W. Faber, was born in Yorkshire, England, on this day in 1814. Though Roman Catholic, his hymns appeal to Protestants as well, and his poems are widely quoted in Dr. A. W. Tozer's *The Christian Book of Mystical Verse.* ● Today is also the birthday, in 1848, of William Thomas Giffe who grew up outside of Portland, Indiana, and served in the Civil War. He became a popular musician and music publisher. His best known gospel song was written in response to attacks being made on the Scriptures: "I'll Not Give Up the Bible." ● And Eliza E. Hewitt was born on this day in 1851. Though an invalid much of her life, her gospel songs are marked by their cheerfulness: "More About Jesus," "My Faith Has Found a Resting Place," "Singing I Go," "Victory in Jesus," etc. ● Today is also the birthday of the Lutheran Church in America, formed on June 28, 1962, at a meeting in Detroit in which four Lutheran synods merged into a denomination of two million members.

PRAYER FOR THE PASTOR'S CLOSET

Fill me with power for service and use me;
Is there not some work my weak hands can do?
Make me a channel of life and of blessing,
And with the Spirit anoint me anew.
—ELISHA A. HOFFMAN from his hymn,
"Power for Service," 1904

WORSHIP HELPS

Call to Worship

Praise the LORD, call upon His name; declare His deeds among the peoples, make mention that His name is exalted. Sing to the LORD, for He has done excellent things; this *is* known in all the earth (Is. 12:4–5).

Welcome

I'd like to share six words with everyone here, whether you're a guest, a regular attendee, or a member: "Christ in you, the hope of glory" (Col. 1:27 NIV). You see, we don't evaluate our standing with God based on how well-dressed we are or whether others view us as super spiritual. Our right-standing before God—the only reason we dare meet together claiming to worship and serve the Creator—is through the shed blood of Christ and His resurrected Spirit who lives in we who accept Him as Savior and Lord. So I want you to take a moment to shake hands with a few people here and repeat those six words to each other as a reminder: "Christ in you, the hope of glory."

Invitation

> *Will you take Jesus to be your Guide?*
> *His love will brighten the way;*
> *Safe in His keeping you may abide;*
> *Will you take Jesus today?*
>
> *For you the Savior was crucified,*
> *Accept His love while you may;*
> *The door of mercy stands open wide;*
> *Will you take Jesus today?*
> —WILLIAM W. ROCK, 1910; from
> "Will You Take Jesus Today?"

Additional Sermons and Lesson Ideas

The God Who Is
Date preached:
By Rev. Melvin Tinker

SCRIPTURE: Exodus 3:1–22

INTRODUCTION: God in all His holiness revealed Himself to Moses. Moses was to approach God on God's terms. He is a God who has chosen a people, One who cares for those people, and One who is personal and is known by name.

1. The God with a People (v. 6).
2. The God with a Heart (vv. 7–10).
3. The God with a Name (vv. 11–15).

CONCLUSION: God sent His Son Jesus Christ to be sacrificed that we might become, through faith, God's chosen people. God made Himself known and gave us His name that we might know Him personally.

A Day in the Life of Jesus
Date preached:
By Dr. Kevin Riggs

SCRIPTURE: Mark 1:21–45

INTRODUCTION: Jesus came to make broken people whole again; spiritually, physically, and emotionally.

1. Spiritually Whole (vv. 21–28). Jesus delivered the man from his demon possession.
2. Physically Whole (vv. 29–34). Jesus physically healed Peter's mother and many others as well.
3. Emotionally Whole (vv. 38–45). Lepers were ostracized in this culture, and so Jesus restored this man to much needed community.

CONCLUSION: If you are an unbeliever, Jesus desires to make whole all of your maladies and fulfill in you the full potential of what you were created to be. If you are a believer, Jesus provides for us an example in verses 35–37 by taking time to spiritually, physically, and emotionally recharge by spending time alone with the Father.

JULY 5, 2009

SUGGESTED SERMON

Do You Want to Be Free?

Date preached:

By Dr. Timothy K. Beougher

Scripture: Mark 5:1–20, especially verse 19
Go home to your friends, and tell them what great things the Lord has done for you, and how He has had compassion on you.

Introduction: As you know, on July 4, 1776, the Declaration of Independence was signed. Representatives from the thirteen American colonies declared, "We hold these truths to be self-evident, that all men are created equal, that they are endowed by their Creator with certain unalienable Rights, that among these are Life, Liberty and the pursuit of Happiness." Yesterday on July 4—233 years later—we again celebrated our freedom. We had parties to mark the occasion because freedom is worth celebrating! But the ironic thing is that at the same time as many Americans celebrated our nation's freedom, they themselves are in bondage. Our nation may be free from control of foreign powers, but many individuals find themselves in bondage to sin. Mark 5:1–20 offers hope for those who want to be set free!

1. **Sin Enslaves You (vv. 2–9).** Mark paints for us a gruesome picture of this demon-possessed man that Jesus and the disciples encounter. Out of the tombs ran a demon-possessed man. It was a fitting place for him to be—among the dead—for he was simply the shell of a human being. Here was a man in total bondage to sin. The local townspeople had attempted to restrain him, but to no avail. He was uncontrollable and dangerous. This man was gashing himself with stones. What a vivid picture of the self-destruction that comes with sin! As Jesus and the disciples landed on the shore, this man ran up to Jesus. The demons within this man knew who Christ was (James 2:19). Ordinary people are often slow to see who Christ is, but this man knew immediately who Christ was. We see a vivid picture of demonic activity in this man, as evidenced by the name "Legion." A legion was a Roman regiment of some six thousand troops. This man was in total bondage to thousands of evil spirits.

2. **Christ's Power Can Transform You (vv. 10–15).** A conversation takes place between Jesus and this great army of intruders that have enslaved this man in sin. The spirits recognize the superior power of Jesus. They know He has the power to send them to the abyss, to the bottomless pit. They plead to be spared from the abyss, but to be allowed to go into a nearby herd of pigs. When Jesus gives them permission, a remarkable sight unfolds. The two thousand pigs stampede to their death. The man "Legion" is totally restored. Jesus gave a visible demonstration of the man's total deliverance. This man's life was radically changed by Christ. In verse 15 the man was "sitting" instead of raging about the tombs as he had before. He was clothed and "in his right mind." The Gerasene demoniac was totally delivered. What a testimony to the transforming power of Christ! Such transformation is impossible without God.

3. **When You Have Been Set Free, You Will Want to Tell Others (vv. 16–20).** When you see the power of God at work, it's hard to remain neutral. Notice first the response of the people whose lives were not changed in verse 17: ". . . they began to plead with Him to depart from their region." They sent Jesus away! They were probably more concerned about the loss of the swine than about the man's soul. What do we value most? Possessions or people? But notice the response of the one whose life was changed—he wanted to tell others about what Christ had done for him. Jesus told this man whose life was changed to go home and tell his friends what had happened to him. He hadn't had any training, hadn't been through an evangelism class, but he knew his life had been changed. He was a living, walking, talking demonstration of what Christ can do for a man. There is no greater testimony for Christ than a changed life.

Conclusion: You may sense a bondage to something so strong that you wonder if you can ever be delivered. If anyone's condition was hopeless, it was this man from Gerasene. There seemed to be no hope, until he met Jesus. Do what this man did; come to the feet of Jesus. The Jesus who calmed the stormy seas, who calmed this man's storm-tossed soul, can calm yours as well.

STATS, STORIES, AND MORE

More from Dr. Timothy Beougher: Demonic Activity
When we talk about the demonic in today's world, people tend to go to one of two extremes. Many want to dismiss this as some ancient superstition, saying "people in Jesus' day believed in the demonic, but we know better in our enlightened and sophisticated age." The other extreme is to become fixated on the demonic realm. C. S. Lewis, in the Preface to his classic book, *Screwtape Letters,* wrote: "There are two equal and opposite errors into which our race can fall about the devils. One is to disbelieve in their existence. The other is to believe, and to feel an excessive and unhealthy interest in them. They themselves are equally pleased by both errors and hail a materialist and magician with the same delight."

Poem by John Oxenham

"Rabbi, begone! Thy powers
Bring loss to us and ours.
Our ways are not as Thine,
Thou lovest men, we—swine.
Oh, get you hence, Omnipotence,
And take this fool of Thine!
His soul? What care we for his soul?
What good to us that
Thou hast made him whole,
Since we have lost our swine?

Cleaned Up
A man named Gene Warr worked with another man in a lumberyard in South America. He shared Christ with him and the man accepted. The next day the man was clean-shaven and had on clean clothes unlike his usual appearance. Gene Warr asked him, "Who told you to clean up?" The man responded: "No one. When you feel clean on the inside, you want to feel clean on the outside."

PRAYER FOR THE PASTOR'S CLOSET

Our Father, teach us not only Thy will, but how to do it. Teach us the best way of doing the best thing, lest we spoil the end by unworthy means. —J. H. JOWETT

APPROPRIATE HYMNS AND SONGS

"Who Can Satisfy My Soul Like You?," Dennis Jernigan, 1992 Shepherd's Heart Music/BMI.

"The Power of Your Love," Geoff Bullock, 1992 Word Music, Inc. & Maranatha Music.

"We've a Story to Tell," H. Ernest Nichol, Public Domain.

"Hallelujah (Your Love Is Amazing)," Brenton Brown & Brian Doerksen, 2000 Vineyard Songs.

"There Is a Fountain Filled with Blood," Lowell Mason & William Cowper, Public Domain.

FOR THE BULLETIN

Sir Thomas More, the devout Roman Catholic Lord Chancellor under King Henry VIII, opposed the king when Henry proclaimed himself as head of the English church. As a result, he was arrested, imprisoned, and condemned to death. On this day in 1535, he wrote his last letter, using a piece of charcoal as "ink." It was to his daughter, Margaret, and he said, "Tomorrow long I to go to God; it were a day very meet and convenient for me." ● Emma Revell, who became the wife of evangelist D. L. Moody, was born on July 5, 1863, in London. ● William Booth started a tent meeting in July of 1875, on a Quaker burial ground in East London. He preached every night to the lower classes who lived in the slums. At midnight on July 5, 1865, while returning home, he said, "I have found my destiny!" This is considered the beginning of the Salvation Army (originally called The Christian Mission). When he started the Salvation Army, he had little support, and few churches shared his vision. When he died forty-seven years later, 40,000 attended his funeral, and the Salvation Army was working in fifty-eight countries of the world. ● On this day in 1925, as seventeen-year-old Bill Wallace of Knoxville, Tennessee, sat in a garage working on an old Ford, the Lord spoke to his heart about missions. He later served sacrificially in China for seventeen years as a Southern Baptist medical missionary before being arrested by the Communists and beaten to death in prison. After his death, the Communists sought to bury him in an unmarked grave, but faithful Chinese Christians found his body and laid him to rest under a headstone that said, "For Me to Live Is Christ."

WORSHIP HELPS

Call to Worship

The LORD reigns, He is clothed with majesty; the LORD is clothed, He has girded Himself with strength. Surely the world is established, so that it cannot be moved. Your throne is established from of old; You are from everlasting (Ps. 93:1–2).

Responsive Reading

Worship Leader: Then Jesus said to those Jews who believed Him, "If you abide in My word, you are My disciples indeed. And you shall know the truth, and the truth shall make you free. . . . whoever commits sin is a slave of sin. And a slave does not abide in the house forever, but a son abides forever" (John 8:31–32, 34–35).

Congregation: Therefore if the Son makes you free, you shall be free indeed (John 8:36).

Worship Leader: We know that the law is spiritual; but I am unspiritual, sold as a slave to sin (Rom. 7:14 NIV).

Congregation: If the Son makes you free, you shall be free indeed (John 8:36).

Worship Leader: Stand fast therefore in the liberty by which Christ has made us free, and do not be entangled again with a yoke of bondage (Gal. 5:1).

Invitation

You may be living in a free country today, but you feel a sense of bondage in your life: bondage to alcohol, lust, anger, jealousy, addiction, work . . . any of these things may be the controlling factor in your life. You realize that it's your passions and not Jesus Christ who is truly Lord. Today, He offers you freedom. Submission to Jesus as Lord and Savior is freedom from sin and death, from your own notions of morality that you'll never live up to. Jesus will empower you to live a victorious life in His freedom. Won't you trust Him today?

Additional Sermons and Lesson Ideas

Faith and Freedom
Date preached:

By Dr. Timothy K. Beougher

SCRIPTURE: Various

INTRODUCTION: Faith in Christ is our means of true freedom:

1. Faith Brings Freedom from Fear (Heb. 13:6). Those who have trusted in Christ never have to walk alone again.
2. Faith Brings Freedom from Performance (Rom. 7:14). While Christ continually works to change us to be more like Him, there is great peace in knowing that He accepts us just like we are.
4. Faith Brings Freedom from Sin (Rom. 8:1). In the face of sin's guilt, we can experience "no condemnation." Through Christ, you now have the power to say "no" to the things that would destroy you.

CONCLUSION: The potential for evil resides within each of us. The Bible is clear; we cannot free ourselves from our own bondage. We are totally dependent on God and His grace. Faith brings true freedom to believers!

Hey, Mr. President
Date preached:

By Pastor Al Detter

SCRIPTURE: 1 Peter 2:13–17

INTRODUCTION: We are to submit to the government that God has put above us.

1. Christians Are to Submit to the Government for the Lord's Sake (v. 13).
2. The Government's Role Is to Promote Good and to Limit Evil Among Its Citizens (v. 14).
3. Law-Abiding Christians Will Make an Impact on Those Who Dislike Them (vv. 15–16).
4. Submission to the Government Is Part of an Overarching Respect for Everyone (v. 17).

CONCLUSION: The context of this passage is that it was written to a people under a brutal and murderous emperor, Nero. Peter's message is "submit." We also are called to humbly submit to the government that God has placed over us. We are called to be different and in so doing, lead others to Christ.

William Sangster

When entrusted to God, even sickness can become a tool for his glory. Asked why the man in John 9 was blind, Jesus replied, "This happened so that the work of God might be displayed in his life" (NIV). Paul's illness, though a "thorn" in his flesh, displayed the sufficiency of God's grace. William Sangster's four rules for facing illness show us how that happens.

Sangster was born in London in 1900 and started attending a Methodist church at age nine. At thirteen he became a Christian and immediately began sharing his faith with friends. Three years later he preached his first sermon on February 11, 1917. After stints in the army and in college, he began pastoring a circuit of Methodist churches, working himself to exhaustion, frequently saying, "I just can't do enough!" His reputation as a powerful preacher and beloved pastor followed him from church to church.

In 1939, Sangster assumed leadership of Westminster Central Hall, a Methodist church near London's Westminster Abbey. During his first worship service he announced to his stunned congregation that Britain and Germany were officially at war. He quickly converted the church basement into an air raid shelter, and for 1,688 nights Sangster ministered to the various needs of all kinds of people. At the same time he somehow managed to write, to preach gripping sermons, to earn a Ph.D., and to lead hundreds to Christ. He became known as Wesley's successor in London and was esteemed as the most beloved British preacher of his era.

After the war, Sangster headed Britain's Methodist home missions department until he was diagnosed with progressive muscular atrophy. For three years he slowly died, becoming progressively more paralyzed, finally able to move only two fingers. But his attitude didn't falter, for when first learning of his illness, Sangster made four rules for himself. Many people have rules for living. Sangster composed four rules for dying: "I will never

Continued on the next page

HEROES FOR THE PASTOR'S HEART—*Continued*

complain. I will keep the home bright. I will count my blessings. I will try to turn it to gain." He did all those things. And thus the work of God was displayed in his life, and God's strength was made perfect in his weakness.[1]

> **Quote for the Pastor's Wall**
>
> *My motto was always to keep swinging. Whether I was in a slump or feeling badly or having trouble off the field, the only thing to do was keep swinging.*
>
> —HANK AARON

[1] "More on the Strange Case of the Worldwide Persecution of Christian" by Herb Denenberg in "The Bulletin: Philadelphia's Family Newspaper, on January 18, 2008, at http://www.thebulletin.us/site/news.cfm?newsid=19210513&BRD=2737&PAG=461&dept_id=623508&rfi=6, accessed on January 22, 2008.

JULY 12, 2009

SUGGESTED SERMON

Lord of All or Not at All

Date preached:

By Rev. Melvin Tinker

Scripture: Romans 14:1–12, especially verse 9
For to this end Christ died and rose and lived again, that He might be Lord of both the dead and the living.

Introduction: Do you consider some of your life to be God's and some to be your own? Does Jesus have control of your Sundays but not your Monday morning? Do you submit your time to Christ but not your bank account? Are you faithful to Bible study but not to serving others in love? If the Christian faith is compartmentalized, we will fall for the common myth that faith is private, that one view is as good as any other and the phrase "Jesus is Lord" will be reduced to an empty mantra of catchy choruses. A proper understanding of what it means to claim that Jesus is Lord is vital to our very salvation, let alone the spiritual health of the church. Let's look at what Paul has to teach us in Romans 14 where we discover three vital relationships which the Lordship of Christ affects.

1. **Our Relationship to God (vv. 7–9).** Only when we acknowledge Jesus as Lord does our relationship with God become right. You cannot find a more vivid contrast between the Christian and the non-Christian than Paul's description in these verses. All of us are either living for ourselves or for the Lord. If Christ is Lord then nothing is outside His dominion. You can't have Christ as your Savior and then later on decide to have Him as your Lord as if this is a two-stage installment plan. It is a package deal. He is Savior precisely *because* He is Lord, the One who has all authority in heaven and earth, seated at His Father's side, and so enabled to bestow salvation and the Holy Spirit on anyone who trusts in Him.

2. **Our Relationship to Each Other (vv. 2–6).** In verse 1 Paul urges these Christians to accept those whose faith is *weak*, the Christian whose understanding isn't well developed and who has a rather over-sensitive conscience. As we see in verses 2–6, Christians differed on what were matters of secondary importance. A modern

day example would be someone who gets converted from a home where alcoholic drink is a major problem and has been a problem for them, so they become teetotalers. What is more they feel they cannot go anywhere near a bar. That is quite understandable. But what is quite unacceptable is the supercilious judgment of other Christians, the superior looking down upon those with whom we disagree.

3. **Our Relationship to the Outside World (v. 11).** Finally, if we acknowledge Jesus Christ as Lord, then our relationship with the outside (the secular, unbelieving) world is right as well. The context of this verse is judgment. Each one of us is going to give an account of himself to Christ the Lord and Christ the Judge. So, in the first instance it applies to Christians. But there is a secondary application as well. In its original context in Isaiah, it's one of the great missionary verses of the Bible, which carries the conviction that not just Israel but the whole world which one day will bow the knee to Yahweh. In the New Testament it's revealed that Jesus is the Lord to which they will bow and confess as Lord (cf. Phil. 2:5–11). At the very least if we really do believe Jesus is Lord, we shall want others to know that truth too! We must tell others about Christ so that they can know the Lord not simply as judge, which is the only alternative, but know the sweet release He brings as Savior and Lord of our lives!

Conclusion: Is Jesus Christ your Lord or are you denying His Lordship in some way? To reject His teaching, to disobey His moral commands, to complain against His providential will—all of this is to deny His Lordship. To boss other Christians around or to despise them because they are not like us is to deny His Lordship. I ask whether you are willing tonight to surrender to Him what it is that you have been withholding for years, whatever it may be. To deny His Lordship, which we can be so good at doing, is to skulk around in the darkness of fantasy. But to acknowledge Jesus is Lord is to come out into the sunshine of reality. Won't you do that today?

STATS, STORIES, AND MORE

Stats on Young People Leaving the Faith
Why do young people abandon their faith? Well, a few years ago a team of social scientists decided to find out. They polled several hundred university students and published the results in *The Review of Religious Research*. The number one reason cited for the abandonment of faith was hypocrisy: 38 percent of the students saw the behavior of church members as contradicting their professed beliefs. The second reason given by 36 percent of the students was that Christianity was not successful in solving the problems of life. Reason number three—at 30 percent—was learning things at school which contradicted what they were taught at church.

Is Jesus Really Your Lord?
It was the broadcaster Steve Chalk who rightly pointed out to a group of young people that you will never know that Jesus is really your Lord until He asks you to do something you don't want to do: such as not going out with a non-Christian, working hard at getting to grips with the Bible, sharing your faith with friends, getting regular at church and so on. The test comes through things which the Bible teaches, but which we find uncomfortable or unpopular. Anyone can sing it; God wants us to live it.

APPROPRIATE HYMNS AND SONGS

"It Is You," Peter Furler, 2002 Ariose Music.

"Everlasting God," Brenton Brown & Ken Riley, 2005 ThankYou Music.

"Awesome God," Paul Garcia & Tim Johnson, 1988 Doulos Publishing.

"Famous One," Chris Tomlin, 2002 Worshiptogether.com Songs/sixsteps Music.

"Rejoice the Lord Is King," Charles Wesley, Public Domain.

FOR THE BULLETIN

On July 12, 1172, England's Henry II allowed himself to be flogged in penance for the murder of Thomas Becket. ● On July 12, 1536, Desiderius Erasmus, Dutch scholar and the first editor of the Greek New Testament, died in Basel. ● On July 12, 1690, Protestant forces led by William of Orange defeated the Roman Catholic army of James II at the Battle of the Boyne in Ireland. ● Colonial missionary David Brainard was converted on this day in 1739. He later described the event like this: "As I was walking in a dark thick grove, unspeakable glory seemed to open to the view . . . of my soul. By the glory I saw I don't mean any external brightness . . . but it was a new inward apprehension or view that I had of God; such as I had never had before . . ." Brainard later died at age twenty-nine, but his influence on subsequent missionaries was profound. ● July 12, 1803, marks the birthday of Thomas Guthrie, distinguished Scottish minister who became one of the most popular preachers of his day and the founder of the "ragged schools" for poor children in Edinburgh. ● Today is also the birthday, in 1817, of American philosopher and naturalist, Henry David Thoreau. ● English divine, Frederick W. Robertson, was ordained into the Anglican Church on July 12, 1840. ● And today is the birthday of Peter Deyneka, Sr., born on July 12, 1898. He came to Christ under the ministry of evangelist Paul Radar on January 18, 1920, as Radar preached at Moody Memorial Church in Chicago. Deyneka went on to become one of the founders of the Russian Gospel Association (now the Slavic Gospel Association).

Quote for the Pastor's Wall

There can be no study without time; and the mind must abide and dwell upon things, or be always a stranger to the inside of them.

—Dr. Robert South (1632–1716)

WORSHIP HELPS

Call to Worship

> *Light of the world!*
> *Whose kind and gentle care is joy and rest;*
> *Whose counsels and commands so gracious are,*
> *Wisest and best;*
> *Shine on my path, dear Lord,*
> *And guard the way,*
> *Lest my poor heart, forgetting,*
> *Go astray.*
>
> *Lord of my life!*
> *My soul's most pure desire,*
> *Its hope and peace;*
> *Let not the faith Thy loving words inspire*
> *Falter, or cease;*
> *But be to me, true Friend, my chief delight,*
> *And safely guide,*
> *That every step be right.*
>   —Henry Bateman, 1869; from "Light
>   of the World! Whose Kind and
>   Gentle Care"

Pastoral Prayer

Who can understand his errors? Cleanse me from secret faults. Keep back Your servant also from presumptuous sins; let them not have dominion over me. Then I shall be blameless, and I shall be innocent of great transgression. Let the words of my mouth and the meditation of my heart be acceptable in Your sight, O Lord, my strength and my Redeemer (Ps. 19:12–14).

Benediction

Now to Him who is able to keep you from stumbling, and to present you faultless before the presence of His glory with exceeding joy, to God our Savior, who alone is wise, be glory and majesty, dominion and power, both now and forever. Amen (Jude 1:24–25).

Additional Sermons and Lesson Ideas

Ruler Over All
Date preached:

By Rev. Robert Norris

SCRIPTURE: Daniel 4:4–37

INTRODUCTION: God will not tolerate human arrogance. He gives grace to the humble and scatters the proud. Nebuchadnezzar was a great man. This confident man, who needed nothing and nobody to make his life complete, was nevertheless humbled and brought to confess a personal faith in God. God, through His grace, allowed Nebuchadnezzar that opportunity.

1. The Rebuke Nebuchadnezzar Received (vv. 4–27).
2. The Disaster Nebuchadnezzar Suffered (vv. 28–33).
3. The Lesson Nebuchadnezzar Learned (vv. 34–37).

CONCLUSION: We need the grace of God. Not only have we been saved by the grace of God, but we continue to live in that grace. We are dependent upon it to have our sin met with forgiveness and our failure with the mercy of heaven that was won for us by Jesus Christ.

A Matter of Conscience
Date preached:

By Rev. Peter Grainger

SCRIPTURE: 1 Corinthians 8:1–13

INTRODUCTION: There are many ethical and moral issues which the Bible and Jesus do not directly address and which are not expressly forbidden or are clearly morally wrong. There are ultimately two ways in which we can address these issues.

1. The Way of Knowledge (vv. 1–8). Knowledge is not the way to resolve an issue.
2. The Way of Love (vv. 9–13). Paul says that love and not knowledge must be the guiding factor in determining our actions in respect of our fellow Christians.

CONCLUSION: If love means forfeiting a freedom for the sake of another believer, then we should gladly be willing to do it rather than risk endangering a fellow Christian for whom Christ died.

JULY 19, 2009

Humble Circumstances

Date preached:

Scripture: James 1:9–11, especially verses 9–10a
Let the lowly brother glory in his exaltation, but the rich in his humiliation.

Introduction: The world says we have to have the right philosophy about money. For example, consider the philosophy of the great American thinker, Henry David Thoreau. The first chapter of his book about Walden Pond is titled "Economy." You don't have to read very far in *Walden* to know that rich people didn't impress Thoreau. He believed the happiest life was the simplest life. He thought all of us should live so simply that if an enemy appeared at the outskirts of town, we could walk out of the gate empty-handed and without anxiety. That's not a bad philosophy. But as Christians we have a theology about money (from theos—God + logos—logic). We have God's logic on the subject. In the Bible, He reveals His thoughts about money and money-management, and the Bible is remarkably consistent in what it says. The epistle of James addresses this subject several times; and in today's passage, James has something to say to two different groups in the church.

1. **Poor Believers Should Be Aware of Their True Wealth (v. 9).** Speaking to Christians (note the word "brother"), James addresses those who are "lowly" or in humble circumstances (NIV). He says that if you're struggling financially, you should rejoice and become more aware of your high position. What does he mean by that? The best commentary on James 1:9 is James 2:5: *Listen, my beloved brethren: Has God not chosen the poor of this world to be RICH IN faith and heirs of the kingdom which He promised to those who love Him?* (my emphasis).

    The two words I want you to notice are: *RICH IN.* . . .

    Compare 1 Timothy 6:17–18, where Paul commands those who are *RICH IN this present age* not to put their hope in wealth, but in God, who richly gives us all things to enjoy. *Let them . . . be RICH IN good works.*

In Luke 12, Jesus spoke of people who were *RICH IN God's sight* (v. 21 GNT).

In 1 Corinthians 1:4–5 (HCSB), Paul spoke to those who . . . *were made RICH IN everything—in all speaking and all knowledge* (see also 2 Cor. 8:7 and 9:11).

So if you're a Christian and don't think you're very rich, you're not cognizant of the Bible's valuation of your assets. The Bible says that in Christ we are RICH IN . . .

- Good deeds
- God's sight
- Knowledge—what we know
- Speech—what we have to say
- Faith
- Every way

2. **Rich Believers Should Be Aware of Their Transitory Lives (vv. 10–11).** The next two verses warn rich believers to remember the brevity of life and the temporary nature of earthly wealth (see also James 4:14). Job said, "Naked I came from my mother's womb, and naked I will depart." Paul said, "We brought nothing into this life, and we can take nothing out of it." So we shouldn't become too enamored with the things of this world. We should use it and invest it and give it as faithful stewards who will have to give an account to God. Psalm 62:10 (NIV) says: *Though your riches increase, do not set your heart on them* (see also 1 Cor. 7:29–31).

Conclusion: CNN recently carried a story of a 62-year-old man who was rushed to Cholet General Hospital in France, suffering stomach pain. His family told doctors the man had a history of mental illness and a penchant for swallowing coins, but nothing could have prepared the doctors for X-rays of the man's stomach. It was filled with 350 coins he had swallowed. The doctors performed surgery to remove the mass, but the man died of complications twelve days later. "What a sick man," you say. But he's illustrative of this world that is gorging itself sick on materialism. The commentator J. B. Mayor made a profound point when he said that this passage in James gives the poor self-respect and it gives the rich self-abasement. Christianity—the message of Jesus and the church and the family of God—obliterates class distinction. If you don't have much money, rejoice in how rich you are in faith, in good deeds, in Christ, in eternal blessings. And if you're getting along pretty well, think about how quickly it's all going to be over and you're going to face the Lord. Are you ready to meet the Lord? Are you laying up treasures in heaven?

STATS, STORIES, AND MORE

I Wrote a Check
I read about a man who was dying and he was quite wealthy. On his deathbed, he told his wife that he wanted to be buried with his money, and he made her promise that she would put a million dollars in the casket with him. Then he died, and at the funeral she took a large envelope and slipped it into the casket just before the lid was sealed. Afterward, her friends said to her, "Did you really put a million dollars in the casket with him?" And she said, "Yes, I always keep my word and I promised I would do it . . . . I wrote a check!" Well, we're not going to cash any checks when we die. We're not going to make any deposits. We're not going to need one thin dime. And our lives are so uncertain. In chapter 5, James is going to warn rich people that their lives are nothing more than a vapor that is here for a moment and then vanishes.

Easy Come, Easy Go
A couple of years ago, I read about a man near Indianapolis who won the lottery. He won thousands and thousands of dollars, and that very night as he was walking to the grocery store near his home where he had bought the winning ticket, he was hit by a car and killed. He never received or enjoyed one dime.[1]

---

[1] "Lottery Winner Dies in Accident Hours After Show," an AP story at www.cnn.com on January 24, 2004.

APPROPRIATE HYMNS AND SONGS

"Unfailing Love," Chris Tomlin, Cary Pierce & Ed Cash, 2004
    Worshiptogether.com Songs/sixsteps Music/Popular Purple
    Publishing/Alletrop Music.

"My Jesus I Love Thee," William R. Featherstone, Public Domain.

"O Love That Will Not Let Me Go," George Matheson, Public Domain.

"How Deep the Father's Love for Us," Stuart Townend, 1995 ThankYou
    Music.

FOR THE BULLETIN

The city of Rome caught fire on this day in A.D. 64, during the reign of unpopular Emperor Nero who deflected blame by attributing the fire to Christians. This triggered the first state-sponsored persecution against believers in the Roman Empire. ● Today marks the birthday, in 1624, of Quaker founder George Fox; and of Edward Winslow in 1649. Winslow became the Governor of Plymouth Colony and one of the principle organizers for the Society for Propagating the Gospel in New England. ● Charles Wesley famously ministered to a group of prisoners condemned to be hanged on July 18, 1738, counseling them, praying for them, and singing on the way to the gallows the old Isaac Watts hymn, "How Sad Our State My Nature Is." ● Samuel Medley died on this day in 1799. He was an English Baptist leader, pastor, and hymnist who was converted after reading a sermon by Isaac Watts. ● Today is the birthday, in 1837 in Louisville, Kentucky, of William Shakespeare Hayes, a journalist and songwriter who was jailed during the Civil War for his songs sympathetic to the Confederates. After the war he became a steamboat captain on the Mississippi, and later a columnist for the Louisville Courier-Journal. He's the composer of the music for the hymn, "I've Found a Friend in Jesus, He's Everything to Me." ● On July 19, 1850, a ship wrecked off the South Shore of Long Island, and a heroic woman named Margaret Fuller, forty-one, refused to leave her husband's side. Both perished, along with the couple's young son. Margaret was an author, editor, poet, and orator, and has been called the most famous woman in America during her life. She was an early feminist leader. She is also the author of the hymn, "Jesus a Child His Course Begun." ● Evangelist Paul Rader died on this day in 1938.

WORSHIP HELPS

Call to Worship
Thus says the LORD, your Redeemer, and He who formed you from the womb: "I am the LORD, who makes all things, who stretches out the heaves all alone, who spreads abroad the earth" (Is. 44:24).

Pastoral Prayer Idea
Remember to pray frequently for the persecuted church around the world. According to a column by Herb Denenberg in a Philadelphia newspaper called *The Bulletin,* there were approximately 45 million Christians killed for their faith across the twentieth century, and 600 million Christians are now suffering persecution and various forms of harassment because of their faith. The worldwide discrimination against Christians is arguably the most under-reported story in the media. According to Nini Shea in her book on Christian persecution, between the resurrection of Christ and the year 1900, approximately twenty-five million Christians died as martyrs. In the twentieth century alone, the number stands at forty-five million. And there's every reason to believe that the twenty-first century will be worse. Ms. Shea wrote, "Millions of American Christians pray in their churches each week, oblivious to the fact that Christians in many parts of the world suffer brutal torture, arrest, imprisonment, and even death—their homes and communities laid waste—for no other reason than that they are Christians."[2] There are a number of good Web sites that document current cases of known discrimination and persecution. Take time to search out specific cases and lead your church to pray during services for the persecuted church.

[2]From the editor's book, *On This Day,* published by Thomas Nelson Publishers, 1997, entry for February 11.

Additional Sermons and Lesson Ideas

Prayer for Discerning Love
Date preached:
By William Graham Scroggie

SCRIPTURE: Philippians 1:9–11

INTRODUCTION: Love is the supreme proof of the reality of our Christian profession.

1. Love's Perfecting Unfolded.
   A. Enlargement of Love (v. 9). "I pray that your love may abound more and more . . ."
   B. Enrichment of Love (v. 9). "In real knowledge and all discernment . . ."
   C. Employment of Love (v. 10). "So that you may approve the excellent things . . ."
2. Love's Perfecting Displayed.
   A. Trueness of Conscience (v. 10). "In order to be sincere . . ."
   B. Consistency of Conduct (v. 10). "In order to be blameless . . ."
   C. Fullness of Character (v. 11). "Having been filled with the fruit of righteousness . . ."
3. Love's Perfecting Revealed.
   A. Ruling Motive (v. 10). "Until the day of Christ . . ."
   B. Divine Secret (v. 11). "Through Jesus Christ . . ."
   C. Ultimate Object (v. 11). "To the glory and praise of God . . ."

CONCLUSION: May we seek and receive true Christian love.

Out on a Limb
Date preached:
By Dr. Michael A. Guido

SCRIPTURE: Luke 19:1–10

INTRODUCTION: Zacchaeus was changed by believing in Jesus.

1. Mark the Curiosity (vv. 1–4). Zacchaeus wanted to see Jesus.
2. Mark the Call (vv. 5–6). Jesus called Zacchaeus down.
3. Mark the Critics (v. 7). The onlookers saw Zacchaeus as unchangeable.
4. Mark the Change (vv. 8–9). Zacchaeus was changed by Jesus.
5. Mark the Commission (v. 10). Jesus states that He came for the lost.

CONCLUSION: Jesus came to seek and to save those who are lost. He came to offer new life to sinners, He came to change us from the inside, and He came and found us.

JULY 26, 2009

SUGGESTED SERMON

Fighting the Battle for Purity *Date preached:*

By Pastor Al Detter

Scripture: 2 Samuel 11–12, especially verse 13
Then David said to Nathan, "I have sinned against the LORD." Nathan replied, "The LORD has taken away your sin. You are not going to die (NIV).

Introduction: Good people of every age fall. People we'd never expect. Sin enters their lives and bad things happen. We need some kind of perspective when good people sin. That's what we find in the Bible— honest accounts of failure and recovery, defeat and forgiveness, weakness and grace. As we look at the story of David's failure, there are five powerful truths that we need to grasp as we fight the battle for sexual purity in our sexually overexposed society.

Truths:

1. **Mismanaged Sexual Lust Is a Very Slippery Slope (11:1–5).** Sexual lust is an intense desire and temptation to satisfy one's sexual appetites outside the marriage relationship. Sexual lust is very controlling and the Bible tells us that our best weapon is to flee sexual lust, to run from it (1 Cor. 6:18; 2 Tim. 2:22). David got himself on such a slope:

   A. **He Wasn't Where He Belonged (v. 1).** In those days, kings were supposed to be with their armies in battle. But where was David? Relaxing in the palace. We are very vulnerable to sexual temptation when we are where we shouldn't be. We set ourselves up for trouble.

   B. **David Coddled Temptation (v. 2).** I chose the word "coddle" on purpose. Its primary meaning is "to cook slowly in water just below the boiling point." David happened to see Bathsheba taking a bath. She was very attractive. Instead of fleeing, he allowed his sexual desire to escalate, to boil. David's glance became a gaze. His gaze became a pursuit as he sent someone to find out about her (v. 3). His pursuit ended in adultery (v. 4).

2. **The Primary Instinct After Sexual Sin Is to Cover It Up (11:6–27).**
   Shortly after their affair, Bathsheba told David something he wasn't
   planning to hear: "I'm pregnant (v. 5)." David began to devise an
   elaborate plot to make Bathsheba's pregnancy look like it was really
   Uriah's child. In the innocence of his integrity, Uriah didn't cooperate. David got desperate and ultimately had Uriah killed (vv. 14–17).
   There are three things we should know about hiding our sin:

   A. **Cover-Ups Are Temporary (12:1–13; cf. Num. 32:23).**

   B. **Innocent People Get Hurt While You Try to Cover Up (2 Sam.
      11:14–17).**

   C. **God Knows (v. 27).**

3. **Confrontation Is the Usual Means by Which Sexual Sin Is Admitted
   (12:1–12).** When absolute proof is put before a person involved in
   sexual sin, usually they'll admit to something. Even then, the whole
   truth is hard to get. God used Nathan the prophet to confront David.
   We learn something very important from how Nathan handled this
   situation: *how one makes the confrontation is just as important as
   making the confrontation.* Nathan approached David with skill, tact,
   and courage and opened up a window for David to eventually see
   himself. If you confront a person with anger and accusations, don't
   expect things to go well.

4. **Deep Godly Sorrow over Major Sin and God's Forgiveness Always
   Run in Tandem (12:13).** David's response was immediate: "I have
   sinned against the Lord (12:13a NIV)." David took full responsibility
   for his sin. He admitted his sins and, according to the law of Moses,
   expected to die because of them. It's amazing what Nathan said
   next: "The LORD has taken away your sin. You are not going to
   die" (12:13b NIV). God forgave Him! After he experienced God's
   forgiveness, David wrote Psalms 51 and 32. These Psalms are extremely impacting; there's no doubt David's repentance was real.

5. **Sexual Sin Always Has Devastating Consequences (2 Sam. 12:10–
   12, 14–23).** It's great to know that God forgives sin, but sin creates
   consequences that cannot be reversed. The truth is, David's life was
   never the same again. From this point on he experienced ongoing
   bad problems in his family and he kept fighting wars (12:10–12) to

the extent that he was unable to build his dream—the temple in which to worship God. But the consequence that broke his heart was the death of the newborn child.

Conclusion: I don't know where you may be today, but no matter what you've done or what you're doing now, you can be restored. It won't be easy, but it's the best thing that can happen. The fall of a good person doesn't have to end with sin and sadness.

STATS, STORIES, AND MORE

Stats

- One survey reported that forty million American adults regularly log onto pornographic Web sites.
- There are over four million pornographic Web sites.
- A survey of Promise-Keeper men found that 53 percent of them had viewed pornography in the week prior to the survey.
- The average age of a person's first exposure to Internet pornography was age eleven.
- Ninety percent of all young people ages eight to sixteen have viewed pornography online, most of them while doing homework.
- Forty-seven percent of all Christian families say that pornography is a problem in their homes.

Responding to the Text

When I read the stories of biblical people who fell, two strong thoughts grip my soul. First, I think, "Oh, God, please keep me from a sin that would blemish Your name, hurt others, and ruin the reputation of Your servant." I don't want to get into the entangled mess of a major sin. These failure stories are examples to us not to do what they did (1 Cor. 10:6, 11). My second thought is about the incredible grace and mercy of God. Some good people have experienced damaging sin. They've fallen hard and it became public. But God is not about throwing people on a garbage heap. These stories are messages of hope, healing, and restoration for good people who fall.   —*Pastor Al Detter*

APPROPRIATE HYMNS AND SONGS

"I Lift My Eyes Up," Brian Doerksen, 1990 Vineyard Songs Canada.

"Lifesong," Mark Hall, 2005 Club Zoo Music/SWECS Music.

"Knowing You," Graham Kendrick, 1994 Make Way Music.

"May the Mind of Christ, My Savior," Kate B. Wilkinson, Public Domain.

"Take Time to Be Holy," William D. Longstaff, Public Domain.

FOR THE BULLETIN

On July 26, 1603, King James VI of Scotland became James I of England. He is the king who authorized the English translation of the Bible that commonly bears his name. ● In 1789, the Christian statesman, William Wilberforce, first spoke against slavery in the House of Commons. He lectured on the subject, wrote books, posted billboards, and lobbied leaders for years. Finally in 1807 after nearly twenty years of work, Wilberforce sat bent in his chair, head in his hands, weeping, as the parliament outlawed the trading of slaves in the British Empire. Wilberforce pressed on for another twenty years for complete emancipation of all slaves in the British Empire. On July 26, 1833, the Bill for the Abolition of Slavery passed in the House of Commons. News was rushed to the bedfast Wilberforce who raised himself on one elbow, smiled quietly, and said, "Thank God that I have lived to witness [this] day." He died three days later, his life's work finished. ● July 26, 1826, marks the death of Jessie Seymour Irvine, composer of the hymn tune CRIMOND, the melody for the popular hymn, "The Lord's My Shepherd," taken from the Scottish Psalter (1650) version of Psalm 23. ● William Jennings Bryan, a leader of the Fundamentalists in the Presbyterian Church and an American political figure and orator, died on this day in 1925. ● Today marks the death, in 1933, of the African-American preacher, Charles Albert Tindley, who became pastor of the church where he once served as janitor, the Calvary Methodist Episcopal Church in Philadelphia. His great song, "I'll Overcome Some Day" serves as the basis of the Civil Rights anthem, "We Shall Overcome." His other popular gospel songs include the classics "Nothing Between," "Stand by Me," and "We'll Understand It Better By and By."

WORSHIP HELPS

Call to Worship

Come to Me, all you who labor and are heavy laden, and I will give you rest. Take My yoke upon you and learn from Me, for I am gentle and lowly in heart, and you will find rest for your souls. For My yoke is easy and My burden is light (Matt. 11:28–30).

Scripture Reading

Have mercy upon me, O God, according to Your lovingkindness; according to the multitude of Your tender mercies, blot out my transgressions. Wash me thoroughly from my iniquity, and cleanse me from my sin. For I acknowledge my transgressions, and my sin is always before me. Against You, You only, have I sinned, and done this evil in Your sight—that You may be found just when You speak, and blameless when You judge. . . . Create in me a clean heart, O God, and renew a steadfast spirit within me. Do not cast me away from Your presence, and do not take Your Holy Spirit from me. Restore to me the joy of Your salvation, and uphold me by Your generous Spirit. Then I will teach transgressors Your ways, and sinners shall be converted to You (Ps. 51:1–4, 10–13).

Benediction

Draw near to God and He will draw near to you. Cleanse your hands, you sinners; and purify your hearts, you double-minded. Lament and mourn and weep! Let your laughter be turned to mourning and your joy to gloom. Humble yourselves in the sight of the Lord, and He will lift you up (James 4:8–10).

Additional Sermons and Lesson Ideas

Principles for Confronting Others About Sexual Sin
Date preached:
By Pastor Al Detter

SCRIPTURE: 2 Samuel 12:1–15

INTRODUCTION: We can learn some principles from Nathan and from later revelation about how to confront others in their sexual sin.

1. Have Absolute Proof (v. 1). The Lord sent Nathan with divine revelation. Nathan had no reason to doubt. When we confront others, it may not be divinely revealed, but we must not confront based on gossip or second-hand information.
2. Never Go Alone (v. 1). Again, the Lord sent Nathan who was a prophet. We're not prophets, so it's best—especially in the case of sexual sin—to have two or three witnesses involved (cf. Matt. 18:16ff; 1 Tim. 5:19; 2 Cor. 12:21–13:1).
3. Realize Confrontation Can Go South (2 Cor. 12:21). Even if people admit to something, it can get nasty. Not all confrontations go like Nathan's did. Confrontation isn't fun. It's very unsettling. But it's the likely means that will bring secret sin out into the open.

CONCLUSION: The Lord has called us to keep the church purified of sin. This often works itself out through confrontation of the sexually immoral (1 Cor. 5). Never attempt to confront someone without following a scriptural pattern!

Understand?
Date preached:
By Dr. Larry Osborne

SCRIPTURE: 1 Corinthians 2:1–16

INTRODUCTION: The Holy Spirit was given to believers in Christ that we may have a Helper present within us.

1. Keep It Simple and Spirit-led (vv. 1–5). When ministering we should stick to the basics and allow the Holy Spirit to guide us.
2. A Rescue Plan No One Ever Thought of (vv. 6–10). God has a plan of redemption that is counter-intuitive to the "wisdom" of this world.
3. The Key to Spiritual Knowledge and Power (vv. 11–16). The Holy Spirit is required in order for us to understand the mind of Christ and receive the power of God.

CONCLUSION: God's plan of redemption is seen as foolishness by the wise of this world. It is only through the Holy Spirit that we are able to understand who God is and what it is He has freely given us in Christ.

PATRIOTIC SERMON

Tired of War

Date preached:

By Pastor Al Detter

Scripture: Various, especially Psalm 120:7
I am for peace; but when I speak, they are for war.

Introduction: I can't imagine the total number of Americans who have given their lives for our country. God knows the number and name of each one, and today we remember and are grateful for their sacrifice! Despite your opinions of various political situations, everyone can agree that we're tired of being at war! We don't want our soldiers dying in battle. Today let's look through the lens of Scripture and to bring the Scriptures to bear on how we view war as Christians. When looking at the words—battle, war, and peace—in the Bible, five realities about war bubble to the surface. I want to present those realities to you today.

Realities:

1. **God Is at War.** In considering the issue of war, this is the place to start. There are actual spirit beings in cosmic war between the forces of God and the forces of Satan. This war began in eternity past when Satan and his followers were cast out of heaven (Is. 14:12; Rev. 12). The war has been constant from that point on. Most worldly observers tend to dismiss cosmic war as something superstitious. But the entire Bible holds to the worldview that God is at war. It records and teaches that war exists in the unseen realms and those wars have a direct bearing on the well-being of human beings and the environment of this earth.

2. **Wars Pervade History.** Someone has said that the history of mankind is the history of wars. Pick up any history book and you'll see this is accurate. What about the Bible, our one-and-only sacred book? It's full of war! The first recorded war in the Bible is in Genesis 14:2 when an assortment of kings went to war near the Dead Sea in the days of Abraham. Later, when Israel came out of Egypt into the Promised Land, they were a virtual war machine. The wars continued into the eras of the judges and kings of Israel and Judah against nations like the Philistines, Assyria, and Babylon.

The prophets spoke of wars that would pervade human history. So whether you pick up a history book at school or a Bible at home, war permeates the pages. But why? This leads to our next reality:

3. **Wars Come from Within.** Classically, we think of war as open hostilities between nations or political factions carried out by weapons. But war goes beyond that. War is basically a condition of hostility and opposition by which injury is inflicted against the opposition to gain a victory. Wars don't just happen between states. They happen in marriages, families, at the work place, in churches, and among people who used to be friends. James 4:1–2 says, "Where do wars and fights come from among you? Do they not come from your desires for pleasure that war in your members? You lust and do not have. You murder and covet and cannot obtain. You fight and war. Yet you do not have because you do not ask."

4. **Wars Will Increase.** If you're tired of war, expect to be fatigued. Wars are part of the human landscape. Things are not going to get better. With all our learning and technological advancements, we haven't learned how to get along in the world. Instead, we've learned how to annihilate much of the globe. There will be periods of respite from war, but the trend line is upward. Jesus, speaking of the end times in Matthew 24, predicts the great Tribulation—that period at the end of this age when the world will experience unprecedented war and destruction. The apostle Paul says that people will be saying, "Peace and safety" (1 Thess. 5:3), but this is false. Sudden destruction will come in the form of the last Great War as Christ returns.

5. **Wars Will Cease in the New Heaven and Earth.** History is moving somewhere. It's going towards a predetermined plan that God is overseeing. Unregenerate mankind will continue to slug it out. At the same time, the gospel of peace will go forth to the four corners of the earth. When the trumpet of God is sounded, Christ will call for His elect, the church, from the four corners of the world. Then He will descend as a mighty warrior and defeat the hostile armies of the world (Rev. 19). All the former things like death and war and sorrow will pass away forever. Until that day, what can we do in a world of war and unrest with no end in sight?

Application:

1. **Prefer Peace.** Psalm 120:7 reads: "I am for peace; but when I speak, they are for war." The singer's plight comes to light in this Psalm. He wants peace. His enemies want war. I believe we need to defend ourselves, but we need to value peace above war. We need to pray for wisdom for our leaders. We need to value the souls of the enemy. We need to pray for the peace of Jerusalem.

2. **Wage Peace.** We know what it means to wage war. Why not wage peace? Here are two key ways we can wage peace:

   A. **Share the Gospel of Peace with Others.** In Ephesians 6:15, Paul tells us to cover our feet with the preparation of the gospel of peace. The best way to stop war in the world is not through military might; it's through changed hearts.

   B. **Make Peace in Your Own World.** Jesus said, "Blessed are the peacemakers, for they shall be called sons of God" (Matt. 5:9). Paul said in Romans 12:18, "If it is possible, as much as depends on you, live peaceably with all men." Let your every action be an action of peace; it will change your world.

Conclusion: Are we putting our hope in political parties, guns, and bombs or in the gospel of the kingdom of God? Do we have a passion for love and justice in the world? Are we saddened by violence, destruction, and war? Are we thankful for the sacrifice made by those who fight for our freedom? Are we committed to being peacemakers in our world? May Jesus and the New Testament determine our worldview and not the culture and policies of our day.

AUGUST 2, 2009

Noah and the Great Flood

Date preached:

By Dr. Woodrow Kroll

Scripture: Genesis 6, especially verse 5
Then the LORD saw that the wickedness of man was great in the earth, and that every intent of the thoughts of his heart was only evil continually.

Introduction: Have you ever thought to yourself, "I can get away with this. Nobody's watching. I can do it"? Well, if you have and the answer is yes, I have a message for you today. The Bible says that God sees everything we do. He takes note of everything. He knows what's going on in our hearts and minds, even before we do what we do. I've always been amazed that people think they can get away with things and God isn't going to know about it, because the Bible teaches just the opposite.

1. **A Bunch That Can't Behave (Gen. 6:5–12).** Notice in Genesis 6:5 the words, "Then the LORD saw. . . ." If we really believed God sees everything we do, we would probably live differently than we do (see Mark 4:22; Jer. 16:17; Luke 12:2–3; Heb. 4:13; Prov. 5:21). And it says, "The LORD saw . . . the wickedness of man" (see Prov. 15:3). And God saw that the intents and thoughts of the human heart were only evil continually. If this isn't an adequate description of the twenty-first century, what is? In verse 6, God condemned the earth and pronounced judgment on this bunch that can't behave, which encompasses all of mankind, all humanity. The passage goes on to say that the earth was corrupt, and all flesh was corrupt.

2. **A Barge That Can't Sink (Gen. 6:13–22).** We've got a bunch that can't behave, so the Lord said, "My answer to it is this—I'm going to bring judgment. But to you, Noah, I'm going to tell you how to escape judgment." That's an amazing thing to me. God is grieved; God is angry; and God is bringing judgment. But in the middle of it all, God is merciful and gracious. He allowed Noah and his family and the animals to escape judgment. Notice the architecture of this boat. It was more of a barge, really, than a ship. It's 450 feet long, seventy-five feet wide, and forty-five feet high. That means that the approximate space inside this barge is about 1.54 million cubic feet.

That's large enough to hold 522 standard-sized train cars. This is a boat big enough to hold all that God wanted in the ark, including the people He was going to save.

3. **A Bird That Can't Land (Gen. 8).** Noah entered the ark, and seven days later it began to rain. It rains forty days. One hundred ten days later, the ark comes to rest on the mountains of Ararat (Gen. 8:4). After 271 days, Noah sent out a raven, and then a dove. The dove can't find any place to land, so it comes back to the ark. A week later, he sent out the dove again and this time it came with an olive leaf in its mouth. At that point, they had been on the ark for 278 days. If you take the time to go through the passage and add up all the time designations, you'll find that Noah and his family were on the ark a total of 377 days—just over a year. Every day was a day of judgment on the outside of the ark, and a day of mercy on the inside. Every day was a token of God's saving strength, and when they exited the ark, the first thing Noah did was to build an altar to the Lord to thank Him for saving his life. The bird that couldn't land shows that the mercy of God just continued and continued and continued.

4. **A Bunch That Can't Behave (Gen. 11).** That brings us to the next major story in Genesis, the Tower of Babel, and we're back to the bunch that can't behave. This group announced three goals—to reach heaven by man-made means, to make a name for themselves, and to keep from being dispersed all over the world. But they failed at all three counts.

Conclusion: God designed the ark not just as a means of mercy, but as a means of mercy in the midst of judgment. Outside the ark, judgment was taking place. Inside the ark, God's mercy and grace was at work. And what we have in the ark is a picture of the salvation of God. Just as He designed the ark, He designed the plan of salvation. Jesus is the door, and inside of Him we are safe. If you are experiencing the judgment of God today, I want you to know you can experience the mercy of God. You can come to the place where God judged your sin at the cross, and falling before Him, you can say, "Lord, take my life and change it completely."

STATS, STORIES, AND MORE

More from Dr. Woodrow Kroll
According to its measurements, the ark was large enough to hold 522 standard, American-size train cars, with each car holding 240 sheep which means 125,280 sheep. Now not all animals in the ark were the size of sheep, but Noah didn't have to take two of every animal on the face of the earth. He had to take two of every *kind* of animal on the face of the earth. Biologists who classify animals say that a *kind* is a larger group than just a *species.* So for example, a horse and a zebra and a donkey would all be of the equine kind. All of them could have come from a single ancestor. The same thing is true with dogs and wolves and coyotes. They all could have come from a single ancestor. So we don't have to have two dogs, two wolves, two coyotes; we have to have a kind of each of these. And by the way, the Bible doesn't say they had to be full-grown adults either. They could have been small animals. They could have been teenage animals. They could have been little animals. This was a boat big enough to hold all that God wanted in that ark, including the people who He is going to save, Noah and all his family.

APPROPRIATE HYMNS AND SONGS

"Jesus Paid It All," Elvina M. Hall, Public Domain.

"Your Love, Oh Lord," Mac Powell, Brad Avery, David Carr, Mark D. Lee & Tai Anderson, 1999 New Spring Publishing, Inc./Vandura 2500 Songs/Gray Dot Songs.

"Again and Again," Claire Cloninger & Robert Sterling, 2004 Juniper Landing Music/Two Fine Boys Music/Word Music.

"Jesus, Draw Me Close," Rick Founds, 1990 Maranatha Praise, Inc.

PRAYER FOR THE PASTOR'S CLOSET

*Grant me grace, O God, I pray Thee, that I may with all my might,
All my lifetime, day and night, love and trust Thee and obey Thee
And, when this brief life is o'er, praise and love Thee evermore.*
—PAUL GERHARDT

FOR THE BULLETIN

When William the Conqueror of England died in 1087, his son Rufus (William II) moved quickly to seize the throne and is remembered as one of history's worst men. He derived perverse pleasure by watching men and animals tortured, and he vowed never to become a good man. Rufus passionately hated Christ, Christianity, and the clergy. On August 2, 1100, while hunting in the woods, he was struck by a powerful arrow from nowhere. He died quickly, and to no one's sorrow. No church bells tolled, no prayers were said for him, no alms given in his memory, no monuments built to his name. His younger brother Henry reigned in his stead. ● During the days of Queen Mary, James Abbes, a shoemaker from Stoke by Nayland, was burned at the stake on this day in 1555, according to John Foxe in his Book of Martyrs. ● French-born Isaac Jogues was a colonial era Roman Catholic missionary to American Native Americans, for whom he was so burdened he was willing to give his life in the effort of reaching them with the gospel. On August 2, 1643, Jogues and his traveling party were ambushed by the Iroquois. The missionary could have escaped, but he willingly joined his captured companions. The group was mercilessly tortured by the Indians. Eventually Jogues was freed, but he returned to his mission and was again captured and killed by tomahawk. His murderer, however, was later converted and took the name "Isaac Jogues" as his baptism name. ● Charles and Susannah Spurgeon declared their love for each other in her grandfather's garden on August 2, 1854. Afterward Susannah retired to an upper room in the house and knelt before God in thanksgiving for giving her the love of such a man as Charles. They were married on January 9, 1856. ● On August 2, 1876, Wild Bill Hickok was shot from behind and killed while playing poker in Deadwood, South Dakota.

Quote for the Pastor's Wall

There are two ways of being creative. One can sing and dance. Or one can create an environment in which singers and dancers flourish.

—WARREN BENNIS

WORSHIP HELPS

Call to Worship

Rejoice today with one accord, sing out with exultation;
Rejoice and praise our mighty Lord, Whose arm hath brought
*   salvation;*
His works of love proclaim the greatness of His name;
For He is God alone Who hath His mercy shown;
Let all His saints adore Him!   —HENRY W. BAKER

Special Hymn

The above verse is the first stanza of Henry W. Baker's "Rejoice
Today with One Accord," which is sung to Martin Luther's
Tune Ein Feste Burg ("A Mighty Fortress Is Our God").

Baker was a prolific British hymnist, the author of such
classics as "The King of Love My Shepherd Is," and the author
of one of history's greatest hymnbooks, *Hymns Ancient and
Modern*, in which "Rejoice Today with One Accord" first
appeared. If you would like to sing it at your church, the other
two verses are:

When in distress to Him we cried, He heard our sad
*   complaining;*
O trust in Him, whate'er betide, His love is all sustaining;
Triumphant songs of praise to Him our hearts shall raise;
Now every voice shall say, "O praise our God alway";
Let all His saints adore Him!

Rejoice today with one accord, sing out with exultation;
Rejoice and praise our mighty Lord, Whose arm hath brought
*   salvation;*
His works of love proclaim the greatness of His name;
For He is God alone who hath His mercy shown;
Let all His saints adore Him!

Additional Sermons and Lesson Ideas

A Redemption Story

Date preached:

By Rev. Melvin Tinker

SCRIPTURE: Ruth 4:1–22

INTRODUCTION: God's work of salvation in history is not intermittent, with God occasionally intervening; it is continuous with God constantly at work.

1. A Costly Redemption (vv. 1–10). Boaz was willing to pay whatever it cost to redeem Ruth.
2. An Effective Redemption (vv. 11–17). The sacrifice of Boaz led to blessings and new life for Boaz, Ruth, and Naomi.
3. A Future Redemption (vv. 18–22). The blessings of this redemption reach to the entire world through the line of Boaz.

CONCLUSION: This story points to a future time when God will bless and redeem the world through Jesus Christ. Jesus' death was costly but effective and points to a future of a new and perfect life.

Essential Encouragement

Date preached:

By Rev. Larry Kirk

SCRIPTURE: Hebrews 10:19–25

INTRODUCTION: Since we have confidence through the death and resurrection of Jesus Christ and because He is our great priest (vv. 19–21):

1. Let Us Draw Near to God (v. 22).
2. Let Us Hold Unswervingly to the Hope We Profess (v. 23).
3. Let Us Consider How We May Spur One Another on to Love and Good Deeds (v. 24).
4. Let Us Not Give Up Meeting Together (v. 25).

CONCLUSION: This is the life we should be living because of Christ.

AUGUST 9, 2009

SUGGESTED SERMON

The Real Road Less Traveled

Date preached:

By Dr. Larry Osborne

Scripture: Psalm 15, especially verses 1–2
LORD, who may dwell in your sanctuary? Who may live on your holy hill? He whose
walk is blameless and who does what is righteous . . . (NIV).

Introduction: The road less traveled isn't found in any woods. The road
of righteousness is the road less traveled. Psalm 15 only has five verses,
but contains powerful teaching that can guide us down this road.
Psalm 15 is similar to Matthew 5:48: ". . . be perfect, just as your Father
in heaven is perfect." In Matthew 5, Jesus sets the bar so high in the
Sermon on the Mount that we have no option but to run to Jesus
Christ. That's exactly the point in Psalm 15. We can never reach this
standard except through Christ, but at the same time we *can* become
more and more like Him day by day. There are four questions worth
asking ourselves that set the standard for what God is looking for in
our lives.

1. **Are My Words Helpful or Hurtful (vv. 2–3)?** This question is easy
    to overlook, but God sets an incredibly high standard for our speech.
    James 1:26 is quite direct about the importance of our speech: "If
    anyone among you thinks he is religious, and does not bridle his
    tongue but deceives his own heart, this one's religion is useless."
    How can we speak the truth in our heart (Ps. 15:2) without back-
    biting with our tongue (Ps. 15:3)? Let's look at two truths to help us
    understand this balance:

    A. **There's a Time and Place for Negative and Harsh Words.** The
        Bible is full of examples of negative and harsh words (cf. 2 Tim.
        4:14–15). Jesus dished out some of the harshest rebukes that can
        be found in Scripture (Mark 12:38–40). Peter did not speak out
        against legalism and was publicly rebuked by Paul (Gal. 2:11–
        14). So there's certainly a time for negative and harsh words, but
        many of us don't use this type of speech in the proper time or
        place.

B. Before You Pass on a Negative Report, Reconsider. Before we open our mouths in a negative or harsh word, we must ask ourselves three questions. First, *is this true and am I sure?* If you pass on negative information without being completely certain it's true, you're guilty of slander. The second question to ask ourselves: *are my words motivated by hurt or a genuine need to know?* Why would we tell someone negative information if it was ultimately for us and not them? When we rebuke others out of our own hurt or anger, it's motivated ultimately by hatred and perversion (Prov. 10:12; 16:28).

2. **Are My Heroes Godly or Godless (v. 4)?** Verse 4 tells us we are to despise a vile man but honor those who fear the Lord. The word *despise* doesn't mean we treat others with disrespect, for even the Lord Jesus was often surrounded by sinners as He ministered to them. Rather, we're to hate evil to the extent that we don't have evil people as role models. The issue here is who we look up to and emulate. Parents, when your children are seriously trying to emulate the godless, it's time to have a serious talk with them.

3. **Do I Keep My Commitments (v. 4)?** ". . . who keeps his oath even when it hurts . . ." (NIV). The things we often consider small, inconvenient, or painful are the things we neglect. Christians should be people who, even in the small things, are people of their word! How often at work do we say "Oh yeah, I'll get that done for you . . ." and then we don't? We do it with our kids: "I had a rough day so I can't take you to the park like I promised." Toughen up and keep your commitments even if it costs you!

4. **Do I Help the Helpless (v. 5)?** ". . . who lends his money without usury and does not accept a bribe against the innocent." The issue here is exploiting the poor. In those days sometimes there was 30–50 percent interest, what today we would call predatory interest. People would make their living on the backs of the disadvantaged (cf. Lev. 23:22). We're called to help those who need it most; to neglect this is to ignore God's Word, His character, and His example.

Conclusion: Take these four questions and use them as a mirror this week. Remember that Jesus is the only human who has ever fully lived up to these things. Rely upon His Spirit as you aspire to become more like Him in these ways.

STATS, STORIES, AND MORE

There's a story of a rabbi who had someone come to him and say, "I passed on some slander about another person and I realize it was wrong. What can I do to get right with God?" The rabbi says, "It's very simple. There are two steps to take—one today and one tomorrow. Today, go get a feather pillow. Walk through the main street of town, cut it open and scatter the feathers. That's all you need to do today and come back tomorrow." The fellow did what he was told and returned the next day asking what his next task was. The rabbi said, "The next step is simple: just go back and pick up all the feathers." The man replied, "I can't . . . that's impossible!" The rabbi said, "Yes. That's the problem with slander."

Lying as a Life Style
It's easy to adopt lying as a lifestyle. A New Hampshire newspaper reported on a case in which police officers stopped a car with a missing taillight. The driver told them he was taking his wife, who was in labor, to the hospital. Three small children were in the back seat, and the couple seemed distressed, so police escorted them to the local emergency room. The woman entered and was checked in. But in the waiting room, the woman asked another woman for a ride to a friend's house. Feeling sorry for the pregnant woman, the other woman gave her a lift. Only later was it discovered that the couple's car was stolen, the woman was not pregnant, and the Good Samaritan discovered $160 missing from her purse. Police were amazed at how quickly the crooks could spin their deceptive stories, but in the end both the man and woman were arrested and charged with theft. We may not go to those extremes, but one small lie can easily lead to another, and before we realize it lying has become a lifestyle.[1]

APPROPRIATE HYMNS AND SONGS

"Better Is One Day," Matt Redman, 1995 Kingsways Music/PRS.

"He Leadeth Me," Joseph H. Gilmore, Public Domain.

"All the Way My Savior Leads Me," Fanny Crosby, Public Domain.

"Jesus, Lover of My Soul," Paul Oakley, 1995 ThankYou Music.

"Blessed Be Your Name," Beth Redman & Matt Redman, 2002 ThankYou Music.

---

[1]"Woman Lands in Jail After Theft, Lying About Pregnancy" by Allison Knab in the Seacoastonline.com, at http://www.seacoastonline.com/apps/pbcs.dll/article?AID=/20080123/NEWS/801230336/-1/NEWS01&sfad=1, accessed January 23, 2008.

FOR THE BULLETIN

On August 9, 1253, Pope Innocent IV issued papers establishing the religious order of Poor Ladies, modeled on the Franciscan order and founded by Saint Clare of Assisi. Two days later, on August 11, Clare died at the age of fifty-nine. ● Jonathan Burr was a humble pastor in Suffolk, England, but because he didn't conform to the Church of England, he was suspended from his church, leading to his immigrating to the colonies with his family. Once in America, he battled smallpox but recovered and rededicated himself to God. In 1641, after preaching a sermon on "Redeeming the Time," he fell ill and died on August 9, at the age of thirty-seven. His last words were to his wife: "Cast thy care upon God; for He careth for thee. Hold fast, hold fast." ● Joseph Addison's hymn, "When All Thy Mercies, O My God," first appeared in *The Spectator* in London on August 9, 1712, at the end of an essay on the subject of gratitude. ● Today is the birthday, in 1788, of America's first foreign missionary, Adoniram Judson. It's also the birthday, in 1813, of Christian Henry Bateman, best known for his enduring hymn, "Come, Christians, Join to Sing." ● Cyrus Field, a devout Christian businessman, worked hard to connect America and Europe by the first transoceanic telegraph cable. The effort had repeatedly failed, but Field believed that God wanted him to keep trying and to succeed. On August 9, 1866, aboard the Great Eastern, he found and repaired the break in the cable, and the two continents were linked. ● On August 9, 1974, Richard Nixon resigned from office, and Gerald Ford was sworn in as America's thirty-eighth president.

WORSHIP HELPS

Call to Worship

"Come, Christians, join to sing Alleluia! Amen!"
—CHRISTIAN H. BATEMAN, born on this day in 1813

Offertory Scripture Reading

Now a man came up to Jesus and asked, "Teacher, what good thing must I do to get eternal life?" "Why do you ask me about what is good?" Jesus replied. "There is only One who is good. If you want to enter life, obey the commandments." "Which ones?" the man inquired. Jesus replied, " 'Do not murder, do not commit adultery, do not steal, do not give false testimony, honor your

Continued on the next page

father and mother,' and 'love your neighbor as yourself.'" "All these I have kept," the young man said. "What do I still lack?" Jesus answered, "If you want to be perfect, go, sell your possessions and give to the poor, and you will have treasure in heaven. Then come, follow me." When the young man heard this, he went away sad, because he had great wealth. Then Jesus said to his disciples, "I tell you the truth, it is hard for a rich man to enter the kingdom of heaven. Again I tell you, it is easier for a camel to go through the eye of a needle than for a rich man to enter the kingdom of God." When the disciples heard this, they were greatly astonished and asked, "Who then can be saved?" Jesus looked at them and said, "With man this is impossible, but with God all things are possible" (Matt. 19:16–26 NIV).

Benediction

> When on Thy glorious works we gaze,
> There Thee we fain would see;
> Our gladness in their beauty raise,
> Our God, in joy to Thee!
> O everywhere, O every day,
> Thy grace is still outpoured;
> We work, we watch, we strive, we pray;
> Behold Thy seekers, Lord!
> —THOMAS G. HILL, from "Not
> Only when Ascends the Song,"
> 1848

Additional Sermons and Lesson Ideas

Painless Giving
Date preached:
By Pastor Al Detter

SCRIPTURE: 2 Corinthians 8:1–7

INTRODUCTION: What do you feel when you give? Do you feel joy like the Macedonians or pain?

1. Painless Giving Happens After We Experience the Deep Grace of God (vv. 1–2).
2. Painless Giving Happens When We Realize We Have the Financial Ability to Do It (v. 3).
3. Painless Giving Happens When We Believe in the Cause (v. 4).
4. Painless Giving Happens When We First Give Something More Valuable Than Our Money, Ourselves, to God (v. 5).

CONCLUSION: In verses 6 and 7, Paul encouraged the Corinthians to make their giving consistent with the way they lived the rest of their lives. Paul also sent Titus to help get them started. Some of us live well, learn well, and love well and yet when it comes to giving, we falter. Instead, "excel in this grace of giving."

The Influence and Integrity of Isaac
Date preached:
By Dr. Melvin Worthington

SCRIPTURE: Genesis 27–28

INTRODUCTION: Genesis 27 records God's providence in controlling the affairs of men and protecting the kingdom of God. Isaac's legacy is one which should encourage every believer.

1. Isaac's Blessing (Gen. 27–28). Isaac's diminishing stature (Gen. 27:1–4), the designed scheme (Gen. 27:5–17), the deceptive son (Gen. 27:18–29), the disappointed son (Gen. 27:30–40), and the despising son (Gen. 27:45).
2. Isaac's Belief (Heb. 11:20). Isaac had the proper attitude regarding his family focus, faith, future, and failures.
3. Isaac's Behavior (Gen. 21–28). The overall bent of Isaac's life was one of loyalty in his place, to his posterity, and as a picture of Christ.

CONCLUSION: Isaac serves as a beacon for believers who would serve God loyally. There are no insignificant Christians; we all have a role in God's work. Every believer has significance in God's eyes.

Study and Power
Dr. Edwards A. Park

Dr. Edwards Park was one of America's best-known theologians when he died at his home in Massachusetts at the age of ninety-one. For over fifty-five years, he labored at Andover Seminary, teaching theology and sacred rhetoric from 1847 to 1881. He also served as the editor of *Bibliotheca Sacra* from 1851 to 1884, and also edited *The Sabbath Hymn Book,* which reached a circulation of over 100,000 copies. He also served as President of the Board of Trustees of Abbott Academy for over thirty years. Perhaps his greatest claim to fame was his marriage to the great-granddaughter of Jonathan Edwards, a man he greatly admired. He died in 1900, but this essay is still as fresh as the day it was first spoken:

> The vigor of mind and heart which is gained from doctrinal investigation is the mainspring of effective preaching. The eloquence of the pulpit is eloquence of thought. Warmth of emotion in the pulpit will not diffuse itself through the pews, unless the great object of that emotion be distinctly and vividly exhibited; and the preacher cannot exhibit what he does not fully possess. He cannot write with interest and zeal, nor can he with earnestness and energy deliver what he has written, unless he can understand and feel the great bearings of his theme.
>
> He may goad up his animal susceptibilities to an immense excitement; he may saw the air, and distort his visage, and beat the pulpit cushion, and stamp with his foot, and thunder with his voice; but this is not the animation which the hearers wish or want.
>
> Rational, educated minds will smile at his nervous agitation and vapid remark, and will demand the excitement which is kindled by thought, and will sympathize profitably with none but intelligent emotion.
>
> When he is preaching on eternity, on the judgment, on the Divine justice in eternal retributions, it will be easy

to distinguish between his antic gestures or vehement contortions of face and that serious, solemn eloquence, which would be breathed into him by the deep study of those doctrines.

Nothing but such deep study can impart the true sober energy, the considerate reasonable excitement, which, wherever seen, is power. The speaker may practice before his mirror, and learn to raise his hand gracefully, and explode vowels forcibly, but, without intense thought on the matter of his discourses, all the rules in the world will never make him eloquent; and with this intense thought awakening appropriate emotion, he will be eloquent without a single other rule.

Other rules are useful; they make the body. This rule is essential; it makes the soul. The soul will live without the body; the body is putrefaction without the soul; both together make the man.

AUGUST 16, 2009

SUGGESTED SERMON

Faith in the Marketplace

Date preached:

By Rev. Peter Grainger

Scripture: 1 Corinthians 10:14–11:1, especially 10:31
Therefore, whether you eat or drink, or whatever you do, do all to the glory of God.

Introduction: Temptation in our society is not hard to come by. Often, whether through work, school, or social settings, we find ourselves in questionable situations. When should we flee to save ourselves from temptation and when should we endure and shine our light as Christ's witnesses in dark situations? We find some of the answers in the New Testament letter of 1 Corinthians.

1. **When to Run (10:14–22).** One of the big issues for the Christians in Corinth related to attendance at the many temples that filled the city of Corinth. The temples were not only places of worship but also acted as the first century equivalent of social and business clubs and restaurants. The meat served there had been sacrificed by the priest to the god of that temple and the feasts that followed often led to an excess of drinking and immorality. So, what was a Christian to do? The only possible response for "wise men" is to run. He gives his reasons for this ruling, why idolatry is to be avoided at all costs, in the verses that follow:

    A. **Divided Allegiance (10:16–18).** How can a person who claims to worship Christ as Lord also join in worship services to some idol? How can a person who drinks from the cup of wine which represents the death of the Lord Jesus also drink to the honor of some god-substitute or idol? How can a Christian share bread with other Christians as a sign of their unity in Christ and also share with non-Christians in the worship of another so-called god? Paul explains this should not be so!

    B. **Demonic Influence (10:19–21).** The fact that the idols worshiped in the temples in Corinth are not real gods at all does not mean that worshiping them is harmless. Demons (maligned spiritual entities) use them as a front to gain a foothold in the lives of idol-worshipers, even though these people may not be aware of their activity or existence.

C. **Divine Jealousy (10:22).** "Or do we provoke the Lord to jealousy? Are we stronger than He?" The obvious answer is that we absolutely should not provoke the Lord who is far greater than we. This is a stern warning that putting ourselves in these situations is gravely dangerous.

2. **When to Ask No Questions (10:22–33).** Paul addresses the issue of eating meat sacrificed to idols. At the Corinthian meat market, there was a good chance that purchased meat had also come from a sacrifice offered in the temple, for the priests often sold excess sacrificial meat. Was it safe for a Christian to eat this meat? Paul's answer is to go ahead and ask no questions. However, he adds a caveat: "All things are lawful for me, but not all things are helpful; all things are lawful for me, but not all things edify" (v. 23). My choice should be based not just on what suits me but based on what is:

A. **For the Good of Others (10:24).** A Christian might choose to forgo his legitimate rights such as eating anything set before him rather than give unnecessary offense to a non-Christian who is present. Paul says this is not a matter of conscience for him and no one should denounce him for something that he has accepted as a gift from God.

B. **For the Glory of God (10:31–33).** The most important factor of all is the glory of God—does what I do honor and please God? What is it that most dishonors God and fails to give Him glory? It's that all human beings have sinned and fall short of His glory (Rom. 3:23). What brings glory to God? When sinners are saved—when people are put right with God through Jesus and begin to live in a way that glorifies Him. The governing factor in every decision should be to follow that course of action which will be most likely to lead to others becoming Christians and to avoid any action which might cause them to stumble.

Conclusion (11:1): In a society where people stand on their rights and put what suits me first, Christians are called to be different. Paul tells us how: "Imitate me, just as I also imitate Christ" (11:1). Will my actions and behavior cause a non-Christian to stumble or help towards their salvation?

STATS, STORIES, AND MORE

More from Rev. Peter Grainger

Some time ago, something very unusual happened: a Christian was headline news in the media. Even more unusual was the fact that he was from Scotland and from a Baptist Church. Perhaps most unusual of all, it was good news and not bad news about a Christian. In the words of the BBC: "Cameron Stout, a thirty-two-year-old religious fish trader from Orkney has won this year's Big Brother Reality TV Show."

I must confess that, when I heard at the start of the show that a committed Christian (vouched for by none other than John Percival!) was one of the occupants of the Big Brother House, I doubted his wisdom in putting himself in such an environment and under such a spotlight. I certainly didn't think (and neither did Cameron) that he had any chance of winning if he remained true to his Christian convictions. However, despite all the temptations that were placed before him, he was able—firmly yet graciously—to state not only what he believed ("to talk the talk") but also to practice what he preached ("to walk the walk").

Very few of us would, I suspect, be prepared to place ourselves under the spotlight in the Big Brother House. Yet every follower of Christ is under the spotlight as people look at us and our lifestyle and choices. It is a cop-out to say, "Don't follow my example, follow Christ." Only when we do that, however poorly (and admit when we get it wrong), are others likely to be saved. The greatest achievement is not to win Big Brother but to win someone for Christ.

APPROPRIATE HYMNS AND SONGS

"Shine on Us," Michael W. Smith, 1996 Milene Music, Inc. and Deer Valley Music.

"The Solid Rock," Edward Mote, Public Domain.

"How Can I Keep from Singing," Chris Tomlin, Matt Redman & Ed Cash, 2006 Worshiptogether.com Songs/sixsteps Music/Alletrop Music/ ThankYou Music.

"Fill Me Now," Michael Hansen & Christina Peppin, 2005 Mercy/Vineyard Publishing.

"Faith Is the Victory," John H. Yates, Public Domain.

FOR THE BULLETIN

Swedish Lutheran missionary John Campanius left Stockholm on August 16, 1642, for America, landing in Delaware the following February 15. For several years, he helped establish Lutheran preaching points in the colonies and among the Lenape Indians. In 1648, he was relieved by other missionaries and returned to Sweden where he pastored until his death in 1683. ● August 16, 1661 marks the death of popular British churchman and historian, Thomas Fuller, who once said, "God's children are immortal while their Father has anything for them to do on earth." ● On August 16, 1722, Count Nikolaus Ludwig von Zinzendorf and Countess Erdmuth Dorothea von Reuss were engaged to be married, forming a partnership that helped establish the Moravian community Herrnhut and the golden era of Moravian missions. ● Rev. Charles Spurgeon, twenty-five, was frustrated that there was no building large enough in London to hold the crowds wanting to hear about Jesus from his lips. The New Park Street Church decided to build a much larger tabernacle. The cornerstone was laid on August 16, 1859, and it opened in May of 1861, with seating for 6,500 people. Here Spurgeon preached regularly until shortly before his death in 1892. ● On the very same day, August 16, 1859, a baby was born in Sweden to a humble carpenter and his wife, and named Carl Gustaf Boberg. He became a Christian at age nineteen and went on to write a number of hymns, including "O Store Gud"—"How Great Thou Art." ● Abraham Lincoln signed the Emancipation Proclamation on this day in 1863. ● Several notable people have died on this day. Evangelist Charles Finney died on this day in 1877. Baseball legend Babe Ruth died on this day in 1948, at the age of fifty-three. And today is the anniversary of the death in 1977 of Elvis Presley at the age of forty-two.

WORSHIP HELPS

Call to Worship
Worthy is the Lamb, who was slain, to receive power and wealth and wisdom and strength and honor and glory and praise" (Rev. 5:12)!

Responsive Reading
Leader: Bless the LORD, O my soul! O LORD my God, You are very great; You are clothed with honor and majesty, who cover Yourself with light as with a garment, who stretch out the heavens like a curtain (Ps. 104:1–2). *Continued on the next page*

WORSHIP HELPS—*Continued*

Congregation: He lays the beams of His upper chambers on the waters, who makes the clouds His chariot, who walks on the wings of the wind (Ps. 104:3).

Leader: You covered it with the deep as with a garment; the waters stood above the mountains. At Your rebuke they fled; at the voice of Your thunder they hastened away. You have set a boundary that they may not pass over, that they may not return to cover the earth (Ps. 104:6–7, 9).

Congregation: He sends the springs into the valleys; they flow among the hills. They give drink to every beast of the field . . . By them the birds of the heavens have their home; they sing among the branches. He waters the hills from His upper chambers . . . (Ps. 104:10–11a, 12–13a).

Leader: The earth is satisfied with the fruit of Your works. O LORD, how manifold are Your works! In wisdom You have made them all. The earth is full of Your possessions. These all wait for You . . . You open Your hand, they are filled with good (Ps. 104:13b, 24, 27a, 28b).

Congregation: May the glory of the LORD endure forever; may the LORD rejoice in His works. He looks on the earth, and it trembles; He touches the hills, and they smoke (Ps. 104:31–32).

All: I will sing to the LORD as long as I live; I will sing praise to my God while I have my being. Bless the LORD, O my soul! Praise the LORD (Ps. 104:33, 35b)!

Additional Sermons and Lesson Ideas

The Great Rule of Life
Date preached:

By Rev. Billie Friel

SCRIPTURE: 1 Corinthians 10:31

INTRODUCTION: "Do all for the glory of God" should become our rule of life for the following reasons:

1. Simplifies Life. When we are faced with a choice, we should simply ask the question "Will this glorify God?" This greatly simplifies our life.
2. Satisfies Life. Only living for the glory of God brings genuine satisfaction in life. Live for God's holy purpose.
3. Saturates Life. We should not compartmentalize our life into spiritual and secular. Everything we do should glorify God, including the elemental tasks of eating and drinking.
4. Saves Life. Only what is done for the glory of God will be rewarded in eternity. Every other impetus is a waste and a loss.

CONCLUSION: Jesus lived to glory His Father (John 17:4). Let us live so our "good works glorify our Father which is in heaven" (Matt. 5:16).

Investing Wisely
Date preached:

By Dr. Larry Osborne

SCRIPTURE: Matthew 6:19–24

INTRODUCTION: As believers, our perspective should be eternal and our treasure in heaven.

1. It Is Wiser to Invest in Something I Can't Lose, Than Something I Can't Keep (vv. 19–20).
2. My Heart Will Always Follow My Time, Energy, and Sacrifices (v. 21).
3. If I want to Do the Right Thing, I Have to Stay Focused on the Right Thing (vv. 22–23).
4. It Is Impossible to Serve God and Money Equally (v. 24).

CONCLUSION: We often get caught up in the materialism of the world around us. Jesus calls us to be investing in His kingdom. We cannot serve God and materialism. We must allow God to be God and trust Him for both our temporal and eternal needs.

AUGUST 23, 2009

SUGGESTED SERMON

The Battle Line Has Been Drawn

By Pastor Jonathan Falwell

Date preached:

Scripture: Various, especially Ephesians 6:10–11
Finally, my brethren, be strong in the Lord and in the power of His might. Put on the
whole armor of God, that you may be able to stand against the wiles of the devil.

Introduction: As a local congregation, we have certain goals that we're
praying and working towards: lives we want the Lord to change, ministry we ask God to bless, new members we hope to have join our family,
etc. When we talk about those kinds of goals, that type of God-sized
vision, you can rest assured there will be opposition. We have drawn
a line in the sand and we are daring Satan to cross it. My friends, he
wants to stop it! He's willing to go to battle to make that happen. There
are four principles I want to share with you this morning that we must
all understand if we are to win this battle.

1. **The Danger Is Real (Eph. 6:10).** "Finally, my brethren, be strong in
   the Lord and in the power of His might. Put on the whole armor of
   God, that you may be able to stand against the wiles of the devil."
   The word "wiles" is where we get our word "methods." Meaning,
   this is the word for specific tricks, traps, and schemes that Satan
   will use to destroy us. He knows our weaknesses and he knows
   how to get to us, to make us fail in our lives.

2. **The Enemy Is Strong (Eph. 6:12).** "For we do not wrestle against
   flesh and blood, but against principalities, against powers, against
   the rulers of the darkness of this age, against spiritual hosts of
   wickedness in the heavenly places." This teaches us that Satan is
   of a spiritual realm, beyond any human ability. To think that we
   can defeat him by conventional, human means is ridiculous.

3. **Our Protection Is Promised (1 John 4:4).** "You are of God, little
   children, and have overcome them, because He who is in you is
   greater than he who is in the world." It's important to resist the
   enemy's attacks to have *spirit-filled prayer, spirit-filled lives,* and *spirit-
   filled service.* Satan can never move the hand of God but he can

always move the hearts of men if we are not grounded in Christ. Those who believe and trust Him are the ones who can be assured that they can endure and overcome any spiritual attack!

4. **The Victory Is Ours (Eph. 6:10–14).** Four times in this passage, the Bible says the word *stand/withstand.* You would think that if there is a battle, the Bible should have used the words *fight, run,* or *move!* But here, the Bible tells the believer that in the middle of the battle, he should "stand." Be immovable, anchored. James 4:7 echoes this idea: "Therefore submit to God. Resist the devil and he will flee from you." The same Greek word for the word *stand* is also the same Greek word for *resist* or literally, *"stand against* the devil and he will flee from you."

Conclusion and Application:

1. **Salvation.** Friend, if you are here today and you are not saved, you are walking around this earth without any protection from Satan! You need spiritual protection! You need a Savior Jesus Christ.

2. **Baptism.** Have you been baptized? Every time a Christian is baptized it's somewhat like a soldier being commissioned for battle. That is, you're making a public profession, a public statement associating yourself with the triune God of Scripture who endured the wrath of God on your behalf.

3. **Church Membership.** We are committed to equipping our members in the Word of God and discipling them to be a committed Christian who is protected from Satan. If you are looking for a church that sees this as a priority, then I invite you to join our church today.

4. **Sanctification.** How protected are you from Satan's attack? Just ask yourself, how often do you commune with God every day? How often do you ask Him to forgive you and cleanse you and give you His thoughts today?

Wherever you are in your Christian walk, even if it has not yet begun, I ask you today to draw a line in the sand. If you're not a believer, do so through faith in Jesus and repentance from sin. If you are, take your stand with us, your brothers and sisters in Christ, as we go into battle!

STATS, STORIES, AND MORE

More from Pastor Jonathan Falwell
If we read further along in Ephesians 6, you will notice that around verses 15 and 16, you hear about "Shoes of the Gospel of Peace" and the "Shield of Faith." In battle, the soldiers who held the shields were given special shoes to wear. The shields were large: the Greek word for this particular shield is translated "door." Literally, these shields were as heavy as a door.

They would take these doors or shields and stand side by side so as to make a make-shift wall during battle. If you stayed behind these shields during battle, you would be safe. They could not afford any of these soldiers who were assigned to hold these shields to slip and fall down, so they gave them special shoes. We need a powerful army of Christians who are fully committed to going to battle: committed to standing arm in arm, locked together, grounded in the gospel as we face the formidable opponent that is Satan.

Quotes About the Devil's Attacks
- "Should I tell, in how many forms the Devil has assaulted me, and with what subtlety and energy his assaults have been carried on, it would strike my friends with horror."
  —from Cotton Mather's diary
- "There is no neutral ground in the universe; every square inch, every split second, is claimed by God and counter-claimed by Satan. *—C. S. Lewis*
- "At the sign of triumph Satan's host doth flee; / On then, Christian soldiers, on to victory."
  —Sabine Baring-Gould in "Onward, Christian Soldiers."

APPROPRIATE HYMNS AND SONGS

"Firm Foundation," Nancy Gordon & Jamie Harvill, 1994 Integrity's Praise! Music & Integrity's Hosanna! Music.

"Stand Up, Stand Up for Jesus," George Duffield, Public Domain.

"Onward, Christian Soldiers," Sabine Baring-Gould, Public Domain.

"Mighty Is the Power of the Cross," Chris Tomlin, Sean Craig & Jesse Reeves, 2004 Ariose Music/Praise Song Press/Worshiptogether.com Songs/sixsteps Music.

FOR THE BULLETIN

On the night of August 23, 1572, as Catherine de Medici and her son, young King Charles IX, were sequestered in the palace, they issued orders to kill the French Protestants (the Huguenots) in France. Protestant leader Gaspard de Coligny was seized and tortured. Huguenots and their children were dragged into the streets and slain. The sun, rising over Paris on St. Bartholomew's Day, revealed thousands of Protestant corpses. ● August 23, 1683 marks the passing of John Owen, greatest of the Puritan theologians. During his lifetime he published eighty different works, and late in his life he accepted his final pastorate at a church in Leadenhall Street in London. He died at the age of sixty-seven and was buried in Bunhill Fields. ● Today is the birthday, in 1744, of the quaint and popular English pastor, Rowland Hill, a disciple of George Whitefield. Hill preached in London for fifty years. ● The British Parliament passed the Slavery Abolition Act on August 23, 1833, outlawing slavery throughout its empire. On August 1st of the next year, 700,000 slaves were freed. (On August 23, 2007, the International Slavery Museum was opened at the Albert Docks complex in London.) ● Salvation Army worker Charles W. Fry died on this day in 1882. He's the author of the gospel song, "The Lily of the Valley." And the author of "Standing on the Promises," Russell Carter, died on this day in 1928. ● Five SIM (Sudan Interior Mission) missionaries, serving the Lord in the Sudan during World War II, were caught in a bombing raid on this day in 1940, when the Italian Air Force dropped eighty-nine bombs on their mission station. Four of the five were either killed or badly wounded, and only one—Zillah Walsh—was uninjured. ● Corrie ten Boom suffered a serious stroke, one effect of which was that she lost her ability to speak. She was unable to travel or speak after that date, either publicly or to me privately. She died on April 15, 1983, without speaking again following her stroke.

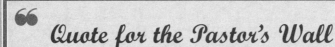

" Quote for the Pastor's Wall

Enthusiasm is like having
two right hands.

—ELBERT HUBBARD

"

Call to Worship

He appeared in a body, was vindicated by the Spirit, was seen by angels, was preached among the nations, was believed on in the world, was taken up in glory (1 Tim. 3:16). Let's join our hearts in worship to this Jesus today!

Reader's Theater

Reader 1: In this world you will have trouble. But take heart! Jesus has overcome the world (from John 16:33 NIV).

Reader 2: Who is it that overcomes the world? Only he who believes that Jesus is the Son of God (1 John 5:5 NIV).

Reader 3: For our struggle is not against flesh and blood, but against the rulers, against the authorities, against the powers of this dark world and against the spiritual forces of evil in the heavenly realms (Eph. 6:12 NIV).

Reader 1: . . . for everyone born of God overcomes the world. This is the victory that has overcome the world, even our faith (1 John 5:4 NIV).

Reader 2: You, dear children, are from God and have overcome them, because the one who is in you is greater than the one who is in the world (1 John 4:4 NIV).

Benediction

Therefore, since we are surrounded by such a great cloud of witnesses, let us throw off everything that hinders and the sin that so easily entangles, and let us run with perseverance the race marked out for us (Heb. 12:1 NIV).

Additional Sermons and Lesson Ideas

The Cost of Discipleship

Date preached:

By Dr. Timothy K. Beougher

SCRIPTURE: Mark 8:31–38

INTRODUCTION: What does it cost to be a follower, a disciple, of Jesus? It seems at times it just costs a Sunday morning and if you're really sacrificial a Wednesday night. But here, Jesus says that it costs you everything.

1. Christ Must Suffer, Die, and Rise Again (vv. 31–33).
2. Deny Yourself (v. 34).
3. Take Up Your Cross (v. 34).
4. Follow Me (v. 34).
5. Lose Your Life (vv. 35–37).
6. Testify of Christ (v. 38).

CONCLUSION: We are not called to comfort and riches and the easy life. We are called to suffering and sacrifice, selflessness and death, and lifelong obedience and proclamation. We are called to follow Christ and to be His witnesses.

The God Who Tests

Date preached:

By Rev. Melvin Tinker

SCRIPTURE: Genesis 22:1–19

INTRODUCTION: What we see here is the ultimate test of a man who loves his God.

1. The God Who Perplexes (vv. 1–2). God after pronouncing His promise now seems to be asking Abraham to forfeit those very promises.
2. The Man Who Obeys (vv. 3–10). Abraham's obedience is immediate and yet tormenting. This is not a callous obedience but a calculated trusting of a faithful God.
3. The Lord Who Provides (vv. 13–19). A ram was sent by God to be sacrificed in Isaac's stead and serves as a picture of Jesus coming as the Lamb to take away the world's sins.

CONCLUSION: It's the Father and the Son together who have agreed on this course of action as being the only course of action to reconcile a sinful world. It cost the Father as much as it did the Son, just as it cost Abraham as well as Isaac. God is faithful and we must give our total obedience to Him who is trustworthy.

The Treasury of Scripture Knowledge

The Bible is its own best commentary, and we often find that the "problem verses" are solved by finding parallel passages that enlighten the subject. I remember the insight I gained when I compared Luke 14:26 ("If anyone comes to Me and does not hate his father and mother . . . he cannot be My disciple") with Matthew 10:37 ("He who loves father or mother more than Me is not worthy of Me").

This principle of comparing Scripture with Scripture makes cross-referencing an indispensable tool. The Bible contains over 31,000 verses, so it's difficult to keep them all in mind all the time. Many reference Bibles provide a few cross-references in the center column; but for generations, one tool has proven essential for sermons for Bible students from the new convert to the seasoned scholar. It's *The Treasury of Scripture Knowledge*.

This book has a fascinating history that harkens back to a man named Thomas Scott, who was born into an English farming family in the mid-1700s in Lincolnshire. He was the tenth of thirteen children. His mother had high hopes for him and sent him off to school to be a surgeon; but he was dismissed for bad conduct and returned home in disgrace like the prodigal son, and he was put to hard manual labor for the next ten years. Growing tired of farm work, he decided to enter the ministry, and at age twenty-five he was ordained as an Anglican priest, although he believed little of what he was required to preach.

It was his correspondence with the far-famed John Newton (author of "Amazing Grace") that changed his life. As the two men became friends, Scott fell under the conviction of his sins and was gloriously transformed in heart. When Newton left his church in Olney for London, Scott took over the church; and then he himself followed Newton to London and became the chaplain for an institution ministering to syphilis sufferers.

It was during this period that Scott began publishing a weekly column of Bible studies. "I had read over the whole Scripture repeatedly," he said, "I trust with constant prayer, and considering how almost every verse might be applied, as if I had been called to preach upon it; I had often thought that I should like to preach through the Bible . . . . While I was in this frame of mind, a proposal was made to me to write notes on the Scriptures, to be published, with the sacred text, in weekly numbers.''

Scott began the project on January 1, 1788, and the first column was published on the following March 22nd. This column ran for 174 weeks, and the strain of it wore Scott out; but his work was well received and later compiled into six volumes under the title *Scott's Commentary on the Whole Bible.*

Years later, and another British preacher, Dr. Reuben Archer Torrey, who gained worldwide fame as a conference speaker, evangelist, and Bible teacher, drew great insight from *Scott's Commentary.* He also discovered the *English Polyglot Bible,* which was published in London by Samuel Bagster and Sons of *Daily Light* fame. This work, too, contained helpful cross references.

Using Scott's Commentary, supplemented by the material from the Polyglot Bible, Dr. R. A. Torrey compiled a massive list of over a half-million references into a single volume called *The Treasure of Scripture Knowledge.*

It became one of the most useful and widely used Bible references of all time. Anyone, young or old, could turn to any verse in the Bible and instantly find a helpful list of cross-references. Bible students could track and trace subjects through the Bible from Genesis to Revelation.

A century later, another man entered the story. In 1955, Jerome H. Smith was attending a high school class during Vacation Bible School at Detroit's Highland Park Baptist Church. His teacher, Miss Ellen Groh, recommended Torrey's *Treasury.* When Jerome later received five dollars as a gift, he rode his bicycle to a nearby Christian bookstore and purchased a copy. Over the years, he poured over this book, tracking down cross-references and comparing Scripture to Scripture, sometimes studying hours at a time with the Bible and the Treasury opened before him. As he found additional references, he jotted them in the corners and margins of the page. *Continued on the next page*

CLASSICS FOR THE PASTOR'S LIBRARY—*Continued*

After thirty years of such study, Smith set out to revise and update the Treasury, but he almost didn't live to finish the job. On March 13, 1986, he was shot in the head by an unknown assailant. Thankfully, he survived the attack and was soon back at work on the project, using his long convalescence to make a more thorough revision than he had originally planned.

The New Treasury of Scripture Knowledge is by far the most extensive collection of Bible cross-references ever published. Dr. John MacArthur calls it the one book aside from the Bible itself that he most values in his studies.

The Treasury is available free on multiple Web sites, and the New Treasury is easier than ever to use with newly published Bible study software. But if you still like the feeling you get with two great books open on the table in front of you—separated perhaps by a pen and notepad—then I recommend the Scriptures and *the Treasure of Scripture Knowledge*. From Scott to Torrey to Smith, it's been a long time in the making.

AUGUST 30, 2009

SUGGESTED SERMON

The Lord Lives

Date preached:

By Dr. Melvin Worthington

Scripture: Various Resurrection Passages, especially 1 Corinthians 15:1–4, 14

Moreover, brethren, I declare to you the gospel which I preached to you, which also you received and in which you stand, by which also you are saved, if you hold fast that word which I preached to you—unless you believed in vain. For I delivered to you first of all that which I also received: that Christ died for our sins according to the Scriptures, and that He was buried, and that He rose again the third day according to the Scriptures . . . And if Christ is not risen, then our preaching is empty and your faith is also empty.

Introduction: The resurrection of Jesus Christ is indispensable if there is any validity and value to Christianity. Consequently, opponents of Christianity concentrate their attacks against the resurrection of Christ while Christians center their defense upon this essential foundational truth.

1. **The Prediction of Christ's Resurrection (Matt. 12:38–40; 16:21; 17:9, 23; 20:19; 27:63; Mark 8:31; 9:9, 31; Luke 9:22; 18:23; John 2:19–21).** The Gospels focus on the resurrection as the completion of the picture of Jesus Christ. Christ announced, affirmed, and anticipated His resurrection. Had He not risen from the dead, He would have been a deceiver and liar.

2. **The Proofs of the Christ's Resurrection.** The theories proposed by unbelievers to explain the empty tomb suggest that Jesus did not die but swooned and later revived. Others suggest that Christ did not rise bodily from the grave but in spirit. The truth that Christ died, was buried, and on the third day rose from the grave is the topsoil of the New Testament. The Scriptures assert, attest, and authenticate the truth of Christ's resurrection.

   A. **The Appearances Recorded (Matt. 28; Mark 16; Luke 24; John 20–21; Acts 1).** Unique to the Christian faith, there is not one individual who claims special, independent, sole divine revelation (as opposed to Islam, Mormonism, etc.). On the contrary, the revelation of Jesus' resurrected body was one shared by many witnesses!

B. **The Apostolic Reminders (Acts 2:22–36; 3:12–18; 1 Cor. 15:1–34; Eph. 1:20–23).** The theme of apostolic preaching was the resurrection of Christ. They were conscious, convinced, consumed, and controlled by the truth of the resurrection.

C. **The Almighty's Revelation.** God's Word declares that Jesus Christ rose from the grave. The only proper explanation of Christianity is the resurrection of Christ. Christianity welcomes all possible sifting and testing by those who honestly desire to arrive at the truth. If they will give proper attention to all the facts and factors involved, we believe they will come to the conclusion expressed years ago by Archbishop of Armagh, that the resurrection is the rock from which all the hammers of criticism have never chipped a single fragment. The eternal truth (God's Word), the empty tomb (God's witness), and the effective testimony (God's work), declare that Jesus Christ was raised from the dead.

3. **The Provisions of Christ's Resurrection (1 Cor. 15; Rom. 1:4).** The resurrection of Christ *attests* His deity (Rom. 1:4) and *authenticates* that He was the preexistent Word (John 1:1–5). The resurrection *assures* us of the atoning character of His death and His divine exaltation (Rom. 1:4). The gospel includes a testimony to the resurrection features, thereby providing to the heavens the assurance of divine redemption (Rom. 4:25; 1 Cor. 15:1–4).

4. **The Pledge of Christ's Resurrection (1 Cor. 15; 2 Cor. 5).** Christ's resurrection assures us that we will be resurrected. The consummation of our redemption will be our glorious resurrection body. This gives us a glorious hope for the future, but also a warning. Those who believe in the resurrection will experience a resurrection unto life. Those who dismiss the resurrection as false, as a peripheral doctrine, or as anything other than physical and bodily will find themselves experiencing a very different resurrection: one that ends in eternal punishment.

Conclusion: Without the resurrection of Christ, Christianity is reduced to the level of just another religion. The eternal truth from the empty tomb is that our Lord lives. One day we shall behold Him and be like Him. John summed it up when he declared, "Beloved, now we are children of God; and it has not yet been revealed what we shall be, but we know that when He is revealed, we shall be like Him, for we shall see Him as He is" (1 John 3:2).

STATS, STORIES, AND MORE

Easter Is Coming

During morning worship on Palm Sunday, 1994, a tornado struck the Goshen United Methodist Church in Piedmont, Alabama. It happened during a dramatic presentation. The electricity failed, and the congregation was trying to get along without its sound system. A window broke, people screamed, and the building exploded, injuring scores of members and killing twenty. Among the fatalities was Hannah Clem, four-year-old daughter of Pastor Kelly Clem.

The night after the tragedy, Kelly was trying to sleep, tossing and turning through the pain of her own injuries. An unusual dream came to her. She saw herself trying to lift bricks and toss them aside, clearing away rubble, trying to rescue the victims. She kept doing the same thing over and over. Everything was gray and dull. But as her dream progressed, she stepped back from the scene and saw right in the spot where Hannah had been buried, children, dressed in beautiful, bright colors. They seemed oblivious to the onlookers, and were playing and laughing with each other. They were standing on grass of the greenest green. When Kelly awoke, a peace settled over her and strengthened her for the funerals ahead.

The next day, a reporter asked Kelly if the disaster had shattered her faith. "It hasn't shattered my faith," she replied. "I'm holding on to my faith. It's holding me. All of the people of Goshen are holding on to each other, along with the hope they will be able to rebuild. Easter is coming."[1]

APPROPRIATE HYMNS AND SONGS

"My Redeemer Lives," Reuben Morgan, 1998 Reuben Morgan/Hillsongs Publishing.

"One Day," J. Wilbur Chapman, Public Domain.

"He Lives," Alfred H. Ackley, 1933 by Homer A. Rodeheaver. Renewed 1961 by Rodeheaver Company.

"Alive Forever, Amen," Travis Cotrell, David Moffitt & Sue C. Smith, 2003 First Hand Revelation Music/Integrity's Hosanna! Music/CCTB Music and New Spring Publishing.

---

[1]Adapted from Dale Clem, "Winds of Fury, Glimpses of Grace," *Christian Reader,* May/June 1998, 88–100.

FOR THE BULLETIN

Today marks the death of Pope Alexander III (born Rolando Bandinelli). He was the first pope to focus attention of missionary activities east of the Baltic Sea. In March of 1179, he also convened the Third Council of the Lateran, which passed a number of laws designed to improve the workings of the church. He is most remembered, however, as the pope who humbled England's Henry II in the affair of the murder of Thomas Becket in 1170. ● The martyrdom of missionaries and nationalist Christians in China during the Boxer Rebellion is a story that should never be forgotten. The Chinese government issued a proclamation by imperial command to exterminate the Christian faith and kill all "foreign devils" (missionaries). In the summer of 1900, 184 foreign missionaries and missionary children were murdered, with most of the causalities occurring in the Shansi Province in the north. Scores of missionaries were hidden by Chinese Christians, among them Willie Peat, his wife Helen, two daughters, and two other single missionaries. For three weeks they were hidden in caves in the region, and in a letter smuggled out of the cave, one of the single missionaries, Edith Dobson, a nurse, wrote, "We know naught can come to us without His permission. So we have no need to be troubled: it is not in my nature to fear physical harm, but I trust, if it comes, His grace will be all sufficient." As they were about to be captured, Willie had just enough time to write a final note to his mother: "The soldiers are just on us," he wrote, "and I have only time to say 'Good-bye' to you all. We can only now be sorry for you . . . . Good-bye! At longest it is only 'til He comes." They were slain on August 30, 1900.

Kid's Talk

Ask Sunday school teachers a week or so previous to this Kid's Talk to ask their students a few questions about the resurrection of Christ. Some ideas are: How many days was Jesus in the grave before He rose from the dead? Did anyone see Jesus after He rose from the dead? Why do you think Jesus rose from the dead? Take a sampling of responses to read, but keep names anonymous. Inevitably, some of the responses will be right on and others will not. Use this occasion to remind your congregation how important it is to read, to teach, and to constantly talk to our children about that which validates our faith: the resurrection of Jesus.

WORSHIP HELPS

Call to Worship
I will exalt you, my God the King; I will praise your name for ever and ever. Every day I will praise you and extol your name for ever and ever (Ps. 145:1–2 NIV).

Scripture Reading
So then, just as you received Christ Jesus as Lord, continue to live in him, rooted and built up in him, strengthened in the faith as you were taught, and overflowing with thankfulness. See to it that no one takes you captive through hollow and deceptive philosophy, which depends on human tradition and the basic principles of this world rather than on Christ. For in Christ all the fullness of the Deity lives in bodily form, and you have been given fullness in Christ, who is the head over every power and authority. In him you were also circumcised, in the putting off of the sinful nature, not with a circumcision done by the hands of men but with the circumcision done by Christ, having been buried with him in baptism and raised with him through your faith in the power of God, who raised him from the dead (Col. 2:6–12 NIV).

Benediction
If we died with him, we will also live with him; if we endure, we will also reign with him. If we disown him, he will also disown us; if we are faithless, he will remain faithful, for he cannot disown himself (2 Tim. 2:11–13 NIV).

Additional Sermons and Lesson Ideas

Stop Fighting and Start Building
By Dr. Larry Osborne

Date preached:

SCRIPTURE: 1 Corinthians 3:1–23

INTRODUCTION: We should grow up, get over our petty differences, and recognize that Christ is our foundation.

1. Stuck in Immaturity (vv. 1–4). Believers should grow in Christ rather than get bogged down in jealousy and fighting.
2. Why Fighting and Dividing Is so Stupid (vv. 5–11). Jesus Christ is the foundation for new life and the only name that matters; the name to be unified under.
3. God's Standard of Judgment (vv. 12–23). God judges us based on our faith in Christ. We are of Christ and Christ is of God, and so all things are ours.

CONCLUSION: It is easy for us to quibble over minor (and major) differences, but it is important to remember that we are all one in Christ. God is interested in what is being built upon Christ's foundation and whether it will last.

Suffering: A Survival Guide
By Pastor Al Detter

Date preached:

SCRIPTURE: 1 Peter 3:13–22

INTRODUCTION: Everyone experiences suffering, but how can we survive it?

1. Remind Yourself That God Blesses People Who Suffer for Doing What's Right (v. 14a).
2. Fear Christ Rather Than People (vv. 14b–15a).
3. Be Ready to Explain Why Your Faith Sustains You During Times of Suffering (v. 15b).
4. Keep a Good Conscience Before God in Difficult Times (vv. 16–17).
5. Realize That Your Suffering Benefits Others (vv. 18–21).
6. Believe That Righteous Suffering Now Will Result in Your Glorious Exaltation in Heaven (v. 22).

CONCLUSION: Suffering is unavoidable in life. But, when we follow God's Word, we will join the suffering company of the ages who discovered God's comfort.

BAPTISM SERMON

Saved from Wrath

Date preached:

By Joshua D. Rowe

Scripture: 1 Peter 3:18–22; 1 Corinthians 10:1–2; Matthew 12:39–40, especially
1 Peter 3:21 (NIV)
". . . this water symbolizes baptism that now saves you also—not the removal of dirt from the body but the pledge of a good conscience toward God. It saves you by the resurrection of Jesus Christ."

Introduction: The wonderful Hymn "Rock of Ages" asks Jesus to "be of sin the double cure: save from wrath and make me pure." When we consider baptism, I'm afraid we often neglect half of this "double cure." Most understand baptism, rightly, to be symbolic of our purification from sin through the death, burial, and resurrection of Christ. However, we often neglect the second truth; baptism is also a symbol of the wrath of God that Jesus came through on our behalf through His death, burial, and resurrection.

1. **Water: The Symbolic Element of Wrath.** In the creation account, the Spirit of God was hovering over the waters (Gen. 1:2). Scripture tells us that everything was formed out of water (2 Pet. 3:5). After the Fall, however, water shifted from being a creative element to become an element of wrath, chaos, and destruction. God destroyed the earth with water (Gen. 6–7; 2 Pet. 3:6). The sea became the home to the twisting serpent (Is. 27:1). In Revelation 13, the beast comes up out of the sea. In the new heaven and new earth, there will be no more sea (Rev. 21:1). All of these Scriptures (and many more) point to the notion that, after the Fall, water became a chaotic element of wrath and judgment.

2. **Jesus: The One Who Saves Us from Wrath.** Three historic accounts help us to understand how baptism relates to our union with Christ as He has secured our passage safely through God's wrath to new life in Him:

    A. **Noah (Gen. 6–7; 1 Pet. 3:18–22).** Peter teaches us, ". . . in the days of Noah while the ark was being built. In it only a few people, eight in all, were saved through water, and this water symbolizes baptism that now saves you also—not the removal of dirt from the body but the pledge of a good conscience toward God. It saves you by the resurrection of Jesus Christ . . ." (1 Pet. 3:20–21 NIV). The floodwaters of God's judgment rained down and wiped out all inhabitants of the earth—except for Noah and his family (Gen. 6–7). They were able to come safely through the judgment of God. Peter teaches us this is symbolic for our union with Christ—that we, too, come through God's judgment safely, but only by the resurrection of Jesus Christ. We undergo God's judgment, but are safely brought through just like Noah through the Flood, since we are hidden with Christ. It's no wonder Peter speaks of this "baptism that now saves you." He doesn't suggest that baptismal water is itself the purifying or saving agent; baptism is symbolic for the baptism we undergo through the death, burial, and resurrection of Christ.

B. **Israel (Ex. 14; 1 Cor. 10:1–2).** Paul gives another historic reference, "Moreover, brethren, I do not want you to be unaware that all our fathers were under the cloud, all passed through the sea, all were baptized into Moses in the cloud and in the sea" (1 Cor. 10:1–2). Again God's judgment comes through water in Exodus 14. The Egyptians were seeking to return Israel to captivity despite God's miracles and wonders. God held back the waters of His judgment for His chosen people Israel, but when the evil ones pursued, God released the full force of His wrath, drowning the Egyptian armies. Paul speaks of the Israelites' Red Sea experience as a baptism: they were safely brought through the judgment of God. In the same way, in Jesus' death, burial, and resurrection, He has become God's chosen One. In Him, we, too, can safely pass through God's judgment as His chosen people. That's what being baptized is all about—symbolizing the incredible act of Christ, proclaiming our union with Him and dependence on Him to escape God's wrath.

C. **Jonah (Jon. 1:17–2:10; Matt. 12:39–40).** Jesus teaches us, "An evil and adulterous generation seeks after a sign, and no sign will be given to it except the sign of the prophet Jonah. For as Jonah was three days and three nights in the belly of the great fish, so will the Son of Man be three days and three nights in the heart of the earth" (Matt. 12:39–40). As Jonah attempted to run from God, he and his seafaring mates experienced God's fury through water. A great storm threatened to drown everyone and ultimately Jonah had to be thrown overboard to appease God's wrath. He was swallowed whole by a great fish and for three days was underwater, encased in the fish's stomach as if he were boxed into a casket—the smells, the darkness, the confinement all symbolizing death. Yet, after three days, he was spit onto dry land, safely rescued from the wrath of God (Jon. 1:17–2:10). This is the sign Jesus said He would fulfill in Matthew 12:39–40. He fulfilled this sign as He suffered God's wrath, underwent judgment for our sins on the cross, was encased in death for three days, and was raised from the grave, vindicated as the chosen One of God. Our physical baptism reflects this amazing gospel.

Conclusion: God is angry because of our sins. Only Jesus can secure our way through His wrath to restore us to a right relationship with God. Have you put your trust completely in Jesus Christ to save you from God's fury? If so, have you been baptized? Jesus commands it (Matt. 28:16ff), and for good reason! Throughout history, God has repeatedly given us examples of how He makes a way to escape His wrath—these all ultimately point to Jesus. That's why we're commanded to physically go through the symbolic act of baptism; it points to Jesus. If Jesus offers to save you from wrath, to purify you from sin, and to restore you to God, why would you reject Him as your Lord and Savior? If Jesus commands you to display an outward sign of this salvation by being baptized; why would you delay?

SEPTEMBER 6, 2009

Doing First Things First

Date preached:

By Dr. David Jeremiah

Scripture: 1 Timothy 4:7
But reject profane and old wives' fables, and exercise yourself toward godliness.

Introduction: In his book, *First Things First,* Stephen Covey employs two images to emphasize living by priorities—a clock and a compass. The clock represents our daily commitments, appointments, schedules, and activities. The compass represents our vision, values, principals, conscience, and direction.[1] For most of us, there's a gap between the two. We say we want live by certain priorities, but that isn't really reflected in our everyday agenda. Take daily Bible reading for example. Nothing's more important for shaping our moral and social behavior, yet only 18 percent of all of us read the Bible daily, according to surveys (see Ezra 7:10 and Acts 17:11). In 1 Timothy 4:7, the word "exercise" is the word "gymnatsio," from which we get "gymnasium." The key to closing the gap between the clock and the compass is spiritual discipline. Along these lines, I'd like to ask four questions today.

1. **Are We Prepared to Respond to the Challenge of Change?** No one ever accomplished a goal by simply writing it down, as important as that may be. Whenever we determine by the grace of God to change something in our lives, we face an incredible war with inertia. We have to take the responsibility and align our clocks with our compasses.

2. **Are We Prepared for the Resistance of Our Spiritual Adversary?** If you're going to make a spiritual goal, hang on, friends! You are going to have some resistance. The devil will do everything he can to keep it from happening (see Eph. 6:12). Before you make new goals in the spiritual realm, understand that you're walking into enemy territory, and you must put on the whole armor of God.

---

[1] Stephen Covey, A. Roger Merrill, Rebecca R. Merrill, *First Things First: To Live, To Love, To Learn, To Leave a Legacy,* (New York: Simon & Schuster, 1994), pp. 19–20.

3. **Are We Prepared to Replace the Urgent with the Important?** "Urgency Addiction" is the self-destructive behavior that temporarily fills the void created by unmet needs. We're masters at responding to urgent things, but do we know the difference between the urgent and the important? The more urgency we have in our lives the less importance we usually have. Let me tell you out of the tenderness of my own heart, you have to be ruthless in pushing some of the urgent things away to create an environment for the important. If you don't do that, you'll never succeed in being the kind of person God wants you to be. There's no way to be holy except to take time for it.

4. **Are We Prepared to Record Our Progress in a Journal?** I haven't been doing this for too long, so I am not an expert at it, but I want to tell you, it's an effective way of tracking activity. Get a book, put the date at the top of each page, and every day take a few moments, whatever your goal is, and jot down both your successes and your failures. Plato said that the unexamined life is not worth living. Keeping a personal journal empowers you to see and improve, on a day-by-day basis, the way you're developing and using your endowments.

Conclusion: Covey tells of a professor who reached under the table and pulled out a wide-mouth gallon and filled it with rocks. When the class thought it was full, he dumped some smaller gravels in the jar and shook it so the gravel went into the smaller spaces. Then, when the class thought it was full, he poured in some sand. Then came a pitcher of water. Asking the class for the point of the experiment, some of them said, "Well, we can always fit more into our lives." But the professor said, "No, the point is this. If I hadn't put the big rocks in first, I wouldn't have gotten them in at all." Boy, does that speak to my heart! I almost want to go home, take five rocks, write my priorities on them, and remind myself everyday that the big rocks have to go into the jar first. Let's all say it again and again and again: The main thing is to keep the main thing the main thing. Let's all live with the first things first and exercise ourselves unto godliness.

STATS, STORIES, AND MORE

More from Dr. David Jeremiah
I recently read the journal of Jim Elliott, the missionary killed by the Auca Indians. Two weeks before he was killed he entered this in his diary: "In studying Spanish, I left off English Bible reading, and my devotional reading pattern was broken. I have never restored it. Translation and preparation for daily Bible lessons is not sufficient to empower my soul. Prayer as a single man was difficult, I remember, because my mind always reverted to Betty. Now it's too hard to get out of bed in the morning. I have made resolutions on this score before now but not followed them up. Tomorrow it's to be—dressed by 6:00 A.M. and study in the Epistles before breakfast. So help me, God." I took great encouragement from that! Here is a man we all revere as a great stalwart of the faith, one of the greatest missionaries who ever lived. Two weeks before he died he was struggling with the fact that he'd been spending all his time reading Spanish and not getting food for his own soul out of the English Bible, and he said by the grace of God he would start all over again tomorrow at 6:00 A.M., and he wrote it in his journal.

Dr. R. C. Sproul said it painfully well: "Here then is the real problem of our negligence. We fail in our duty to study God's Word, not so much because it is difficult to understand, not so much because it is dull and boring, but because it is work. Our problem is not a lack of intelligence or a lack of passion. Our problem is that we are lazy."[2]

APPROPRIATE HYMNS AND SONGS

"Sweeter," Israel Houghton, Meleasa Houghton & Cindy Cruse-Ratcliff, 2003 Integrity's Praise! Music, Lakewood Ministries Music and My Other Publishing Company.

"Still," Reuben Morgan, 2002 Reuben Morgan/Hillsong Publishing.

"We Fall Down," Chris Tomlin, 1998 Worshiptogether.com Songs.

"How Great Thou Art," Carl Boberg; Trans. by Stuart K. Hine, 1953 Stuart K. Hine: 1955 Manna Music.

"Wonderful Grace of Jesus," Haldor Lillenas, 1946 Hope Publishing Company.

[2]Dr. R. C. Sproul, *Knowing Scripture* (Downers Grove, IL: InterVarsity Press) 17.

FOR THE BULLETIN

Georg Blaurock, an Anabaptist leader in Geneva and the first person in the modern era to be baptized upon profession of faith rather than in infancy, was arrested on September 6, 1529, and burned at the stake. ● On September 6, 1620, the *Mayflower* set sail from Plymouth to the New World. ● On this day in 1651, Rev. Obadiah Holmes was whipped at the post in Boston Commons for his Baptist preaching in Puritan New England. ● Today is the birthday, in 1711, of Henry Melchoir Muhlenberg, the German theologian who was sent to America to help establish Lutheran churches in Pennsylvania. He also frequently traveled across the eastern part of the country from New York to Georgia during a forty-five year ministry. He's considered the patriarch of the Lutheran Church in the United States. A larger-than-life statue now stands in Allentown, Pennsylvania, at Muhlenberg College, which is named for him. ● America's first missionary, Adoniram Judson, twenty-four, was sent to India/Burma by the General Association for the Congregationalists in Massachusetts under the direction of the American Board of Foreign Missions. But during the four-month voyage, as Judson and his wife Ann studied the Bible, they became convinced in the importance of believer's baptism. Arriving in India, they were baptized by Rev. William Ward in Calcutta on September 6, 1812. When news reached America, Baptists organized the American Baptist Missionary Union for their support. ● On this day in 1837, Oberlin College in Ohio granted equal status to men and woman, becoming the first college in America to do so. Oberlin was a distinctively Christian school, the purpose of which was "to train teachers and other Christian leaders for the boundless, most-desolate fields of the West."

" Quote for the Pastor's Wall

Any fool can criticize, condemn, and
complain—and most fools do.

—Benjamin Franklin

"

WORSHIP HELPS

Call to Worship

> On this day, the first of days,
> God the Father's name we praise;
> Who, creation's Lord and Spring
> Did the world from darkness bring.
>
> On this day the eternal Son
> Over death His triumph won;
> On this day the Spirit came
> With His gifts of living flame.
>
> O that fervent love today
> May in every heart have sway,
> Teaching us to praise aright
> God, the Source of life and light
> —From *Die Parente Temporum*,
> translated from the Latin by
> HENRY W. BAKER, 1861

Hymn Story: "Dear Lord and Father of Mankind"
John Greenleaf Whittier, a Quaker, was one of America's best-known poets. His best-known hymn, "Dear Lord and Father of Mankind," is adapted from a long narrative poem entitled "The Brewing of Somo." After describing a pagan worship ceremony in which heathen priests drink themselves into stupor trying to have a spiritual experience, Whittier described the true worship that should characterize the people of God. In 1884, a hymnal editor named W. Garrett Horder extracted this portion of "The Brewing of Soma" and adapted it as a Christian hymn that still ranks as one of the finest ever written by an American author. The music usually associated with this hymn is a melody called REST, written by the English organist Frederick Charles Maker.

Additional Sermons and Lesson Ideas

iTell: A Lesson in Evangelism for the iPod Generation

Date preached:

By Pastor Jonathan Falwell

SCRIPTURE: Various

INTRODUCTION: We are charged with the responsibility of telling others about Christ.

    1. Why We Tell (1 Tim. 2:3–4; Luke 11:33).
    2. What We Tell (Rom. 3:23; 6:23; 10:9–10).
    3. How We Tell:
        A. With Knowledge (1 Pet. 3:15a).
        B. With Love (1 Pet. 3:15b).
        C. With Understanding (1 Cor. 1:18).
        D. With Prayer (1 Tim. 2:1–2).
        E. With Your Testimony (Matt. 5:16).
    4. Where We Tell (Luke 14:23).

CONCLUSION: We must go out from this place with a passion to win souls, to see people understand the gospel as we've presented here today, as we present it often in this place.

Rest for the Weary

Date preached:

By Dr. Timothy K. Beougher

SCRIPTURE: Mark 3:13–19

INTRODUCTION: Jesus did four things in His ministry when the overwhelming needs of people began to drain Him:

    1. Get Away (v. 13).
    2. Pray (Luke 6:12).
    3. Share Responsibility with Others (v. 14).
    4. Cultivate Replenishing Relationships (vv. 14–19).

CONCLUSION: If we are to be effective, we must learn to slow down, focus on God, humble ourselves, and seek to build others up.

SEPTEMBER 13, 2009

SUGGESTED SERMON

Life Together

Date preached:

By Dr. Ed Dobson

Scripture: Romans 15:1–14, especially verses 5–6
Now may the God of patience and comfort grant you to be like-minded toward one another, according to Christ Jesus, that you may with one mind and one mouth glorify the God and Father of our Lord Jesus Christ.

Introduction: We often focus on how we are to live our own lives as Christians; perhaps we tend to be too individualistic in that, for Scripture tends to focus more on the body of believers than the individual. Today we're going to look at some of the principles that Paul lays out for us to teach us how to live together as a community of believers.

1. **We Do Not Live to Please Ourselves (v. 1).** If we're to live together from different backgrounds, across generations, bringing different baggage to the family of God, if we really want to live together in unity, then we must understand that our goal as followers of Jesus is not to live our lives to please ourselves. Paul says those who are strong have an obligation and a debt that they owe to those who are weak. Paul reminds us that in the body we're all on a journey. Some are further down the road in spiritual maturity than others, but we're all in the process of continually growing. By the way, none of us have yet arrived; we all need to grow.

2. **We Should Strive for Unity (vv. 5–6).** Do you know where disunity comes in? When you decide to follow somebody other than Jesus and you are brought into conflict. Paul says it's our responsibility to be devoted, unconditional, without reservation, followers of Jesus Christ. Whatever our culture, however we express it, what ultimately matters is that we're followers of the same Person, Jesus Christ. In fact notice what he goes on to say: ". . . be like-minded . . . that you may with one mind *and* one mouth glorify the God and Father of our Lord Jesus Christ" (vv. 5–6). We tend to think that we glorify God when we sing and we certainly ought to. But Paul says when you follow Jesus and I follow Jesus, there's a unity between us that brings glory and honor to God.

3. **We Should Accept Each Other (v. 7).** Accept one another, then, just as Christ accepted you, in order to bring praise to God. How did Jesus accept you? When I was lost, Jesus accepted me totally, without conditions, and Jesus accepts me exactly where I am. Paul says just as Christ accepted you, we are to welcome. Welcome means to embrace, to invite into one's life, to invite into one's circle, to invite into one's family. He says accept one another in the same way that Jesus Christ accepted you.

4. **We Are to Correct Each Other (v. 14).** Spiritual maturity is more than knowing the right stuff. Spiritual maturity is being the right kind of person—full of goodness and complete in knowledge and therefore, verse 14: "able also to admonish one another." When you're full of kindness and you're competent in knowledge, you have a responsibility to instruct, to warn, and to admonish each other. We don't grow in the Lord independently of each other. We need each other and we're responsible for each other. When a brother or a sister begins to wander or to take a wrong turn, we have a responsibility—in gentleness, goodness, but with the truth— to confront, to warn, and to admonish.

5. **We're to Pray for Each Other (vv. 30–33).** "Now I beg you, brethren, through the Lord Jesus Christ, and through the love of the Spirit, that you strive together with me in prayers to God for me . . ." (v. 30). How often have we told another believer "I'll pray for you" only to completely forget within the hour of that promise? How much of your prayer life is devoted to praying for people other than yourself and your immediate family? Brothers and sisters, prayer is the means by which God works in His church. If we neglect to pray for one another, we might as well close our doors.

Conclusion: Growing in Christ cannot happen when we are disconnected from His body of believers. As we have seen, this involves much more than a "get together" once a week. We need to be intentional about our relationships with each other and committed to living out life in the body according to Scripture.

STATS, STORIES, AND MORE

More from Dr. Ed Dobson

My wife and I heard Bill Bright speak at the graduation at Liberty. He was eighty years old, having walked with God a long, long time. I believe he said they had twenty thousand full-time staff members all over the world. It's a massive organization. He said, "I'm here to testify that at eighty years of age (he was dying) I still struggle with the flesh." I thought WOW! All the way down the road, further than I've ever been and he still struggles. So Paul says in the body you have people in all sorts of stages of spiritual growth. And Paul says we who are strong, who are spiritually mature have a debt that we owe to those who are spiritually weak, those who are beginning the journey, those who are struggling on the journey. It's our responsibility to help. The word literally means to pick up and carry their burden. Those who are strong have a responsibility to bear with, to pick the burden up, of those who are weak and not to please ourselves. The Christian life is not lived in individualistic isolation. We are connected to each other and we have a responsibility, those who are spiritually mature, to pick up and to carry along those who are spiritually weak, and we are not to please ourselves."

APPROPRIATE HYMNS AND SONGS

"These Hands," Jeff Deyo, 2000 Emack Music/Sonic Flood Music.

"Ancient Words," Lynn Deshazo, 2001 Integrity's Hosanna! Music.

"The Family of God," Gloria Gaither & William Gaither, 1970 by William J. Gaither & Gaither Music Company.

"Brethren, We Have Met to Worship," George Atkins, Public Domain.

"If We Are the Body," Mark Hall, SWECS Music.

FOR THE BULLETIN

On September 13, A.D. 81, the Roman emperor Titus died at age forty and was replaced by his brother, Titus Flavius Domitianus, twenty-nine, who reigned until ninety-six as Domitian and unleashed terrible persecution against the church. ● Catherine Winkworth was born on this day in 1827 in London, but spent most of her life in Manchester, England. Her passion and legacy was in translating German hymns into English, and she's largely responsible for bringing the German chorale tradition to the English-speaking world. Among her most popular translations are the Christmas carol, "All My Heart This Night Rejoices," originally written in German by Paul Gerhardt, and the thanksgiving hymn, "Now Thank We All Our God," originally written by Martin Rinkart in the seventeenth century. ● The hymn, "Sweet Hour of Prayer," first appeared in *The New York Observer* on this day in 1845. ● Missionary Robert J. Thomas arrived on the coast of Korea on September 13, 1865, becoming the first Protestant missionary to the region. He was later martyred, reportedly by having his head whacked off by a machete, but his last known words were, "Jesus! Jesus!" The man who killed him, haunted by the missionary's face, kept one of the Bibles and used its pages to wallpaper his house. People came from everywhere to read the words, and a church was born. ● Today is the anniversary of the passing, in 1904, of the British pastor, Frederick Whitfield, best remembered as the author of the hymns, "I Saw The Cross of Jesus" and "O How I Love Jesus."

PRAYER FOR THE PASTOR'S CLOSET

Lord, I believe, but would believe more firmly; O Lord, I love, but yet would love more warmly. I offer unto Thee my thoughts, that they may be towards Thee; my deeds, that they may be according to Thee; my sufferings, that they may be for Thee—Amen.

—from *Treasury of Devotion*, 1869

WORSHIP HELPS

Call to Worship
I will praise the LORD, who counsels me; even at night my heart instructs me. I have set the LORD always before me. Because he is at my right hand, I will not be shaken (Ps. 16:7–8 NIV).

Offertory Scripture Reading
Jesus sat down opposite the place where the offerings were put and watched the crowd putting their money into the temple treasury. Many rich people threw in large amounts. But a poor widow came and put in two very small copper coins, worth only a fraction of a penny. Calling his disciples to him, Jesus said, "I tell you the truth, this poor widow has put more into the treasury than all the others. They all gave out of their wealth; but she, out of her poverty, put in everything—all she had to live on" (Mark 12:31–44 NIV).

Pastoral Prayer
Lord, this is our prayer that You, the only wise God, may receive the glory forever through Jesus Christ our Lord. Teach us what it means to be a community of faith. Teach us what it means to love each other and serve each other and carry each other's burdens. Teach us what it means to exercise our giftedness. Grant that we would carry Your gospel to every nation of the world. This is Your heart, Lord. Remind us that You use people to do it. Thank You for the times that we have shared together from this marvelous book, and grant especially that it's practical truths would be lived out in our lives. We yield ourselves to You today. Dismiss us with Your blessing and in Christ's name. Amen.
—*Ed Dobson*

Additional Sermons and Lesson Ideas

Caleb: Model Senior Citizen
By Rev. Billie Friel

Date preached:

SCRIPTURE: Joshua 14:6–10

INTRODUCTION: Some people dread growing old. Caleb exemplifies the senior adult characteristics that every person should desire to have.

1. Caleb: An Unusual Senior Adult.
   A. Volunteer (v. 6). Caleb offered his service.
   B. Vitality (vv. 10–11). Caleb enjoyed good health and remained vigorous.
   C. Vision (v. 12). Caleb had a clear vision of service for the Lord and of His plan.
2. Caleb: An Unusual Young Man.
   A. Convictions (v. 7). Caleb lived by God's truth in his heart.
   B. Courage (v. 8). Caleb had learned to stand with God against the favor of others.
   C. Commitment (vv. 8–9). Caleb "wholly followed the Lord."

CONCLUSION: The reason Caleb was an unusual senior citizen is because he was an unusual young man. What kind of senior citizen will you be? Follow Caleb's example and be unusual.

The Body of Christ
By Dr. Larry Osborne

Date preached:

SCRIPTURE: 1 Corinthians 12:12–31

INTRODUCTION: The body of Christ is a group of diverse people made equal by one baptism in the Spirit and gifted particularly by God.

1. We Need Each Other (vv. 12–20). There is beauty in the diversity.
2. The Least Important Gifts Are the Most Honored Gifts (vv. 21–26). There is honor in the equality.
3. God Gifts and God Assigns (vv. 27–31). There is design in the appointment.

CONCLUSION: God gifts as He sees fit and it is for us to learn that we are all one in Christ Jesus. Each gift is for the encouragement and edification of the body and it is important to remember that we are all in this together.

CLASSICS FOR THE PASTOR'S LIBRARY

The Poems of Helen Steiner Rice

Okay, so it's a stretch to use the word "classic" to describe the simple, almost childlike poetry of Helen Steiner Rice. Some of them are little more than old-fashioned sentimental verses designed for greeting cards. But for pastors, these poems are very helpful. Even today, long after their composition, they are very quotable, recite-able, and readable in sermons, funerals, and in all sorts of talks.

There's a prevailing theory today that modern and post-modern audiences don't want to hear any sing-song poetry; but that's only because so few preachers attempt it anymore. A good poem with rollicking rhyme and rhythm can still catch an audience un-awares, alter the mood of the meeting, and bring a tear or a smile.

And then there's this—sometimes great depth resides in great simplicity. Helen Steiner Rice wasn't a theologian, but, as I'll explain, she was a pastor of sorts, ministering to people through verse at poignant moments in life; and there is a certain pastoral benefit to her work, which makes it transferable to our ministries. I've been surprised to find some of the unexpected deep insights woven through Rice's poems, but it's not surprising knowing her story. Her life was pockmarked with tragedy.

Helen Steiner was born in Ohio in 1900, and in high school she dreamed of going on to college and of running for Congress—lofty ideas for a woman in the early years of the twentieth century. But her father's death in the flu epidemic of 1918 changed all that, for she had to become the family breadwinner. She eventually became the spokesperson for an electric light and power company and traveled across America giving speeches on the advantages of having electricity in the home.

After several years, she opened her own speaker's bureau and became a popular motivational speaker. While on a gig in Dayton, Ohio, she met her future husband, banking executive Franklin Rice, and the two were married in 1929, just in time to lose everything in the stock market crash and Great Depression. While Franklin, having lost his job, sank into despair, Helen went out and found a job as the "Ambassador of Sunshine" for the Gibson Art Company in Cincinnati. One day in October of 1932, as she was at work in Cincinnati, Franklin committed suicide and left her a widow at age thirty-two.

Shortly afterward when the greeting card editor at Gibson died suddenly, Helen applied for the job, and for the next forty years she churned out cards, verses, and poems like an assembly line—over two million of them by one estimation. There were poems for every occasion—Christmas, birthdays, Easter, graduation, funerals, weddings, and holidays. Since Gibson frowned on religious sentiments, most of Rice's poems were sentimental and secular. But in the 1960s, she began writing poems expressing the truths of Scripture. When one of them, "The Priceless Gift of Christmas," was read nationwide on the Lawrence Welk Show, Helen Steiner Rice became a household name, and she was soon known as "America's Poet Laureate of Inspirational Verse."

Books of her poems hit the shelves of bookstores around the world, and her time was consumed in writing poems and in responding personally to her reading public.

Late in life, Helen suffered from increasingly painful and crippling arthritis, and at about age eighty she had to give up her work.

"I'm ready to go be with the Lord," she told one visitor in her convalescent home. "I can't wait to shed this aching body.... I'm ready for heaven."

She passed away on April 23, 1981.

I think there's still a place for poetry in sermons; and *if it's well practiced*—or memorized—imagine how effectively this Helen Steiner Rice poem could be used on a Sunday morning:

Brighten Up the Corner
Where You Are

We cannot all be famous
or be listed in "WHO'S WHO,"
But every person great or small
has important work to do,

Continued on the next page

For seldom do we realize
the importance of small deeds
Or to what degree of greatness
unnoticed kindness leads
For it's not the big celebrity
in a world of fame and praise,
But it's doing unpretentiously
in undistinguished ways
The work that God assigned to us,
unimportant as it seems,
That makes our task outstanding
and brings reality to dreams
So do not sit and idly wish
for wider, new dimensions
Where you can put in practice
your many "GOOD INTENTIONS"
But at the spot God placed you
begin at once to do
Little things to brighten up
the lives surrounding you,
For if everybody brightened up
the spot in which they're standing
By being more considerate
and a little less demanding,
This dark old world would very soon
eclipse the "Evening Star"
If everybody BRIGHTENED UP
THE CORNER WHERE THEY ARE!

SEPTEMBER 20, 2009

SUGGESTED SERMON

Becoming an Excellent Church *Date preached:*

Scripture: 2 Corinthians 8–9, especially 8:7 (NIV)
Just as you excel in everything—in faith, in speech, in knowledge, in complete earnestness, and in your love for us—see that you also excel in this grace of giving.

Introduction: In the 1980s, Tom Peters was given a generous expense account and sent around the world to interview successful leaders. From his research, he put together a two-day presentation with 700 slides for the leadership of PepsiCo. But Peters, worried that Pepsi's Andy Pearson wouldn't endure a long presentation, sat at his desk mulling over his presentation. He leaned forward and jotted down eight things on a pad of paper. Those eight principles became the basis for the book he co-authored that changed the landscape of corporate America—*In Search of Excellence.* To this day, "excellence" is a buzzword in the daily life of successful corporations. But in our church life, sometimes we're still searching for excellence. In this passage, Paul is exhorting the Corinthians to be generous in giving to the special offering he was collecting for the poverty-stricken churches of Judea; and chapters 8 and 9 of 2 Corinthians are perhaps his most profound writings on the subject of stewardship. But notice how he begins in verse 7—by appealing for excellence in six vital areas of church life.

1. **We Should Excel in Faith.** The New Testament doesn't just emphasize the personal faith of individual Christians but the corporate faith of individual churches. The book of Acts talks about specific churches that were growing in faith (see Rom. 1:8; Col. 1:3–4; 2 Thess. 1:3). How do you recognize a church that excels in faith? One way is by the works they do, the missionaries they send, and the ministries they sustain (see 1 Thess. 1:3). We believe God is real, the Bible is true, Jesus is alive, and because of that we plunge into His work with all our hearts. We invest our time, money, and energy in children's ministry, youth ministry, music ministry, benevolence, and global outreach. We demonstrate our faith by our works. We just tear into it, expecting God to bless our efforts.

2. **We Should Excel in Speech.** The Greek word here is that familiar term *logos,* and it seems to refer to the church's public ministry of

teaching and preaching. We have the gospel that liberates and satisfies us. We have the Bible that tells us how to live. We have the way, the truth, and the life. In our sermons, lessons, and conversations, we should share that message with excellence, rightly dividing and correctly applying the Word.

3. **We Should Excel in Knowledge.** Connected with that is the third area of excellence—knowledge. Professor Steve Prothero of Boston University recently wrote a book entitled *Religious Literacy*, in which he claims that even churchgoers in America are woefully deficient in Bible knowledge. According to his studies, 60 percent of Americans can't name half of the Ten Commandments, and 50 percent of high school seniors think Sodom and Gomorrah were married. We need to be lifelong students of the Bible.

4. **We Must Excel in Earnestness.** Some translations use "zeal" here, and that's a strong but frequently forgotten Bible word. Jesus said, "The zeal of Thy house hath eaten me up."

5. **We Should Excel in Love.** Healthy church members love each other. (See Stats, Stories, and More for an illustration from Julia Child's life.)

6. **We Should Excel in Giving.** Having said all that, Paul was gearing up for his main point. He is advocating that we be a church of excellent givers. That's what these two chapters are about, and it's very interesting how Paul begins. He anticipates that the Corinthians might say, "Well, we can't do very much. We don't have the funds right now." That's one excuse the Bible doesn't allow. In this paragraph, Paul tells them about the congregations to the north whose extreme poverty welled up in rich generosity and they gave beyond their ability (see Mark 12:41–44).

Conclusion: I've read stories about prisoners in concentration camps who were given scraps of bread and watery bowls of soup, and that's all they had. But they found a way of tithing from it. One man fasted every tenth day and gave his full meal on that day to someone else. The principle of the Bible is proportional giving—this passage says that we are to give "as God has prospered us." Are you doing that? The Bible says, just as you excel in everything—in faith, in speech, in knowledge, in complete earnestness, and in your love for one another, see that you also excel in the grace of giving.

STATS, STORIES, AND MORE

It's Because of You, Jesus
In the memoirs of Julia Child, she tells of moving to Paris with her husband, Paul, and having a conversation about the reported rudeness of French people. Paul told Julia that in the 1920s, he found 80 percent of the people difficult and 20 percent charming. Now the reverse was true—80 percent of the Parisians were charming and only 20 percent were rude. But Paul admitted that the difference wasn't really in the French. It was he himself who had changed, and this is the way he put it: 'I am less sour now than I used to be," he said. "It's because of you, Julia."[1] Most of us are prone to be sour by nature, and we get ourselves into a state in which people easily offend us, upset us, get on our nerves, but Jesus makes a difference in our attitude. We can say, "I'm more pleasant than I used to be, easer to get along with. I'm less sour now—and it's because of You, Jesus." It's because of Him that we can excel in love.

Stewardship Quotes

- *The only investments I ever made which have paid constantly increasing dividends is the money I have given to the Lord*—J. L. Kraft, head of Kraft Cheese, who for many years gave 25 percent of his income to Christian causes.

- *I have tithed every dollar God has entrusted to me: And I want to say, if I had not tithed the first dollar I made, I would not have tithed the first million dollars I made*—John D. Rockefeller, Sr.

- *I am totally dependent on God for help in everything I do. Otherwise I honestly believe I would start to fall apart in months*—Wallace Johnson, founder of Holiday Inn and a Christian steward.

APPROPRIATE HYMNS AND SONGS

"The Church's One Foundation," Samuel J. Stone & Samuel S. Wesley, Public Domain.

"This Is Your House," Randy Phillips, 2002 Awakening Media Group.

"Because We Believe," Nancy Gordon & Jamie Harvill, 1996 Mother's Heart Music & Integrity's Hosanna! Music & Integrity's Praise! Music.

"A Glorious Church," Ralph E. Hudson, Public Domain.

---

[1]Julia Child and Alex Prud'homme, *My Life in France* (New York: Alfred A. Knopf, 2006), p. 25.

FOR THE BULLETIN

In the sixteenth century, French Protestants, under persecution in their homeland, migrated abroad, a number of them coming to the New World and settling in what is now called Florida. On September of 1565, the Spanish captain Pedro Menendez landed in Florida with nearly 3,000 men, and on the 20th, Menendez and his troops massacred the Protestant immigrants. He later reported to the king, "I had their hands tied behind their backs and themselves put to the sword." ● Charles and Susannah Spurgeon had twin boys, Charles and Thomas born on this day in 1856. The proud father wrote, "Charlie and Tommy are good little boys; when they're asleep, they don't make any noise." He later baptized both boys on their eighteenth birthday, and both became preachers. Thomas later succeeded his father as pastor of the Metropolitan Tabernacle. ● On this day in 1871, the English missionary to Melanesia, John Coleridge Patteson, went ashore Nukapu Island to preach the gospel. He was seized by natives and clubbed to death. The next day, grieving friends buried him at sea. ● Today marks the death in New York City of music publisher, Will Lamartine Thompson, who became ill during a tour of Europe and rushed home in hopes of recovery. He's remembered for his spontaneous gift of writing hymns on the spot. "No matter where I am," he wrote, "at home, at the store, or traveling, if an idea or theme comes to me that I deem worthy of a song, I jot it down in verse. In this way I never lose it." He's the author of the words and melodies for "Jesus Is All the World to Me," "There's a Great Day Coming," and the invitational hymn, "Softly and Tenderly Jesus Is Calling." ● Another great American hymnist, William Kirkpatrick, died on this day in 1921. He composed the tunes to "We Have Heard the Joyful Sound," "'Tis So Sweet to Trust in Jesus," "Redeemed, How I Love to Proclaim It," and "He Hideth My Soul in the Cleft of the Rock."

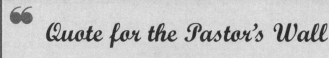

" Quote for the Pastor's Wall

*A room without books is like
a body without a soul.*

—G. K. CHESTERTON

WORSHIP HELPS

Call to Worship
Be exalted, O LORD, in your strength; we will sing and praise your might (Ps. 21:13 NIV).

Scripture Reading Medley
Why are you cast down, O my soul? And why are you disquieted within me? Hope in God; for I shall yet praise Him, the help of my countenance and my God. Our soul waits for the LORD; He is our help and our shield. For our heart shall rejoice in Him, because we have trusted in His holy name. Let Your mercy, O LORD, be upon us, just as we hope in You. The LORD is my strength and my shield; my heart trusted in Him, and I am helped; therefore my heart gladly rejoices, and with my song I will praise Him. God is our refuge and strength, a very present help in trouble. Be still, and know that I am God; I will be exalted among the nations, I will be exalted in the earth! The LORD of hosts is with us; the God of Jacob is our refuge. I will lift up my eyes to the hills—from whence comes my help? My help comes from the LORD, who made heaven and earth. He will not allow your foot to be moved; He who keeps you will not slumber. Behold, He who keeps Israel shall neither slumber nor sleep. The LORD is your keeper; the LORD is your shade at your right hand. The sun shall not strike you by day, nor the moon by night. The LORD shall preserve you from all evil; He shall preserve your soul (Ps. 42:11; 33:20–22; 28:7; 46:1, 10–11; 121:1–7).

Benediction
Blessed are the people whose God is the LORD (Ps. 144:15b NIV).

Additional Sermons and Lesson Ideas

The Christian's Armor

By Dr. Michael A. Guido

Date preached:

SCRIPTURE: Ephesians 6:11–18

INTRODUCTION: We daily fight a spiritual battle against an enemy that is not seen. It is important then to outfit ourselves with the armor of the Lord (vv. 11–13).

1. The Belt of Truth (v. 14a). Let God's Truth support you.
2. The Breastplate of Righteousness (v. 14b). Let God's Righteousness protect you.
3. The Shoes of Peace (v. 15). Let God's Peace equip you.
4. The Shield of Faith (v. 16). Let God's Faithfulness protect you.
5. The Helmet of Salvation (v. 17a). Let God's Salvation re-form you.
6. The Sword of the Spirit (v. 17b). Let God's Word defend you.

CONCLUSION: After we put on the armor; Paul encourages us to be prayerful in the Spirit and vigilant at all times (v. 18). Without prayer, we fight in our own power and will suffer defeat.

Moses' Mandate and Mission

By Dr. Melvin Worthington

Date preached:

SCRIPTURE: Exodus 3–4

INTRODUCTION: Moses was called by God to do a specific work. A renewed emphasis must be given to the call of God on an individual's life for God's service. God's divine call includes the following elements:

1. The Occasion (Ex. 3:1–6). Note the flock, the fire, the focus, and the fear.
2. The Objective (Ex. 3:7–10). The oppression included the afflicted people, the affirmed promise, the accurate perception, and the announced plan.
3. The Objections (Ex. 3:11–4:17). Here we read of Moses' insignificance, his lack of information, his ignorance, and his inadequacy.
4. The Obedience (Ex. 4:18–31). The obedience of Moses is played out in this sequence: the request, the rod, the reminder, the ritual, the rehearsal, and the revelation.

CONCLUSION: Disobedience to God's call brings devastating consequences. Moses obeyed the Word of the Lord and embarked to fulfill his calling. So likewise should each of us.

SEPTEMBER 27, 2009

SUGGESTED SERMON

What Does It Take to Get God's Blessing?

Date preached:

By Rev. Larry Kirk

Scripture: Galatians 3:6–14, especially verse 14
Through Christ Jesus, God has blessed the Gentiles with the same blessing he promised to Abraham, so that we who are believers might receive the promised Holy Spirit through faith (NLT).

Introduction: Do you know that it's possible to be at complete peace with God, not basing your peace with Him on your performance at all, and yet still be passionate about pursuing Him and pressing on in your spiritual growth and discipleship? God wants you to know that. He wants you to glorify Him by your gladness in Him because of His grace to you. That's the purpose of Galatians 3.

I. **God's Blessing Has *Always* Come Through Faith in Christ (vv. 6–9).** Galatians 3:6 takes us all the way back to Genesis, the first book in the Bible, and to the man Abraham. Paul quotes and refers to Genesis all through this passage. In verse 6, he uses the example of Abraham to tell us how God's blessing is received and enjoyed.

   A. **God's Blessing Is a Central Theme of Scripture.** In the beginning, when God created the world He blessed it. That doesn't just mean that He wished it or us well. When God blesses something, He empowers it to fulfill His purposes. Later, God promised Abraham a family that would outnumber the stars, a land to call his own, and a blessing to empower him for life. The story of the Bible becomes the progressive development of that promised blessing. It's the theme that runs through the whole Book and is fulfilled in Christ.

   B. **God's Blessing Has Always Been Received by Faith.** Look at how many times the words believe or faith appear in verses 6–9. Abraham's misdeeds and failures did not exclude him from God's blessing, just as his good deeds did not earn him God's blessing. God still works this way today with you and me. His blessing has always come through faith.

2. **God's Blessing Can *Only* Come Through Faith in Christ (vv. 10–12).** Notice how clearly verse 10 makes this point. "But those who depend on the law to make them right with God are under his curse" (NLT). No one can obey the law perfectly. So receiving God's blessing cannot possibly come by works, which lead to a curse. God's blessing can only come by God's grace through faith.

   A. **This Truth Is Humbling.** If we are justified by faith and not by works, no one can boast (Eph. 2:8–9). No one can look down on others. We're all in need of the saving grace that only comes through faith in Christ.

   B. **This Truth Is Liberating.** When you understand that the blessings of God's grace come only through faith in Christ, the knowledge is humbling, but it is liberating as well: "For you have been called to live in freedom, my brothers and sisters" (Gal. 5:13a NLT).

3. **God's Blessing *Richly* Comes Through Faith in Christ (vv. 13–14).** "But Christ has rescued us from the curse pronounced by the law. When he was hung on the cross, he took upon himself the curse for our wrongdoing. For it is written in the Scriptures, 'Cursed is everyone who is hung on a tree.' Through Christ Jesus, God has blessed the Gentiles with the same blessing he promised to Abraham, so that we who are believers might receive the promised Holy Spirit through faith" (NLT).

   A. **Blessed with the Richness of Complete Redemption.** The word *redeem* means to set someone free by paying a price for his freedom. As a result of what Christ has done for us, we are saved from the curse of judgment and receive the blessing of grace.

   B. **Blessed with the Richness of His Promised Spirit.** When you receive Christ, you are not only redeemed from something, but you are also redeemed for something. You were forgiven so that you might be filled. The ultimate blessing is God living in you in grace. The promise of the Spirit means that you can practice the presence of Christ.

Conclusion: Is God's blessing, received through faith in Christ, the source of your strength? Is your heart softened, sweetened, and strengthened because you know that through faith in Christ you are blessed by God? When you know, that through your faith in Christ, God has given you these blessings of grace that you could never deserve, that is a life-changing understanding.

STATS, STORIES, AND MORE

More from Rev. Larry Kirk

In his book *Healing Grace,* David Seamonds tells of a man named Stypulkowski, who was a fighter in the Polish underground during World War II. He was captured by the Russian army and placed on trial for displeasing the Communists. His compatriots broke under the pressure, but Stypulkowski did not, despite 141 interrogations. For over two months, his tormentors relentlessly examined every aspect of his life, work, marriage, church, and concept of God. He faced a starvation diet, sleepless nights, and calculated terror. He never broke and was eventually freed.

The most impressive part of his story was the completely unselfconscious way he witnessed to his Christian faith. It was obvious that he was not free from weaknesses. His accusers pointed them out to him time after time, but he was never shattered by them. He knew he was accepted, loved by God, and forgiven. So whenever they accused him of some personal wrong, he freely admitted it, even welcomed it. He said: "I never felt it necessary to justify myself with excuses. When they showed me a reflection of myself with all my inadequacies, I said to them, 'But, gentlemen, I am much worse than that.' For you see, I had learned it was unnecessary for me to justify myself. One had already done that for me— Jesus Christ![1]

APPROPRIATE HYMNS AND SONGS

"The Name of the Lord," Clinton Utterbach, 1989 Polygram International Publishing & Utterbach Music.

"You Are Good," Israel Houghton, 2001 Integrity's Praise! Music and Champions for Christ Publishing.

"You Are God Alone," Billy Foote & Cindy Foote, 2004 Billy Foote Music.

"Showers of Blessings," Daniel Whittle & James McGranahan, Public Domain.

"Lord Most High," Don Harris & Gary Sadler, 1996 Integrity's Hosanna! Music.

---

[1] David Seamonds, Healing Grace (Victor, 1988), pp. 115 ff.

FOR THE BULLETIN

The Society of Jesus—the Jesuits—was founded by St. Ignatius of Loyola, and on this day in 1540, when Pope Paul III issued a papal bull, the Regimini militantis eccelesiae, confirming the new order. ● Jacques Benigne Bossuet, one of the most eloquent French Catholic orators and the court preacher for King Louis XIV, was born in Dijon on September 27, 1627. His sermons were "unexcelled upon earth," it was said. In some sermons, he addressed the king by name; and on one occasion he earnestly implored Louis to abandon his adulteries and return to his wife. ● September 27, 1785 marks the birth of the Protestant Episcopal Church in the United States, founded after the American Revolutionary War when U.S. Anglicans met in Philadelphia to establish a denomination independent from the Church of England. ● George Mller was born on this day in 1805. He was a prodigal son and jailbird who, following his conversion, became a powerful evangelist and is best known for his faith-based orphanages in Bristol, England. During his lifetime he cared for over 10,000 orphans without ever appealing for funds. ● Today's also the birthday, in 1872, of Bentley DeForest Ackley, Pennsylvania-born musician who became the pianist for the Billy Sunday and Homer Rodeheaver evangelistic campaigns. He wrote over 3,000 melodies to gospel songs, some of them for his poem-writing younger brother, Alfred Henry Ackley. ● And James Ellor, hat maker, died on this day in 1899, Newburgh, New York at his son's home. When he wasn't making hats, James was writing music, and he's the composer of the tune DIADEM, to which "All Hail the Power of Jesus Name" is frequently sung.

Quote for the Pastor's Wall

There can be no really powerful preaching without deep thinking, and little deep thinking without hard reading.

—BISHOP JOHN RYLE

WORSHIP HELPS

Call to Worship
Lift up your heads, O you gates; be lifted up, you ancient doors, that the King of glory may come in. Who is this King of glory? The LORD strong and mighty, the LORD mighty in battle (Ps. 24:7–8 NIV).

Scripture Reading
Praise be to the God and Father of our Lord Jesus Christ, who has blessed us in the heavenly realms with every spiritual blessing in Christ. For he chose us in him before the creation of the world to be holy and blameless in his sight. In love he predestined us to be adopted as his sons through Jesus Christ, in accordance with his pleasure and will—to the praise of his glorious grace, which he has freely given us in the One he loves. In him we have redemption through his blood, the forgiveness of sins, in accordance with the riches of God's grace that he lavished on us with all wisdom and understanding. And he made known to us the mystery of his will according to his good pleasure, which he purposed in Christ, to be put into effect when the times will have reached their fulfillment—to bring all things in heaven and on earth together under one head, even Christ (Eph. 1:3–10 NIV).

Benediction
Bless those who persecute you; bless and do not curse. Rejoice with those who rejoice; mourn with those who mourn. Live in harmony with one another. Do not be proud, but be willing to associate with people of low position. Do not be conceited (Rom. 12:14–16 NIV).

Additional Sermons and Lesson Ideas

Unexpected Heroism
Date preached:

By Rev. Robert M. Norris

SCRIPTURE: Judges 6:11—7:19

INTRODUCTION: Like many of us Gideon was a man with many issues and yet he was still a man who was used by God. He offers to each of us an encouragement to know that we may be useful to the Lord and His service despite our own human weakness.

1. Gideon Had a Personal Encounter with God (6:11–24).
2. Gideon Was Required to Take a Stand for God (6:25–32).
3. Gideon Was Equipped by God (6:33–35).
4. Gideon Received Special Assurance from God (6:36–40).
5. Gideon Was Required to Exercise a Practical Faith (7:1–19)

CONCLUSION: The lesson of Gideon's victory is the lesson for us too. Humble, frightened, and inadequate people may yet hope to be mighty warriors. God calls us to be His instruments for change in a world that needs changing.

Family Ties
Date preached:

By Rev. Melvin Tinker

SCRIPTURE: 1 John 3:11–24

INTRODUCTION: Loving other Christians is basic to what it means to be a Christian. If you are a believer you will imitate your Father. God is love (1 John 4:16) and so we must love others. We can find our confidence in this passage.

1. The Opposite of Love Is Seen in Cain (vv. 11–15).
2. The Measure of Love Is Seen in Christ (vv. 16–18).
3. The Fruit of Love Is Confidence (vv. 19–24).

CONCLUSION: If you are not trusting you will not love; if you are trusting then you will love. Faith in Christ is the root, loving Christians is the fruit, and if we are doing both authentically then we can rest assured we are His.

OCTOBER 4, 2009

Blessed Perseverance

Date preached:

Scripture: James 1:12
Blessed is the man who perseveres under trial, because when he has stood the test,
he will receive the crown of life that God has promised to those who love him (NIV).

Introduction: The great tenth-century ruler in Spain, Abd Er-Rashman III,
is famous for his quotation about happiness: "I have now reigned
about fifty years in victory or peace, beloved by my subjects, dreaded
by my enemies, and respected by my allies. Riches and honors, power
and pleasure, have waited on my call, nor does any earthly blessing
appear to have been waiting to my felicity. In this situation, I have
diligently numbered the days of pure and genuine happiness which
have fallen my lot. They amount to fourteen." The words "happy" and
"happiness" come from the old Middle English word *hap* which means
"luck." We get *happen, happening, haphazard, happenstance, mishap,*
and *hapless* from this term. But the Bible uses a different and better
word—"blessed," which is the English translation of a Greek word
found fifty times in the New Testament—*makarios.* The simplest definition is this—it is God's kind of happiness. James 1:12 gives us one
of the secrets to this "blessed life."

1. **The Reality: Blessed Are Those Who Persevere Under Trial.** The
   first part of the verse gives us the reality of tests and trials. In this
   life we must learn to persevere. Romans 5:3–4 indicates this is the
   very core of character. Tenacity and perseverance is foundational to
   the success of all our other attitudes and actions. Robert Louis
   Stevenson said, "Saints are sinners who keep on going." William
   Barclay used the British author, Samuel Coleridge, as a negative
   example of this: "Nothing was ever achieved without discipline; and
   many an athlete and many a man has been ruined because he
   abandoned discipline and let himself grow slack. Coleridge is the
   supreme tragedy of undiscipline. Never did so great a mind produce
   so little. He left Cambridge University to join the army; but he left
   the army because, in spite of all his erudition, he could not rub
   down a horse; he returned to Oxford and left without a degree. He

began a paper called *The Watchman* which lived for ten numbers and then died. It has been said of him: 'He lost himself in visions of work to be done, that always remained to be done.' Coleridge had every poetic gift but one—the gift of sustained and concentrated effort. In his head and in his mind he had all kinds of books, as he said himself, 'completed save for transcription. I am on the eve,' he said, 'of sending the press two octavo volumes.' But the books were never composed outside Coleridge's mind, because he would not face the discipline of sitting down to write them out. No one ever reached any eminence, and no one having reached it ever maintained it, without discipline."[1]

Life is hard, but we've got to trust the Lord and keep going. We can't give up. Temptations come, but we've got to keep resisting. Disappointments come, but we've got to keep believing. Failures appear, but we've got to keep trying. Hardships come, but we've got to keep moving forward.

2. **The Reward: They Will Receive the Crown of Life.** The reward of perseverance is given in the middle part of the verse—the crown of life. Commentators are divided about what this means. James may be using the symbol of a crown as a picture of heaven and eternal life. Other commentators believe the "crown of life" is a special reward God will give those who persevere through adversity or persecution (Rev. 2:10). The New Testament speaks of various crowns to be awarded in heaven. There's the crown of life, the crown of glory, the crown of righteousness, etc. In either case, it bears out the message of that old song that says, "When all my labors and trials are o'er, / And I am safe on that beautiful shore, / Just to be near the dear Lord I adore, / Will through the ages be glory for me."

3. **The Reason: To Those Who Love Him.** The final part of the verse gives us the reason we persevere. What's the driving force behind it all? It's our love for the Lord Jesus Christ. It isn't just that we're stubborn people, or that we're superhuman, or that we're strong-willed. It's that we're filled with a love for Him that bears us along, sustains our spirits, and triggers our songs.

---

[1] William Barclay, The Gospel of Matthew (Philadelphia, PA: Westminster, 1958), vol. 1, 284.

Conclusion: If we love the Lord Jesus above all else, He will give us day by day the persevering grace we need and crown of life we seek, and we can say, "Oh, that will be glory for me!"

STATS, STORIES, AND MORE

As I researched for this message, I came across an article in a New York newspaper. It was written by a woman named Dr. Rachel Bryant, and the title was "Children Learn When They Persevere." The column begins this way: "The power to persevere is one of the most important, and yet hardest, things to teach kids. If we teach them to persevere, then we give them their goals. If we don't teach them how to apply themselves, then all the love and tutoring in the world will never result in their reaching their potential."

Dr. Bryant goes on to say: "Success requires ability, but ability is not enough. Many bright kids who sail through the early grades find themselves suddenly overwhelmed in fifth or sixth grade when the work requires much more effort. If a ten-year-old student has never learned to apply herself, she may struggle and even feel like a failure, because suddenly the answers don't come so easily. Often, she just needs help learning what most kids have to learn by second grade: I have to work hard and practice to learn the lesson.

"Learning how to persevere is more than learning how to study, but studying does provide us with daily opportunities to develop this in our school-age kids . . .

"Imagine two six-year-olds with the same level of intelligence and the same fine motor skills. Both are trying to learn to tie their shoes. One fumbles with the laces for five to ten seconds and says, "Oh forget it. It's no use." The other, goes off and spends five full minutes carefully trying to get the laces to go the right way. Even if this second child meets with failure, he has demonstrated that he is developing a life skill that will give his potential every chance to grow.

"Whatever the task, building a tower, gluing a model airplane, reading a social studies chapter or doing a page of math problems, first let your child know that you are pleased to see them trying, and with your presence help them to stretch themselves just a few more minutes."[2]

---

[2]"Children Learn When They Persevere" by Dr. Rachel Bryant, at http://www.star gazettenews.com/apps/pbcs.dll/article?AID=/20080102/MOMS02/301020002/-1/ ARCHIVES%20date=20070417, accessed January 22, 2008.

APPROPRIATE HYMNS AND SONGS

"Your Grace Is Enough," Matt Maher & Chris Tomlin, 2003–2005 Matt Maher. Published by spiritandsong.com.

"Unchanging," Chris Tomlin, 2002 Worshiptogether.com Songs/sixsteps Music.

"I Sing the Mighty Power of God," Isaac Watts, Public Domain.

"Word of God, Speak," Peter Kipley & Bart Millard, 2002 Wordspring Music, LLC. Songs from the Indigo Room and Simpleville Music.

FOR THE BULLETIN

Madame Guyon grew up in the seventeenth century in an aristocratic French family and married into more wealth. When she was twenty, she found assurance of salvation, but her life was dominated by all that was worldly and external. On October 4, 1670, at age twenty-two, she was stricken with smallpox. "When I was so far recovered as to be able to sit up in my bed," she wrote, "I ordered a mirror to be brought, and indulged my curiosity so far as to view myself in it. I was no longer what I once was. It was then that I saw my heavenly Father had not been unfaithful in His work, but had ordered the sacrifice in all reality." She went on to become one of the most beloved and quoted of the French mystics. ● Miles Coverdale, rector of St. Magnus Church near London Bridge, is best known as the translator and publisher of the English Bible. Visitors today can read a memorial plaque on the east wall of his church: . . . *he spent many years of his life preparing a translation of the Scriptures.* On this day in 1535, the first complete printed English version of the Bible was published under his direction. ● The early American "hellfire and brimstone" frontier preacher, Peter Cartwright, who helped start the Second Great Awakening and personally baptized over 12,000 people, was ordained on this day in 1808. His autobiography is a classic in American church history. ● Today is the birthday, in 1880, of Homer Rodeheaver, one of the best-loved songleaders in the Christian world who traveled widely with evangelist Billy Sunday and who also became an influential publisher of gospel music. ● Catherine Booth, the "Mother of the Salvation Army," died at age sixty-one in Clacton-on-Sea at Crossley House on October 4, 1890, in the arms of her husband, William Booth, and surrounded by her family.

WORSHIP HELPS

Call to Worship

But you are a chosen generation, a royal priesthood, a holy nation, His own special people, that you may proclaim the praises of Him who called you out of darkness into His marvelous light (1 Pet. 2:9).

Pastoral Prayer Idea

Today's message is about persevering in times of trial and testing. You might preview your subject during the prayer portion of the service, and sympathize with those who are burdened. Remind the church of the old saying, "In every pew there sits a broken heart." Invite people to bow their heads, and during a quiet moment (or with the instruments playing softly), allow time for everyone to offer their own quiet and personal prayers to the Lord. Then offer the pastoral prayer using the promises found in Psalm 55:22 and 1 Peter 5:7.

Offertory Comments

> "It is an anomaly of modern life that many find giving to be a burden. Such persons have omitted a preliminary giving. If one first gives himself to the Lord, all other giving is easy."
>
> —*John S. Bonnell (1893–1992)*

> "I do not believe one can settle how much we ought to give. I am afraid the only safe rule is to give more than we can spare. In other words, if our expenditure on comforts, luxuries, amusements, etc., is up to the standard common among those with the same income as our own, we are probably giving away too little. If our charities do not at all pinch or hamper us, I should say that they are too small. There ought to be things we should like to do and cannot do because our charitable expenditures exclude them."   —*C. S. Lewis*

Additional Sermons and Lesson Ideas

iKnow: A Lesson in Truth for the iPod Generation
By Pastor Jonathan Falwell

Date preached:

SCRIPTURE: 2 Timothy 3:14–17 NIV

INTRODUCTION: Where do we turn in a world that convolutes truth? Scripture is the source of truth, able to pierce through the lies of this age. Paul teaches us in 2 Timothy that the Word of God does six things for us:

1. The Word of God Saves Us (v. 15): "make you wise for salvation."
2. The Word of God Teaches Us (v. 16): "teaching."
3. The Word of God Confronts Us (v. 16): "rebuking."
4. The Word of God Corrects Us (v. 16): "correcting."
5. The Word of God Guides Us (v. 16): "training."
6. The Word of God Equips Us (v. 17): "thoroughly equipped."

CONCLUSION: If you want to be able to be an effective witness in this iPod generation, you have to know the Scriptures and be wise in your use of it in order to reach this world!

Paul's Thorn in the Flesh
By Rev. Billie Friel

Date preached:

SCRIPTURE: 1 Corinthians 12:1–10

INTRODUCTION: Sometimes God allows us to experience strange things and go through painful things so that we might grow deeper in our relationship with Him.

1. Paul's Experience.
    A. Perplexity (vv. 1–3). Strange experience.
    B. Paradise (v. 4). Third heaven.
    C. Preview (v. 4). Inexpressible things.
2. Satan's Emissary.
    A. Prohibition (v. 7). Kept Paul grounded.
    B. Physical (v. 7). Not a spiritual affliction.
    C. Painful (v. 7). Educative suffering.
    D. Prayer (v. 8). Specific, repeated, and fervent.
3. God's Explanation.
    A. Purpose (v. 8). Revelation of God and self.
    B. Power (v. 9). God gave sufficient grace.
    C. Pleasure (v. 10). Consider trials joy (James 1:2).

CONCLUSION: God desires growth and change in us. When crises come, pray for relief. If God does not deliver, He has a purpose and will give sustaining grace.

OCTOBER 11, 2009

SUGGESTED SERMON

Fighting the Battle of Unbelief

By Pastor Al Detter

Date preached:

Scripture: Genesis 18:1–15, especially verse 14
Is anything too hard for the LORD?

Introduction: We tend to think that if we don't commit a major sin, we're doing okay. But we often fall into something more subtle—living a life of unbelief, living with a small God who's at work only in the possible, the reasonable, and the doable. Let's learn six lessons that will help us fight the battle of unbelief.

1. **We Need Some Impossible Situations Occasionally.** Sarah was ninety and Abraham was one hundred (Gen. 17:17). People don't have babies at that age. Sarah had infertility problems when she was young, and Romans 4:19 says that at her age her womb was dead. As a couple, they were childless. A baby now would be impossible. Sometimes God allows impossible things to come into our lives. Sure, they frustrate us. Yes, they can hurt us. But throughout the course of our lives, God will allow us to encounter situations that no human being can solve. That's God's opportunity to show us His glory and His power.

2. **God Wants to Speak to Us About Our Impossibility.** Years before, God had promised Abraham a special land and a host of descendants (Gen. 12:2; 15:4, 18; 17:2, 5, 8). But Abraham and Sarah had no children and they were past the age of having children. The fulfillment of that promise now looked impossible. But God hadn't forgotten His promise. He came to Abraham to speak to him about what seemed impossible. In verse 10, God said, "I will surely return to you about this time next year, and Sarah your wife will have a son." God spoke into their situation to build their faith. In our day, He does this through the Bible.

3. **We Need to Be Careful About Our Reaction to What God Says.** Sarah was inside the tent baking for the guests. One of the guests asked in verse 9, "Where is your wife, Sarah?" That caught her

attention and she listened up. She heard the stranger say by that time the next year she would have a son (v. 10). She laughed. Had she believed God, I think she would have either been very excited or very fearful. But she laughed because it sounded so ridiculous. In verse 14, God asks why she laughed as if that would be too hard for the Lord; she insulted the same God who came to visit her. Don't we do the same when we disbelieve the promises of Scripture?

4. **We Must Settle the Question of God's Ability to Perform Miracles in Our Lives.** God said something very powerful to Abraham in verse 14: "Is anything too hard for the LORD?" That's the issue we've got to settle. Just how powerful *is* this God we serve? Is there *anything* that goes beyond His power? What do we really believe?

5. **Activating God's Power Often Requires Illogical Obedience.** For Sarah to have a baby, she had to have sex with Abraham. And she knew it. She said in effect, "Do you mean that I'm going to have sex with that old man?" (v. 12). It wasn't going to happen any other way. They tried to have a child many times before and it didn't work. They had to do it again. Here's the point: people are often unwilling to do the very thing they need to do because they've tried it before and it didn't work.

6. **God Does Impossible Things When They Are in His Will.** The birth of Isaac and the nation of Israel were all in the plan of God. So something like old age and a dead womb wasn't going to get in God's way. God did the impossible. Sarah had a baby. Not all possible things are in the will of God. But sometimes there are things in life that seem so impossible yet not unreasonable to the will of God. How are we to know what God's will is and what it isn't? Here are some sure things that are God's will:

A. **The Salvation of Every Person (2 Pet. 3:9).**

B. **The Health of Every Marriage (Matt. 19:8–9).**

C. **Our Likeness to Christ (Phil. 2:13).**

Conclusion: The good news is, Sarah stopped laughing and started believing (cf. Heb. 11:11), and so can we! For the rest of our lives, we need to live in the knowledge that with God, all things are possible!

STATS, STORIES, AND MORE

More from Pastor Al Detter
We were called to the emergency room to identify our oldest son some years ago. He'd been in a car crash. He was on life support in ICU, and no one knew if he would live or die. There was nothing more anyone could do. I went home that night and sat on the edge of my bed. I took my Bible and cried out, "God, You need to speak to me." Then I opened the Bible at random. Of all places, it opened to Psalm 113. Verse 9 was underlined. I read it: "He makes the barren woman abide in the house as a joyful mother of children."

I couldn't believe my eyes. Marie and I were married seven years and had no children. When we adopted Jason, that was the very verse on the card we sent to announce to all our friends that we finally had a baby. I began to weep because I knew God had spoken to me in an impossible situation. I knew He was telling me that Jason would not die. I was grieving about the situation but that night I believed God. I was confident my son would live. If you're facing an impossible situation, God wants to knock on the door of your heart and speak a word of faith to you about your situation. Be listening!

APPROPRIATE HYMNS AND SONGS

"I Know Whom I Have Believed," Daniel Whittle, Public Domain.

"My Faith Has Found a Resting Place," Lidie H. Edmunds, Public Domain.

"There Is None Like You," Lenny LeBlanc, 1991 Integrity's Hosanna! Music.

"Great and Mighty Is He," Todd Pettygrove, 1987 Integrity's Hosanna! Music.

"Refresh My Heart," Geoff Bullock, 1992 Word Music and Maranatha! Music.

FOR THE BULLETIN

When Islamic Arabian armies swept westward during the Dark Ages, threatening to seize the remnants of the old Roman Empire, Charles Martel and his Franks met the invaders on October 11, 732, at the plain between Tours and Poitiers. For five days the attacks came in waves. On the sixth day the Arabs cut through the lines only to find themselves surrounded and trapped. The surviving invaders fled, and Europe was saved for Christianity. ● On another European battlefront on October 11, 1531, the Swiss Reformer Ulrich Zwingli received a fatal wound from a lance to his neck. He is said to have uttered, "What does it matter? The body they can kill, but not the soul." The enemy cut his body into four pieces and burned it, but his heart was later said to have been found unharmed. ● Today is the birthday, in 1884, of Eleanor Roosevelt. ● And Avis Christiansen was born in Chicago on this day in 1895. In childhood she was greatly influenced by a godly grandmother who loved hymns; and as a teenager and adult, she was influenced and associated with the Moody Bible Institute. Avis is the author of a number of several popular hymns, including, "Blessed Redeemer" and "It Is Glory Just to Walk with Him." ● The Second Vatican Council convened on this day in 1962. Sixteen documents were eventually adopted. Catholic liturgy was simplified, with permission given to celebrate the rites of the church in the languages of the peoples rather than in Latin. ● Toronto-native Isobel Kuhn, following training at Moody Bible Institute, sailed for China on October 11, 1928, where she and her soon-to-be husband John worked with great results among the Lisu. Isobel left China at the last moment, escaping over a hair-raising route from the Communists in 1950.

WORSHIP HELPS

Call to Worship

The Spirit and the bride say, "Come!" And let him who hears say, "Come!" And let him who thirsts come. Whoever desires, let him take the water of life freely (Rev. 22:17).

Welcome

Through Scripture, God speaks to the impossibilities in our lives. What situation are you facing today? You might be facing a financial impossibility. He'll tell you that if He feeds the sparrows, He'll feed you (Matt. 6:25–26). Maybe you're facing an impossible marriage situation. He'll tell you how to love and forgive your spouse (Matt. 6:14–15; Eph. 5:25). Maybe you have rebellious kids and you can't see any way through. He'll tell you that if you've trained that child in the faith, the child is positioned to get his life right with God when he gets older (Prov. 22:6). God will speak to our impossibility through His Word. So it's to His Word that we turn today to hear from Him.

Reader's Theater

Reader 1: Now faith is being sure of what we hope for and certain of what we do not see (Heb. 11:1 NIV).

Reader 2: By faith we understand that the universe was formed at God's command, so that what is seen was not made out of what was visible (Heb. 11:3 NIV).

Reader 1: By faith Abraham, even though he was past age—and Sarah herself was barren—was enabled to become a father because he considered him faithful who had made the promise (Heb. 11:11 NIV).

Reader 2: It is by grace you have been saved, through faith—and this not from yourselves, it is the gift of God—not by works, so that no one can boast (Eph. 2:8–9 NIV).

Reader 1: So then, just as you received Christ Jesus as Lord, continue to live in him, rooted and built up in him, strengthened in the faith as you were taught, and overflowing with thankfulness (Col. 2:6–7 NIV).

Additional Sermons and Lesson Ideas

Beware, the Bible Can Mess You Up
Date preached:

By Dr. Larry Osborne

SCRIPTURE: 1 Timothy 1:1–13

INTRODUCTION: The Word of God can be misused. We must be aware of what Scripture says to avoid straying away from God's truth. Paul gives us some guidelines to follow.

1. How to Recognize Dangerous Bible Teaching (vv. 3–7). Dangerous Bible teaching often involves conjecture, myths, and controversies and does not promote God's work by faith.
2. How to Recognize the Real Deal (vv. 5–6). True biblical teaching includes love; it comes from and encourages a pure heart, a good conscience, and a sincere faith.
3. How to Read and Understand the Old Testament (vv. 8–13). The law is good when used appropriately. It combats unsound doctrine which stands in contrast to the gospel.

CONCLUSION: All Scripture ultimately points us to Christ and should push us to become more like Him.

Why Are You Afraid?
Date preached:

By Dr. Timothy K. Beougher

SCRIPTURE: Mark 4:35–41

INTRODUCTION: God reminds us, through Mark's account of Jesus calming the storm, that His Son has power over nature. If Jesus has this power over the wind and the waves, we can certainly trust Him to guide us through storms in our own lives.

1. The Reality of the Storm (vv. 35–37).
2. The Anxiety of the Disciples (v. 38).
3. The Calm Brought by the Savior (vv. 39–41).

CONCLUSION: Don't live your life in fear of the next storm. Jesus Christ is one who rules over land and sea; He has the power to calm the storms that come into our lives.

OCTOBER 18, 2009

SUGGESTED SERMON

Kaleidoscope of Grace

Date preached:

By Rev. Todd M. Kinde

Scripture: 1 Peter 4:7–11, especially vv. 7 and 10

But the end of all things is at hand. . . . As each one has received a gift, minister it to one another, as good stewards of the manifold grace of God.

Introduction: This paragraph summarizes how we are to live as followers of Christ in the last days since He is coming to judge the living and the dead (4:5). This paragraph also rounds out a larger section in the letter which began at 2:11–12. Our behavior, our moral code, as Christians, is rooted upon the glory of God and the return of Christ. Peter tells us, since the end is near, to:

1. **Be Self-Controlled and Sober-Minded So You Can Pray (v. 7).** We are to live in constant expectation of Christ's return. We know it will be sudden as a thief comes in the night. We are to be self-controlled and sober-minded. These are fruits of the Holy Spirit which equip us for prayer. A disciplined mind is a mind that prays for the coming of Christ and for the sovereign grace to stand before Him on that day (Luke 21:33–36). A disciplined mind is the mind that is praying in the Spirit.

2. **Love One Another (v. 8).** From prayer comes love. The measure of our capacity to love one another seems to be related to the clarity and earnestness of our prayers. This means that our love for others comes from God not from ourselves. "We love because He first loved us" (1 John 4:19 NIV). We are to love earnestly and fervently. The test of love, therefore, seems to be most intense at the point of forgiveness: "Love will cover a multitude of sins" (4:8, cf. 1 Cor. 13:4–7).

3. **Show Hospitality to One Another (v. 9).** Now from Spirit-controlled prayer flows love and forgiveness and from love and forgiveness flows hospitality. The practice of opening the Christian home began perhaps with the apostles who traveled an itinerate schedule proclaiming the message of Christ and establishing local churches in new towns. Our understanding of this practice of hospitality is

broadened to include opening the Christian home to those members of our own local church (Acts 2:42–47; 5:42; 20:20). The meal is designed by God to express relationships of loyalty, intimacy, and obligation (Ps. 23). So when we eat with one another we renew our commitment to one another in and under the Lord Jesus Christ.

4. **Serve One Another with Your Gifts (vv. 10–11a).** God's grace comes in various forms of gifts. We are instructed to use those gifts of His grace for the benefit of one another (v. 10). Some of these gifts are speaking gifts while others are serving gifts (v. 11). The grace of God is distributed by His spirit in infinite diversity. Even among those who share the same gift the use and application of that gift will be unique to the person's temperament, background, experience, and style. Here then we see the kaleidoscope of God's manifold grace manifest in the body of believers. God's grace is infinitely multifaceted. Now that you have trusted the person and work of Christ your talents are sanctified, set apart by the Holy Spirit of God to advance His kingdom and the ministry to His people (v. 10).

5. **Glorify God Through Christ (v. 11b).** The form of the sentence here is not a command like those we have just studied. Here it is presented more as motive or even as a purpose or a result. You are to use the gifts of God's grace by His supply of resource and power in order that God Himself may receive the glory in everything. Of course other verses do put this in the command form (1 Pet. 4:16). God has given gifts to you so that you may glorify Him. This is the way you will be truly satisfied: when you come to the point of saying, "I am happiest most when God gets the glory."

Conclusion: Will you give up your own pursuit of glory and self-advancement for the sake of Christ? Will you allow your gifts to be sanctified for His service rather than your own?

STATS, STORIES, AND MORE

"Living with an awareness" is a common phrase indicating that a life-altering condition has occurred that has cast a great shadow—for good or ill—over a person's everyday perspective. The phrase was originally introduced through Yoga and Eastern mysticism, which advocates "living with an awareness of the divine." But the phrase appears in various ways in today's conversations. Cancer patients talk about living with an awareness of their disease, and ecologists talk about living with an awareness of our eco-footprint. As Christians, we should live with an awareness of the imminent return of Christ. Every beautiful sunrise is a symbol of His coming. We should train ourselves, whenever we see stunning formations in the clouds or gorgeous sunsets at the close of day, to say, "Even so, come, Lord Jesus!"

Great Quotes

- Has not our Lord Jesus carried up our flesh into heaven and shall He not return? We know that He shall return.   —*John Knox*
- The Spirit in the heart of the true believer says with earnest desire, Come, Lord Jesus.   —*John Wesley*
- We must hunger after Christ until the dawning of that great day when our Lord will fully manifest the glory of His kingdom.
  —*John Calvin*
- Many times when I go to bed at night I think to myself that before I awaken Christ may come.   —*Billy Graham*
- The coming again of Jesus Christ and the end of the age occupies some 1,845 scriptural verses.   —*John Wesley White*

APPROPRIATE HYMNS AND SONGS

"Let It Rise," Holland Davis, 1997 Maranatha Praise, Inc.

"Show Me Your Ways," Russell Fragar, 1995 Russell Fragar/Hillsong Publishing.

"Grace, Greater Than Our Sins," Julia H. Johnston, Public Domain.

"Amazing Grace (My Chains Are Gone)," John Newton, Chris Tomlin & Louie Giglio, 2006 Worshiptogether.com Songs/sixsteps Music.

FOR THE BULLETIN

Edward Winslow was born on October 18, 1595, in Worcestershire, England. He and his wife sailed to America aboard the Mayflower, and when his wife died during the first winter in the New World, he married Susanna White, a widow. Theirs was the first pilgrim marriage in America. ● Today is also the birthday of pastor and commentator Matthew Henry, born this day in 1662. He is best known for his *Matthew Henry's Commentaries on the Holy Scriptures*. ● The Edict of Nantes, issued in 1598 by French King Henry VI, granted freedoms to the Calvinist Protestants of France. For many years, the edict formed the basis of French unity and religious protection, but on October 18, 1685, King Louis XIV, revoked the Edict of Nantes and declared Protestantism illegal, sending Protestants fleeing to Great Britain, Prussia, Holland, and Switzerland. ● Robert Moffat, a Scottish gardener who became a Congregationalist missionary, sailed for South Africa on October 18, 1816. His fiancé, Mary Smith, followed him three years later, and the two became one of the most remarkable missionary couples of the nineteenth century. They returned home on furlough only once during their long career. Their oldest daughter, Mary, married missionary David Livingstone. ● John Owen became the first person in modern history to run the 100 yard dash in under ten seconds, on this day in 1890. ● On October 18, 1949, cowboy singer and entertainer Stuart Hamblen was converted during the Billy Graham Los Angeles Crusade, and the news helped extend the length of the meetings and catapulted Graham to worldwide prominence. Hamblen later penned the song, "It Is No Secret What God Can Do."

WORSHIP HELPS

Call to Worship

In the beginning, O Lord, you laid the foundations of the earth, and the heavens are the work of your hands. They will perish, but you remain; they will all wear out like a garment. You will roll them up like a robe; like a garment they will be changed. But you remain the same, and your years will never end" (Heb. 1:10–12 NIV).

Pastoral Prayer

Lord, please penetrate our lives, our hardened hearts, through your Word today. As it is written: "For the word of God is living and active. Sharper than any double-edged sword, it penetrates even to dividing soul and spirit, joints and marrow; it judges the thoughts and attitudes of the heart. Nothing in all creation is hidden from God's sight. Everything is uncovered and laid bare before the eyes of him to whom we must give account" (Heb. 4:12–13 NIV).

Offertory Quote

No one has ever become poor by giving.
—ANNE FRANK

Benediction

Once you were alienated from God and were enemies in your minds because of your evil behavior. But now he has reconciled you by Christ's physical body through death to present you holy in his sight, without blemish and free from accusation—if you continue in your faith, established and firm, not moved from the hope held out in the gospel . . . (Col. 1:21–23 NIV).

Additional Sermons and Lesson Ideas

True Religion

Date preached:

By Rev. Melvin Tinker

SCRIPTURE: Deuteronomy 4:1–24

INTRODUCTION: We must be unwilling to exchange the true experience of God for false experience. God, through His servant Moses, goes to great lengths to warn His people not to do so. What are the characteristics of true religion?

1. True Religion Is God Given Not Man-Made (vv. 1–8).
2. True Religion Is Rooted in the Past Not Driven by the Present (vv. 9–14).
3. True Religion Involves Hearing the Objective Words of God Not Being Swayed by the Subjective Feelings of Men (vv. 19–24).

CONCLUSION: The true experience of the one true God comes from His Word. We see this culminated in the life, death, and resurrection of Jesus Christ (Col. 2:6–10).

When a Christian Dies

Date preached:

By Dr. Michael A. Guido

SCRIPTURE: Various

INTRODUCTION: How do you see death? Is it perplexing or is it precious?

1. Look at the Certainty (Eccl. 9:5; 1 Sam. 20:3; Rom. 5:12; Heb. 9:27).
2. Look at the Compassion (2 Kin. 13:23; Ps. 139:1–18; Rom. 8:38–39).
3. Look at the Control (Dan. 6:10–23; Acts 12:1–11; Rom. 8:28).
4. Look at the Concern (Ps. 116:15; Acts 7:55).
5. Look at the Cancellation (2 Tim. 1:8–10).
6. Look at the Change (2 Cor. 5:1–10; Phil. 1:20–24).
7. Look at the Colonization (2 Pet. 1:13–15).
8. Listen to the Call (Rev. 22:17).

CONCLUSION: As believers we ought to find rest in knowing that our God cares for us and loves us even to our deaths (Phil. 1:21). If you're not a believer, heed the call to rest in Christ (Matt. 11:28–30).

HEROES FOR THE PASTOR'S HEART

John Williams

Before he was murdered in Polynesia, John Williams had a full and fruitful ministry. He had been a wild youth back in England, but all that had changed on a Sunday night when he ducked into a church to hide from the wild gang that chased him. There in the back row he heard the gospel. And there, on another Sunday, he heard the call of God to missions. He was sent to Polynesia from the London Missionary Society in 1816 and immediately began going from island to island sharing Christ.

Several of the islands were ruled by an evil chief named Romatane, to whom Williams preached from Isaiah 44:15–17 on the folly of idolatry. A man cuts down a tree and uses some of it for firewood, "And the rest of it he makes into a god, his carved image. He falls down before it and worships it, prays to it and says, 'Deliver me, for you are my god!'" How foolish!

That day the chief began to glimpse the truth of the gospel, and he stayed up all night talking to John. In the morning, he called together his people and ordered them to destroy all their idols.

"Will not the gods punish us?" cried the people.

"No," said Romatane. "Each god is a worthless piece of wood that we have decorated. Pile them up and make a bonfire."

They did, and it was indicative of John's success everywhere. During his ministry, fifty different South Sea islands received the gospel.

He was only forty-three when he set off for a new group of islands, the New Hebrides. After a difficult passage, he disembarked with seven others on the cannibalistic island of Erromanga and began following a small creek inland. He heard a noise behind him, turned, ran, tripped, and fell. His skull was smashed in two blows, and then his backbone was broken.

His soul went to heaven. His body was eaten.[1]

---

[1]From the editor's book, *From This Verse,* published by Thomas Nelson Publishers in 1998, entry for May 4.

OCTOBER 25, 2009

REFORMATION DAY   SUGGESTED SERMON

Faith in Three Dimensions

Date preached:

Scripture: James 2:14–26, especially verse 17
Thus also faith by itself, if it does not have works, is dead.

Introduction: Today is Reformation Sunday around the world, the day in which we remember Martin Luther's famous action on October 31, 1517, of nailing his ninety-five theses to the cathedral door in Wittenberg, thus initiating the Reformation. But Luther certainly wasn't infallible in everything, and one of the interesting footnotes of history is that he wasn't overly fond of the book of James. Luther's great message was justification by grace through faith alone (Rom. 1:16–17; Rom. 4; Eph. 2:8–9). This was Luther's clarion cry. So when he read our paragraph for today in James 2, he just couldn't understand it. When Luther translated the Bible from the Latin into the German language, he took James out of the Bible, along with three other New Testament books, and put them in the back of his Bible as a special supplement, and he did not list those books in the Table of Contents. Well, I love the book of James. I am so glad it's in the Bible. James did approach things differently than Paul, but not in a way that provides contradiction. Paul and James compliment one another. If we do not have James, we cannot understand fully what Paul was trying to say. The great theme of James is: The kind of faith that saves us and really transforms us has got to be the kind of faith that exists in three different dimensions. James taught a three-dimensional faith.

1. **We Need an Intellectual Faith.** Faith it is not anti-intellectual, it is not antiacademic. Genuine faith corresponds to what is true. Faith is not "believing in something *despite* the evidence," it is "believing in something reasonably and logically *because* of the evidence." James 1:19 says that even the demons have intellectual faith, and they shudder! In James 5:19, he talks about someone who drifts from faith or faithfulness to the gospel as "wandering from the truth." Faith is when our thinking corresponds to what genuinely is true. Biblical faith is looking at the evidence and saying, "Hey, this is logical, this is reasonable." This is intellectual belief. It is

believing there is a Creator and a God, there is Christ, He lived, He died, and He rose again! The Bible is true. These things are factual. These things correspond to the truth. That's the intellectual dimension of faith. It is necessary, we've got to have it, but if that is all we have, if that is as far as our faith goes, it doesn't do you any good because even the devils believe like that . . . and shudder.

2. **We Need an Internal Faith.** This second dimension of faith is the internalization of faith, when we say, "I'm going to not only believe this in my mind, I'm going to receive it into my heart and I'm going to derive peace and joy and hope and excitement and enthusiasm in my life because of this faith." This is what James is talking about in James 1:2–8. Our faith gives us piety, peace, hope, and the ability to count all things as joy.

3. **We Need Incarnational Faith.** The third dimension of faith is incarnational, when our faith becomes flesh and we begin to live it out in kindness and benevolence every day. It affects the way we live and it results in obedience. It results in helping people and it results in having a different attitude towards life. It manifests itself in tithing and it manifests itself in generosity and caring for the poor; and because we have faith, we're kinder to people and we do good works and people recognize we're Christians. This is the kind of faith the world is looking for, and Jesus said that when they see our good works, they will glorify our Father in heaven. Our faith should wear work clothes and have work-gloves on. That's the kind of faith that James is concerned about (see James 1:22; 1:26; 2:1; 2:14; 3:13; 4:17, etc.).

Conclusion: The theme of James is: It's not enough to have intellectual faith. It is not even enough to have intellectual and internal faith. We have got to have intellectual, internal and incarnational faith, the kind of faith that shows up every single day in the way we befriend other people, and the way we keep our lives pure, and the way we're generous, and the way we love people, and the way in which we live—the attitudes we have at home, the way we manage our tongue, the way we manage our anger, the way we treat people, the way that we notice when someone has a need. This is genuine Reformation living. Is your faith three-dimensional?

STATS, STORIES, AND MORE

More from Rev. Robert J. Morgan
There are two ways to put this message into action. First, we need to find people and befriend them. Just find somebody every day that you can befriend in some simple little way. Maybe let someone have your parking space. Maybe help someone out if they are having a problem, maybe a neighbor, maybe a friend, maybe just ten minutes talking to a youngster when you really don't have time, maybe turning off the TV and focusing on someone. The Bible commands us to feed the hungry, cloth the naked, treat the wounded, and care for the dying. This is Christianity in action. We need to do this as a church, but it begins as we do it as individuals.

Second, find someone to evangelize, and evangelize them. When we give a cup of cold water, we're to do it in Jesus' name. That means we're concerned about the *physical* and the *spiritual* needs of those to whom God has called us to minister.

An Old Story
Following World War II, some German students volunteered to help rebuild a cathedral in England that had been badly damaged by the Luftwaffe bombings. As the work progressed, they weren't sure how to best restore a large statue of Jesus with arms outstretched and bearing the familiar inscription, "Come unto Me." They repaired everything except Christ's hands, which had been completely destroyed. After considerable thought, they decided to leave the hands off, and underneath to place this inscription: "Christ has no hands but ours."

APPROPRIATE HYMNS AND SONGS

"A Mighty Fortress Is Our God," Martin Luther, Pubic Domain.

"Alas and Did My Savior Bleed?," Isaac Watts, Public Domain.

"Thou Art Worthy," Pauline Mills & Tom Smail, 1975 by Fred Brock Music Company.

"Thank You," Dennis Jernigan, 1991 Shepherds Heart Music, Inc.

FOR THE BULLETIN

Henry II ascended to the throne of England on this day in 1154. He is chiefly remembered for his participation in the assassination of his former friend, Thomas Becket, whom he named Archbishop of Canterbury. ● As copies of William Tyndale's English translation of the New Testament began to appear in England, civil and church authorities became alarmed. On October 25, 1526, Bishop Tonstall warned all London booksellers against the importation and sales of "Lutheran" works. He also issued an injunction to all his archbishops, which said: "Certain children of iniquity, maintainers of Luther's sect, blinded by extreme wickedness, declining from the way of truth and the orthodox faith, have with crafty trickery translated the holy gospel of God into our vulgar English tongue." ● On Sunday morning, October 25, 1787, William Wilberforce sat at his desk thinking of his conversion to Christ, he decided to pour his energy into a crusade to abolish slavery in the British Empire. He wrote in his journal on that day, "Almighty God has set before me two great objectives, the abolition of the slave trade and the reformation of manners," by which he meant public morality. ● Today is the birthday of a one-handed French winemaker named Palcide Cappeau, who was also an occasional politician and mayor of the town of Roquemaure. He is best remembered, however, for writing the words of the Christmas carol, "O Holy Night." He was born on October 25, 1808. ● Jonathan Goforth, missionary to China, was ordained on October 25, 1885. ● On October 25, 1890, the Door of Hope was opened by Emma Whittemore. She was a wealthy New Yorker, who, following her conversion, developed an intense burden for abused and orphaned girls on the streets of New York City. Within four years, the Door of Hope had helped over 300 girls, and by the time of Emma's death in 1931, there were ninety-seven homes operating in seven countries.

WORSHIP HELPS

Call to Worship
I am not ashamed of the gospel of Christ, for it is the power of God to salvation for everyone who believes, for the Jew first and also for the Greek. For in it the righteousness of God is revealed from faith to faith; as it is written, "The just shall live by faith."

Hymn Story: Faith of Our Fathers, 1849
Frederick William Faber was raised in an Anglican parsonage in Calverley, Yorkshire, England; but when he moved to Oxford University as a young man, he came under the influence of the Roman Catholic, John Henry Newman, author of "Lead, Kindly Light." Following graduation, Faber entered the Anglican ministry, but his soul was troubled. He was drawn to the historic, reverent liturgy of the Catholic faith. On Sunday night, November 16, 1845, he announced to his congregation that he intended to leave the Church of England and be ordained as a Roman Catholic. For the remainder of his short life—Faber died at 49—he endeavored to provide a body of hymns for English Catholics to sing. Perhaps his most enduring is "Faith of Our Fathers," which was actually written to remind the Catholic Church of its martyrs during the days of the Protestant King Henry VIII and Queen Elizabeth I. Now, of course, this great hymn reminds us all of the noble sacrifices made those in every branch of the Christian family who have passed on their faith to us ". . . in spite of dungeon, fire and sword."

Additional Sermons and Lesson Ideas

The Prayer for Enlightened Behavior
By William Graham Scroggie

Date preached:

SCRIPTURE: Colossians 1:9–12

INTRODUCTION: This prayer embraces the entire Christian life.

1. Fundamental Equipment (v. 9).
   A. Pursuit of Blessing: A persistent prayer and definite desire.
   B. Nature of Blessing: Being filled with, knowing, and living God's will.
   C. Acquirement of Blessing: "All spiritual wisdom and understanding."
2. Progressive Experience (v. 10a).
   A. Practical Energy: To walk implies effort, progress, and steadiness.
   B. Lofty Standard: "Walk in a manner worthy of the Lord."
   C. Ideal Aim. We are to please Him in all things at all times.
3. Manifold Expression (vv. 10b–12).
   A. Service to Men: Progressing in knowledge and good works.
   B. Character of Self: Providing patience through His power and glory.
   C. Gratitude for God: Praising Him for inheritance and grace.

CONCLUSION: Let us rise to our true calling and tell all people of His redeeming love.

Treasure in Jars
By Rev. Peter Grainger

Date preached:

SCRIPTURE: 2 Corinthians 4:7

INTRODUCTION: God has chosen to use human beings to propagate His message of salvation.

1. A Striking Paradox (v. 7). There is a contrast in quality, beauty, and durability.
2. A Surprising Privilege (v. 7). Poor, unworthy, and frail humans entrusted with the treasure of the gospel of Jesus Christ (2 Cor. 4:6).
3. A Special Purpose (v. 7). In our weakness we experience and display God's power.

CONCLUSION: God has chosen weak and foolish creatures to be the vessels in which His message of good news is presented. But, we must remember that it is not because of anything we have done, but that His desire is to give us the pleasure of taking part in His plan of redemption and demonstrating His power to the world.

SINGLES SERMON

The Single Life Is Good

Date preached:

Scripture: 1 Corinthians 7:32–35, especially verse 32
He who is unmarried cares for the things of the Lord—how he may please the Lord.

Introduction: We know that the single life is good because the Christian life is good, and the Christian life is good because, as Psalm 100 says, the Lord is good. There's admittedly a certain amount of loneliness with being single, and here in 1 Corinthians 7 the apostle Paul speaks bluntly about some of the physical and emotional pressures of singleness. But the passage we've read today is the most proactive and optimistic portion of Scripture dealing with these things. It is the Bible's premier text on the single life, and what it says is that the single life is *good*. The Lord makes this point three times in 1 Corinthians 7:

- Verse 1 (NIV): *Now for the matters you wrote about: It is good for a man not to marry.*

- Verse 8 (NIV): *Now to the unmarried and the widows I say: It is good for them to stay unmarried, as I am.*

- Verse 26 (NIV): *Because of the present crisis, I think that it is good for you to remain as you are* (that is, single).

I. **Singles Are Freer from Concern.** Verse 32 (NIV) says: *I would like you to be free from concern.* The phrase "free from concern" is one word in the Greek, *amérimnos*, made up of the alpha-negative, coupled with the Greek word for worry, *merimnáō*. It's the idea of less in our lives. There is a fine line between concern and worry. It isn't a sin to be concerned; but being anxious is a sin, and that's bad. Being concerned is evidence of love; being anxious is evidence of unbelief. But sometimes we have a hard time knowing how to draw the line between healthy concern and unhealthy worry. But even when it doesn't become unhealthy, it can be distracting, and that's the point Paul is making in 1 Corinthians 7. The Lord doesn't want us to suffer anxiety, but He also doesn't want us to become so distracted by the valid and legitimate concerns of life that we fail to do the very best things. Sometimes the *good* is the enemy of the *best*. We can become so sidetracked doing good things that we fail to do the very best. When a person is married, when they have a husband or wife, when they have children or grandchildren, their lives become very busy and very complicated. There are more cares in life, more responsibilities, more problems, and more distractions. The great thing about being single is that it's Gods' way of freeing us from those sets of concerns so that we can devote ourselves more fully to our walk with Christ and to our work for Christ (see vv. 32–35 in a newer translation).

2. **Singles Have Two Ultimate Priorities.** Notice that according to this passage there are two ultimate priorities here for singles.

   A. **We Should Be Committed to Pleasing the Lord.** It's remarkable how much the Bible has to say about this. If you want to do an interesting Bible study, just get a concordance and look up every reference to the subject of pleasing God (for example, Ps. 19:14; Prov. 15:8; Rom. 12:1–2; 2 Cor. 5:9; Heb. 11:6). It's obviously not a bad thing to please your husband or wife. That's a good thing; but the great advantage of being single is that you're free from responsibilities to a husband or wife so that you can be more fully focused on pleasing the Lord.

   B. **We Should Live in Undivided Devotion to the Lord.** The last verse in this paragraph says: *I am saying this for your own good, not to restrict you, but that you may live in a right way in undivided devotion to the Lord* (NIV). In her autobiography, Bertha Smith, missionary to China, wrote that she had been in China less then two years when she received tragic news that back in the States her father had died in the 1918 flu epidemic. As a result, it was necessary for her to go to the city of Chefoo to sign some papers. That meant eight days travel there and back, and Bertha passed from one mission station to another, staying with missionaries along the way. In all, she visited seven happy missionary families and their children. On the last leg of the trip, she found herself crying all the time, because she was single and so badly wanted to have children and to be a mother. Finally she knew that something had to be done to settle the matter in her heart, and so she walked very fast to get ahead of her guides and to have some quiet time to herself. There, calling on a nearby mountain peak to be her witness, she made a covenant with the Lord, speaking out loud and later recording these words: *Lord, I want* *to enter into an agreement with You today. You called me to China and you gave me grace to follow in coming. I am here to win souls to You. The only thing that will take the place of my own children will be spiritual children. If You will take from my heart this pain, I will be willing to go through with just as much inconvenience, self-denial, and pain to see children born into the family of God, as is necessary for a mother to endure for children to be born in the flesh.* Many years later, when she was aged and tenured, she gave this testimony, "From that moment forward there were no more tears, for the Lord met my every heart need. I became content with my lot and began to study the Bible and books on soul-winning with a new interest. Prayer become more definite for individuals, and every opportunity to speak for the Lord was seized. The transaction has lasted until this day, and many, many times I have praised the Lord for the privilege of being a single woman with the other person's soul-need having first place in my heart."[1]

Conclusion: All of us in this room have been, are, or will be single. Unless my wife and I perish together in a plane crash or a car wreck or a similar disaster, one of us will be single for a period of our lives at some point in the future. Most of our teens are single, and we have many single adults in their 20s, 30s, 40s, and so on. We have single mothers and single fathers, and we have divorced singles, and we have widows and widowers, and many of our senior adults are single. There are disadvantages to the single life, but his overriding emphasis of the Bible is positive. The single life is the life in which we are liberated from certain concerns in life that we may be more fully consecrated to the Lord, in both our walk with Him and in our work for Him, to please Him and to live in undivided devotion to His cause.

[1] Bertha Smith, *Go Home and Tell* (Nashville, TN: B&H Publishers, 1995), pp. 25–27.

The Ministry of Marriage

Date preached:

Scripture: Romans 16:3–4
Greet Priscilla and Aquila, my fellow workers in Christ Jesus. They risked their lives for me. Not only I but all the churches of the Gentiles are grateful to them (NIV).

Introduction: For thousands of years, the concept of marriage as a commitment between one man and woman has served as the foundation of home life and social order; but in the last few years, those foundations are being destroyed in the civil arena. This is disturbing, but not exactly new. The devil has been trying to destroy marriage from the beginning. In the Bible, Adam and Eve had no sooner been married in the Garden of Eden than the devil attempted to destroy their marriage. It's remarkable how many troubled marriages we see in the Bible. The Bible profiles hundreds of men and women, but only a handful had truly exemplary marriages. One of the best was the marriage of Aquila and Priscilla.

1. **Background: The Story of Aquila and Priscilla.**

    A. **Acts 18:1–3, 18–19, 24–28:** This couple first appears in Acts 18. Paul entered Corinth with fear and trembling (1 Cor. 2:1–3), and he was evidently broke. To generate some funds, he found a job in an area of town that sold tents, for he was a tentmaker. Here he found himself working alongside Aquila and Priscilla. We don't know if they were Christians at this point or whether Paul led them to the Lord, but soon they were copartners with him in gospel labor. They left town with Paul; and he passed through the city of Ephesus, which had not yet been evangelized, he left them as an advance team for his future campaign there. Their primary convert there was Apollos.

    B. **Romans 16:3–4:** Some years later, when Paul wrote to the church at Rome, and who should be there but Priscilla and Aquila, with a church meeting in their home.

    C. **Both 1 Corinthians 16:19 and 2 Timothy 4:19** give us the Bible's additional references to this couple. Aquila is never mentioned alone. There is no reference in the Bible to Priscilla alone. They are always named together in the Bible; we never saw one without the other. What that tells us is that *marriage* is *ministry*—and that's the point I want to make. Marriage is ministry; and it is ministry in two ways.

2. **Marriage Is Ministry to One Another.** Marriage is that relationship, ordained by God, in which we are given the opportunity to meet the needs and fulfill the desires of one other person on this planet whom God brings into our lives. The golden rule of marriage is that we meet our spouse's needs as we would have our own needs met. Marriage is about being a caregiver to one another. As long as the husband's primary endeavor is to please his wife and the wife's primary endeavor is to please her husband, there will be a good marriage under that roof. It's when we stop meeting one another's needs and stop ministering to each other that marriages begin to fail.

3. **Marriage Is a Ministry to Others.** Notice how this couple served as a team for the Lord. They worked side-by-side in their tentmaking business, and that brought them into contact with people whom they evangelized. Together they instructed Apollos. Together they entertained the church in their home, not only opening their house but also in teaching and working and risking their lives and mentoring and discipling others. Perhaps you noticed that in the passages we studied, sometimes Priscilla's name came first. I have a feeling she was the fireball of the two, but they were a team and they represent one of the great marriages of the Bible. I believe God wants strong marriages, not just so we can meet each other's needs, but also so husbands and wives can labor side-by-side in the kingdom. That doesn't mean every couple should be in fulltime ministry in the sense of being vocational pastors or missionaries. But it does mean that every couple should be devoted to serving the Lord side by side, not only in raising godly children for the kingdom but in also in working hard in the church and in the world for the Lord.

Conclusion: Marriage is the relationship God gives you for the primary purpose of pleasing and meeting the needs of one other person on this planet. And marriage is that relationship God gives for the purpose of serving side-by-side with someone whose gifts and abilities compliment your own. Don't think of marriage as *misery* but as *ministry*, even as the Son of God came not to be served but to serve and to give His life as a ransom for many.

STATS, STORIES, AND MORE

More from Robert J. Morgan
There's a clinical psychologist named Willard F. Harley who has devoted his life to helping couples stay married. He said that early in his practice he was frustrated because, despite his best efforts, he was unable to save most of the marriages he dealt with. Then he began to realize that in his counseling he'd been focusing on why marriages were failing and trying to correct it. He said that he changed his approach and begin to focus on what made marriages succeed, and the answer, when he found it, was very simple. Marriages succeed when the husband does what it takes to make the wife happy, and when the wife does what it takes to make the husband happy. "From that point on, each time I saw a couple, I simply asked them what the other could do that would make them the happiest, and whatever it was, that was their first assignment."[1]

Some Current Statistics
According to a 2008 report in the UPI, 70 percent of those surveyed in Great Britain see nothing wrong in sex before marriage. In a similar survey in 1984, that figure was 48 percent, demonstrating a rapid shift of societal ethics. In the new survey, 66 percent said there is little difference socially between being married and living together, and only 28 percent said that married couples make better couples than unmarried ones.[2]

APPROPRIATE HYMNS AND SONGS

"Sing to the King," Billy James Foote & Charles Silvester Horne, 2003 Worshiptogether.com Songs/sixsteps Music.

"Made to Worship," Chris Tomlin, Stephan Sharp & Ed Cash, 2006 Worshiptogether.com Songs/sixsteps Music.

"Majestic," Lincoln Brewster, 2005 Integrity's Praise! Music.

"Nothing But the Blood," Robert Lowry, Public Domain.

"Your Name," Paul Baloche & Glen Packiam, 2006 Integrity's Hosanna! Music/Vertical Worship Songs.

---

[1]Willard F. Harley, Jr., *His Needs Her Needs* (Grand Rapids: Baker Book House, 2001), p. 12.
[2]"British Survey: Sex Before Marriage OK," dateline London (UPI), January 23, 2008.

FOR THE BULLETIN

On November 1, 1755, at 9:40 in the morning as many people gathered in churches and cathedrals for All Saints Day services, a massive earthquake stuck Lisbon, Portugal, followed by a tsunami and a fire, causing the near-destruction of the city and the deaths of as many as 100,000 people. ● The hymn "O Jesus Christ, Grow Thou in Me" was published on November 1, 1860, in the *British Messenger* by translator Elizabeth L. Smith. Originally written in German by Johann C. Lavater, the words say: "O Jesus Christ, grow Thou in me, / And all things else recede! / My heart be daily nearer Thee, / From sin be daily freed." ● Today is the birthday, in 1887, of Bill Borden, heir to the Borden Dairy Estate of Chicago, who felt God's call to become a missionary to the Muslims of China. He died en route there, having contracted spinal meningitis in Cairo. He was twenty-five, and his life's slogan was: "No Reserves, No Retreats, No Regrets." ● Today is also the birthday (1921) of the popular twentieth-century composer, John W. Peterson, who passed away in 2006. He's the author of such modern classics as "It Took a Miracle," "Heaven Came Down," and "Surely Goodness and Mercy." ● Evangelist Mordecai Ham died on this day in 1961. Born in Allen County, Kentucky, Mordecai wanted to be a salesman rather than a "poor preacher" like his father and grandfather, but God's call on his life proved too great, and he quit business to enter the ministry. He was a gifted and anointed evangelist who won at least 300,000 people to Christ, including Billy Graham, who was saved at a 1934 Ham meeting in Charlotte, North Carolina. ● On exactly the same day, Helen Lemmel passed away in Seattle, Washington. Born in England to a Methodist preacher and his wife, Helen became a popular musician who is best remembered for writing the words and music for the hymn, "Turn Your Eyes Upon Jesus."

WORSHIP HELPS

Call to Worship

For the grace of God that brings salvation has appeared to all men, teaching us that, denying ungodliness and worldly lusts, we should live soberly, righteously, and godly in the present age, looking for the blessed hope and glorious appearing of our great God and Savior Jesus Christ (Titus 2:11–13).

Service Ide

Testimonies are a powerful tool for reinforcing the truth of a sermon or lesson. In advance of today's service, select two or three couples who have enjoyed long and happy Christian marriages. Ask them in advance to think of the advice they'd like to give to younger couples. During the worship service, walk into the congregation with a microphone and have each couple stand in turn and share their insights with the church.

Pastoral Prayer
Our Heavenly Father, in this room are children and adults, single people and married people, younger couples and older couples. But only the Lord Jesus Christ, who is here among us, is perfect, and all of us need to work on our relationships. Forgive us, Lord, for being ill-tempered, self-centered, and shortsighted. Teach us to see the needs of others, and help us become more concerned for others than for ourselves. Bless our homes, Lord. Bless our marriages. Let all bitterness, wrath, anger, clamor, and evil speaking be put away from us, and may we be kind to one another, tenderhearted, forgiving one another, even as God in Christ has forgiven us. We pray in Jesus' name. Amen.

Additional Sermons and Lesson Ideas

Practicing a Converted Life
Date preached:
By Pastor Al Detter

SCRIPTURE: 1 Peter 4:1–5

INTRODUCTION: Salvation is about two major things. First, it is about salvation from sin. Second, it is about salvation from self. Peter talks about three things that will help us to practice this converted life:

1. Determine to Use Suffering as a Deterrent from Sin (vv. 1–2).
2. Live for the Will of God and Not Your Lusts (vv. 2–3).
3. Change Your Friends If Need Be (vv. 4–5).

CONCLUSION: Your life as a Christian won't change unless you practice a converted life in the power of the Holy Spirit.

Revealed
Date preached:
By Rev. Larry Kirk

SCRIPTURE: Psalm 19

INTRODUCTION: This tells us that we have all the revelation we need to live life. We need to receive that revelation and live in light of it.

1. Look at the Skies and Rejoice in God's Revelation of His Glory (vv. 1–6). God reveals Himself through His creation.
2. Look at the Scriptures and Receive God's Revelation for Life (vv. 7–11). God reveals Himself through His Word.
3. Look at Yourself and Respond to God's Revelation (vv. 12–14). Our response to God's revelation is a desire for freedom through obedience and a life truly pleasing to God.

CONCLUSION: The revelation of God is all the more appealing and authoritative because the God who reveals Himself in His creation and through His Word redeems us by His grace in Christ.

CLASSICS FOR THE PASTOR'S LIBRARY

Borden of Yale '09

And Other Books by Mrs. Howard Taylor

Mrs. Howard Taylor (Mary Geraldine Guinness) was a British missionary to China—and the daughter-in-law of Hudson Taylor—who became the official biographer of the early missionaries connected with the China Inland Mission (OMF International).

Geraldine grew up in London, the daughter of the Irish evangelist Henry Grattan Guinness whose preaching helped usher in the Ulster Revival of 1859 and who had a passionate missionary heart. At one point, Henry wanted to join the China Inland Mission, but Hudson Taylor advised him to continue his evangelistic work in Great Britain, so Guinness stayed in London and began the East London Missionary Training Institute (Harley College), which eventually trained over 1,300 missionaries, and is continuing today as Cliff College.

Henry Guinness had seven children who entered the ministry,[3] including daughter Mary who, in her youth, taught a Bible class for factory girls in London's East End. At age twenty-two, she left for China, arriving at her mission station at Yangzhou of March 23, 1888. "Oh!" she wrote, "If English Christians only knew the need and the longing willingness of these dear souls to hear the glad tidings, and the joy, the unspeakable joy of a missionary's life, they would surely cry from the depths of their yearning hearts, "Lord, here am I, send me, send me."

Soon she was writing the stories that unfolded all around her, recording the history of the pioneer works in China. After falling in love with Howard Taylor, son of CIM founder Hudson Taylor, Geraldine took up her pen in earnest to write the incredible stories of the missionaries, including a two-volume biography of her father-in-law (condensed into the classic *Hudson Taylor's Spiritual Secret*), the story of her brother, Dr. Gershom Whitfield

Continued on the next page

---

[3] His great-grandson is Os Guinness.

CLASSICS FOR THE PASTOR'S LIBRARY—*Continued*

Guinness (*Guinness of Honan*), *The Triumph of John and Betty Stam*, *Behind the Ranges: Fraser of Lisuland*, and *Borden of Yale*.

Mrs. Taylor writes sparingly about herself, but one of her books, *With P'u and His Brigands*, she described her adventures of being kidnapped by Chinese bandits.

All these books are treasures, and Mrs. Taylor's writings have inspired every succeeding generation of missionaries. *Borden of Yale* is a particularly gripping tale because of its unique subject—a wealthy young American who left everything to become a missionary to China, but died before arriving on the field.

William Borden was a millionaire, heir to the vast Borden estate of Chicago. At age sixteen, he spent a year touring the world and visiting Asia and Europe, and his trip laid a great burden on his heart for the multitudes of unreached souls around the globe. As he returned to the States, he stopped in Rome and penned a note to his mother, saying, "Darling Mother, I am glad that you have told Father about my desire to be a missionary. I am thinking about it all the time, and looking forward to it with a good deal of anticipation. I know that I am not at all fitted or prepared yet, but in the next four or five years I ought to be able to prepare myself."

Returning home, he enrolled at Yale University where he instantly became a leader among students and very heavily invested in student and community ministries, helping to found the Yale Hope Mission in New Haven. After Yale, he attended Princeton Theological Seminary.

In 1912, having bequeathed a million dollars to Christian missions, Borden sailed for Cairo, Egypt, where he planned to study Arabic before continuing on to China. But while in Egypt, he contracted cerebrospinal meningitis and died in 1913 at the age of twenty-six.

I was especially moved by the determination of William's mother to journey to Cairo to be with her son on his deathbed. Knowing she was on her way, William would groan in his semi-consciousness, "Poor Mother! Poor Mother!" She arrived in Cairo at 1 P.M. on April 9, 1913. William had passed away at nine o'clock that morning. A few days later Mrs. Borden wrote about the experience: *As yet, it is all more like a dream than reality. But I wanted to tell you just one thing that you may not hear from anyone else: and that is that, when we saw him, it seemed as though William had been transformed into the very likeness of Christ through suffering. I should not have known him, his beard and moustache had grown and the contour of his face was changed. We had been in doubt as to whether to go to the hospital to see him altered as he would inevitably be; but thank God, we did. . . . We were told not to go near the bed, but that at a distance it would be safe. We approached a long, low building, standing right on the ground, so that it seemed as though we might be going to the tomb itself, and the question, "Who will roll us away the stone?" was almost on my lips. The door was opened, and immediately we were in the presence of all that remained here of our William.*

I was so shocked at the change that I turned to beg Joyce not to look or to come in, but she had already done so, and in the gentlest voice—afterward, I thought, it was like the voice of an angel: "But Mother, did you see how he looks like all the pictures of Christ?"

I looked again, and then indeed I saw.

One hardly dared speak of it to others, fearing it would be though irreverent or fanciful. But I did mention it to Douglas in Mr. Gairdner's hearing, who quietly said: "Yes, and you only stood at the threshold. If you had gone nearer you would have seen the resemblance more clearly . . ."

It was as though we had been permitted a glimpse into the mystery of suffering, human and Divine, and had seen that through it God had, so to speak, given the final touches to William's life.

Some of Mrs. Taylor's books, including *Borden of Yale*, are still in print (most in soft cover editions) and some are available on-line for downloading, but all are available from used books sites. I recommend them to pastors because these stories shouldn't be lost, they are full of sermon illustrations, they are almost as motivational as the actual stories found in the Bible, and they make great gifts for young people.

NOVEMBER 8, 2009

INTERNATIONAL DAY OF PRAYER FOR THE PERSECUTED CHURCH
SUGGESTED SERMON

Where Is God When All Hell Breaks Loose?

Date preached:

By Dr. Larry Osborne

Scripture: Psalm 73, especially verse 28
But as for me, it is good to be near God. I have made the Sovereign LORD my refuge;
I will tell of all your deeds (NIV).

Introduction: It's often easy for us to see God in the good times, but where is God when it seems like all hell is breaking loose? When evil seems to surround us, when tragedy seems to chase us down, or when the hard times just won't stop, where is God?

1. **Stinking Thinking: A Recipe for Depression (vv. 1–16).** The psalmist Asaph who was likely a musician for David was probably in the midst of a crisis with David as they ran for their lives from his enemies who did not want him on the throne. The psalmist begins with a statement that he begins to doubt, "Surely God is good to Israel, to those who are pure in heart" (v. 1). The psalmist began to envy the wicked for their prosperity (vv. 1–12). When he considered this, he began to believe he had followed the Lord in vain (v. 13). However, Asaph also realized that acting on that belief would have betrayed God (v. 15). The psalmist then says, "When I tried to understand all this, it was oppressive to me" (v. 16). What a great example of all hell breaking loose and a believer struggling to understand the situation. In these verses, the psalmist displays two characteristics we tend to display in hard times:

   A. **It's All About Me.** In thinking about how God fits into our situation, we tend to evaluate everything based on what happens to *us*. We often think we're the center of the universe. That's the first trap: when we judge God completely by how it impacts us.

   B. **It's All About Now.** Asaph judges his walk with God not only by what is happening with him, but by what is happening to him today, right now. Whenever the enemy can get us thinking only about ourselves and only about now, he has us right where he wants us.

2. **Perspective: How It Changes Everything (vv. 17–28).** Verse 17 is the key pivotal verse where the psalmist describes the way God transformed his thinking: "till I entered the sanctuary of God; then I understood their final destiny. The psalmist describes the utter destruction that will fall upon the wicked, even if not immediately (vv. 18–20). He then contrasts that to his own future: one full of the presence and favor of God (vv. 23–28). He concludes the psalm saying, "But as for me, it is good to be near God. I have made the Sovereign LORD my refuge; I will tell of all your deeds" (v. 28 NIV). The word *refuge* means "hiding place"—the place where someone would go during a storm. Asaph has moved from the brink of counting his faith worthless and speaking that lie to others to an evangelist for the deeds of God. The amazing thing is: *nothing has changed materially* for the psalmist; the bad guys seem to still be winning. But now he has the proper perspective. It's the same for us. God gives us the Scriptures so that we know there's a larger picture than what we see. We must develop the discipline of stepping back, coming to God, and gaining that perspective when hard times come.

3. **From God Is Nowhere to God Is Now Here (vv. 12–19).**

   A. **Judge God's Goodness and Power by the Cross and Eternity (vv. 16–17).** There may be times in all of our lives where we will cry out "God are You good? Are You powerful?" Our conclusion in these times should never come out of a glance at the here and now but should always be evaluated in light of the Cross of Christ and His eternal plan.

   B. **Embrace the Sorrow—Reject the Bitterness (vv. 12–19).** Christians often have a hard time when others express their doubts about God. We often respond with clichés rather than real understanding. We should feel freedom to embrace the sorrow of tragic situations rather than trying to give an artificial pat answer. When people embrace the pain around you, don't give them a cliché, a tract, or even a Bible verse—give them a hug.

Conclusion: Next time it seems that all hell is breaking loose, take a step back, come before God's presence, and reevaluate your situation in light of the cross and eternity.

STATS, STORIES, AND MORE

Fear Has to Leave
In her book of devotions, *Not I, But Christ,* holocaust survivor Corrie ten Boom wrote, "When I was in a concentration camp I did not know that I would be one of the twenty percent of women who left it alive. I looked death in the eyes. When we touch eternity we see all things so simply. It was as if I saw the devil who was much stronger than I. But then I saw Jesus, who is much stronger than the devil, and together with Him I am much stronger than the devil. Then fear has to leave. Those who are with us are more and stronger than those who are against us. 'Greater is He that is in you, than he that is in the world' (1 John 4:4)."[1]

Hold Thou My Hand
Psalm 73:23 says, "Nevertheless . . . You hold me by my right hand." Hymnist Fanny Crosby once wrote of a time when her spirits had been depressed. Normally happy and effervescent, she had been dark and troubled. Then she cried in prayer, "Dear Lord, hold Thou my hand!" and the burden lifted and the oppression fled. She expressed her gratitude by writing a hymn titled, "Hold Thou My Hand," which said:

> *Hold Thou my hand; so weak I am, and helpless,*
> *I dare not take one step without Thy aid;*
> *Hold Thou my hand; for then, O loving Savior,*
> *No dread of ill shall make my soul afraid.*

APPROPRIATE HYMNS AND SONGS

"Rock of Ages," Rita Baloche, 1997 Maranatha Praise, Inc.

"Did You Feel the Mountains Tremble?" Martin Smith, 1994 Curious? Music U.K.

"'Tis So Sweet to Trust in Jesus," Louise M. R. Stead, Public Domain.

"Through It All," Andrea Crouch, 1971 Manna Music.

[1]Corrie Ten Boom, *Not I, But Christ* (Nashville: Thomas Nelson Publishers, 1983), p. 94.

FOR THE BULLETIN

John Duns Scotus, Medieval theologian and brilliant Christian logician, died on this day in 1308. ● Today is the birthday, in 1656, of Sir Edmond Halley, of Halley's Comet fame. ● America's oldest college for women, Mount Holyoke Female Seminary in South Hadley, Massachusetts, opened on November 8, 1836, through the efforts of Mary Lyon, a devout Christian educator with a vision of providing affordable Christian education for all who wanted it. Its motto was from Psalm 144:12: "That our daughters may be as cornerstones, polished after the similitude of a palace." ● James Hannington was known as the "Lion-hearted Bishop of Africa." Hailing from Sussex, England, he became a small-town British pastor who developed an intense burden for Africa. He sailed for Zanzibar on May 17, 1882, and labored faithfully until being imprisoned by King Mwanga II of Buganda. After eight days of captivity, Hannington was speared in both sides (some accounts say he was shot with his own rifle). His last words, on October 29, 1885, were, "Go, tell Mwanga I have purchased the road to Uganda with my blood." On November 8th, four men from Hannington's party who survived martyrdom emerged with news of the Bishop's death. ● Today is the birthday of the Canadian pastor, evangelist, and author Dr. Oswald J. Smith, who was born in a bedroom above the train station in Odessa, where his father was a telegraph operator for the Canadian Pacific Highway. He was converted at age sixteen in an evangelistic campaign led by R. A. Torrey and Charles Alexander, and went on to pastor in Toronto from 1915 to 1959. He was a champion of global missions, and raised some fourteen million dollars for international missions, a history-breaking record in its day. When he died at age ninety-six, Billy Graham conducted his funeral.

WORSHIP HELPS

Call to Worship

Now let us come before Him,
With song and prayer adore Him.
—PAUL GERHARDT

Scripture Reading Medley

Give us help from trouble, for the help of man is useless. Through God we will do valiantly, for it is He who shall tread down our enemies. O LORD my God, I cried out to you, and You healed me. Oh LORD you brought my soul up from the grave . . . weeping may endure for a night, but joy comes in the morning . . . You have turned for me my mourning into dancing; you have put off my sackcloth and clothed me with gladness . . . that my glory may sing praise to You and not be silent. O LORD my God, I will give thanks to You forever. The king shall have joy in Your strength, O LORD; and in Your salvation how greatly shall he rejoice! You have given him his heart's desire, and have not withheld the request of his lips. Blessed be the LORD God, the God of Israel, who only does wondrous things (Ps. 60:11–12; 30:2–3a, 5b, 11–12; 21:1–2; 72:18).

Pastoral Prayer

Lord, we know that You are Lord over all. We know that You know the suffering of our brothers and sisters around the world. We trust that You thwart what was meant to destroy Your church to build it up. And yet, Lord, we feel pain for their sake. We pray that Your justice would be served and that those who have suffered loss for the sake of the gospel would not become embittered but empowered. Deliver our brothers and sisters from the hands of the enemy and allow peace to pervade this earth so Your gospel can spread. We ask in Jesus' name, Amen.

Suggested Scriptures

- 1 Peter 1:3–7; 4:12
- 2 Corinthians 4:17 (cf. 11:23–27)
- Romans 8:18–39; 12:15
- James 2:15–16

Benediction

O righteous God, who searches minds and hearts, bring to an end the violence of the wicked and make the righteous secure (Ps. 7:9 NIV).

Additional Sermons and Lesson Ideas

A Short History of the World
By Dr. Larry Osborne

Date preached:

SCRIPTURE: Various

INTRODUCTION: Every Christian should understand the big picture of Scripture. Let's take a brief overview of the whole of history as revealed in Scripture:

1. Creation (Gen. 1–2): God Made It All.
2. The Fall (Gen. 3): Why It's a Mess.
3. Cain and Abel (Gen. 4): The Bad Guy Wins.
4. Paid in Full (John 19:30): Paid in Full.
5. The Return (Rev. 5:1–6:1): Escrow Closes.

CONCLUSION: We have been given an amazing privilege of knowing both where we've been and where we're going from God's perspective. This should help us gain perspective since our job as believers is to understand our lives within the context of God's plan rather than our own.

The Communion of Saints
By Rev. Larry Kirk

Date preached:

SCRIPTURE: Philippians 1:3–11

INTRODUCTION: God wants you to treasure not only your connection to Him but to every other person who is connected to Him through Christ.

1. The Communion We Share as Christians Should Make Us Patient with the Progress of Others (vv. 3–6).
2. The Communion We Share as Christians Should Make Us Thankful for the Grace We See at Work in One Another (vv. 7–8).
3. The Communion We Share as Christians Should Move Us to Love One Another from the Heart (vv. 9–11).

CONCLUSION: A Christian community is one that is thankful for the work of grace in imperfect people, patient with the progress of people, and loving with a love that both holds people accountable for their actions and cares graciously for their needs. It is this kind of communion that brings change to a world in need.

NOVEMBER 15, 2009

Nature's Fury—God's Faithfulness

By Dr. Kevin Riggs

Date preached:

Scripture: Mark 6:45–52, especially verse 51
Then He went up into the boat to them, and the wind ceased. And they were greatly amazed in themselves beyond measure, and marveled.

Introduction: Hurricane Wilma hit Florida in mid-October, 2005, killing twenty-one people. After the storm a meteorologist explained how Wilma had cleaned out the atmosphere. This got me thinking. Could "cleaning out the atmosphere" be part of the reason God allows storms in the first place? What about personal storms? Why does God allow storms to happen in our lives? Could it be to clean out the junk in our lives? The story of Jesus walking on water gives us some guidance on the topic.

1. **Jesus Watches Over Us, Even When We Are Unaware.** The word "strain" in verse 48 carries the idea of being tormented. Where was Jesus while they were fighting for their lives? He was watching them, fully aware of what was taking place. For reasons unknown you are in the middle of a storm. Jesus seems like He is a million miles away. But in reality, He is standing on the side of a mountain, looking out at you, and looking out for you. But why does Jesus wait so long to help? Why did He allow His disciples to go through so much pain before He intervened?

2. **We Have to Reach the End of Our Own Strength Before We Will Allow Jesus to Take Over.** Nowhere in the story do you see the disciples praying, or crying out to Jesus for help. They just keep rowing, doing things their own way, wearing themselves out (v. 48). What storm are you in? Are you trying to solve the problem on your own? Quit tormenting yourself. Quit wearing yourself out. Allow Jesus to get in the boat and take the controls.

3. **Jesus Waits to Intervene So We Will Recognize Him When He Does Intervene.** In the middle of their storm, trying to do things their own way, ". . . He (Jesus) came to them, walking on the sea,

and would have passed them by. And when they saw Him walking on the sea, they supposed it was a ghost . . ." (6:48–49). The phrase, "would have passed them by," is better translated, "He intended to pass their way." Jesus was not trying to walk by them without being seen, rather He was walking toward them, but they did not recognize Him; as a result, they were afraid.

4. **When We Fail to Recognize Jesus, We Live in Fear.** We fear the worst because we fail to recognize who Jesus is, and then, when Jesus does show up, it scares us even more. But notice; in the middle of their storm, in the midst of their fear, Jesus said to His disciples, "Be of good cheer! It is I; do not be afraid" (6:50). The disciples did not recognize Jesus, so Jesus told them exactly who He was. The phrase, "It is I," literally reads, "I am." Jesus was claiming to be God . . . and this time the disciples got it! When they finally "got it," the storm died down.

5. **Once You "Get It" (Jesus Is God), Your Storm Becomes Nothing but a Shower.** Until you invite Jesus to climb into your boat and take the oars of your life, you will always be at the mercy of the storm. The storms of life may have blown you off course, but right now Jesus is walking toward you. Recognize who He is. Allow Him to come aboard, and the direction you were going in will become the destiny He has for you.

6. **Not All the Storms You Face in Life Are Your Own Fault.** The only reason the disciples were in a storm was because Jesus made them get into the boat and sent them on their way. The storm was not their fault; but there they were, right in the middle of a hurricane. Jesus used the storm to drive the disciples to Himself.

Conclusion: Sometimes things happen in your life in which you have no control. But in the middle of nature's fury, Jesus is faithful. You may not be able to control the situation, but you can control your attitude and your reactions. It may not be your *fault* that you are in the mess you are in, but it will be your *faith* that gets you out.

STATS, STORIES, AND MORE

Due to an accident with a welding torch, David Snitker was burned over 80 percent of his body. While in the Intensive Care Unit, he heard of the many people who were praying for him, and he felt himself slowly regaining strength, slowly starting to heal. But then a strange thing happened. He began to feel self-conscious about the number of people praying for him, and he began to feel guilty. He knew that his entire church was in prayer. He heard that the children were gathering to pray for him. He found out that friends and well-known community leaders were endeavoring to raise money for his family's bills.

He said to himself, "Why do I deserve all this love? I've made a lot of mistakes. I've done things I'm ashamed of." And he slipped into a relapse. His temperature climbed and he stopped making progress. Feelings of guilt hindered his own prayer life, and the doctors became concerned about his survival.

Then one night in his haze and fog and pain, a nurse came into his cubicle, and he asked her to read to him from the Bible. She picked up the Bible on the nightstand and turned at random to Psalm 130 (KJV): *Out of the depths have I cried unto Thee, O LORD. . . . If Thou, O LORD, shouldest mark iniquities, O LORD, who could stand, but there is forgiveness with Thee, that Thou mayest be feared. With the LORD there is mercy . . .*

He felt like his soul and his very body was being washed in God's unfailing love. The nurse closed the Bible, put it on the nightstand, and took his temperature. A surprised look came over her. His temperature had returned to normal, and his physical healing resumed.

This morning you can take a turn for the better. You can have a positive mood swing. You can move from anguish to anthem in your heart, from a sigh to a song because of the privilege of coming to the Lord in prayer and reminding yourself of His unfailing love expressed through Jesus who never, never fails!

APPROPRIATE HYMNS AND SONGS

"All Creatures of Our God and King," St. Francis of Assisi, Public Domain.

"Indescribable," Laura Story & Jesse Reeves, 2004 Worshiptogether.com Songs/sixsteps Music/Gleaning Publishing.

"Great Is Thy Faithfulness," Thomas O. Chisholm, 1951 Hope Publishing Company.

"He's Been So Good to Me," R. Douglas Little, 1978 Heartwarming Music Company.

"It Is Well," Haratio Spafford, Public Domain.

FOR THE BULLETIN

The melancholy British poet and hymnist, William Cowper, was born on this day in 1731. He and his pastor in Olney, John Newton, produced the famous Olney Hymns, and William is the author of "God Moves in a Mysterious Way" and "There is a Fountain Filled with Blood." ● On November 15, 1824, Peter Cartwright, the Methodist frontier preacher, and his wife Frances, arrived from Kentucky at their new and permanent home in Illinois, to "get entirely clear of the evil of slavery." They met tragedy en route, however, when a faulty tree near their campfire toppled over and crushed their young daughter Cynthia. ● A group from the University of Oxford met in Town Hall on November 15, 1838, to plan a memorial to three great English martyrs. The work was completed in 1841, and the inscription reads: "To the glory of God and in grateful commemoration of His servants, Thomas Cramner, Nicholas Ridley, Hugh Latimer . . . who, near this spot, yielded their bodies to be burned, bearing witness to the sacred truths which they had affirmed . . ." The actual site of the burning is marked by an iron cross set in the pavement. ● Oswald Chambers, the Scottish minister who came to Christ under the ministry of Charles Spurgeon and who is best known for his devotional *My Utmost for His Highest* (which was complied from his sermons after his death), died on this day in 1917, while serving as a chaplain with British troops in Egypt during World War I, as the result of a ruptured appendix.

WORSHIP HELPS

Call to Worship

Praise the LORD. I will extol the LORD with all my heart in the council of the upright and in the assembly. Great are the works of the LORD; they are pondered by all who delight in them. Glorious and majestic are his deeds, and his righteousness endures forever (Ps. 111:1–3 NIV).

Invitation

Perhaps you've never turned control of your life over to Jesus. You believe in Him and you know what He wants of you, but you are fighting for control. The storms in your life rage, yet you refuse to desperately cry out to Jesus. Maybe you've been a Christian for a while, but something you've experienced has made you bitter or angry. Instead of trusting Jesus amidst storms, you blame Him. Jesus is Lord of the wind and the waves, but have you allowed Him to be Lord in your life whatever the climate? Whatever situation you find yourself in, trust in Jesus today. Give Him command of the wheel and you'll find He's much better at being the Captain than you are.

Pastoral Prayer

What an amazing God You are that even the wind and the waves obey You. Lord, the storms rage around us and, just like Your disciples, we so quickly forget Your power and Your faithfulness that You have displayed to us so many times before. Today we ask that You would strengthen our faith and increase our dependence upon You. We ask in Jesus' name, Amen.

Benediction

Peace to the brothers, and love with faith from God the Father and the Lord Jesus Christ. Grace to all who love our Lord Jesus Christ with an undying love (Eph. 6:23–24 NIV).

Additional Sermons and Lesson Ideas

Wisdom from Above

Date preached:

SCRIPTURE: James 3:13–18

INTRODUCTION: There's a little town in Southwest Montana called Wisdom—Wisdom, Montana. It's situated along the trail explored by Lewis and Clark; and, is so named because it grew up beside the river Meriwether Lewis dubbed the "Wisdom River" in honor of the purported wisdom of President Thomas Jefferson. Well, this world would be so much better if everyone lived in the town of Wisdom and drank the waters of Wisdom River.

1. The Embodiment of Wisdom (v. 13). Wisdom is evidenced by living a good life with deeds done in humility. A great example of this is Dorcas in Acts 8.
2. The Opposite of Wisdom (vv. 14–16). The absence of wisdom is bitter envy, selfish ambition, and disorder. It seems that James might have been concerned about conflicts in the various congregations and churches that he was addressing (see ch. 4).
3. The Qualities of Wisdom (vv. 17–18).
   A. Pure.
   B. Peace-loving.
   C. Considerate.
   D. Submissive.
   E. Full of Mercy and Good Fruit.
   F. Impartial.
   G. Sincere.

CONCLUSION: Are you living in the town of Wisdom and drinking from its river?

Unity in the Church

Date preached:

By Rev. Billie Friel

SCRIPTURE: Ephesians 4:1–6

INTRODUCTION: Paul urges us to live a life worthy of the call we have received (v. 1).

1. Evidences of Unity (v. 2). This is what a church will look like when unity prevails. There will be humility, gentleness, patience, and enduring love.
2. Endeavoring to Keep the Unity (v. 3). God desires that each member gives diligence to preserve the peace in His family.
3. Essentials of Unity (vv. 4–6). There are seven areas of oneness we must have to walk in unity: one body, one Spirit, one hope, one Lord, one faith, one baptism, and one God and Father.

CONCLUSION: If the body of Christ is not unified, then we will not be effective and we will not truly know what it means to be in Christ. Let us live according to our calling.

NOVEMBER 22, 2009

SUGGESTED SERMON

What Does the Future Really Hold?

By Rev. Melvin Tinker   *Date preached:*

Scripture: 2 Peter 3:1–9, especially verse 9

The Lord is not slack concerning His promise, as some count slackness, but is longsuffering toward us, not willing that any should perish but that all should come to repentance.

Introduction: It's the end of the world as we know it. You see, in the spectrum of world faiths the Bible gives a unique appreciation of the future; the passage of time is meaningful and directed, we are going somewhere. The Christian message isn't just about having Jesus in your heart, or even just a message about going to heaven when you die. It is a message about a new heaven and a new earth which in one shattering future event will replace this old and corrupt world of ours. So turn with me to 2 Peter 3.

1. **The Relationship Between God and History (vv. 5–6).** Peter refers to Noah's flood. God does act in history; He is not someone who set the whole show in motion and then retired like a cosmic clock maker. God is passionately concerned about the world He has made and our place within it. Yes He meets us daily with blessing, causing the sun to shine on the just and unjust alike, but He will also meet us in judicial discipline as He did then. If we ignore our Creator and instead live selfish lives, like we all are prone to do, God will hand us over to the logical consequences of our practical atheism as two world wars tragically show. Say good-bye to God and you can say good-bye to social stability. If God is working in history then it makes perfect sense that He will guide it to one grand conclusion with one final and climactic scene before the curtain comes down. Will He come again? You can bet your life on it.

2. **The Relationship Between God and Time (v. 8).** "But, beloved, do not forget this one thing, that with the Lord one day *is* as a thousand years, and a thousand years as one day." Time can only be measured in an arena where change can take place. Our bodies grow old. Our cars wear out. But what if we lived in eternity? What would our

time look like from that perspective? Such a being would see everything within one moment, the end from the beginning. Nothing would take Him by surprise. God is not thwarted by anything we might do; He is God the Eternal One. So whether it is five seconds or five millennia, from the standpoint of His plans it's all the same to Him. Does two thousand years seem a long time to you? It's a mere blink in the eye of eternity as far as God is concerned. So don't be fooled into falsely thinking that because Jesus has not yet returned He will never return. As Peter remarks in verse 10, the day will come like a thief in the night. God expects us to be ready to meet Him at anytime.

3. **God's Relationship with Us (v. 9).** "The Lord is not slack concerning His promise, as some count slackness, but is longsuffering toward us, not willing that any should perish but that all should come to repentance." How do I know that God passionately loves you and doesn't want you to perish? You have offended God by the sins you have committed; your conscience tells you that. How do I know? Some two thousand years ago the God of history came into history as a baby. The God who is so passionately committed to us became one of us, going to a lonely cross, and taking upon Himself the judgment which is rightly yours and mine. So He the Judge was judged in your place and mine. He took the punishment which was yours and mine. And then was raised from the dead, He now reigns in the glory of heaven, and He is going to come back to claim the world and His people for His own.

Conclusion: Are you ready? Do you long for meaning and direction in your life? Do you desperately desire to get back in touch with the One who made you, who loves you, and who is so patient with you? Well, you can, you know. And the way you do it is to come to Christ turning away from sin—accepting Jesus as Savior and Lord.

STATS, STORIES, AND MORE

More from Rev. Melvin Tinker

In July 1994, twenty-one pieces of a comet slammed into Jupiter, causing bruises on the surface almost as big as the earth. One scientist has concluded that every thousand years or so, our planet is visited by an asteroid with the diameter of a football field, traveling at twenty thousand miles per second. It doesn't take the mind of a rocket scientist to imagine what affect such an invader would have if it were to land in one of our oceans. Hollywood has done the job for us with such films as *Deep Impact* and *Armageddon.* But we might shield ourselves from such pessimistic prognostications by contemplating the statistics involved; the likelihood of this happening in our own lifetime is rather remote.

For others of us, it's not so much the fear of what lies in deep space which is of concern, but what we ourselves are busy doing on earth. After all we are the first generation to be raised under the specter of nuclear war. The menace of universal famine is real as is the shadow of economic chaos. Arthur C. Clark, the author of *2001 Space Odyssey* said, "No age has shown more interest in the future than ours, which is ironic, since it may not have one."

Either we live in a cold impersonal universe with no meaning, or what the Bible teaches is true: the universe is the work of a glorious, loving Author, whose signature is written in the heavens He has made. This Divine Author—this Word—has declared that we matter and that the whole history is moving toward a dramatic climax.

APPROPRIATE HYMNS AND SONGS

"God Is Great," Marty Sampson, 2001 Marty Sampson/Hillsong Publishing.

"I See the Lord," Chris Falson, 1993 Maranatha Praise.

"I Know Who Holds Tomorrow," Ira F. Stahphill, 1978 by Singspiration Music/ASCAP.

"Be Still My Soul," Katherina A. von Schlegel, Public Domain.

FOR THE BULLETIN

On November 22, 1718, Blackbeard the Pirate (Edward Teach) was killed during a battle off the North Carolina coast when cornered by British sailors who shot and stabbed him more than twenty-five times. ● Today is the birthday, in 1840, of Daniel Webster Whittle, the Civil War major who was converted to Christ while in a Confederate POW camp. He later entered the field of evangelism. He also wrote some of our favorite gospel songs, including "The Banner of the Cross," "Moment by Moment," "There Shall Be Showers of Blessings," and "I Know Whom I Have Believed." ● On the night of November 22, 1873, the *Ville du Havre* collided with an iron sailing vessel, the *Lochearn,* and sank within two hours. The 226 fatalities included the children of Chicago businessman Horatio Spafford. Out of the experience, Spafford, who rushed to Europe to join his wife, wrote the hymn, "It Is Well with My Soul." ● The lowest scoring game in NBA history was played on this day in 1950 when the Fort Wayne Pistons (later of Detroit) defeated the Minneapolis Lakers (later of Los Angeles) by a score of 19 to 18. ● On this day in 1963, President John F. Kennedy was gunned down in Dallas, Texas. On the same day, the Oxford professor and Christian apologist, C. S. Lewis, collapsed in his bedroom at 5:30 P.M., and died a few minutes later at age sixty-four. (Aldous Huxley, the author of *Brave New World,* died on the same day.)

WORSHIP HELPS

Call to Worship
And He has on His robe and on His thigh a name written:
KING OF KINGS AND LORD OF LORDS (Rev. 19:16).

Scripture Medley
I am the Alpha and the Omega, the Beginning and the End,
says the Lord, who is and who was and who is to come, the
Almighty . . . . Do not be afraid; I am the First and the Last. I
am He who lives, and was dead, and behold, I am alive
forevermore. Amen. And I have the keys of Hades and of
Death. Take heed that no one deceives you. For many will come
in My name, saying "I am the Christ," and will deceive many.
And you will hear of wars and rumors of wars. See that you are
not troubled; for all these things must come to pass . . . For
nation will rise against nation, and kingdom against kingdom.
And there will be famines, pestilences, and earthquakes . . . But
he who endures to the end shall be saved. And this gospel of
the kingdom will be preached in all the world as a witness to all
nations, and then the end will come. And behold, I am coming
quickly, and My reward is with Me, to give to every one
according to his work. I am the Alpha and the Omega, the
Beginning and the End, the First and the Last . . . . I am the
Root and the Offspring of David, the Bright and Morning Star"
(Rev. 1:8, 17–18; Matt. 24:4–14; Rev. 22:12–13, 16).

Benediction
> *Alpha, Omega, beginning and end,*
> *Who is, who was, and who is yet to come—*
> *May grace and peace now upon us descend*
> *From Father, Spirit, and Christ the Son.*
> —SUSAN H. PETERSON

Additional Sermons and Lesson Ideas

Walk This Way
By Dr. Ed Dobson

Date preached:

SCRIPTURE: Philippians 2:5–11

INTRODUCTION: Jesus Christ lived the ultimate life and made the ultimate sacrifice. Paul shows how Jesus lived and how Jesus died and told us that we are to be the same.

1. Selflessness (v. 6).
2. Sacrifice (v. 7).
3. Servant Hood (v. 7).
4. Identification (v. 7).
5. Submission (v. 8).
6. Humility (v. 8).
7. Obedience (v. 8).

CONCLUSION: Have the same attitude as that of Christ Jesus. Be willing to humbly walk in obedience becoming a servant. Be willing to die to yourself so that He may give you new life.

Charge!
By Pastor Al Detter

Date preached:

SCRIPTURE: 2 Timothy 4:1–5

INTRODUCTION: Paul gives Timothy an extremely serious charge or directive on how to conduct his ministry. It centers on the matter of sound doctrine in the church.

1. The Seriousness of the Charge (v. 1). The forcefulness and gravity of Paul's charge comes across as he makes it in the presence of God and in view of His coming judgment and kingdom.
2. The Execution of the Charge (v. 2). The instruction Paul gives is to preach God's Word and to ". . . Convince, rebuke, exhort, with all longsuffering and teaching."
3. The Reason for the Charge (vv. 3–4). Sound doctrine is vital to the church. Paul taught, and we see even today, that many would distort Scripture to suit their own agenda or preferences.
4. The Keeping of the Charge (v. 5). Those who minister God's Word should be watchful, for affliction will come. We must continue to share the gospel nonetheless.

CONCLUSION: We must not ignore the importance of scriptural preaching and sound doctrine. We must reject any teaching that rebels against biblical teaching and commit ourselves to share the gospel of Jesus Christ.

HEROES FOR THE PASTOR'S HEART

John Newton, Hymnist

John Newton's story is well known—believing mother, pagan father, prodigality, became a sailor, deserted ship, flogged, became a slave trader, became a slave, saved, became a pastor, Olney, London, became a champion of Wilberforce, helped abolish slavery in the British Empire, wrote "Amazing Grace."

What isn't as well known is that Newton spent almost as much time each week preparing his closing hymn as he did his weekly sermon. As Newton selected his texts and prepared his expositions, he liked to summarize his points in a concluding poem; and most of these great hymns have been lost to popular usage. A great example is this poetic overview of the story of Elisha's servant in 2 Kings 6:

> *Alas! Elisha's servant cried,*
> *When he the Syrian army spied,*
> *But he was soon released from care,*
> *In answer to the prophet's prayer.*
>
> *Straitway he saw, with other eyes,*
> *A greater army from the skies;*
> *A fiery guard around the hill,*
> *Thus are the saints preserved still.*
>
> *When Satan and his host appear,*
> *Like him of old, I faint and fear;*
> *Like him, by faith, with joy I see,*
> *A greater host engaged for me.*
>
> *The saints espouse my cause by prayer,*
> *The angels make my soul their care;*
> *Mine is the promise sealed with blood,*
> *And Jesus lives to make it good.*

What audience wouldn't be thrilled with an original poem, deftly stated and easily recited at the end of Sunday's sermon! Many of us would do well to incorporate a little more poetry into our sermons, and some of us could write our own closing hymns as Newton did, if not every week, at least on special occasions. What a way to assimilate, summarize, and apply the text; and what a great way to set your church to singing. If your people sing your sermons, they'll be more likely to live them.

John Newton had an amazing knack for taking the simple stories of the Bible and retelling them with rhyme and rhythm, and with personal application. Much of his imagery and terminology are outdated, but the underlying truths are much needed by today's church. If you take the time to search out Newton's more obscure hymns, you'll find some jewels like this rendering of Elijah's miracle of the flour and oil.

By the poor widow's oil and meal
Elijah was sustained;
Though small the stock it lasted well,
For God the store maintained.

It seemed as if from day to day,
They were to eat and die;
But still, though in a secret way,
He sent a fresh supply.

Thus to his poor he still will give
Just for the present hour;
But for tomorrow they must live
Upon his word and power.

No barn or storehouse they possess
On which they can depend;
Yet have no cause to fear distress,
For Jesus is their friend.

Continued on the next page

Then let not doubts your mind assail,
Remember, God has said,
"The cruse and barrel shall not fail,
"My people shall be fed."
And thus though faint it often seems,
He keeps their grace alive;
Supplied by his refreshing streams,
Their dying hopes revive.

Though in ourselves we have no stock,
The Lord is nigh to save;
His door flies open when we knock,
And 'tis but ask and have.

NOVEMBER 29, 2009

FIRST SUNDAY OF ADVENT   SUGGESTED SERMON

Dying from the Inside Out   *Date preached:*

By Rev. Timothy K. Beougher

Scripture: Mark 6:14–29; Luke 23:6–12, especially Mark 6:25–26
Immediately she came in with haste to the king and asked, saying, "I want you to give me at once the head of John the Baptist on a platter." And the king was exceedingly sorry; yet, because of the oaths and because of those who sat with him, he did not want to refuse her.

Introduction: Are you dealing with terrible sin inwardly and yet you're going through your daily routine convincing others everything is fine? You know you can't keep it up long because it's eating away at you. Today we are going to study a passage which describes for us King Herod, a man who died from the inside out. We are going to see how his inner sense of right and wrong—his conscience—went from confused to seared to hardened.

1. **A Confused Conscience (vv. 17–20).** Herod made numerous wrong decisions in his life. He made decisions not based on what was right, but based on what would bring him power and prestige and pleasure. Herodias had been the wife of Herod's brother, Philip. The early church historian Josephus helps shed further light about what was going on in this family. On one occasion, while he was visiting his brother Philip, Herod had an affair with Philip's wife, Herodias. Herod and Herodias decided to divorce their spouses and to marry each other. So Herodias became Herod's wife and moved into the palace. John had the courage to call this relationship what it was: sinful! Herodias wanted to kill John, but Herod protected him because he feared to touch him. Herod was struggling with sin and he compromised his conscience. He put John in prison because it silenced John's continual criticism of his sinful practices. But he also was afraid to kill John and in a strange way, he was actually attracted to this courageous preacher of God's Word.

2. **A Seared Conscience (vv. 21–28).** Herodias had been plotting, trying to find a way to kill John; it was Herod's birthday. All the who's who in society were there. Toward the end of the banquet, when

everyone had had their fill of wine, Herodias sent her daughter in to entertain the guests with a dance that was no doubt erotic. Herod responded just as Herodias knew he would, offering the young girl anything she wanted up to half his kingdom (vv. 22–23). The girl took her mother's advice to ask for John's head. Herod was sorry (v. 26); his conscience was still working to some degree, but ultimately Herod seared his conscience because of his lust and because of his pride: "because of the oaths and because of those who sat with him, he did not want to refuse her" (v. 26). Spiritual truth would never again have the effect on him that it had up to that point in his life. Mark's account of Herod's life ends here but we see elsewhere in Scripture that this is not the end of the story.

3. **A Hardened Conscience (Luke 23:6–12).** After John was dead, Herod continued to die from the inside out. Remember, Herod used to enjoy listening to John. At one point he showed some signs of spiritual interest, but he allowed his sinful impulses to carry the day. Now, Herod finally got to meet Jesus. The text says he was "very glad" when he saw Jesus. Why? Because he was seeking spiritual truth? No, the text tells us Herod wanted to be entertained; he wanted to see Jesus perform a great miracle. Christ did not respond to his improper motives, and then Herod mocked Him. Here is a picture of a man who has died from the inside out—one who has gone from some interest in the truth to a man who ignores the truth to a man who mocks the truth. That's what sin does to us: the longer we harbor it, the harder it becomes to leave it. It first confuses our conscience, then sears our conscience, and then can ultimately harden our conscience. The longer one waits to repent, to turn from his or her sin, the harder it becomes to repent.

Conclusion: What about you? Are you dying from the inside out? Are you living for self or for Christ? If you are living for self, the Bible says you are heading for the experience of Herod—the experience of being very sorry one day. As the Scriptures say, "today if you will hear His voice, do not harden your hearts . . ." (Heb. 3:15).

STATS, STORIES, AND MORE

Dying from the Inside Out

I grew up on a farm in Kansas. Over the years, we had all different kinds of livestock: milk cows, beef cattle, pigs, even a horse. When I was a freshman in high school my parents decided we should save money on eggs by having our own chickens. There are many different varieties of chickens, but for our purposes we only need to know about two: tame and wild. Somehow we got a batch of chickens that didn't like to lay eggs in the chicken coop like they were supposed to; they would lay them in various places all over the farm. They were wild with a capital "W."

One hot summer day I was up in the hayloft in the top of our barn and found about three dozen eggs on some straw in the corner. I wasn't sure if they were still good or not, having been in the heat for who knows how long. So I took one egg and cracked it open on a board. What happened when I cracked that egg could best be described as a small explosion. The eggs had spoiled; they had rotted on the inside and the decaying material had built up such unbelievable pressure that they exploded like a bomb when the shell was cracked.

Now remember, when I found these eggs I was a teenager. I won't tell you all the uses I invented for those eggs—some things are best left unexplained. These eggs were unusual; they looked okay on the outside, but they were rotten and dead on the inside. Did you know it is possible for a person to be like those eggs? On the outside, a person can look perfectly normal, perfectly healthy, but on the inside, their soul is decaying and rotting.   —*Dr. Timothy K. Beougher*

APPROPRIATE HYMNS AND SONGS

"Hungry," Kathryn Scott, 1999 Vineyard Songs.

"Beautiful One," Tim Hughes, 2002 ThankYou Music.

"Better Than Life," Cindy Cruse-Ratcliff & Israel Houghton, 2001 Integrity's Praise! Music/Lakewood Ministries Music & My Other Publishing Company.

"Joy Unspeakable," Barney E. Warren, Public Domain.

"Come Thou Fount," Robert Robinson, Public Domain.

FOR THE BULLETIN

The early Christian missionary and bishop in Toulouse, France, Saturninus, was seized on November 29, A.D. 257, and given an ultimatum to worship pagan gods or perish. He replied, "I adore one only God, and to Him I am ready to offer a sacrifice of praise. Your gods are devils . . ." The enraged accusers had him whipped then dragged through town by a galloping bull until he was dead. ● Marcus and Narcissa Whitman, pioneer medical missionaries to the Cayuse Indians of Oregon, were attacked by a band of braves on November 29, 1847, and killed along with twelve victims. ● When missionary James Gilmore in China saw a picture of Miss Emily Prankard of London, he wrote to her and proposed, though he had never met her. She wrote back and accepted! By autumn Emily was in China, arriving on this day, November 29, 1874. A week later they were married. Gilmore acquired both wife and colleague, and they labored faithfully side by side for years, reaching northern China for Christ. ● Composer Joseph Lincoln Hall died on November 29, 1930, at his brother's home in Philadelphia. He left behind some of our best hymn tunes, including the melody to "Does Jesus Care," which he claimed as his favorite. ● Today is the birthday, in 1893, of C. S. Lewis, the Oxford scholar who, following his radical conversion to Christ, wrote some of the most popular Christian works of the twentieth century, including *Mere Christianity* and *The Chronicles of Narnia.*

Kid's Talk

Bring two boxes wrapped as gifts—one very large and one very small. Stuff the larger one with paper scraps and in the small one place a $1 bill. Show them to the children and ask them which one they would pick if they could choose only one gift. Allow them to answer and then explain:

"The natural choice is the bigger gift. But it's not which one looks better on the outside . . . [open both gifts] . . . it's the inside that really counts! You know it's the same with us. God doesn't judge us based on how we look on the outside. There's a verse in the Bible that says 'The LORD does not look at the things man looks at. Man looks at the outward appearance, but the LORD looks at the heart'" (1 Sam. 16:7 NIV).

WORSHIP HELPS

Call to Worship
Let us come before him with thanksgiving and extol him with music and song. For the LORD is the great God, the great King above all gods (Ps. 95:2–3 NIV).

Advent Scripture Reading Medley
"Behold, I send My messenger, and he will prepare the way before Me. And the Lord, whom you seek, will suddenly come to His temple . . . Behold, He is coming. Prepare the way of the LORD; make straight in the desert a highway for our God. But you, Bethlehem Ephrathah, though you are little among the thousands of Judah, yet out of you shall come forth to Me the One to be Ruler in Israel. And out of Egypt I called My son. Therefore the Lord Himself will give you a sign: Behold, the virgin shall conceive and bear a Son, and shall call His name Immanuel" (Mal. 3:1; Is. 40:3b; Mic. 5:2a; Hos. 11:1; Is. 7:14).

Additional Sermons and Lesson Ideas

The Power in Persistence
By Dr. Larry Osborne

Date preached:

SCRIPTURE: Matthew 7:7–12

INTRODUCTION: Jesus encourages the people to seek God because He is a good God and to treat others well.

1. A Call to Persistence (vv. 7–8). We are to be seeking God and His good gifts.
2. A Reminder of God's Goodness (vv. 9–11). God is good and gives to those who ask.
3. An Appropriate Response (v. 12). We are also to offer good gifts to others around us.

CONCLUSION: We must realize that our seeking after God must be on His terms and not on ours. Likewise, we must ask for His will and He will provide appropriately for us. Lastly, Jesus exhorts us to treat others as we like to be treated and in so doing give of ourselves to them.

You Just Call Out My Name
By Dr. Michael A. Guido

Date preached:

SCRIPTURE: Various, especially Jeremiah 33:3

INTRODUCTION: God invites us to speak with Him, to bring our concerns and requests before Him, and to praise Him through prayer. It is through prayer that our relationship with Him is strengthened and our lives transformed.

1. Mark the Subject (Jer. 33:3). Prayer is us asking and God answering.
2. Mark the Source (Jer. 33:3; John 16:24; Rom. 15:30). Prayer begins with God.
3. Mark the Scope (1 Sam. 1:1–19; James 5:17–18; Matt. 14:30). Anyone can pray about anything at anytime.
4. Mark the Simplicity (Jer. 33:3a). God invites us to call on Him.
5. Mark the Surety (Jer. 33:3b; Matt. 7:11; Matt. 6:8). God will answer us.

CONCLUSION: "Call to Me and I will answer you and tell you great and unsearchable things you do not know" (Jer. 33:3 NIV).

THANKSGIVING SERMON

Thankfulness Reexamined

Date preached:

By Pastor Al Detter

Scripture: Various, especially 1 Thessalonians 5:18
In everything give thanks; for this is the will of God in Christ Jesus for you.

Introduction: I'd like us to take a fresh look at what it means to be thankful and to venture into the truer depths of thanksgiving. To have a full and biblical view of thankfulness, I believe we must experience three levels of gratitude on a consistent basis. It's not until we get to "level three" that our understanding of gratitude is complete. As we talk about these three levels today, ask God to speak to your heart.

Levels:

1. **Gratefulness for Getting What We Want.** This is the easiest and most natural level of gratitude. We are almost automatically happy about getting what we want. We feel good emotions, perhaps excitement. Giving thanks is easy at this level. It's great to be thankful even at this level, but the Bible pushes us to go beyond. If we don't move beyond this level, we will almost certainly develop:

   A. **An Entitlement Mentality (Gen. 3:4–7).**

   B. **A Forgetful Spirit (Deut. 6:10–12; 8:11–18).**

   C. **A Discontented Heart (Prov. 13:25; Eccl. 4:8).**

2. **Gratefulness for Getting What We Don't Want.** Scripture teaches us plainly, ". . . in everything give thanks; for this is the will of God in Christ Jesus for you" (1 Thess. 5:18). It's not hard to thank God for getting what we want, but how wonderful to learn to thank Him for what we'd rather not experience. Sometimes we get upset and angry because undesirable and painful circumstances invade our lives, but 1 Thessalonians 5:18 teaches us four truths about thankfulness:

   A. **Thankfulness Is All Inclusive: "in everything."** It's hard to give thanks for getting things we don't want. It's hard to give thanks for tragedies. It's hard to give thanks for the consequences of evil. Gratitude in bad circumstances goes counter to our natural inclinations. But we are told to give thanks under every circumstance of life (see Eph. 5:20)

B. Thankfulness Is a Command: "give thanks." The scriptural order is not first feel then obey; it's first obey then feel. It is a lie of the devil to say that you'll be a hypocrite by doing something you don't feel. God knew it would be a tall order. That's why He gave us the command. The commands of God are designed to help us break through barriers that are unnatural and harmful to us.

C. Thankfulness Is God's Will for Us: "this is the will of God." Thanking God in everything is not just good advice. It is the will of God to thank Him in circumstances that we do not like. Part of pleasing God is to do His will. When we do not thank God in everything, we move outside the will of God.

D. Thankfulness Is Accomplished Through Our Connection with Christ: "in Christ Jesus for you." Jesus is the Source of our ability to thank God when we get what we don't want. Only our union with Him makes thankfulness possible. When we are connected with Jesus in a vital way, the dynamic life of Jesus in us gives us the power to give thanks.

3. **Gratefulness for Not Getting What We Deserve.** This level might be the most revolutionary. When we get to this level, there is a change of mindset. In our text today, Paul tells us to give thanks in everything. "Give thanks" is one word in Greek and it is built from the word meaning "grace." Grace in the New Testament means unmerited favor or kindness (even mercy) extended to the undeserving." The idea behind giving thanks in the New Testament is extreme gratitude that God has given us incredible blessings that we don't deserve. If we grasp that we deserve hell and hell alone, then we'll be filled with gratitude for everything we get that we do not deserve—from our salvation and home in heaven to the sun and rain, our food, our house, our car, our health, our appliances, our comforts, the people in our lives. It's all God's grace to us. We deserve none of it. Anything less than overwhelming gratitude should be unthinkable. God owes us nothing. We owe Him everything. Christ took the hell He didn't deserve to give us the multitude of good things we don't deserve!

Conclusion: Which level have you reached in your thankfulness? When we get to "level three" gratitude, God's grace in our lives will never seem anything less to us than astonishing. And we will be able to give thanks in everything! May God help us to become experienced in all three levels!

DECEMBER 6, 2009

An Unexpected Inheritance   *Date preached:*

By Dr. Robert M. Norris

Scripture: 2 Thessalonians 2:13–17, especially verse 13
. . . God from the beginning chose you for salvation through sanctification by the
Spirit and belief in the truth.

Introduction: There are lots of things that you cannot change about
yourself. There is, however, one thing that as a Christian you can
change. If you don't have a sense of joy about life, then you can and
must gain it. Grace at work produces a deep sense of peace and secures
our hope. The nature of that grace is made clear to us as we see how
the activity of God in each of the steps in our salvation brings us eternal
comfort and good hope. Paul makes an orderly progression of God at
work in us:

1. **He Chooses Us (v. 13a).** ". . . God from the beginning chose you
   for salvation . . ." (v. 13). The first step that brought us to our eternal
   comfort and good hope is the election of God who chose us for
   salvation. Paul makes clear that our election is an election of grace.
   Grace is God's disposition to elect for Himself a people apart from
   any of their works. When God chose us for Himself, He did not
   base His choice on any works that we might do, but solely on the
   gracious counsel of His will. We did not deserve it or do anything
   to merit it. It was free.

2. **He Calls Us (v. 14).** We are summoned by God through His Holy
   Spirit by the sound of the gospel, which we believed: ". . . to which
   He called you by our gospel" (v. 14). How incredible that God's
   extending the gospel to our lives is born out of His will and purpose
   and not by virtue of anything in us. He called and wakened us from
   the slumber of spiritual death and raised us to life in Christ. We
   are chosen and we are called through grace.

3. **He Sanctifies Us by the Spirit (v. 13b).** We attain salvation not as
   rebels against God, but as people who are being changed by the
   Holy Spirit. This change is called sanctification, which is the process

of becoming like Jesus: "through sanctification by the Spirit" (v. 13b). It's the day-by-day working out of what it means to be chosen and called by God. Paul repeatedly affirms that this transformation is owing, not to himself, but to the grace of God. This is the way a believer ought to think and feel and talk about their sanctification. Your life is a work of grace. No matter how hard you work—and hard work is encouraged—the lasting fruit of your labor is always owed to God's grace.

4. **He Gives Us Faith (v. 13c).** No one is saved apart from faith in the truth of the gospel. Wherever the Holy Spirit is at work to sanctify, there is faith, and wherever faith is alive, there the Holy Spirit is at work to sanctify: "God from the beginning chose you for salvation through sanctification by the Spirit and belief in the truth" (v. 13). Sanctification and faith really happen together. Sanctification by the Spirit describes God's side of the activity, and faith in the truth describes our side. Nobody changes his own stance as skeptic to become an obedient and loving child of God. It's all done by God who is the giver of faith. We have believed the truth by grace, not by our effort, energy, and will.

5. **He Secures Our Hope (vv. 14–17).** Paul ensures us that we will obtain the glory of Christ forever, which is the goal of our salvation: ". . . He called you by our gospel, for the obtaining of the glory of our Lord Jesus Christ" (v. 14). How can we be sure our salvation will really turn out in glory and not destruction? The answer is the grace of God. When we are finally glorified in Jesus Christ, and our salvation is complete, that, too, will accord with the grace of our God.

Conclusion: From beginning to end our salvation, our election, our calling, our faith, our sanctification, and our glorification, is a work of divine grace. The reason we have eternal comfort and good hope is that our salvation is a great work of God. He elected, He called, He sanctifies, and He preserves us for glory. This is the truth in which we believe and rest. This is an eternal comfort, and this is a good hope.

STATS, STORIES, AND MORE

The Sovereign Shepherd

Anna Talbott McPherson in her book, *They Dared to Be Different,* tells a story about the great gospel singer, Ira Sankey. I do not know if this story is true or not; I haven't found it confirmed elsewhere. But as she tells it, Ira Sankey was traveling by steamboat up the Delaware River on Christmas Eve of 1875. The sky was clear, the stars were out, and the air was balmy. Many of the passengers were gathered on deck, and someone recognized Mr. Sankey and asked him to sing something for them. He agreed to do so, but he paused and whispered a prayer to heaven for the choice of the song. Then he began singing in a clear voice that rang out over the quiet waters of the Delaware: "Savior, Like a Shepherd Lead us, Much We Need Thy Tender Care." When the song was over, a rough-looking man came up to him and said, "Mr. Sankey, did you ever serve in the Union Army?"

"Why, yes," said Sankey, "in the spring of 1860."

"Do you remember doing picket duty on a bright moonlight night?"

"I remember some bright, moonlight nights," said Sankey.

"So do I," said the man, "but I was serving in the Confederate Army. When I saw you standing at your post on that particular night, I thought to myself, *That fellow will never get away from here alive.* I raised my musket and took aim. I was standing in the shadow completely concealed while the full light of the moon was falling on you. At that instant, just as a moment ago, you raised your eyes to heaven and began to sing. . . . I took my finger off the trigger . . . The song you sang then was the song you sang just now. I heard the words perfectly. . . . These words stirred up many memories in my heart. I began to think of my childhood and my God-fearing mother. She had sung that song to me many, many times. . . . When you had finished your song it was impossible for me to take aim at you again. . . ."

Ira Sankey threw his arms around the man and shared with him on that Christmas Eve the story of the Christ of Christmas, the Prince of Peace, and the man confessed his sins and acknowledged Jesus Christ as his Lord and Savior.[1]

---

[1] Anna Talbott McPherson, *They Dared to Be Different* (Chicago: Moody Press, 1967), 22–24.

APPROPRIATE HYMNS AND SONGS

"Of the Father's Love Begotten," Prudentius, Public Domain.

"O Come, O Come, Emmanuel," Thomas Helmore & Henry Sloane Coffin, Public Domain.

"Hallelujah! Christ Jesus Is Born," Dennis Jernigan, 1994 Shepherds Heart Music, Inc.

"King of Love," Martin Smith, 1994 Curious? Music U.K.

FOR THE BULLETIN

Thomas Aquinas, born about 1225, was one of the most brilliant thinkers in Christian history, best known for his *Summa Theologica.* Thomas's towering intellect was accompanied by pulpit prowess. He would sometimes have to pause in mid-sermon to give congregations time to recover from their weeping. On December 6, 1273, while conducting Mass in the Chapel of St. Nicholas, a tremendous mystical experience broke over him. Thomas never again wrote theology. "I can do no more," he told his servant. "Such things have been revealed to me that all that I have written seems to me as so much straw. Now I await the end of my life." ● Anabaptist Hans Hut, a traveling bookseller, preacher, and mystic, was a significant Anabaptist leader in South Germany and Austria. He was arrested and tortured, but died accidentally on this day in 1527, as the result of a fire in the Augsburg prison. ● Today is the birthday of Dorothy Greenwell, in Durham, England, who wrote the hymn, "I am not skilled to understand / What God hath willed, what God hath planned; / I only know that at His right hand / Is one Who is my Savior!" ● Today marks the death, in 1925, of Pastor Russell Conwell, who as a young man was an atheist and a lawyer, but who, following his conversion, became a prominent and popular minister in Philadelphia, and the pastor of the largest Baptist congregation in America. He also founded Temple University and is famous for his lecture, "Acres of Diamonds."

Call to Worship

Sing to the LORD a new song, and His praise from the ends of the earth. . . . Let the wilderness and its cities lift up their voice. . . . Let them shout from the top of the mountains. Let them give glory to the LORD, and declare His praise in the coastlands (Is. 42:10–12).

Advent Scripture Reading Medley

"Now the birth of Jesus Christ was as follows: The angel said to [Mary], "Rejoice, highly favored one, the Lord is with you; blessed are you among women!" And behold, you will conceive in your womb and bring forth a Son, and shall call His name JESUS. He will be great, and will be called the Son of the Highest; and the Lord God will give Him the throne of His father David. And He will reign over the house of Jacob forever, and of His kingdom there will be no end." Then Mary said, ". . . Let it be to me according to your word." So all this was done that it might be fulfilled which was spoken by the Lord through the prophet, saying: "Behold, the virgin shall be with child, and bear a Son, and they shall call His name Immanuel," which is translated, "God with us." (Matt. 1:18a; Luke 1:28, 31–33, 38a; Matt. 1:22–23).

Benediction

Now may our Lord Jesus Christ Himself, and our God and Father, who has loved us and given us everlasting consolation and good hope by grace, comfort your hearts and establish you in every good word and work (2 Thess. 2:16–17).

Additional Sermons and Lesson Ideas

The Prayer for Spiritual Illumination
By William Graham Scroggie

Date preached:

SCRIPTURE: Ephesians 1:15–23

INTRODUCTION: Paul prayed that the church would grow to a greater understanding of their relationship with Christ.

1. Occasion of the Prayer (vv. 15–16).
   A. The Ephesians' Faith in Jesus (v. 15a).
   B. The Ephesians' Love for the Saints (v. 15b).
   C. Paul's Gratefulness of Heart (v. 16).
2. Object of the Prayer (vv. 17–19a).
   A. That God May Give You a Spirit (v. 17).
   B. That God May Open Your Heart (v. 18a).
   C. That God May Increase Your Understanding (vv. 18b–19a).
3. Outlook of the Prayer (vv. 19b–23).
   A. The Resurrection of Christ (vv. 19b–20a).
   B. The Exaltation of Christ (v. 20b).
   C. The Dominion of Christ (vv. 21–23).

CONCLUSION: We serve a powerful God who is able to grant us a growing faith by His unending and unmatched power.

What's Wrong?
By Rev. Melvin Tinker

Date preached:

SCRIPTURE: Ezekiel 28:1–19

INTRODUCTION: There is obviously something wrong with the world. In this passage God speaks to the King of Tyre and tells him that he is full of pride. This is our problem too. The very cause of the issue is the human heart.

1. Man's Folly (vv. 1–5).
2. God's Verdict (vv. 6–10).
3. Man's Tragedy (vv. 11–19).

CONCLUSION: If left like this, we have no hope. But God has a remedy; Jesus Christ. Do you want to be restored into the presence of God? Do you want to regain some of the dignity and value you have lost? Then there is only One we can go to and that is the Lord Jesus Christ.

HEROES FOR THE PASTOR'S HEART

James Renwick

Andrew and Elizabeth Renwick, a young couple, weavers, lived in the hills of Glencairn, Scotland, in the 1600s. All their children had died. Andrew accepted his grief, but Elizabeth cried to the Lord day and night for another child.

The Lord answered, and little James was taught the Holy Scriptures from infancy. Growing up, his conscience was tender; his mind, sharp. He excelled at the University of Edinburgh, but was denied a degree because he refused to accept Charles II as head of the Scottish church.

Remaining in Edinburgh, James watched with alarm as nonconformists were martyred, their severed heads and hands nailed to the city gates as a warning to others. He left Scotland for training and ordination abroad, but his heart was still in the highlands, and he soon returned to preach, teach, organize, counsel, and wear himself out. "Excessive travel," he told a friend, "night wanderings, unseasonable sleep and diet, and frequent preaching in all seasons of weather, especially in the night, have debilitated me." He trudged with diligence through moors and mountains, in the cold stormy nights and by day. His study was often a cold glen or cave; his pillow, a rock or log. He managed a hundred escapes, but at length one winter's night in Edinburgh he was captured, put in irons, and convicted of treason.

His widowed mother visited him in prison, her heart breaking apart. "O James!" she cried, "How shall I look up to see your head and hands upon the city gate? I shall not be able to endure it." He comforted her as he could, and on February 16, 1688 smuggled a message to her, "There is nothing in the world that I am sorry to leave but you. . . . Farewell, mother. Farewell, night wanderings, cold, and weariness for Christ. Farewell, sweet Bible and preaching of the gospel. Welcome, crown of glory. Welcome, O Thou blessed Trinity and one God! I commit my soul into Thy eternal rest."

The next morning he embraced his weeping mother once more, then went to the scaffold.

He was twenty-six.[2]

---

[2]From the editor's book, *On This Day,* published by Thomas Nelson Publishers, 1997, entry for February 16.

DECEMBER 13, 2009

Christmas and the Cause of Hope

By Rev. Larry Kirk

Date preached:

Scripture: Luke 1–2, especially 1:45 (NIV)
Blessed is she who has believed that what the Lord has said to her will be accomplished!

Introduction: As we read and think about great Christmas passages of the Bible, one of the things we need to do is to resist the influence of our culture to trivialize Christmas and its powerful meaning for our lives. The true message of Christmas is about hope. Hope is one of the greatest needs of the human heart and one of the greatest messages of the Christmas story. Sometimes in English the word "hope" describes a wish. In the Bible hope is a kind of confidence. Let's look together at the hope that Christmas brings:

1. **Hope Is Confident Expectation That God Will Fulfill His Promises (1:45).** When Mary the mother of Jesus meets her cousin Elizabeth, she says: "Blessed is she who has believed that what the Lord has said to her will be accomplished!" (Luke 1:45). That's the language of hope. Hope is believing that what the Lord has said to you will be accomplished. We need the confident expectation that God can be relied on to fulfill the hopes He has awakened in our hearts through the promises of His Word.

2. **Hope Trusts in God in Spite of Problems (2:25).** The whole Christmas story takes place against the backdrop of all kinds of serious problems. Yet its entire message is filled, not only with deep happiness in the midst of great darkness, but also profound hope in the face of perplexing problems. For example, "Now there was a man in Jerusalem called Simeon, who was righteous and devout. He was waiting for the consolation of Israel, and the Holy Spirit was upon him" (Luke 2:25). Simeon was waiting and believing. That's hope. Simeon's hope was not based on a denial of the problems of the day but rather on a decision to trust in God despite the problems of the day.

3. **Hope Trusts God to Transcend Understanding and Expectations (Luke 1–2).** Mary, Joseph, Simeon, the shepherds, and all the others in the Christmas story are not given full explanations that describe in detail how God will fulfill His promises. Mary and Joseph don't understand the spiritual and biological details of the miracle of the virgin birth. Simeon doesn't know precisely how this little baby will be a light of revelation to the Gentiles and the glory of his people Israel. But Mary, Joseph, and Simeon do not allow the limitations of human understanding to determine the height of their hope in God. Hope trusts God to fulfill His promises in ways that transcend our understanding and expectations.

4. **Hope Waits for God to Accomplish His Will His Way (2:28–30).** One of the most revealing things about this man, Simeon is the way he describes his own relationship to God: "Sovereign Lord, as you have promised, you now dismiss your servant in peace" (v. 29). The word "Lord" here is the word from which we get the English word *despot*. It is not the common word for Lord that is found throughout the Bible. It's the word for an absolute master who has complete rule over the lives of those under him. To hope in God for Simeon is not to come to God with his agenda and ask God to bless it and "hope" that He will do it. In every life something rules as sovereign. What is it that rules as sovereign in your life as you prepare for Christmas?

5. **Hope Does Not Disappoint (1:45–47).** The exchange between Elizabeth and Mary shows how hope does not lead to disappointment, but sees the fulfillment of God's promises for our greater good and His greater glory: "'Blessed is she who has believed that what the Lord has said to her will be accomplished!' And Mary said: "My soul glorifies the Lord and my spirit rejoices in God my Savior" (vv. 45–47). Mary trusted the promises for good reason. They were all fulfilled in Christ as He was born that first Christmas in a manger with heavenly signs and hosts, with shepherds and wise men bowing at His feet, with kingly gifts, and so much more than Mary could have expected; not to mention His ultimate role as Savior.

Conclusion: God's Spirit speaks to us in the stories of Christmas, strengthening our hearts with great hope in Him. He will certainly fulfill the promises of grace He has given to us.

STATS, STORIES, AND MORE

More from Rev. Larry Kirk

David Aikman holds a Ph.D. in Russian and Chinese history. He worked for over twenty years as a respected journalist for *Time Magazine.* A few years ago he took some time off and wrote a book titled: *Hope—The Heart's Great Quest.* Through extensive study and interaction with people, he came to the conclusion that every human heart yearns for hope even if he or she doesn't know what hope is. He wrote: "Hope is the distinguishing feature of Christianity compared to any other belief system. It is far more evident in Christianity than in any other religion or philosophy. In New Testament times, the two other prevailing philosophies did not offer hope. Stoics were educated, civilized, thoughtful, and kindly but were grieved at the condition of humankind and were unable to do anything else but live in quiet dignity. Meanwhile, the Epicureans simply sought pleasure. So people were cynics or hedonists. Christianity changed the prevailing attitude."[1]

The Foundation of Hope

Edward Mote was born into poverty on January 21, 1797, in London. His parents, innkeepers, wouldn't allow a Bible in their house, but somehow Edward heard the gospel as a teenager and came to Christ. He eventually became a skilled carpenter and the owner of his own cabinet shop. "One morning," he recalled, "it came into my mind as I went to labor to write a hymn on the 'Gracious Experience of a Christian.' As I went up to Holborn I had the chorus: *On Christ the solid Rock I stand / All other ground is sinking sand.* In the day I had four first verses complete, and wrote them off." In 1852, Edward, fifty-five, gave up his carpentry to pastor the Baptist Church in Horsham, Sussex, where he ministered twenty-one years. He resigned in 1873, in failing health, saying, "I think I am going to heaven; yes, I am nearing port. The truths I have been preaching, I am now living upon and they'll do very well to die upon." Today his hymn, "The Solid Rock," is still popular with Christians around the world: "My hope is built on nothing less than Jesus' blood and righteousness."

---

[1]Aikman, The Revelation of Hope. www.hfe.org.

APPROPRIATE HYMNS AND SONGS

"My Hope Is You," Brad Avery, David Carr, Johnny Mac Powell, Mark D. Lee, & Sam Anderson, 1997 New Song; Vandura 2500 Songs & Gray Dot Songs.

"The First Noel," English Carol, Public Domain.

"Joy to the World," Isaac Watts & George Frederic Handel, Public Domain.

"Thou Didst Leave Thy Throne," Emily Elliott & Timothy Matthews, Public Domain.

FOR THE BULLETIN

The Council of Trent was convened in the Italian Alps in the city of Trento on this day in 1545, in response to the Protestant Reformation. During this Council, the details of the Catholic Counter-Reformation were formulated, including the standardization of the Mass and a decision to commission the first Catholic catechism (The Roman Catechism) and to undertake a revision of the Vulgate. ● The first of the Moravian missionaries, Leonhard Dober and David Nitschmann, arrived on the island of St. Thomas on December 13, 1732, eager to evangelize the slaves, even if it meant becoming slaves themselves. ● Mourners in Lancaster, England, gathered on this day in 1793, to conduct the funeral of musician John Hatton, who reportedly died after being thrown from a stagecoach. He is best known as the composer of the music, DUKE STREET, to which the hymn, "Jesus Shall Reign" is often sung. ● Today is the birthday, in 1823, of William How, British pastor, bishop, and hymnist, author of "For All the Saints," "Jesus, Name of Wondrous Love," "O Word of God Incarnate," "Soldiers of Christ Arise," and "We Give Thee But Thine Own." ● The great Boston pastor and Episcopalian leader, Phillips Brooks, was born on December 6, 1835, and a great statue of him stands today outside Trinity Church in Boston. In additional to his other accomplishments, he is remembered as the author of the Christmas carol, "O Little Town of Bethlehem."

WORSHIP HELPS

Call to Worship

Lo, He comes! His throne the manger,
Shepherds, seek His shrine the stall;
Ox and ass behold the Stranger,
God, who made and governs all!
Mortals, raise your loudest voices,
Jesus lifts on high your horn;
Earth redeemed today rejoices,
For today her Lord is born!
—RICHARD R. CHOPE, 1894,
"Hark! The Full-Voiced Choir
Is Singing"

Advent Responsive Reading

Leader: For unto us a Child is born, Unto us a Son is given; and the government will be upon His shoulder. And His name will be called Wonderful, Counselor, Mighty God, Everlasting Father, Prince of Peace.

Congregation: Of the increase of His government and peace there will be no end, upon the throne of David and over His kingdom, to order it and establish it with judgment and justice from that time forward, even forever.

Leader: "But you, Bethlehem Ephrathah, though you are little among the thousands of Judah, yet out of you shall come forth to Me the One to be Ruler in Israel, whose goings forth are from of old, from everlasting."

Congregation: Jesus was born in Bethlehem of Judea in the days of Herod the king.

Leader: And when (Herod) had gathered all the chief priests and scribes of the people together, he inquired of them where the Christ was to be born.

All: So they said to him, "In Bethlehem of Judea, for thus it is written by the prophet: 'But you, Bethlehem, in the land of Judah, are not the least among the rulers of Judah; for out of you shall come a Ruler who will shepherd My people Israel'" (taken from Is. 9:6–7; Mic. 5:2; Matt. 2:1, 4–6).

Benediction

May the God of hope fill you with all joy and peace as you trust in him, so that you may overflow with hope by the power of the Holy Spirit (Rom. 15:13 NIV).

Additional Sermons and Lesson Ideas

A Light Has Dawned
By Rev. Larry Kirk

Date preached:

SCRIPTURE: Isaiah 9:1–7

INTRODUCTION: This is a message of hope to Israel; however, it also stands as a message of hope in our lives today.

1. The Dawn of God's Light Will Bring Relief for the Distressed (v. 1).
2. The Dawn of God's Light Will Bring Honor for the Humbled (v. 2).
3. The Dawn of God's Light Will Bring Joyful Blessing (v. 3).
4. The Dawn of God's Light Will Bring Freedom for the Oppressed (v. 4).
5. The Dawn of God's Light Will Bring Peace for the Earth (v. 5).
6. The Dawn of God's Light Will Come Because a Child Is Born (vv. 6–7).

CONCLUSION: Jesus came to be our Counselor, our Mighty God, our Eternal Father, and our Prince of Peace. He came to bring the Light of hope to a darkened and hopeless world.

What If Jesus Had Never Been Born?
By Pastor Jonathan Falwell

Date preached:

SCRIPTURE: 1 Corinthians 15:13–20

INTRODUCTION: If Jesus had never been born:

1. Jesus Could Not Have Risen from the Dead (v. 13).
2. Our Faith Is All in Vain (vv. 14–16).
3. The Entire World Is Lost in Their Sins (v. 17).
4. Our Believing Loved Ones Who Have Preceded Us in Death Are Not in Heaven (v. 18).
5. We Have No Hope (v. 19).

CONCLUSION: It is in verse 20 that we get our hope for Paul says, "But Christ has indeed been raised from the dead." During the Christmas season we often remember the little Baby that came to this earth to be our Savior. But let us not forget that He came to die that we might be cleansed by His sacrifice. If He had not been born, He could not have died.

DECEMBER 20, 2009

FOURTH SUNDAY OF ADVENT   SUGGESTED SERMON

Jesus Water of Life

Date preached:

Scripture: Isaiah 55, especially verse 6
Seek the LORD while He may be found, call upon Him while He is near.

Introduction: The book of Isaiah is often called "The Fifth Gospel" because of its many references to the coming Messiah and His good news of salvation. One of the best sections of Isaiah is chapter 55, which is very relevant for this Christmas season. At a time when we're spending record amounts of money on Christmas presents for friends and family, it's good to ask once again the question the Lord asks in Isaiah 55:2: "Why do you spend money for what is not bread, and your wages for what does not satisfy?" In other words, at Christmas of all times, why do we highlight the material at the expense of the spiritual? We can make and spend all the money in the world, and we can give and receive the most expensive presents on earth, but those things can never satisfy the soul. Why don't we focus more on Jesus? Why don't we realize that what we really need this Christmas are the three great commands of Isaiah 55:

1. **Come (vv. 1–5).** There are three stanzas or divisions to this chapter, and we can sum them all up in three different words. The first word is *Come*, which encompasses the material in verses 1–6: "Ho! Everyone who thirsts, come to the waters . . . come, buy and eat. Yes, come, buy wine and milk without money and without price . . . Incline your ear and come to Me." Jesus said: *Come, follow Me . . . . Come unto Me all you who are weary and burdened . . . Let the little children come unto Me. . . . Come and see. . . .* Here in Isaiah 55, the Lord is addressing this passage to the thirsty. Thirst is a metaphor for spiritual need. Remember how the psalmist said, "As a deer thirsts for springs of water, so my soul longs after God"? Jesus began His ministry by saying, "Blessed are those who hunger and thirst after righteousness." He told the people of His own day that He was the water of life. Whoever came to Him and drank from Him would never thirst. The very last invitation in the Bible in Revelation 22 says, "Whoever is thirsty, let him come. . . ." The

Lord is simply saying here, "If you have a spiritual longing, if you want something deeper in your life, if you are thirsty on the inside, all you have to do is to come to Christ. Come and drink. That is, come and believe and receive.

2. **Seek (vv. 6–11).** The second section of this chapter can be summed up with the word *Seek*. We must seek the LORD while He may be found and call on Him while He is near (v. 6). One of the biggest frustrations of my ministry is how many people procrastinate getting saved. I've had so many people say to me, "Well, I know I need to make some changes, but this isn't a good time. I'll get to it later." It seems to us that we have lots of time. But verses 8–11 tell us that God doesn't see things as we do. His thoughts are higher than our thoughts, and His ways than our ways. But He has recorded His thoughts in words (in the Bible, in the gospel message) that have descended to earth like the rain and snow, to quench our thirst and to produce a harvest (vv. 10–11). Just as God sends rain from above to water the earth, so He sends His message from above to revive and transform our hearts. That's why we need to come to Him and drink. That's why we need to seek Him while He may be found.

3. **Go (vv. 12–13).** That leads to the third word: *Go*. We will go out with joy and be led forth in peace. The mountains and the hills shall break forth in singing. In other words, as we come and see and drink and receive, we discover the joy of an enthusiastic life. According to etymologists, the word *enthusiasm* has a Christian origin. When people in the early church came to Christ, they were filled with a joy, zeal, and power they'd never before known. Since no one term described all these things, they put together the Greek words for "in"—*en*—and "God"—*Theos*, creating the term en-theos-ism: *enthusiasm*.

Conclusion: As we celebrate the birth of Jesus this year, come to the waters, seek the Lord while He may be found, and you will go out with joy and be led forth in peace, and the mountains and the hills will burst into singing, and the trees of the field will clap their hands.

STATS, STORIES, AND MORE

More from Rev. Robert J. Morgan

I read about an Italian-American evangelist named John Carrara who was greatly used to bring multitudes of people to Christ. Being of Italian descent, he had grown up in a Roman Catholic family and he was familiar with the rituals and sacraments of the church, but somehow those things didn't really satisfy something deep within him. When he was a teenager in Fairview, New Jersey, a school buddy invited him one day to church, and that evening John's attention was drawn to a verse of Scripture inscribed over the baptistery.

Nothing the preacher said that night impressed him, but John couldn't get away from a phrase from that verse over the baptistery. It struck him like a bolt from the blue. The verse was John 3:16, and the phrase was: . . . *shall not perish! . . . shall not perish! . . . shall not perish!*

John Carrara returned to church the following Wednesday night and there in the pew he gave his heart without reservation to Jesus Christ. When his dad heard the news, he beat him so badly that John's shoulder was dislocated, but nothing could pound the joy from John's heart. He went on to become a greatly used evangelist throughout the twentieth century. The message of Christmas is the message of God. He so loved this world that He gave His only begotten Son that whoever believes in Him shall not perish but have everlasting life.

APPROPRIATE HYMNS AND SONGS

"Infant Holy, Infant Lowly," Anonymous, Polish Carol, Public Domain.

"O Holy Night," John Dwight & Adolphe Adam, Public Domain.

"It's All About Jesus," Henry Seeley, 2003 Planet Shakers Publishing.

"Angels We Have Heard on High," French Carol, Public Domain.

FOR THE BULLETIN

Today marks the death, in 1552, of Katherine von Boro, whom Reformer Martin Luther had married, having smuggled her out of a convent in a herring barrel. Katherine's optimistic spirit and generous hospitality helped define parsonage life for Protestant pastors. ● Edmund Grindal, the English churchman who became Archbishop of Canterbury, was ordered by Queen Elizabeth I to curtail preaching throughout the kingdom. On December 20, 1576, Grindal responded in a long letter, saying in part: *The speeches it hath pleased you to deliver me concerning abridging the number of preachers and the utter suppression of conferences among ministers have exceedingly dismayed and discomforted me. Alas, Madam, is the Scripture more plain in any one thing than that the Gospel of Christ should be plentifully preached? . . . I choose rather to offend your earthly Majesty than to offend the heavenly Majesty of God.* Elizabeth, furious, placed Grindal under house arrest. But the gospel was not shut up, and despite the queen's misgivings gospel preaching spread to every corner of the British Isles. ● The state of Missouri enacted legislation on this day in 1820 to tax bachelors between the ages of twenty-one and fifty for being single. ● The British medical doctor turned expositor, Martyn Lloyd-Jones, was born on December 20, 1899, over the grocery shop that his father owned in Cardiff. ● Adelaide Addison Pollard, seventy-two, was traveling from her New York City home to spend the Christmas holiday and hold meetings in New Jersey. She fell ill in the New York City train station of a ruptured appendix and died on this day in 1834. She is best known for her invitational hymn, "Have Thine Own Way, Lord." ● The Far East Broadcasting Company (FEBC) was incorporated as an international radio ministry on December 20, 1945.

WORSHIP HELPS

Call to Worship
O come, all ye faithful! Come to the waters; and you who have no money, come. You who are thirsty, come! Come, let us adore Him—Christ our Lord!

Advent Reader's Theater:
Reader 1: Then an angel of the Lord appeared to [Zacharias] . . . and when Zacharias saw [the angel], he was troubled, and fear fell upon him (Luke 1:11–12).

Reader 2: ". . . the angel Gabriel was sent by God . . . to . . . Mary. And . . . the angel said to her, 'Rejoice, highly favored one, the Lord is with you; blessed are you among women!' But when she saw him, she was troubled at his saying . . ." (Luke 1:26–29).

Reader 1: "But the angel said to him, 'Do not be afraid, Zacharias, for your prayer is heard; and your wife Elizabeth will bear you a son, and you shall call his name John . . . And he will turn many of the children of Israel to the Lord their God'" (Luke 1:13, 16).

Reader 2: "The angel said to her, 'Do not be afraid, Mary, for you have found favor with God. And behold, you will conceive in your womb and bring forth a Son, and shall call His name JESUS. He will be great, and will be called the Son of the Highest; and the Lord God will give Him the throne of His father David . . . of His kingdom there will be no end' (Luke 1:30–33).

Reader 1: "And Zacharias said to the angel, "How shall I know this? For I am an old man, and my wife is well advanced in years" (Luke 1:18).

Reader 2: "Then Mary said to the angel, "How can this be, since I do not know a man?" (Luke 1:34).

Reader 1: "And the angel answered and said to him, 'I am Gabriel, who stands in the presence of God, and was sent to speak to you and bring you these glad tidings' (Luke 1:19).

Reader 2: "And the angel answered and said to her, 'The Holy Spirit will come upon you, and the power of the Highest will overshadow you; therefore, also, that Holy One who is to be born will be called the Son of God . . . For with God nothing will be impossible' (Luke 1:35, 37).

Additional Sermons and Lesson Ideas

The Real Meaning of Christmas
By Rev. Larry Kirk

Date preached:

SCRIPTURE: Various

INTRODUCTION: What does Christmas really mean?

1. God's Plan and Heart for Everyone.
   A. The Magi—Wealthy, Educated, and Gentile (Matt. 2:1–12).
   B. The Shepherds—Poor, Uneducated, and Jewish (Luke 2:8–20).
2. God Understands.
   A. The World Will Hate His Followers, But They Hated Jesus First (Matt. 10:22).
   B. Jesus Was Tempted in Every Way We Are Tempted (Heb. 4:15–16).
3. We Can Be Forgiven and Changed.
   A. We Have Been Reconciled to God Through Christ (Col. 1:21–23).
   B. Being Connected to God Enables a Change in Us (John 15:4–5).
4. Decision Time: Will God Be Your Ruler or Rival?
   A. Fight Against Jesus and Glorify Self (Matt. 2:1–23).
   B. Fight with Jesus and Glorify Him (Matt. 16:13–19).

CONCLUSION: Jesus came to deliver the world from sin. Give your life to Him today (John 14:6).

Setting Things Straight
By Pastor Al Detter

Date preached:

SCRIPTURE: Various

INTRODUCTION: Christmas is a time to celebrate that God sent His Son to be our Savior. God's plan was to redeem us as His people through the beautiful birth, despicable death, and radiant resurrection of His Son Jesus Christ. Forgiveness came through His sacrifice.

1. Jesus Is Our Only Hope (Matt. 1:21; John 14:6; Acts 4:12; 1 Tim. 2:5; Eph. 2:8–9).
2. Our Sin Has Disrupted Our Relationship with God (Rom. 3:23; 2 Tim. 3:2–4; James 2:10).
3. Jesus Came to Provide Forgiveness for Each of Us (Luke 19:10; Mark 10:45; Heb. 9:15).

CONCLUSION: There are four aspects to forgiveness and salvation (Rom. 3:22–24): Forgiveness involves a violation (v. 23); forgiveness involves the payment of a penalty (v. 24b); forgiveness involves a pardon (vv. 22, 24a); and forgiveness involves a response from the guilty (v. 22).

The Power and the Perils of the Web in Ministry
A Conversation with Joshua D. Rowe

Joshua Rowe is a summa cum laude graduate of Columbia International University and a M.Div. student at The Southern Baptist Theological Seminary. He also works full-time as a Web designer/developer, database designer, and multimedia specialist.

Why do you think the topic of the Internet as it relates to ministry is important to today's pastor?

We could talk all day about how the Internet is changing the world. The Web is the most versatile medium in existence. It's incredibly powerful, specifically in terms of productivity, entertainment, and communication. Like any powerful tool, though, the Web can be dangerous and harmful. I'm concerned with helping pastors and churches avoid major pitfalls. If you're not convinced of the tension between the Web's power and its perils, let me give you two examples:

First, consider the 2008 elections. A presidential candidate didn't dare add his or her name to the ballot without having pages on MySpace and Facebook.[1] However, these are the same social networking sites that have proven themselves fertile grounds for online predators.[2] A second example is the workplace, where there's increasing dependence on the power of the Internet to both promote and conduct business. Yet businesses fight to keep their employees from wasting company time and resources on

Continued on the next page

---

[1]Rawlinson, Linnie for CNN: *Will the 2008 USA election be won on Facebook?* http://edition.cnn.com/2007/TECH/05/01/election.facebook/ accessed December 10, 2007.
[2]Williams, Pete for MSNBC: *MySpace, Facebook attract online predators: Experts say be careful what you post online—somebody is always watching.* http://www.msnbc.msn.com/id/11165576/ accessed December 5, 2007.

CONVERSATIONS IN THE PASTOR'S STUDY—*Continued*

personal online ventures.[3] From schools to libraries to our own households, two things are sure: people are embracing the Web more than ever—and the dangers on the Web increase proportionally to its popularity.

With its rise in popularity and utility, do you think every church should use the Internet as a ministry tool?

Every medium used in ministry needs to be contextualized. A pastor should exegete his congregation like he would a passage of Scripture. If a church body simply doesn't use the Web much, wisdom would tell us to invest time and resources elsewhere. Having said that, I think most pastors will find these tools increasingly relevant to their members.

It seems more and more pastors are streaming video and/or audio of their sermons and worship services. Do you think this is a good idea?

Absolutely! Streaming audio and video is becoming easier to accomplish, whether through podcasts or a number of other tools. You don't have to be a megachurch or have a megabudget to utilize this kind of technology. Streaming sermons can be an incredible blessing to church members who are bedridden, or just sick or away for a weekend. They can also be excellent for reinforcement—anyone at his own convenience could listen to an old sermon series that helped him in the past. Some churches use recorded portions of their sermons in small group sessions to help members further internalize and apply the teaching. Additionally, random Web site visitors may see your videos or tune in to your podcasts; these can be evangelistic tools as well.

However, ministers should remind their congregations that the Web is **not** a substitute for church fellowship (Heb. 10:25). Video and audio can be an excellent extension of pulpit ministries but they're poor substitutes for face-to-face interaction and fellowship promoted by the New Testament.

---

[3]Swafford, Michelle, MSNBC: *Workers' Web Habits Are No Secret.* Aired January 6, 2003 on MSNBC.

Blogs are also increasing in popularity. Do you think pastors should have them?

Blogs (Weblogs) can be a great way for a congregation to become more connected to their pastor or church leadership team. Some pastors' blogs provide commentary on world or local events from a Christian perspective. Others post more devotional content or share personal spiritual insights throughout the week. All of these are wonderfully useful in allowing busy members to receive insight and encouragement from their pastor (or other church leaders) throughout the week.

I might be in the minority here, but I think a pitfall to avoid with church blogs is allowing user feedback—something most blogs allow. Much research has been done to document the increase in aggression people tend to experience online.[4] If an angry member is in front of the computer, steaming at his pastor, he will likely be tempted to lash out where his face cannot be seen but his "virtual" voice can be heard by all—to the detriment of the body. Even if a moderator catches snide remarks before publicizing them, the angry member will likely feel added tension next time he attends worship.

A conversation about the Web as it relates to ministry would be incomplete without a discussion of online tithing.

Online giving is an expansive and difficult topic, the subject of much heated debate. Some view online giving as an unhealthy severing of tithe from corporate worship. Others are wary of enabling online giving technology that makes no distinction between credit and debit cards. They feel that this sends an unhealthy message in our debt-ridden, buy-now-pay-later culture. The issues are too broad to adequately discuss in one conversation. Suffice it to say, every pastor, finance committee, and congregation needs to decide for themselves whether to implement an online tithing system. *Continued on the next page*

---

[4]For more complete analysis and research concerning online aggression, see *The Psychology of the Internet* by Patricia M. Wallace (Cambridge University Press, 2001) pp. 110–130.

CONVERSATIONS IN THE PASTOR'S STUDY—*Continued*

What do you see as the greatest danger to avoid in utilizing the Internet in ministry?

Our culture is saturated with individualistic thinking and living; the Internet provides a unique means to promote the unhealthy aspects of our individualism. It provides an avenue for people to assume virtual identities. Online, we can communicate with a mass audience while simultaneously retaining anonymity. The idea of the church in Scripture is that of a unified body that meets together, people held accountable for their actions and their character—not a virtual community of social networkers who will one day be judged based on their chosen persona.

Are there any other tools or issues you would like to address?

Yes, too many. I'd love to dive into the power and perils of lots of other online tools like calendars, forums, online directories, curriculum reviews, Web sites for Sunday school or small groups, etc. We could talk a lot about the Web not only in terms of ministry tools, but in terms of its use in the daily life of church members and pastors. We could also discuss mediums other than the Internet as they relate to ministry . . . but it's just too much for one conversation. I do have a Web site devoted to these topics: technologyandministry.com—readers can visit to continue the discussion and share their own experiences.

How would you summarize a healthy approach to the use of the Internet in ministry?

The Internet can be a wonderful supplement to ministry but never a substitute. As ministers of the gospel, we're not called to imitate popular culture or technology, but to have a redemptive mindset as we work to reclaim them for the kingdom of Jesus Christ.[5] I believe we can, through the wisdom of the Spirit of Christ, successfully navigate through the perils to harness the power of the Internet for the sake of His kingdom.

---

[5]For an excellent and more complete analysis of Christianity and pop-culture, see *Retaking Mars Hill: Paul Didn't Build Bridges to Popular Culture* by Dr. Russell D. Moore: http://www.touchstonemag.com/archives/article.php?id=20-07-020-f accessed December 4, 2007.

DECEMBER 27, 2009

SUGGESTED SERMON

The Path of Wisdom: Practical Proverbs

By Dr. David Jackman

Date preached:

Scripture: Proverbs 25:1–28, especially v. 11
A word fitly spoken is like apples of gold in settings of silver.

Introduction: The second greatest commandment, to love our neighbor as ourselves, is the focus of our passage for today. The Bible tells us that words and actions are the very way we relate to one another.

I. **Accentuate the Positive.** Many of the proverbs in this chapter are comparisons. They lay out two similar concepts that we might look at them and discern the connection between the two halves. It causes us to stop and think, to savor the wisdom given.

   A. **Speak Appropriately (v. 11).** Here we see the relationship between craftsmanship and a word fitly spoken. The gold and the silver can produce an item of beauty, but it needs a craftsman who takes time and trouble to make it. The emphasis is on the appropriateness and timeliness of our words. The right word is a delightful gift. This requires thought, wisdom, and skill. Think about how you speak to others.

   B. **Reprove Wisely (v. 12).** Reproof is a very positive use of speech, provided it's motivated by wisdom. There are two pieces of jewelry in verse 12 that compliment one another and are much more valuable together than apart. The one who gives wise reproof bases his reproof on God's wisdom revealed in Scripture. Within the Christian family, this is how we support and strengthen one another both giving and receiving biblical reproof.

   C. **Narrate Faithfully (v. 13).** The cold snow here refers not to bitter cold, but to refreshment during a time of great heat. The refreshment comes to the one who has sent the messenger. The messenger achieves his task with integrity and truthfulness and thus refreshes the one who sent him. When someone asks us to represent what happened in a meeting or convey the details of a document, can we be relied on to be truthful in an age of spin?

44444444444

D. Persuade Patiently (v. 15). The situation here is of seeking to win over someone in authority over you. This does *not* mean pulling the wool over someone's eyes as the fool would. The godly wise person with quiet persistence and gentleness will win all sorts of victories that bluster and anger will never see.

E. Report Refreshingly (v. 25). Think about all the ways we can build each other up by bringing good news to one another. Don't pass one another by; think of how you can encourage one another.

2. **Eliminate the Negative.** As much as it helps to have positive commands, we often need negative commands since we naturally gravitate towards doing the wrong things.

A. Don't Gossip (vv. 8–10). Various forms of careless speech sprinkle these verses. There's a hastiness to testify against one's neighbor (v. 8). Wisdom recognizes this may backfire on us since we rarely know all the facts and our motives are rarely as pure as we think.

B. Don't Boast (v. 14). Clouds without rain in Israel symbolized promises without substance. Either the braggart wants you to believe he has money that he doesn't have or to think that he's generous when he isn't. In all our speech we must avoid this type of boasting.

C. Don't Lie (v. 18). The neighbor here is broad in definition; we're to be scrupulously truthful in all we say about others. A false tongue is a highly dangerous weapon. It escalates conflict and hostility like the weapons of death in this verse. When we lie about others we kill their reputation.

D. Don't Provoke (v. 20). This is using speech without sensitivity to the condition of the hearer. It's very provoking. Don't impose your mood on others, but empathize with them.

E. Don't Slander (v. 23). Here the point is the inevitability of the north wind bringing the rain in the same way that a backbiting tongue surely results in hostility and anger. That secret word behind someone's back, that suspicion we cast on others' motives, or that "juicy" information we pass on will all tend to become known.

F. **Don't Nag (v. 24).** The rooftop in this verse is an escape from a quarrelsome wife. Such marriages don't reflect the love of Christ. We're not to use speech (or lack of it) as weapons against each other. We're to live in a common house, speaking and spending time together.

Conclusion: Where does this wisdom leave us? Convicted of how short we fall? I trust so. We should also be aware of God's grace, asking for help to make progress. We need to ask Him for the strength to live wisely and grow in likeness to the Lord Jesus Christ.

STATS, STORIES, AND MORE

More from Dr. David Jackman
I remember reading a story about a pastor in the United States who had become trapped by sexual temptation which led him into sin and actually ruined his whole ministry. He was writing many years later about what he'd been through. He said he had been warned by two friends. They were close friends who reproved him because they saw the direction in which he was going. Someone asked him afterwards, "Didn't you hear the warning bells ringing?" He said, "Oh yes, I heard them all the time. But I wasn't listening." It's one thing to have wise reproof, but another to have a listening ear.

Friendliness
According to D. A. Benton in her book *Executive Charisma,* the ability to work well with other people accounts for 85 percent of our success in getting, keeping, and advancing in our jobs. Our technical skills account for the remaining fifteen percent. "In a thirty-five-year career, " Benton writes, "you'll experience over 100,000 hours of decision making and 400,000 hours interacting with others." Ritz-Carlton Hotels uses a very telling sentence to train their workers: "Elegance without warmth is arrogance."[1]
  Sam Walton, who founded Wal-Mart understood the same thing. Years ago, when the company reached $100 billion, he had a meeting and announced, "We just went out of the retail business. With 30 million coming in our stores a day, we're in the people business. Anybody can put product on the shelves. We'll be the best in how we treat people."[2]
  Well, the Bible gave that same advice nearly 3,000 years ago: "Reliable friends . . . are like cool drinks in sweltering heat" (Prov. 25:13, MSG).

---

[1] D. A. Benton, *Executive Charisma* (New York: McGraw-Hill, 2003), p. 116.
[2] Ibid., p. 117.

APPROPRIATE HYMNS AND SONGS

"Be Thou My Vision," Irish Hymn, c. eigth century; Trans. by Mary E. Byrne & Versified by Eleanor Hall, Public Domain.

"One Pure and Holy Passion," Mark Altrogge, 1992 Dayspring Music, LLC/ Sovereign Grace Praise.

"More of You, Jesus," Michael Farren, 2005 Word Music/Pocket Full of Rocks Publishing.

"Agnus Dei," Michael W. Smith, 1990 Milene Music, Inc.

FOR THE BULLETIN

Ulrich Zwingli arrived in Zurich on December 27, 1518, bringing with him the Protestant Reformation. ● Francis Asbury, thirty-nine, was ordained as the first bishop of the Methodist Church in America on December 27, 1784. ● Missionaries Robert and Mary Moffat were married before a handful of friends on December 27, 1819. And there they labored side by side for fifty-three years, becoming one of the greatest husband-wife teams in missionary history. ● Alexander Whyte, Scottish preacher and author of a famous set of studies on Bible characters, was ordained on December 27, 1857, at the Free St. John's Church in Glasgow. ● Classical organist and composer Peter Christian Lutkin, who gave us the wonderful melody for the Aaronic Benediction ("The Lord Bless You and Keep You"), which often ends with a moving sevenfold "Amen," died on this day in 1931, in Evanston, Illinois. ● Peter Vins was a faithful gospel minister in Russia who was imprisoned by Stalin's Communist government for his faithful preaching. At first, he was sometimes able to see his wife and wave to his son through his prison window, but authorities noticed the practice and covered the windows to deny him the pleasure. His family never saw him again and subsequently learned he died in captivity on December 27, 1943, at the age of forty-five. ● Pope John Paul II visited Rome's Rebibbia prison on December 27, 1983, to meet with the Turkish terrorist who had shot him in an assassination attempt on May 13, 1981.

WORSHIP HELPS

Call to Worship

I will exalt you, my God the King; I will praise your name for ever and ever. Every day I will praise you and extol your name for ever and ever. Great is the LORD and most worthy of praise; his greatness no one can fathom. One generation will commend your works to another; they will tell of your mighty acts (Ps. 145:1–4 NIV).

Scripture Reading

And now . . . what does the LORD your God ask of you, but to fear the LORD your God, to walk in all His ways, to love Him, to serve the LORD your God with all your heart and with all your soul, and to keep the commandments of the LORD and His statutes which I command you today for your good? (Deut. 10:12–13).

Pastoral Prayer

Lord, we ask that You would write Your wisdom in our minds and on our hearts. Because we know that it's out of the abundance of the heart that the mouth speaks, we pray that in our hearts those changes may be happening. We pray that You would change us by the Spirit of Jesus Christ who not only died but was raised and gave His Spirit that we could be conformed into His likeness. Make us responsive to Your Word. Help us to use this great gift of speech gently, graciously, and proactively to build one another up in truth and love. Grant that we, as Your people in the world, may be known for our truth, our honesty, our integrity, and our gentle, persuasive commitment to everything that is revealed in Your Word. We ask in Jesus' name, Amen.

Additional Sermons and Lesson Ideas

Leaving a Legacy
By Pastor Jonathan Falwell

Date preached:

SCRIPTURE: Various

INTRODUCTION: In order to leave a legacy that will have value for generations, there are some basic thoughts that we must understand.

1. Put Your Life in His Hands (Prov. 3:5).
2. Escape from Your Past (1 John 1:7; Ps. 1:1).
3. Continue in Faith (2 Tim. 1:1–5).
4. Finish (2 Tim. 4:6).

CONCLUSION: God didn't create us to start well and finish poorly. He didn't create us to have value today but none tomorrow! God created us to have value today but more value tomorrow. And through Him, because of Him, it really is possible!

Death Knell for Death
Adapted from a Sermon by Dr. Robert M. Norris

Date preached:

SCRIPTURE: Hebrews 2:14–18

INTRODUCTION: Being at one with us in the unity of our humanity, Jesus represents us. We can claim the victory through Him because He has accomplished everything on our behalf.

1. Because We Are Human, Jesus Christ Became Human (v. 14a).
2. Jesus Christ's Death Destroyed Satan's Power in Death (v. 14b).
3. Jesus Christ's Death Destroyed Our Fear of Death (v. 15).
4. Jesus Christ Became Like Us to Save Us from Our Sin (vv. 16–17).
5. Because of Jesus Christ's Experiences, He Is Able to Help Us (v. 18).

CONCLUSION: You are free from death. When you are tempted to despair or unbelief, Christ will come to help you. He will come as One who knows just what you are experiencing and will give you what you need to endure to the end.

CHURCH BUILDING/RELOCATION SERMON

Moving with God

Date preached:

By Pastor Al Detter

Scripture: Numbers 9:15–23, especially verse 17
Whenever the cloud was taken up from above the tabernacle, after that the children of Israel would journey; and in the place where the cloud settled, there the children of Israel would pitch their tents.

Introduction: Building a church or moving to a new location is an extremely ambitious operation. We should go to the Scriptures and look at the dynamics of God's people on the move. It would be a mistake not to see what God has to say to us during this monumental chapter in our church life. As God moves us along on our journey, there are three key lessons we need to learn.

1. **We Need a Sense of God's Presence (vv. 15–23).** Let me refresh your minds to the story. One year almost to the day (Ex. 40:2), God had led Israel out of slavery in Egypt. God led them into the wilderness to Mount Sinai where He gave them the Ten Commandments. From there God would lead them to the Promise Land. From start to finish, God would lead them by some kind of cloud by day and fire by night. The cloud and fire first appeared the night of the Passover as Israel fled Egypt (Ex. 13:21–22). Now that the tabernacle was complete, the cloud and fire stood over the tabernacle when it was not in transit. The cloud and fire was the supernatural manifestation of the personal presence of God with His people (Ex. 40:34–38). We need to live moment by moment with a sense of God's presence. Our text is telling us to look continuously for the cloud and fire and not to make a move unless we see it. In the absence of a literal symbol of God's presence like the cloud and fire, what can we do today to have a continual sense of God's presence in our lives? We need to take measures every day to put ourselves in the presence of God.

2. **We Need a Signal Indicating God's Direction (v. 17).** In verse 17, the text says that whenever the cloud was lifted from over the tent, the people would set out and when the cloud would settle down,

Israel would camp. The cloud would rise and move then fall and stop. Talk about a divine guidance system! There is a key repeated phrase in verses 18, 20, and 23: "At the command of the LORD." To Israel, the movement of the cloud was equivalent to the command of the Lord. When the cloud moved, it was God telling them to set out. When the cloud stopped, it was God telling them to camp. God wants to control all the movements of our lives. Where we live, what we buy, who we marry, where we work, what we do. The cloud did not follow the movements of the people; the people followed the cloud.

3. **We Need a Spirit of Mobility (vv. 20–23).** When we realize that we're living in the wilderness and traveling to another destination, the last thing that should happen is for us to develop a sense of permanence. Israel had to be ready at a moment's notice. They never knew how long a movement or stopping place would be. They just knew they had to be ready to move when the cloud was lifted and camp when it fell. A spirit of mobility is so important if God is going to move His people along on the journey. This lesson is crucial. We need to be able to move when God gives us direction. There are three critical parts to this lesson:

A. **Movement Is Inevitable.** God has a journey in mind for every believer and every church. It's amazing how resistant God's people are to change. Every day Israel looked at the cloud and wondered either, "Will it move today or will it stop?" They never knew. But the expectation was movement. God will lead us all through a lot of change before we complete the journey. We need to understand this. We need a spirit of mobility.

B. **It's Foolish to Put Our Stakes in Too Deep.** At any moment, God may say, "It's time to pack and move on." If our stakes are in too deep or we are too attached to where we are, we may not be able to move on in our journey. We may not even want to.

C. **Knowing Everything About the Move Is Unnecessary.** Even though Israel knew they were headed for Canaan, they never knew where they were going or how long they would be moving or stopping. We live in a day where we want to know everything about the move first. The reality is—God doesn't always tell us. He may take us on a detour like He did Israel (Ex. 13:17). He may move us quickly or He may move us slowly (Num. 9:22). He may move us into some unexpected difficulties (Ex. 14; Num. 20–21). Our desire to see the pathway should never overshadow our desire to see the Lord. Wherever His presence is—that's all we need and that's where we should want to be, whether moving or stopping. A spirit of mobility says, "I want to be with God and move with Him."

Conclusion: The Lord is teaching us through Israel's experience in the wilderness that it's His will to be present and completely in charge of the journey of our lives, and that we need to be flexible, whether as a church, a family, or as individual believers. Who is in charge of leading your life? Are you moving at the command of God or are you directing your journey? Israel spent thirty-nine unnecessary years in the wilderness because they tried to run things. You cannot run your life any better than God. Let's follow the cloud!

WEDDING SERMON

Where You Go I Will Go

Friends, family, loved ones, brothers and sisters in Christ, it's an honor to be a part of this ceremony. As believers in Jesus Christ, _____ and _____ recognize Scripture as their ultimate authority, and so a portion of Scripture from the book of Ruth will be read and briefly discussed. Before we read this passage, let me give a short overview of the story of Ruth and her mother-in-law, Naomi. Naomi moved from her home in Israel to a foreign land to escape famine, but instead of finding relief, intense tragedy struck. Her husband and two sons died within eleven years of their move. She was left with only her two daughters-in-law in the country of Moab. Naomi did not want to hinder her daughters-in-law from living as they pleased, so she released them from their responsibility to care for her. One of them left, but the other—Ruth—clung to her, refusing to leave. The words that Ruth spoke to Naomi are the words _____ and _____ have asked to be read as their commitment to each other and as a challenge to all of us:

> *Scripture:* Ruth 1:16–17 (NIV):
> Ruth replied, "Don't urge me to leave you or to turn back from you. Where you go I will go, and where you stay I will stay. Your people will be my people and your God my God. Where you die I will die, and there I will be buried. May the LORD deal with me, be it ever so severely, if anything but death separates you and me."

I would like to take this passage phrase by phrase to challenge _____ _____, _____, and all of us today. First, Ruth said: "Don't urge me to leave you or to turn back from you. Where you go I will go, and where you stay I will stay." _____ (groom), don't ever push your bride away because you feel unworthy or like you're holding her back. It's often easier to push others away in anger or frustration or discouragement, but it's not healthy. A true commitment involves sharing joys and sorrows, successes and failures, strengths and weaknesses. Where you go, _____ (bride) is committed to go. If you spiral into depression, it's likely she'll do the same. If you stay complacent in your spiritual life, you will neglect to grow closer to the Lord as a couple. But if you make yourself vulnerable, and if you push yourself to grow and to reveal yourself more and more, for better or for worse, you will find great joy and companionship. When trouble comes, hold her close; don't push her away. _____ (bride), in this statement that Ruth makes, it's apparent that she is submitting herself to Naomi's leadership. Even though the rest of the world might not consider Naomi capable of leadership, this is not true. If we had time to read the rest of Ruth, we'd find that God uses Naomi to lead and guide Ruth to a life of joy. In the same way, submit yourself to _____'s leadership. His leadership is not a dictatorship as we read in Ephesians 5; husbands are to reflect the same love that Jesus Christ displayed by laying down his life. Remember that _____ is literally willing to die for you, so you can certainly trust his leadership.

Second, Ruth said: "Your people will be my people and your God my God." Share everything. One of the most enjoyable things about a marriage is sharing common families and friendships. If you spend most of your spare time with different sets of friends, you will begin to drift apart. Sometimes you may find it difficult to find friends who fit you both well, but it's worth the effort. Make it a priority to share a common social circle. Most importantly, share your spiritual lives with each other. Remain committed members to a local church wherever you find yourselves, and always build up and encourage each other's faith. You have a God who has acted in history, who has sent His son in the flesh, who has risen from the grave and now sits at God's right hand as Ruler of All. He's given us His Word to live by. Share your devotion to Him as the focus of your relationship. Let Scripture guide you to strengthen each other with encouragement, sharpen each other with truth, and support each other with your prayers.

Finally, Ruth said: "Where you die I will die, and there I will be buried. May the LORD deal with me, be it ever so severely, if anything but death separates you and me." Friends and family, in our culture commitments are broken as quickly as they are made. But Scripture understands commitment to be a life-and-death matter. In this passage, Ruth takes a vow to cling to her mother-in-law until one of them dies. Scripture tells us that marriage is something that God joins together and no man should dare separate. When the words of the vows, "until death do us part," are spoken, they are not meaningless tradition. This is a Christian wedding, and _____ and _____ are committed to living according to the Word of God and not according to our cultural norms. This marriage is truly a life-long commitment. I think I can accurately say that all of us are excited to continue being a part of these two lives as they are now being joined as one. What an honor to watch this incredible commitment being made before our eyes. May it challenge us to be completely committed to our own families and ultimately to the Lord.

Vows

_____ and _____, if you then have thus been led by the Holy Spirit to take one another as life-partner, and if this marriage is, from the beginning, to be committed to Jesus Christ, will you please join your right hands for the exchanging of your vows and repeat after me:

To groom: *In taking the woman I hold by the right hand to be my wedded wife, before God and these witnesses I promise to love her, to honor her and cherish her in this relationship, and leaving all others, cleave only unto her, in all things a true and faithful husband, as long as we both shall live.*

To bride: *In taking the man I hold by the right hand to be my wedded husband, before God and these witnesses I promise to love him, to honor him and cherish him in this relationship, and leaving all others, cleave only unto him, in all things a true and faithful wife, as long as we both shall live.*

Then you are each given to the other for richer or poorer, for better or worse, in sickness and in health, till death shall you part.

(Insert ring ceremony, pronouncement, and presentation at this point in the ceremony).

WEDDING SERMON

Two Walking Together

Friends and family, we are gathered today to celebrate the union of
_____ and _____. Recognizing
the authority of God and Scripture over their lives and marriage,
_____ and _____ have agreed that a
portion of Scripture should be read as the focus of their ceremony.

> *Scripture Reading:* Ecclesiastes 4:9–12
> Two are better than one, because they have a good reward
> for their labor. For if they fall, one will lift up his companion.
> But woe to him who is alone when he falls, for he has no
> one to help him up. Again, if two lie down together, they
> will keep warm; but how can one be warm alone? Though
> one may be overpowered by another, two can withstand him.
> And a threefold cord is not quickly broken.

Charge

The book of Ecclesiastes was written by the great and wise teacher,
King Solomon, thousands of years ago. If you read through the book
of Ecclesiastes, it can be a bit depressing. Solomon was an old man
looking back over his life and saw that his pursuits of earthly wisdom,
of riches, of happiness were all meaningless. He said in essence: "If
you live a life of chasing after your own selfish desires, you'll find it's
all meaningless, it's worthless!" And yet, sprinkled throughout this
book are God's truths that Solomon found comfort in. One such truth
has applications to the union we are establishing today, for the Bible
says that relationships are not meaningless like so many things in life;
they are worth pursuing. Let's look at two truths from Ecclesiastes that
can help form the basis of a meaningful marriage:

First, Strengthen Your Companionship. Ecclesiastes gives us four ways
that two can be better than one—four ways to strengthen your companionship: (A) We can work together. Verse 9 says: "Two are better than
one, because they have a good reward for their labor." You'll find that
you'll get much more out of life as you enjoy it together. Additionally,
as you find and attend a church, you'll see that you will be much more

effective in others' lives as together you serve others. (B) We can heal together. Verse 10 says: For if they fall, one will lift up his companion." _____ and _____ as all of us who are married can agree, you will fall from time to time. There's nothing worse than a husband or wife who kicks you when you're down. Sympathize with each others' hurts, and always help each other back up. (C) We can stick together. Verses 11–12 say: "Again, if two lie down together, they will keep warm; but how can one be warm alone? Though one may be overpowered by another, two can withstand him." Lots of marriages end up with two people living completely separate lives. If you ever find yourself saying "I'd rather spend time with so-and-so than with my spouse," you can bet the other person feels left out and your marriage is weakened and defenseless. Make time for each other; spend as much time together as you can; and always be each others' best friend. Remember that marriage in Scripture is always taught as a lifetime commitment. (D) We can branch out together. The last part of verse 12 says: "And a threefold cord is not quickly broken." It's true that you should stick together as best friends, but be careful not to push others away in the process. The point of this verse mentioning a cord of three strands is to highlight the importance of outside relationships, both with God and other people. If you have mutual friends, if you're involved in a church together, if your relationship with God is the center of your relationship with each other, if you love to spend time with others and each other, then you will add more and more strands to the cord—more strength to the backbone of your marriage. So strengthen your companionship by working together, healing together, sticking together, and branching out together.

And, Second, Keep Your Commitments. Ecclesiastes 12:13–14 says: "Let us hear the conclusion of the whole matter: Fear God and keep His commandments, for this is man's all. For God will bring every work into judgment, including every secret thing, whether good or evil." These verses are the conclusion of all of Solomon's great wisdom. Fear God and obey what's in His Word. Keep His commandments, including what He's given to us about marriage. Study the Scriptures and what they say about husbands and wives. You'll find that God's wisdom will strengthen your marriage and like an invincible cord, it will not be broken.

Vows

_____ (groom) will you take _____ to be your wedded wife, to live life together as God ordained in Scripture? Will you love her, comfort her, honor and keep her, for better or for worse, for richer or for poorer, in sickness and in health, and forsaking all others keep yourself pure unto her, as long as you both shall live?

Groom says, I do.

_____ (bride) will you take _____ to be your wedded husband to live life together as God ordained in Scripture? Will you love him, comfort him, honor and keep him, for better or for worse, for richer or for poorer, in sickness and in health, and forsaking all others keep yourself pure unto him, as long as you both shall live?

Bride says, I do.

Shall we pray: Heavenly Father, we ask You today to be the third cord in this marriage by being the first and greatest affection in the hearts of these two, Your servants. Enable them to (strengthen their companionship with one another, and to keep their commitments, especially the vows they have here made in the presence of these assembled friends. Guard, guide, bless, and hallow them all their lives, and bring glory to Yourself through their union. We pray in Jesus' name. Amen.

(Insert ring ceremony at this point in the ceremony)

_____, you may now kiss your bride.

Ladies and gentlemen, it is my pleasure to present to you _____ and _____ _____.

WEDDING SERMON

The Lift of Love

Dear friends, we have gathered here in the presence of God and of one another to witness the uniting of vows of the two people who stand before us, having declared their intention to become husband and wife in holy matrimony. Marriage is a biblical concept and a divine institution. Its beginnings are found in the Garden of Eden when God created a man and a woman, Adam and Eve, and brought them together with the words of Genesis 2:24: "Therefore a man shall leave his father and mother and be joined to his wife, and they shall become one flesh."

Our Lord Jesus Christ performed His first miracle at a wedding. The apostle Paul wrote in the seventh chapter of the book of 1 Corinthians: "Let each man have his own wife, and let each woman have her own husband. Let the husband render to his wife the affection due her, and likewise also the wife to her husband" (1 Cor. 7:2–3). The book of Hebrews states, "Marriage is honorable among all." And the New Testament teaches that the social and spiritual graces of Jesus Christ—love, joy, peace, mutual submission, cheerfulness, faithfulness, and the like, have their primary application and demonstration in the home, as we read in Ephesians 5 and Colossians 2.

Husbands and wives are lifters. We lift one another's hearts in joy. We lift one another's loads in labor. We lift one another's names in prayer. We lift one another's reputations before society. We lift one another's spirits as we live side-by-side in the sunshine of God's goodness.

The American poet, Ella Wheeler Wilcox (1850–1919) wrote about this in her composition, "Lifting and Leaning."

> *There are two kinds of people on earth today,*
> *Just two kinds of people, no more, I say.*
> *Not the good and the bad, for 'tis well understood*
> *The good are half bad and the bad are half good.*
> *Not the happy and sad, for the swift-flying years*

Bring each man his laughter and each man his tears.
Not the rich and the poor, for to count a man's wealth,
You must first know the state of his conscience and health.
Not the humble and proud, for in life's busy span,
Who puts on vain airs is not counted a man.
No! The two kinds of people on earth I mean
Are the people who lift and the people who lean.
Wherever you go you will find the world's masses
Are ever divided in just these two classes.
And strangely enough you will find, too, I ween,
There is only one lifter to twenty who lean.
In which class are you? Are you easing the load
Of overtaxed lifters who toil down the road?
Or are you a leaner who lets other bear
Your portion of worry and labor and care?

Well, there will be times _____ and _____
when you will have to lean on the other, but how wonderful to make it
every day's goal to be a lifter, and to lift up the heart and the spirits
and the morale and the emotions of the other. If you are committed
to lifting up one another day by day, your marriage will be lifted to the
very heavens and will be blessed by our gracious Lord Jesus Christ
whose love has lifted us all.

If you, then, _____ and _____, are
prepared in heart and mind to enter into this hallowed relationship,
would you please join hands for the repeating of your vows.

The Groom's Vows: *In taking the woman I hold by the right hand to be
my lawfully wedded wife, I promise to love her, to cherish her, to lift her up
always, and to remain faithful to her and to her alone in the sacred
relationship of marriage as long as we both shall live.*

The Bride's Vows: *In taking the man I hold by the right hand to be my
lawfully wedded husband, I promise to love him, to cherish him, to lift him
up always, and to remain faithful to him and to him alone in the sacred
relationship of marriage as long as we both shall live.*

Then you are each given to the other for richer or poorer, for better or worse, in sickness and in health, from this day forward till death shall you part.

The Ring Ceremony

The wedding ring is a symbol of marriage in that its shape is endless, like the vows you have just spoken, and its metal is pure, like the purity of your love.

_____ (groom), will you place the ring on _____'s finger and repeat after me: With this ring, I thee wed, in the name of the Father, and of the Son, and of the Holy Spirit.

_____ (bride), will you place the ring on _____'s finger and repeat after me: With this ring, I thee wed, in the name of the Father, and of the Son, and of the Holy Spirit.

What God has joined together, let no one put asunder. According to the authority vested in me as a minister of the gospel of Jesus Christ, I pronounce you husband and wife.

FUNERAL SERMON

Suitable for a Christian's Funeral
Sorrow Not as Those Who Have No Hope

Today we have gathered here in memory of _____.

Personal Comments About the Deceased.

Scripture: 1 Thessalonians 4:13–18

Introduction: At a time like this, we can be overwhelmed with anguish; the grief, depression, despair, anger, and sorrow can almost drown us. But one thing bears us up and keeps us going—the biblical truth of the resurrection. If only we can focus our minds on 1 Thessalonians 4:13–18, we'll be all right; so I'd like to look at that passage today phrase by phrase.

Brothers, I do not want you to be ignorant . . .
This is information God wants us to know. It isn't just Paul speaking; the Lord is speaking in the first person to you and me. He says, "My child, I don't want you to be uninformed about something that's going to happen or about those who have fallen asleep." When we die in Christ, the Lord doesn't think of us in terms of being dead, but asleep. When you and I die in Christ, we won't be dead. We are not dead. Our bodies are sleeping and our spirits are still alive with Christ. That's what Jesus taught, and that's what Christians of all the ages have believed. The very word *cemetery* literally means "sleeping place."

. . . lest you sorrow as others who have no hope.
This information keeps our sorrow from becoming despair. Jesus doesn't tell us to grieve, because there's an understandable sadness when a Christian passes away. We miss them terribly, and we long for

"the touch of a vanished hand and the sound of a voice that is still," as Tennyson put it. Jesus Himself wept by the tomb of Lazarus. But we're not to grieve as non-Christians do, like those who have no hope.

For if we believe that Jesus died and rose again, even so God will bring with Him those who sleep in Jesus.
Since God raised Jesus for us all, He will raise all in Jesus when He returns, and our souls will be reunited with our resurrected bodies on that coming day of gladness and grandeur. That's the basic fact He wants us to know.

We who are alive and remain until the coming of the Lord will by no means precede those who are asleep.
Somehow the Thessalonians were concerned that their loved ones who had passed away would miss out on the return of Christ, but Paul said, "Not at all. It would be wonderful to be alive when Jesus returns, but those who are alive at that moment will really have no advantage over those who are sleeping in Christ. In fact, the ones asleep in Christ will rise to meet Him first. Four great events will occur almost simultaneously at the moment of our Lord's return for His children.

For the Lord Himself will descend from heaven . . .
First, the Lord Himself shall descend from heaven. At this very moment, our Jesus is seated in the heavenly realms at the right hand of the Almighty Father. But when the moment comes, He will literally rise from the throne, step into the corridors of light, and descend to the atmospherics of earth.

. . . with a shout . . .
Second, He will shout a loud command. The Greek word used here for "shout" or "loud command" was the word the classical Greek writers used for the shout of soldiers as they charged toward the enemy. It was also the word chariot drivers used to spur on their horses. It was like a wild cry of command and forward charge.

. . . with the voice of an archangel . . .
As Jesus issues the command for the saints of all the ages to rise from the dead, the archangel will issue commands to all the host of angels

under his authority as they participate in the process and escort God's children into the skies.

. . . and with the trumpet of God.
Fourth, there's going to be a blast from a trumpet that will stun and startle the whole earth. In a flash, in the twinkling of an eye, the Lord will descend, He will shout a loud command, the archangel will summon his troops, and a trumpet will blast with a retort loud enough to make the whole world tremble. And then what?

And the dead in Christ will rise first. Then we who are alive and remain shall be caught up together with them in the clouds to meet the Lord in the air. And thus we shall always be with the Lord.
Try to visualize that day. Suddenly in an instant, a billion people will disappear from the face of the earth. You'll be walking around the office or school, and suddenly it'll appear to be de-populated, and those left behind will ask, "Where did everyone go?" Well, this passage tells us that we will be reunited with our Savior and our loved ones forever.

Conclusion: At a time like this, it's appropriate to ask: Are you ready for that day? Are you ready for His return? Have you claimed Jesus Christ as your eternal Lord and Savior? For the Lord Himself shall descend from heaven with a shout, with the voice of the archangel, and with the trumpet call of God, and the dead in Christ will rise first. After that, we who are still alive and are left will be caught up together with them in the clouds to meet the Lord in the air. And so shall we ever be with the Lord.

FUNERAL SERMON

Suitable for the Funeral of One Who Dies Suddenly and Unexpectedly
All Things for Good

Today we have gathered in memory of _____.

Personal Comments About the Deceased.

Scripture: Romans 8:28

Introduction: We are stunned. No one can know how bewildered we feel today. The question "Why?" hangs in the air like a recurring whisper. But Christians don't live by explanations, but by promises. Today I'd like to share with you the most all-inclusive promise in the Bible, and then show you some other passages where this promise is repeated in similar words. Perhaps one of these Scriptures will bring supernatural comfort and calmness to your heart.

1. **All Things Work Together for Good (Rom. 8:28).** The first words of this verse say "And we know. . . ." There's certainty there. We don't have the answers to life's tragedies, but there's one thing we do know: We know that all things will work together for good. The word "all" means everything that happens to us; nothing is excluded. Someone said, "All means all, and that's all all means." The Bible doesn't say that all things *are* good, but that all things *work together* for good in the providence of God. He brings everlasting benefits from earthly sorrows. And He does it particularly for those who love Him and who are living for His purposes.

2. **He Works All Things According to the Counsel of His Will (Eph. 1:11).** The same author who wrote Romans 8:28 also gave us Ephesians 1:11, and the two verses go together wonderfully. The first is from our perspective on earth and the second is from God's perspective in heaven. The reason all things work together for good for us down here on earth is because God, in His sovereign power, has purposed all things to work together according to the counsel of

His will. He is Lord. He reigns. He moves in mysterious ways His wonders to perform.

3. **God Meant It for Good (Gen. 50:20).** There is a corresponding verse in the Old Testament, in Genesis 50:20. The patriarch Joseph told his brothers—the ones who kidnapped him, sold him into slavery, and abandoned him to the prisons of Egypt—that while they meant evil against him, God meant it for good. The Lord used all Joseph's distresses to prepare and place him in a position of great influence and power. The devil intends these things as evil against us, but God intends them for good.

5. **These Things Turn Out for the Furtherance of the Gospel (Phil. 1:12).** In this passage, the apostle Paul is reassuring the church of the Philippians that all his sorrows and problems would turn out all right. In fact, it would have an evangelistic result. He was referring especially to His imprisonment in the city of Rome. He was taken off the road, chained to a post or a soldier, and locked inside the dungeon of the Mamertine Prison in Rome. But there he was able to evangelize the soldiers who guarded him. There he was able to write his epistles. There he was able to embolden the church. As remarkable as it seems, the Lord is able to take the disappointments and disasters of life and turn them into arenas for the sharing of His gospel.

Conclusion: Perhaps the Lord allowed this tragedy to bring you face to face with your need for salvation. Our brother (or sister) was a Christian, and he is happier now than he has ever been. He's walking the streets of the heavenly city. He's with Jesus. His labors and trials are over. But if he could come back for just a moment and speak to us, he would say, "Make sure that you know Jesus Christ as your own Savior. Make sure you're ready for death." Life is unpredictable and uncertain; none of us knows if we'll be alive when the sun sets this evening. Jesus died and rose again, and nothing takes Him by surprise. He has gone to prepare a place for us. Are you His follower? This is your day to give yourself to Him and let's rest in His promise that all things work together for good for those who love Him and are called according to His purposes.

FUNERAL SERMON

Suitable for an Unbeliever's Funeral

The Lord Is Merciful!

Today we have gathered in memory of _____.

Personal Comments About the Deceased.

Scripture: Psalm 103:8

Introduction: None of us knows the heart of another. I do not know what was in (the deceased's) heart, but I do know the heart of God, for it is revealed to us in Scripture. He is a God of mercy. The word *mercy* occurs 359 times in the Bible, and it's one of God's great qualities.

1. **"The Lord Is Merciful."** As we read through the book of Psalms, we come across this word again and again: *The LORD is merciful and gracious, slow to anger, and abounding in mercy. . . . For the LORD is good; His mercy is everlasting. . . . His mercy endures forever. . . . Gracious is the LORD, and righteous; Yes, our God is merciful. . . . Do not remember the sins of my youth, nor my transgressions; according to Your mercy remember me, for Your goodness' sake, O LORD. . . . Turn Yourself to me, and have mercy on me, for I am desolate and afflicted. The troubles of my heart have enlarged; bring me out of my distresses! Oh, give thanks to the LORD, for He is good! For His mercy endures forever. Oh, give thanks to the God of gods! For His mercy endures forever. Oh, give thanks to the Lord of lords! For His mercy endures forever* (Ps. 103:8; 100:5; 106:1; 116:5; 25:7; 25:16–17; 136:1–3). And so we trust our friend into the merciful hands of God. There is nothing more we can do for him (or her). But as we think of the mercy of God, we can trust Him on this day; and we can also apply this truth to ourselves, making sure of our own standing with the Lord.

2. **"Have Mercy on Us."** In the Gospels, we read about the Lord Jesus Christ who came into the world to save sinners like you and me. The Bible teaches that all of us have fallen short of the standards and glory of God, and our sins have separated us from His presence.

In love, God Himself became a man, entering the world through the womb of a virgin. He lived, preached the good news of the gospel, died on the cross, and rose from the dead on the third day. By His death and resurrection, He took upon Himself the sins of the world. His blood provided for our forgiveness. The people of His own day often received His mercy simply by asking for it with contrite, humble, and dedicated hearts.

- In Matthew 9:27, two blind men cried out to Him, saying, "Son of David, have mercy on us!" Jesus healed and saved them.

- In Matthew 15:22, a woman from Canaan cried out, saying, "Have mercy of me, O Lord, Son of David!" Jesus helped her in her distress.

- In Matthew 17:15, a troubled father fell at Jesus' feet and cried, "Lord, have mercy on my son . . . ." And Jesus intervened.

- In Matthew 20:30–31, two blind men in Jericho, sitting by the road, called out, "Have mercy on us, O Lord, Son of David . . . Have mercy on us!" Jesus helped and healed them.

- In Luke 17:13, ten lepers saw Jesus coming in the distance and lifted up their voices, calling out, "Jesus, Master, have mercy on us!" Jesus gladly healed them (though only one of them later came back to thank Him).

- In Luke 18:13, a dishonest tax collector beat his breast, saying, "God, be merciful to me a sinner." And Jesus said that man was justified before God.

3. **God Is Rich in Mercy.** Perhaps the greatest passage in the Bible on this subject is Ephesians 2:4–9: *But God, who is rich in mercy, because of His great love with which He loved us, even when we were dead in trespasses, made us alive together with Christ (by grace you have been saved), and raised us up together, and made us sit together in the heavenly places in Christ Jesus. . . . For by grace you have been saved through faith, and that not of yourselves; it is the gift of God, not of works, lest anyone should boast.* I know that our hearts are broken today, but there is One who can forgive our sins, heal our hearts, and give us hope. He is rich in mercy. We entrust

our departed loved one into His hands, even as we ourselves take seriously our own need to seek and receive God's mercy. Jesus died on the cross. He bore our sins. He died in our stead. He rose for our sakes. He wants to extend His mercy to us. He's ready to forgive our sins. He wants to save us and give us a sure and certain hope of eternal life. Are you ready to say, "Lord, have mercy on me, a sinner?"

I've nowhere else to go,
Dear Jesus, but to Thee,
And so I lift my voice and cry,
Have mercy, Lord, on me.
—FANNY CROSBY, 1896

Special Services Registry

The forms on the following pages are designed to be duplicated and used repeatedly as needed. Most copy machines will allow you to enlarge them to fill a full page if desired.

Sermons Preached

Date	Text	Title/Subject

Sermons Preached

Date	Text	Title/Subject

Marriages Log

Date	Bride	Groom

Funerals Log

Date	Name of Deceased	Scripture Used

Baptisms/Confirmations

Date	Name	Notes

Baby Dedication Registration

Infant's Name: _____

Significance of Given Names: _____

Date of Birth: _____

_____

Siblings: _____

_____

_____

_____

Maternal Grandparents: _____

Paternal Grandparents: _____

Life Verse: _____

Date of Dedication: _____

Wedding Registration

Date of Wedding: _____

Location of Wedding: _____

Bride: _____

    Religious Affiliation: _____

    Bride's Parents: _____

Groom: _____

    Religious Affiliation: _____

    Groom's Parents: _____

Ceremony to Be Planned by Minister: _____ By Couple: _____

Other Minister(s) Assisting: _____

Maid/Matron of Honor: _____

Best Man: _____

Wedding Planner: _____

Date of Rehearsal: _____

Reception Open to All Wedding Guests: _____ By Invitation Only: _____

Location of Reception: _____

Wedding Photos to Be Taken: _____ During Ceremony

                        _____ After Ceremony

Other: _____

Date of Counseling: _____

Date of Registration: _____

Funeral Registration

Name of Deceased: _____

Age: _____

Religious Affiliation: _____

Survivors: _____

    Spouse: _____

    Parents: _____

    Children: _____

    Siblings: _____

    Grandchildren: _____

Date of Death: _____

Time and Place of Visitation: _____

Date of Funeral or Memorial Service: _____

Funeral Home Responsible: _____

Location of Funeral or Memorial Service: _____

Scripture Used: _____ Hymns Used: _____

Eulogy by: _____

Other Minister(s) Assisting: _____

Pallbearers: _____

_____

Date of Interment: _____ Place of Interment: _____

Graveside Service: _____   No _____

Subject Index

Scripture Index

END USER LICENSE AGREEMENT

CAREFULLY READ THE FOLLOWING LICENSE AGREEMENT. BY CLICKING ON THE "I ACCEPT THE TERMS OF THE LICENSE AGREEMENT" BUTTON AND CLICKING THE NEXT BUTTON, YOU ARE CONSENTING TO BE BOUND BY AND ARE BECOMING A PARTY TO THIS AGREEMENT. THIS PRODUCT REQUIRES USER REGISTRATION AND WILL CEASE TO FUNCTION IF USER REGISTRATION IS NOT CONFIRMED. IF YOU DO NOT AGREE TO ALL OF THE TERMS OF THIS AGREEMENT, CLICK THE "CANCEL" BUTTON, AND, IF APPLICABLE, RETURN THIS PRODUCT TO THE PLACE OF PURCHASE FOR A FULL REFUND.

LICENSE GRANT

The package contains software ("Software") and may contain electronic text, graphics, audio, or other resources ("Content") and related explanatory written materials ("Documentation"). "Software" includes any upgrades, modified versions, updates, additions and copies of the Software. "You" means the person or company who is being licensed to use the Software, Content and Documentation. "We" and "us" means Libronix Corporation and its parent company, Logos Research Systems, Inc.

We hereby grant you a nonexclusive license to use one copy of the Software and "unlocked" Content on any single computer, provided the Software and Content are in use on only one computer at any time. The Software is "in use" on a computer when it is loaded into temporary memory (RAM) or installed into the permanent memory of a computer—for example, a hard disk, CD-ROM or other storage device.

If the Software and Content are permanently installed on the hard disk or other storage device of a computer (other than a network server) and one person uses that computer more than 80% of the time, then that person may also use the Software and Content on a portable or home computer.

The package may contain Content that is NOT licensed to you. This Content is "locked" in electronic form and is included for your convenience should you desire to "unlock" it by purchasing a license for it. Content that you "unlock" is covered by this agreement.

TITLE

We remain the owner of all right, title and interest in the Software and Documentation. Ownership of the Content remains with Copyright holders.

ARCHIVAL OR BACKUP COPIES

You may either:
—make one copy of the Software solely for backup or archival purposes, or
—transfer the Software to a single hard disk, provided you keep the original solely for backup or archival purposes.

THINGS YOU MAY NOT DO

The Software, Content, and Documentation are protected by United States copyright laws and international treaties. You must treat the Software, Content, and Documentation like any other copyrighted material—for example a book. You may not:
—copy the Documentation,
—copy the Software or Content except to make archival or backup copies as provided above,
—modify or adapt the Software or merge it into another program,
—reverse engineer, disassemble, decompile or make any attempt to discover the source code of the Software,
—place the Software or Content onto a server so that it is accessible via a public network such as the Internet,
—sublicense, rent, lease or lend any portion of the Software, Content, or Documentation, or
—reverse engineer, disassemble, decompile or make any attempt to "unlock" or circumvent the digital copyright protection of the Content.

TRANSFERS

You may transfer all your rights to use the Software, Content, and Documentation to another person or legal entity provided you transfer this Agreement, the Software, Content, and Documentation, including all copies, update and prior versions to such person or entity and that you retain no copies, including copies stored on computer.

LIMITED WARRANTY

We warrant that for a period of 90 days after delivery of this copy of the Software to you:
—if provided, the physical media on which this copy of the Software is distributed will be free from defects in materials and workmanship under normal use, and
—the Software will perform in substantial accordance with the Documentation.
To the extent permitted by applicable law, THE FOREGOING LIMITED WARRANTY IS IN LIEU OF ALL OTHER WARRANTIES OR CONDITIONS, EXPRESS OR IMPLIED, AND WE DISCLAIM ANY AND ALL IMPLIED WARRANTIES OR CONDITIONS, INCLUDING ANY IMPLIED WARRANTY OF TITLE, NONINFRINGEMENT, MERCHANTABILITY OR FITNESS FOR A PARTICULAR PURPOSE, regardless of whether we know or had reason to know of your particular needs. No employee, agent, dealer or distributor of ours is authorized to modify this limited warranty, nor to make any additional warranties.

SOME STATES DO NOT ALLOW THE EXCLUSION OF IMPLIED WARRANTIES, SO THE ABOVE EXCLUSION MAY NOT APPLY TO YOU. THIS WARRANTY GIVES YOU SPECIFIC LEGAL RIGHTS, AND YOU MAY ALSO HAVE OTHER RIGHTS WHICH VARY FROM STATE TO STATE.

LIMITED REMEDY
Our entire liability and your exclusive remedy shall be:
—the replacement of any diskette(s) or other media not meeting our Limited Warranty which is returned to us or to an authorized Dealer or Distributor with a copy of your receipt, or
—If we or an authorized Dealer or Distributor are unable to deliver a replacement diskette(s) or other media that is free of defects in materials or workmanship, you may terminate this Agreement by returning the Software and Documentation and your money will be refunded.
IN NO EVENT WILL WE BE LIABLE TO YOU FOR ANY DAMAGES, INCLUDING ANY LOST PROFITS, LOST SAVINGS, OR OTHER INCIDENTAL OR CONSEQUENTIAL DAMAGES ARISING FROM THE USE OR THE INABILITY TO USE THE SOFTWARE (EVEN IF WE OR AN AUTHORIZED DEALER OR DISTRIBUTOR HAS BEEN ADVISED OF THE POSSIBILITY OF THESE DAMAGES), OR FOR ANY CLAIM BY ANY OTHER PARTY.

SOME STATES DO NOT ALLOW THE LIMITATION OR EXCLUSION OF LIABILITY FOR INCIDENTAL OR CONSEQUENTIAL DAMAGES, SO THE ABOVE LIMITATION MAY NOT APPLY TO YOU.

TERM AND TERMINATION

This license agreement takes effect upon your use of the software and remains effective until terminated. You may terminate it at any time by destroying all copies of the Software and Documentation in your possession. It will also automatically terminate if you fail to comply with any term or condition of this license agreement. You agree on termination of this license to either return to us or destroy all copies of the Software and Documentation in your possession.

CONFIDENTIALITY

The Software contains trade secrets and proprietary know-how that belong to us and it is being made available to you in strict confidence. ANY USE OR DISCLOSURE OF THE SOFTWARE, OR OF ITS ALGORITHMS, PROTOCOLS OR INTERFACES, OTHER THAN IN STRICT ACCORDANCE WITH THIS LICENSE AGREEMENT, MAY BE ACTIONABLE AS A VIOLATION OF OUR TRADE SECRET RIGHTS.

GENERAL PROVISIONS

1. This written license agreement is the exclusive agreement between you and us concerning the Software, Content, and Documentation and supersedes any and all prior oral or written agreements, negotiations or other dealings between us concerning the Software.
2. This license agreement may be modified only by a writing signed by you and us.
3. In the event of litigation between you and us concerning the Software or Documentation, the prevailing party in the litigation will be entitled to recover attorney fees and expenses from the other party.
4. You agree to register this product with Libronix Corporation within 30 days. (Registration may be accomplished via the Internet or by mail. Registration helps protect the owners and publishers of copyrighted Content and encourages more publishers to release their Content electronically.) You may register anonymously but we may not provide certain types of support or opportunities to participate in certain online features if you choose to do so. After 30 days the software may cease to function until it receives confirmation of registration.
5. You represent that if you choose to provide name, address, credit card, or any other information that it will be your true information. You may choose or be assigned a user name, confirmation code, and/or password in connection with your use of the Software. You agree to keep your confirmation code and password confidential. We disclaim responsibility for unauthorized use of your credit card or password.
6. Registration with Libronix Corporation implies registration with the Content owners whose Content you have licensed for use with the Software. We may share your registration information with the owners of Content you have licensed. We will honor your indication that you do not want registration information shared with any other third party. (You may indicate this during registration if you choose to provide name, address, etc.)
7. You agree that the Software may detect the presence of a connection to the Internet and communicate with servers controlled by Libronix in order to submit anonymous statistical information on use of the Software and Content and to detect and download updates to the Software and Content and new Software and Content for which you may have chosen to purchase licenses. You agree that new and updated Software and Content downloaded by the Software from the Internet are covered by this license.
8. This license agreement is governed by the laws of the State of Washington, USA.
9. You agree that the Software will not be shipped, transferred or exported into any country or used in any manner prohibited by the United States Export Administration Act or any other export laws, restrictions or regulations.
10. The controlling language of this agreement is English. Any translation of this agreement that you may have received is provided only for your convenience.